# BIOLOGICAL BASES
# OF HUMAN
# SOCIAL BEHAVIOUR

# BIOLOGICAL BASES OF HUMAN SOCIAL BEHAVIOUR

**R. A. HINDE**

*Medical Research Council*
*Unit on the*
*Development and Integration of Behaviour*
*Madingley, Cambridge, England*

**McGraw-Hill Book Company**
*New York   St. Louis   San Francisco   Düsseldorf   Johannesburg   Kuala Lumpur*
*London   Mexico   Montreal   New Delhi   Panama*
*Paris   São Paulo   Singapore   Sydney   Tokyo   Toronto*

This book was set in Palatino by Monotype Composition Company, Inc.
The editors were William J. Willey and Andrea Stryker-Rodda;
the designer was Barbara Ellwood;
the production supervisor was Leroy A. Young.
Most of the drawings were done by Priscilla Edwards.
The printer was Halliday Lithograph Corporation;
the binder, The Maple Press Company.

**Library of Congress Cataloging in Publication Data**

Hinde, Robert A
  Biological bases of human social behaviour.

  Bibliography:  p.
  1.  Social behavior in animals.  2.  Psychology,
Comparative.  I.  Title.  [DNLM: 1.  Biology.
2.  Social behavior.  HM106 H662b 1974]
QL775.H53        301.1        74-2151
ISBN 0-07-028932-8
ISBN 0-07-028931-X (pbk.)

**BIOLOGICAL BASES
OF HUMAN
SOCIAL BEHAVIOUR**

1234567890  HDMB  7987654

*for*

**IAN HEPBURN**

**BILL THORPE**

**NIKO TINBERGEN**

**JOHN BOWLBY**

# CONTENTS

# PREFACE

Understanding human behaviour involves problems infinitely more difficult than landing a man on the moon or unravelling the structure of complex molecules. The problems are also more important and more urgent. If we are to tackle them, we must use every source of evidence available to us. Studies of animals are one such source. Sometimes such studies are useful to the extent that animals resemble man, and sometimes they help just because animals are different and permit the study of issues in a simplified, isolated, or exaggerated form. They may assist us in understanding the behaviour of man not only through factual comparison between animal and man, but also by helping us to refine the categories and concepts used in the description and explanation of behaviour and social structure. But the use of animals involves dangers: it is so easy to make rash generalizations, to slip from firm fact to flight of fancy, to select examples to fit preconceptions. Studies of animals must therefore be used circumspectly, and the limitations of their usefulness specified.

In this book I have attempted to review some studies of non-human species which may help us to understand human social behaviour. In doing so I have selected for consideration topics to which the animal data seemed most clearly relevant. Thus I have concentrated on questions of causation and development, at the expense of those of evolution and ecology. And, because their behaviour is most likely to be relevant to our own, I have drawn most of the material from studies of non-human primates—though I have discussed data on other species when issues or principles could be better illustrated by doing so. This has involved the omission of many fascinating aspects of social behaviour—for instance, I have hardly mentioned the social insects, and have included little material on lower vertebrates—but this seemed necessary if I were to pursue my chosen theme in adequate depth.

Since I am a biologist by training, it is the animals on which I have focussed. In some instances I have pointed out the relevance to man, but in many I felt that this would be obvious to the reader and required no comment. In other cases it seemed that the task of a biologist was merely to present the data, the drawing of parallels being properly left to the psychologist, sociologist, or anthropologist. And sometimes I felt that there could properly be some traffic the other way, our intimate knowledge of the human case being allowed to throw light on the behaviour of animals.

The first section (A) contains a discussion of the relevance of the animal data to human problems, and attempts to specify the contexts in which they may be useful. The nature of social behaviour is also considered, and some of the issues with which later chapters are concerned are outlined. Two problems relevant to the study of all behaviour—motivation and development—are considered in the second section (B). Section C concerns communication, which is, of course, basic to social behaviour. Whereas the earlier sections were concerned with non-primate species as much as with primates, from here on the discussion is concerned more and more with monkeys, apes, and man. Section D concerns the development of early social relationships, and Sections E and F discuss two important types of social behaviour—aggressive and sexual. The final section (G) is concerned with various aspects of the structure of groups.

The writing of this book owed much to discussion with a number of colleagues, and to the advice and criticism they offered. I would like to mention especially Pat Bateson, Carol Berman, Judy Bernal, David Bygott, John Flynn, Esther Goody, David Hamburg, Jeannette Hanby, Sandy Harcourt, Nick Humphrey, John Hutchison, Lynda McGinnis, Juliet Oliver, Michael Simpson, Joan Stevenson-Hinde, and Mitzi Thorndahl. Several colleagues have allowed me to quote unpublished work—David Bygott, John Deag, Dian Fossey, Lynda McGinnis, Pat McGinnis, Nicholas Owens, Michael Simpson, and Mitzi Thorndahl. Much of the research in which I have participated was carried out in collaboration with Jeannette Hanby, Lynda McGinnis, Lilyan White, and the late Yvette Spencer-Booth: it was supported by the Royal Society and the Medical Research Council. Finally, I am especially indebted to Priscilla Edwards for her illustrations and to Marion Leslie for help with the preparation of the manuscript.

**R. A. Hinde**

# SECTION

# A

# INTRODUCTION

# ANIMAL AND HUMAN BEHAVIOUR

This book is primarily about the social behaviour of non-human species. At many points, however, there are implications that discussion of the nature of animal behaviour is relevant to an understanding of our own, and in some places direct comparisons are made. It is therefore as well to be clear on the extent to which such comparisons are legitimate.

A biologist, considering this question, is pulled in two directions. On the one hand, with his science unified by the theory of evolution by natural selection, he must hold that there are continuities between the behaviour of animals and that of man. At the same time, much of his training has been concerned with the nature of species differences. He has been taught how even closely related species are adapted to different environments, and how the resulting differences are superimposed on broad phyletic changes of a more fundamental nature, including differences in complexity of organization (e.g., Schneirla, 1949). Such a training engenders awe at the diversity of nature, and emphasizes the need for humility when generalizations are being attempted—or if it does not, it should.

The behavioural gap between animals and man is in fact enormous. In their level of cognitive functioning, in the degree of foresight and awareness of which they are capable, in their ability to reflect on their own behaviour, all animals are markedly inferior to man. Some birds can learn to respond differentially to five or six marks presented in separate groups (Köhler, 1955), but this "counting" without naming numbers is on quite a different level from the counting that forms the basis not only of mathematics and science, but of many aspects of our everyday life. Chimpanzees, given brushes and paper, may produce crude designs, but even to compare them with the Mona Lisa or the Water Lilies is manifestly absurd. Many animals live in complex societies, but the signals which integrate their social lives are on quite a different level of complexity from human language. Chimpanzees use simple tools, but no animal has a culture involving symbolic values, beliefs, and norms of behaviour which even approaches that of our own species. And not only are there these tremendous differences between animal and man, but there are also great differences in social behaviour both among animal species and among human societies, making generalizations even more dangerous.

Some of the differences between animal and man tend to be exaggerated by the methods the biologist uses, for at almost every stage in his work he is forced to simplify. This is not merely a consequence of insufficient knowledge. To describe behaviour, the biologist must abstract regularities, and in doing so he must gloss over the irregularities. In making generalizations, he must focus on the phenomena they encompass and neglect those to which they are inapplicable. In analyzing the behaviour of a species, he is forced to forget individual differences. A bias toward simplification is thus built into his work, and his explanatory concepts are likely always to lag behind the phenomena he is trying to explain. The application of concepts derived from the study of relatively simple animals to the immeasurably more complex human case is rendered even more hazardous if those concepts tend to simplify even the animal case from the start.

It is thus clear that studies of animals can help us only to a limited extent in understanding human behaviour. But they can help in some ways, and many of these arise from the very fact that animals are simpler than man.

First, the study of animals permits the development of methods which can then be adapted for the human case. In most medical sciences this is a commonplace: techniques for diagnosis and treatment are first worked out with animals, and only then applied to man. Some of the techniques used in the diagnosis and treatment of behavioural disorders were also first developed with animals. At a more fundamental level, adequate methods for the description and classification of behaviour were first worked out with animals. Description and classification may seem not very difficult tasks, but their neglect hampered many aspects of psychology for half a century. The continuous stream of behaviour shown by an individual must be broken into elements, and those elements must then be classified, before analysis can proceed. This descriptive phase, essential in the development of every science, was bypassed by those experimental psychologists who attempted to model their strategies on classical physics. These workers overlooked the fact that classical physics was a special case in that its subject matter—falling apples, the apparent bending of sticks in water, floating logs—were everyday events, so that the descriptive phase was part of common experience, and not particularly a job for the scientists. Of course, the way people behave is also part of everyday experience, but to describe behaviour precisely is much more difficult than appears at first sight. As we shall see later, we are not even conscious of some of the signals which we use in communicating with one another, even though they affect our behaviour. And clinicians have come to recognize that it is important for them to know what people actually do, as well as what they say that they do and say that they think. It must be added that every scientific technique must be tailored to the context in which it is to be used. The suggestion is not that the methods of description found useful with animals are immediately applicable to all investigations of human behaviour, but that they can provide a valuable starting point.

Second, animals can be used for the study of particular problems. Sometimes, indeed, the use of animals is essential, since experiments ethically impossible with man can in certain circumstances justifiably be carried out with animals. We shall be considering an example later (Chap. 13)—the use of monkeys to study the effects of separating infants from their mothers, a subject on which evidence from planned experiments cannot be obtained in man. The findings of such experiments must of course be generalized to man only with the greatest caution, and assessed wherever possible against more direct sources of evidence.

Third, the study of animal behaviour can provide principles or generalizations whose relevance to man can subsequently be assessed. It is with issues of this nature that this book is primarily concerned. We shall attempt to understand the principles involved in, for instance, non-verbal communication in animals, the ways in which experience influences their aggressive behaviour, and the nature of mother-infant interaction, and then see to what extent the findings apply to our own species. The animal data are useful here in part because we can experiment with animals, rear them under controlled conditions, or engage in selective breeding experiments which would not be possible with human subjects. In such contexts their relevance to man may depend on similarities between animal and man, but they are also rewarding to study just because they are different. For one thing, their relative simplicity highlights theoretical issues, or permits the isolation of problems, which might be shrouded in the complexity of the human case. Furthermore it is possible to select for study species in which particular aspects of behavior are well-developed or are more accessible for study than in man. For example, infant monkeys spend nearly all their early weeks clinging to their mothers, and the "contact comfort" they obtain from their mothers plays an important part in their development: its study has led to a better appreciation of the importance of contact comfort for the human child.

Comparative study of different species also gives us some understanding of the biological functions of behaviour, the ways in which it has become adapted in evolution to enhance survival and reproduction. The concept of function depends on the study of differences between organisms, and we could make little progress if we confined our studies to one species.

Of course, where we use animals just because they are different from man, even greater care is needed in generalizing the findings to man. Animals are so diverse that it is easy to select facts to fit theories and to neglect awkward cases. Indeed, evidence from animals can be used to bolster up practically any ethical, social or political system, and it is easy to slip from the use of animal metaphors to the implication that they contain something biological and therefore basic also for man. Another difficulty, which we shall meet frequently in later chapters, is to know at what level of abstraction to look for parallels between animal and man. The same principle may find quite different expression in different species, and we may draw false conclusions if we compare at too superficial a level. It is essential to remember that it is the principles for which we must seek, not superficial similarities in overt behaviour. And we must never permit knowledge of principles useful in understanding other species to blind us to our specifically human qualities.

Finally, the study of animal behaviour can give perspective to the behaviour of man. Not only does it emphasize those features that he shares with lower forms, giving depth to our inevitably (and properly) anthropocentric view, but it also highlights his uniqueness. As a biologist, I might add that the reverse is also true. Knowledge of human behaviour, if used with discipline, can sometimes give us increased understanding of that of animals. Students of animal behaviour are so aware of the horrors of anthropomorphism that they sometimes shy away from the most interesting aspects of their subject matter: the over-simple view they get could be corrected by a little disciplined indulgence.

$$\boxed{2}$$

# WHAT IS
# SOCIAL
# BEHAVIOUR?

## The problem of classification

With what sort of category of behaviour are we concerned? Before tackling that question, it is necessary to say a few words about categories in general. Classifying is a basic human activity: our very perception of the world depends on our classifying the sensations we receive. Classification also forms the basis of all science, because to study natural phenomena it is necessary first to describe and classify them. But the pigeonholes we use are often artificial, and our dependence upon them may conceal the fact that they do not quite fit nature. For example, it is convenient for us to divide living organisms into animals and plants, and most of the time it matters little that there are many organisms with characteristics of both categories—not to mention others that have few characteristics of either, so that it is difficult to say whether they are alive or not. But when one of these intermediates is the focus of interest, it is easy to be misled by the usefulness of the initial dichotomy into worrying whether they are "really" animals or plants. The same difficulty occurs again and again in biology. Is a skua, which feeds on the fish that it has caused terns to regurgitate, a parasite or a predator? Is a chaffinch, which eats both insects and seeds, an insectivore or a herbivore? Although science depends on classifying, one of the first lessons to be learnt is that most classificatory systems, if pressed far enough, do not work. What we must do, therefore, is to use our categories as tools and not to dignify them as absolutes, bearing constantly in mind the sorts of distinctions for which they are useful and the nature of their limitations. Every one of the categories of behaviour used in this book is shady at the edges, but this does not mean the categories are disreputable. Every conceptual tool has limitations to its usefulness, and these must be recognized.

### Relations of social behaviour to other categories of behaviour

Social behaviour is no exception. In everyday speech it implies behaviour involving two or more individuals, and it seems quite distinct from behaviour such as feeding, self-grooming, or elimination. But in man, feeding has many social aspects, and may indeed be used as a means of signalling between individuals (e.g., Lévi-Strauss, 1966). In animals, individuals are attracted to food by the stimulus of others eating, and the presence of other individuals may influence what and how much is eaten (e.g., puppies, James and Gilbert, 1956; birds, Tolman, 1968; primates, see pages 243–245). Similarly, self-grooming is closely related in a number of ways to grooming others, an important social activity in most primates and many other species (e.g., page 332); and even urination may be used as a means of signalling to other individuals. On this basis, it might seem that almost all activities are, or can be, social.

The distinction between social and other behaviour also poses difficulties when we come to consider development. We shall see in Section D that the development of relations with social companions may depend upon previous experience with the physical environment and with the individual's own body, as well as interaction with other individuals. Conversely, the development of visuo-motor skills may depend on interactions with the mother and with the subject's own body, as well as with the physical environment. The complexity of the physical environment affects an infant primate's interactions with its mother (Jensen et al., 1968), and the presence of its mother affects its responsiveness to the physical environment (Harlow and Harlow, 1965). The development of social behaviour is thus closely interwoven with that of other types of behaviour.

The student of social behaviour must therefore sometimes extend his interests beyond responses to other individuals. On the other hand, there are some types of behaviour that appear to be social but are not usefully classed as such. For instance, when a cloud of moths gathers round a lamp, the moths are probably responding to the lamp, not to one another: they form an "aggregation" but not a social group. And amongst social groups we find all degrees of complexity from those that are united by responses to simple stimuli from other individuals, through those involving interactive relationships between pairs of individuals, to those involving a complex social nexus.

In view of all these difficulties, is it worthwhile to pursue the question of the definition of social behaviour at all? If we hope ultimately to arrive at a water-tight definition which will be acceptable to all, it clearly is not. But since so many of the difficulties in the study of behaviour involve misunderstandings over definitions, we must at least see where we stand. In doing so we shall not reach any firm conclusions about social behaviour, but we shall come to grips with some of the issues that arise in classifying behaviour, and see the relations of "social" to other categories of behaviour such as feeding, grooming, and sexual behaviour. Let us first see what the latter involve.

## The labelling and classification of behaviour

Whatever species of animal we look at, we can identify a number of more or less stereotyped patterns of movement. These include movements of locomotion, such as walking, running, or flying; movements used in hunting or preparing food, such as the strike of the peregrine falcon or the chewing movements of a cat; movements used in communication, such as those that give rise to vocalizations, gestures, or facial expressions; movements used in fighting, copulation, and so on. These movements differ considerably from one another in their variability. Some, like the soliciting posture of the female chaffinch, vary little in form except that various stages of intensity are possible (Fig. 2.1). Others, like the threat posture of a European robin (Fig. 2.2) or the movements of a chaffinch picking up nest-material, may be oriented in special ways to other individuals or to the environment. In the case of gathering nest-material, the behaviour may be more readily identified in terms of its orientation to the environment or its consequences ("nest-material picked up") than in terms of its actual form.

Now in the natural behaviour of an animal these recognizable movement patterns are usually combined into sequences. For instance, a great tit (a bird related to North American chickadees) may hop over the ground, picking up

FIGURE 2.1
*Successive intensity stages in the soliciting posture of the female chaffinch.* (Drawing by Yvette Spencer-Booth.)

leaves and flinging them aside. Then it may pick up a nut, fly off with it to a bush, place the nut under its foot, open it with its beak, and remove the contents. On another occasion it may hop over the ground, pick up a piece of moss, fly with it to a hole in a tree and there perform certain special movements as it incorporates the moss into its nest. On yet another, it may fly up to a female, perch near her with quivering wings, and then fly onto her back and copulate (Fig. 2.3). We describe these sequences respectively as feeding, nest-building, and sexual behaviour, basing our labels primarily on the conclusion to which each sequence leads. It is notable that each sequence contains some movement patterns that are peculiar to it (e.g., ingestion, circling in the nest-cup, the body movements leading to cloacal contact) and others which are common also to other sequences (e.g., hopping, flying, pecking). Often we cannot identify the early stages of the sequence from the movement patterns alone. We must then either (1) use evidence from the way in which the movement patterns are oriented (i.e., hopping under a tree bearing nuts, or over a mossy path) or (2) wait for a movement characteristic of feeding or sexual behaviour or some other category.

Now let us examine just what it is that the behaviour patterns within each sequence may have in common. First, they may share causal factors.[1] Thus all the movement patterns in the feeding sequences are more likely to occur if the bird has not fed for some time. All those in the nest-building sequence are more likely to occur if the bird is in a suitable hormonal condition, possesses a territory and a nest-site, and so on. Causal factors can be either positive or negative —that is, they may result in either an increase or a decrease in the frequency or intensity of a given pattern of behaviour. Thus the various nest-building patterns are also all suppressed as a consequence of stimuli from a complete nest:

---

[1] Causal factors are discussed in more detail in Chap. 3.

FIGURE 2.2

*Threat postures of European robin, showing orientation of breast toward rival. The bird on the left is displaying toward a rival perched slightly above it; that on the right, to a rival at the same level. (Drawing by Priscilla Edwards, from Daanje, 1950.)*

such stimuli are referred to as "consummatory stimuli" in that they consummate the nest-building sequence.

Second, the behaviour patterns in each sequence have similar consequences. All those in the feeding sequence lead to the end result of food in the stomach, all those in the sexual sequence lead to cloacal contact with the female. Here we must note that each sequence, indeed each pattern of behaviour, has many consequences. For instance (to adapt an example used by Tinbergen, 1951), the incubation behaviour of a herring gull facilitates the development of the embryo, slightly expands the eggshell, and hinders the adult's food-getting behaviour. These consequences are respectively potentially beneficial, neutral, or harmful in terms of natural selection: warming the embryo increases the chances that the gull will leave offspring, expanding the eggshell (probably) does not affect them, and hindering the parents' food-seeking could harm them. A useful type of classification of behaviour is that based on adaptively useful consequences—i.e., in the examples given above, the ingestion of food, the building of a nest, the insemination of the female. Such a classificatory system is usually termed a functional one (Hinde, 1974).

FIGURE 2.3
*Courtship display of great tit.* (Drawing by Priscilla
Edwards.)

We must note here that each of the functional categories so far considered
contains patterns of behaviour that lead to a *particular* adaptive consequence. A
related type of category includes patterns which lead to a range of consequences
which themselves have something in common. Examples here are "care-of-the-
body-surface" behaviour, which includes diverse activities relating to the body
surface no matter how they contribute to its welfare; and "communicatory
behaviour", which may include all patterns of behaviour which may affect the
behaviour of others (though see pages 49–52), no matter what the nature of the
effect.

There are in fact other ways in which we could classify the types of behaviour shown by an animal, though these need not concern us here. But it is important to emphasize that the two we have considered—causal and functional—
need not coincide. For example, reproductive behaviour, considered as a
functional category to include activities that promote reproductive success,
embraces sexual, nest-building, and parental types of behaviour which, in many
species at least, have more or less distinct causal bases (i.e., they depend on different hormones, external stimuli, and/or neural mechanisms). Again, we may
classify the aggressive behaviour of a great tit in spring as territorial behaviour,
since the acquisition of a territory is an adaptive consequence, but this does not
necessarily mean that the acquisition of a territory is the consequence which
brings each episode of aggressive behaviour to an end: thus the label "territorial
behaviour" refers to a function, not necessarily to a (negative) cause. In practice,
where a sequence of behaviour is directed toward a goal situation (see pages 89–
90), such as sitting in the nest-cup in the case of nest-building or food in the

stomach in the case of feeding, stimuli from that situation are consummatory to the sequence and thus play a (negative) causal role, while further consequences (the finished nest, nutritional consequences) can be regarded as functions: in such cases cause and function are related, but not identical.

To summarize three main points from the preceding paragraphs:

1 We usually identify a pattern of behaviour by its form or by its orientation or consequences with respect to the environment. A sequence of behaviour is often (though not invariably) identified by the behaviour or stimulus situations to which it leads.

2 We can classify behaviour in a variety of ways. One generally useful system involves grouping items of behaviour which share causal factors— those factors either enhancing (e.g., eliciting stimuli, hormonal state; see pages 29–31) or reducing (e.g., consummatory stimuli; see pages 31–33) the probability of occurrence of the behaviour in question. Another involves grouping items with a common adaptive consequence.

3 These two systems of classification are by no means coincident.

### The status of social behaviour

In the light of this discussion, what is the status of "social" behaviour?

When, around the turn of the century, psychologists tended to explain much of the behaviour of man and animals in terms of "instincts", an instinct of "sociability" (James, 1892) or "gregariousness" (McDougall, 1923) was usually included. We shall discuss the reasons for which the instinct concept has fallen into disrepute later (Chaps. 3 and 4); the point here is that at that time its use implied that the activities belonging to any one instinct had a common causal basis. Thus social behaviour was then regarded as a causal category. When social behaviour is actually studied, however, it is usually in relation to some other category of behaviour—behaviour to members of the other sex in pair formation and sexual behaviour, behaviour between parents and offspring in parental and filial behaviour, relations with other members of the species in such contexts as feeding and migrating. It has thus been argued that social behaviour is not an exclusive category, but merely a label for types of behaviour involving other members of the species, and that it thus cuts across the more basic categories such as feeding, sexual, and parental behaviour (Tinbergen, 1951).

The attractive nature of this view is apparent as soon as one considers the nature of social behaviour. Generalizing broadly across species for the moment, social behaviour usually consists of an appetitive phase which is brought to an end by the proximity of one or more other individuals, and is then succeeded by some other activity—feeding behaviour, sexual behaviour, or perhaps just sleeping. Thus when a great tit becomes separated from its flock in winter it hops up in the bushes, looks around, calls in a characteristic fashion, and flies around until it finds its companions. It then continues feeding or preening with them. There are thus no special movement patterns, except perhaps for the calls, by which the social appetitive behaviour can be identified. The whole sequence could be regarded as appetitive for feeding or preening behaviour, with the additional proviso that the presence of social companions is part of the stimulus situation normally necessary for these activities.

Furthermore, there appear to be no special positive causal factors which promote social behaviour. In the winter the integration of great tit flocks is to some extent correlated with the intensity of feeding behaviour: both tend to be greater in the morning than at midday, in mid-winter than in autumn, on cold days than on warm. Similarly, in early spring the male keeps closest to the female at the time when copulation occurs most frequently, suggesting that both have causal factors in common. Thus in each case the factors that promote the seeking of proximity with another individual seem not to be specifically social, but to be the same as those for activities performed with or in the company of that individual. The view that "there is . . . no 'social instinct' " (Tinbergen, 1951) thus receives considerable support.

However, activities in the appetitive phase could be classed together as social on the grounds not that they share *positive* causal factors but that they lead to a particular *consummatory situation*—namely, the proximity of another member of the species. True, at some times it seems that any other member of the species will do (e.g., in the winter flocks), while at other times it must be a particular individual (e.g., after pair formation in spring), but in either case the searching behaviour is switched off by proximity, and other types of behaviour follow. From this point of view, then, within one species all types of social behaviour have in common a causal factor—they are affected by the proximity of another individual, just as nest-building activities are affected by stimuli from a completed nest. The effect may be either negative or positive—negative in the initial appetitive phase which is brought to an end by the proximity of another individual, positive in the case of the activities that follow.

However, the validity of a causal basis for the category of social behaviour must not be pressed too far, for the precise stimuli from the second individual that are relevant vary with the type of social behaviour under consideration. As we have seen, the requirement that they come from a particular individual differs between flocking and sexual behaviour. And, when we come to consider man, a moment's consideration of the diversity of factors involved in human social behaviour (the satisfaction of various basic needs; comfort and reassurance; sharing of common problems, interests, and attitudes; the opportunity for self-evaluation; and so on) indicates that common causal factors for all behaviour that would normally be labelled as "social" can be found only at a very superficial level of analysis.

Whether or not the use of a category of "social behaviour" with causal implications is feasible, some treat it instead as a functional category, to include all types of behaviour that have the consequence of promoting proximity with other individuals of the species. This also runs into some difficulties. One is the problem of identifying the precise function (in terms of natural selection) of much social behaviour: this becomes particularly acute with human social behaviour, much of which cannot profitably be considered from that point of view. Another difficulty arises with aggression: although aggressive behaviour may involve proximity-seeking as well as repulsion, its consequence is usually dispersion (but see page 333).

Thus definition neither in causal nor in functional terms is wholly satisfactory, and it is better to return to common usage—social behaviour is a category of patterns of behaviour that lead to the proximity of, or involve interactions with, another individual of the species. The category is thus of the same general type as "care-of-the-body-surface" or "communicatory behaviour", and overlaps with or embraces many of the other categories into which behaviour is conventionally classified, such as feeding or sexual behaviour. From this point of view, aggressive behaviour is "social", though its consequences could be described as anti-social.

In summary, "social behaviour" can have implications of either a causal or a functional nature, but definition in terms of either is not satisfactory. It is best used, as in common speech, with reference to interactions with other individuals, recognizing that the category is a loose one and that further discussion of definition is unprofitable.

### Qualities of social relationships

There are, however, certain important distinctions to be drawn within social behaviour (in the broad sense). The first concerns the extent to which bonds are formed between particular individuals. In many species animals are drawn together by responses to stimuli characteristic of any other individual: although unproved, it seems likely that the fish in a shoal of mackerel have no special bonds with particular individuals, but are equally responsive to all other members of the species of similar size. Social insects are one stage more specific: in many species, members of the same colony or hive distinguish one another from individuals of another colony. Over the animal kingdom as a whole, responsiveness specific to particular individuals is characteristic of only a small minority of species.

Amongst the species in which individuals do respond specifically to each other, a second important distinction concerns the nature of the relationships formed. Are they specific to one particular type of behaviour, or do they transcend the activities in which the animals are involved? Von Uexküll (1934) pointed out that animals sometimes associate together only for the performance of one particular type of behaviour. This is analogous to the sort of human relationship which we describe by such phrases as "drinking companion" or "business colleague": von Uexküll used the German word *Kumpan* to refer to one who is a partner in only one type of activity. In animals, such a relationship may depend on the fact that another individual carries the stimuli for only one type of behaviour: for instance, an adolescent moorhen may respond to the stimuli for feeding presented by a younger individual, and become a temporary "parent companion" to it. Such limited relationships are perhaps most conspicuous when artificial conditions of rearing cause different responses to become attached predominantly to different individuals. A classic example was a jackdaw reared by Lorenz, which in its youth treated Lorenz as a parent companion, later performed all its courting activities to a maid, fed a young jackdaw and treated it as a filial companion, and (after Lorenz had proved his inadequacy in this respect) attached itself to hooded crows as flock companions (Fig. 2.4; Lorenz, 1931). In this case, an element of chance clearly entered in, the jackdaw associating each response with a companion who happened to be available around the time that that response appeared.

By contrast, jackdaws reared normally associate with companions with whom they perform a wide range of activities. Similarly, an infant rhesus monkey may direct toward its mother filial responses, grooming, soliciting for grooming, socio-sexual presenting, aggressive behaviour, play behaviour, and so on. In such cases, the relationship with one individual embraces a variety of types of behaviour. The way in which this comes about will be discussed in Chap. 12: the issue here is the difference in complexity between uniplex relationships, involving only one type of behaviour, and multiplex ones, involving many.

FIGURE 2.4

*Lorenz's jackdaw Jock and her four companions.* (Drawing by Priscilla Edwards from von Uexküll, 1934.)

A reservation is of course necessary. The distinction depends in part on the level of analysis. To take a human example, parent-infant interaction could be said to be uniplex (involving only the parental-filial mode) if it was being compared with the interaction between two friends who do many different things together, or multiplex (involving suckling-nursing, grooming, protection, play, etc.) if it was being compared with the relationship between a nurse with limtied duties and a child in a day care centre. The important issue is not the dichotomy between "single stranded" or "uniplex" and "multiplex", but a dimension of complexity of relationships—the number of modes of interaction involved.

Whether a relationship involves one or many types of behaviour, it may differ in quality in many ways. For one thing, in each type of interaction the roles of the two partners may be fixed and complementary, depending perhaps on masculine and feminine or dominant and subordinate characteristics of the individuals, or they may be variable and equivalent. For another, relationships vary greatly in stability. Often stability depends on complementary relationships between the partners—if one becomes more masculine the other becomes more feminine; if one becomes more dominant, the other becomes more subordinate. The range of such adjustments that are possible is usually limited. Yet again, the complexity of the mutual behaviour of the participants may vary enormously. At one extreme, it may consist merely of simple stimulus-response sequences— as with the adolescent moorhen mentioned above. More usually it involves inter-actions between the two of varying degrees of sophistication—and we must not be surprised to find, even in animals, that the behaviour of one participant in an interaction is determined by its assessment of the probable behaviour of the other.

Beyond this, it is sometimes useful to describe relationships with terms which have some measure of independence from particular types of activities. In our own species, for example, we may speak of relationships as being "affection-ate", "loving", "demanding", "competitive", and so on. These are the sorts of terms which scientists have too often shied away from because it is easier to forget that even in animals relationships can have such qualities than to devise hard-headed ways of coming to grips with them. When we apply such terms to a person, they refer in the first place to qualities which may be exhibited in diverse activities: there is an implication of an intrinsic property of the indi-vidual which is exhibited in several types of behaviour and which could con-ceivably be described in physiological terms (cf. discussion of drive concepts, Chap. 3). Often, however, such terms apply only to a limited range of his activities: we may say that a man is affectionate in his dealings with his family but merciless with his employees. This underlines an important issue—that qualities concern modes of interaction with others, and thus intrinsic properties of an individual, only insofar as he interacts similarly with diverse others. This is especially crucial when we come to apply such terms to relationships. Here they refer to qualities of the possibly diverse types of interaction which an individual shows in relations with another. However there is no necessary implication that all the relationships formed by an individual should have the same qualities—he may have an affectionate relationship with one person and a competitive one with another. Indeed even within one relationship, some modes of interaction may have qualities not present in others, as with parents who are affectionate in private but disciplinarians in public. Thus whether they are applied to persons or relationships, these qualities refer to modes of interacting, to the manner in which individuals *mesh*, in particular contexts: this is affected, but *not* determined, by intrinsic properties of either individual.

There is, however, a further difficulty when such terms as "affectionate" or "competitive" are applied to a relationship, and that is that they are often multi-dimensional. Attempts to measure affection along one scale are found to fail, because it involves many different properties of a relationship. But we can at least try to specify which dimensions are relevant. A human relationship is said to be affectionate to the extent, for example, that one individual directs a variety of (non-aggressive) types of behaviour toward one other individual, that the relationship is of long duration and survives temporary absences, that the presence of the partner provides security in anxiety-provoking situations, that the behaviour of one participant is ordered in relation to the ongoing behaviour of the other, and so on. Each of these qualities may transcend particular motivational contexts. How relationships with qualities of this sort develop in the individual is a problem of the greatest importance, to which we shall return later (Chaps. 12–15).

Again, it must be stressed that any one of the characteristics of affectionate relationships just mentioned embraces cases which may differ greatly in complexity. For instance, ordering of behaviour by one partner in relation to that of the other may at one extreme depend on simple stimulus-response sequences comparable to that of the stickleback's courtship (Fig. 3.2). At the other, it implies that the behaviour of each individual involves goals formulated on the basis of predictions about the other's real (or intended) behaviour. Between these two lie many intermediates—learning to respond to the partner on the basis of previous experience of the partner's behaviour, as when a rhesus monkey infant learns that it can approach its mother to suckle when she is showing some types of behaviour but not others (page 202). Thus affectionate relationships, or "bonds" to use a more neutral term, may differ in the number of qualities of the type mentioned in the previous paragraph that they possess, and in their complexity. Clearly cross-phyletic comparisons require great caution.

We have seen that a relationship between two individuals may involve many types of interaction: in behavioural terms the relationship in fact *is* the nature, quality and patterning of the interactions between them. In practice, of course, it is even more than this, because it involves the perceptions and expectancies that each has of the other: however, these are manifest to an observer primarily through the interactions that occur. Now interactions between two individuals rarely occur *in vacuo*. Each of the participants interacts also with other individuals, and these interactions affect their mutual interactions and thus their relationships with each other. The study of social behaviour thus inevitably leads to the study of groups. And just as the relationship between two individuals is the nature, quality and patterning of interactions between them, so the structure of the group is the nature, quality and patterning of relationships within it.

These, then, are some of the problems with which we shall be concerned. The matter of defining social behaviour is one that we shall disregard from now on: the qualities of social behaviour, how it is determined and how it develops, the nature of social relationships, and how social relationships affect each other, will be our main concern. In some cases it is possible to do little more than formulate the problems, but perhaps that is a not unimportant step towards their solution.

### Summary

Nearly all the categories that we use are to be regarded as working tools, not as absolutes. Social behaviour is no exception: definitions in causal or functional terms could be elaborated, but none would be wholly satisfactory.

Social relationships may differ in quality in a number of ways. The nature and bases of those differences present one of the most challenging problems in the study of behaviour.

# SECTION

# B

## TWO
## BASIC
## PROBLEMS

# 3

# THE PROBLEM
# OF
# MOTIVATION

### Why "instinct" has become a disreputable concept

Around the turn of the century, psychologists tended to explain most of the behaviour of man and animals in terms of "instincts". Amongst these was an instinct of "sociability" or "gregariousness" (see page 13). Now, however, instinct has ceased to be a useful concept. A brief examination of the reasons for this will put us in a better position to proceed with the study of social behaviour.

The instinct concept ran into difficulties because it was used to explain two different properties of behaviour which are not necessarily correlated with each other, and for both of which the concept is valid at only a rather superficial level of analysis. These properties are first that the behaviour develops independently of types of experience that might be considered essential for it, and second that it is in some sense driven from within. For example, nearly all species of birds build fairly elaborate nests. In every case that has been investigated, individuals reared from the egg by foster-parents in a strange type of nest will, on reaching reproductive age, build a nest not like that in which they were reared, but of the type characteristic of their own species. What is more, the nest is normally built at a time appropriate for the laying of the eggs. How did the bird know how to build a nest? And what made it do so at just the right time? The simple answer, that it built the nest "instinctively", was merely a cloak for ignorance. Used in this way, "instinct" explained nothing, and it was inevitable that it should fall into disrepute.

We shall return later to the question of the development of behaviour (Chap. 4); here we shall consider the problem of immediate causation.[1] The tendency to postulate instinctive forces which propel the organism into action is specially strong when we are unable to identify any external change which elicited the behaviour, and when the animal persists in showing a variety of types of behaviour all directed toward the same end. How can we explain the behaviour of a swallow which "spontaneously" starts off on a journey of thousands of miles, during which it crosses seas and mountain ranges and surmounts untold dangers? To postulate a migratory instinct or urge is merely circular: we postulate the instinct because we observe the behaviour, and then explain the behaviour by the instinct we have postulated. It is just as circular to explain human behaviour in terms of instincts labelled as aggressive, sexual, and so on —indeed even to ask the question, "Does man have any instincts?" involves a misunderstanding.

### The basic phenomena

How, then, are we to proceed? Consider first a number of inter-related facts, which all seem to imply changes in the internal state of the animal.

1 Even though an animal remains in a constant external situation, the frequencies with which it shows particular types of behaviour vary with time. For example, a canary kept in a cage, or a great tit living in a wood, is more likely to show nest-building behaviour at some times of year than at others.

2 Even when it is showing a particular type of behaviour, the intensity or frequency of that behaviour varies with time. In the spring, a bird builds more in the early morning than in the afternoon. During an outburst of singing, the notes or phrases come more frequently at some times than at others.

3 At different times, organisms select different categories of stimuli to respond to: sometimes those indicative of food, sometimes warmth, sometimes a sex partner, and so on.

[1] For more detailed discussion, see Bolles (1967), Hinde (1970).

4 The strength of the stimulus necessary to elicit a response of standard intensity varies with time: the longer a person has been without food, the more unappetizing the food that he will accept.

5 The strength of the aversive stimulus that an animal will tolerate varies with time: the longer a rat has been without food, the more highly charged the electric grid it will cross to obtain food.

In all these cases, even though the external stimulus situation for the behaviour in question is constant, the behaviour of the animal changes. We must therefore ascribe the changes in behaviour to changes in the animal's internal state.

To these we may add yet another fact, touched on in the previous chapter —certain types of behaviour tend to occur together. For instance, a male canary is more likely to sing and to court females in the spring than at other times of year. This presumably means that internal factors for these two activities are stronger in spring: since both activities tend to fluctuate together, they may mutually depend on internal factors which are present at that time of year but not at others. Again, a female canary tends to show the activities of picking up nest-material, flying to a nest-site, and weaving material into the nest, in quick succession. This may in part be because each type of behaviour in the sequence leads the animal into the stimulus situation for the next, but it may also be that common causal factors are involved.

The problem of the nature of these internal factors is the problem of "motivation", and we may refer to the presumed changes in the internal state of the animal as involving changing "motivational factors". Note that motivation is *a set of problems, not a thing*. Changes in behaviour with a constant external situation must imply internal changes which we may describe as "motivational" changes or changes in motivational factors, but this does not explain them.

In practice, it is usual to limit the problem of motivation somewhat. Only changes in responsiveness that are reversible and non-permanent are considered. Furthermore, changes in responsiveness that can be accounted for in terms of peripheral factors, such as sensory adaptation and muscular fatigue, are usually excluded.

### The use of intervening variables

In everyday speech, we meet these problems by postulating changes in our internal state which account for the changes in our behaviour, using terms such as "hunger", "thirst", or "aggressiveness" to account for observed changes in behaviour. In the first instance, this sounds as bad as postulating an instinct (see pages 23–24)—we may say a man is hungry because he eats, and we explain his eating in terms of hunger. But there are circumstances in which such concepts are useful. If we find that seeing dogs, waiting in a queue, and engaging in verbal disagreements, all cause a man to clench his fists and strike out, we label him as aggressive. If he did all these things yesterday but not today, we may say, "He was aggressive yesterday". We gain some measure of understanding of these diverse characteristics of his behaviour when we see that they all reflect a single predisposition or temporary state. Similarly, the concomitance of clenched fists, raised arm, and menacing posture we can ascribe to a common internal state, which we may call aggressiveness or aggressive motivation or drive. The postulation of this common internal state is of even more explanatory value if we find that all these aspects of behaviour are likely to be elicited by the same situations (e.g., dogs, queues, and verbal disagreements). We now have three types of situation or "treatment" (dogs, queues, etc.) and three types of response (clenched fist, raised arm, etc.). If we suppose that each treatment independently affects each response, then we must postulate nine treatment-response relationships. If, however, we can postulate an intervening variable, which in turn produces the three responses, we are concerned with only six relationships: economy has been achieved. We can if we like refer to this intervening variable as "aggressiveness" or "aggression", but this carries no necessary implications as to its nature, or as to the existence of any corresponding neural mechanism.

We can represent these relationships by the diagrams in Fig. 3.1, which are modified from diagrams used in a slightly different context by N. E. Miller (1959). From these diagrams, two points are apparent. First, that the degree of economy achieved depends on the number of treatments (referred to more generally as "independent variables") and responses (or "dependent variables"). If there are only two of each, then four relationships have to be established whether or not an "aggressive internal state" (or, in more general terms, an "intervening variable") is postulated.

Second, the postulation of an intervening variable is useful only if the several dependent variables are correlated with one another and with each independent variable. If, for instance, a man hits his dog but is considerate to people in queues and enters into balanced discussion with those who disagree with him, it is less useful to label him as aggressive. And if he hit a dog yesterday but was considerate in queues, it is less useful to say he was aggressive yesterday. Only where the extent to which the various possible dependent variables are correlated with one another is of primary interest, is an intervening variable a valu-

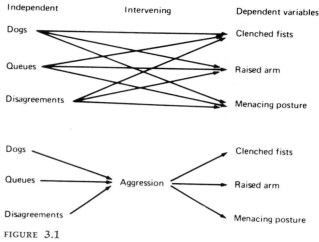

FIGURE 3.1

(a) *The relations between three independent variables and three dependent variables.* (b) *The relations between three independent variables, one intervening variable, and three dependent variables.*

able tool: as soon as any lack of correlation becomes important, such a concept is misleading and can be a positive hindrance.

In the preceding paragraphs it has been implied that intervening variables may be used in a number of different ways. In experimental psychology they are commonly used for more or less temporary motivational states such as hunger or thirst, to link the various ways in which those states may be induced (e.g., deprivation of water, injection of hypertonic saline solution) and assessed (e.g., volume of water drunk, rate of bar-pressing to acquire water, concentration of quinine tolerated in drinking water). Sometimes, however, they are used to explain correlations between dependent variables: for instance, the use of several types of threat posture by a fighting bird may be explained by reference to a postulated internal state, even though the determinants of that state are quite unknown.

Of course, the use of intervening variables is much more widespread than this. For example, they may be used for long-term dispositions or aspects of personality rather than temporary motivational states: as we have seen, we label a man "aggressive" on the basis of his behaviour in a variety of contexts. Furthermore, we may use them with reference to entities larger than a single individual (e.g., mass hysteria).

So far, we have used these intervening variables merely as a convenient device to provide understanding of the relationships between different aspects of behaviour or between behaviour and factors which influence that behaviour. If the intervening variables that we postulate (e.g., "hunger drive") appear to have some relationship to subjective experiences ("feeling hungry"), this may seem to give them a little more substance. However, the temptation to reify these intervening variables, to imagine that they correspond to some entity or process in the organism, is always present and usually dangerous. Let us consider this in relation to the problem of "spontaneity".

### Spontaneity

We referred just now to the swallow which started off on migration "spontaneously". Just what is meant by this term? We use it to describe the swallow's behaviour because we cannot see just what set it off. For the same reason, when a caged canary starts to sing, we might say it started "spontaneously". In both cases, to put the matter in more general terms, the output (in this case, the behaviour in question) of a system (the swallow or canary) has changed without a corresponding change in input. The ringing (output) of an alarm clock (system) can be described in the same terms. This last example makes it clear that when we use the term "spontaneous", we must specify the system we are considering: although the alarm clock rang when there was no change in its environment, we know that the alarm mechanism inside the clock was in fact triggered by a change in *its* environment. Thus a change may be spontaneous at one level of analysis but not at another: changes in output may appear to be spontaneous at the level of the group, individual, nervous system, or nerve cell, but depend on a change in the environment of elements at the next lower level. It will be apparent that "spontaneous" must be used strictly descriptively, and must not be used in an explanatory fashion or it, too, will become a cloak for ignorance.

Because the behaviour of animals and man so often appears to be spontaneous, many psychologists writing in the first half of the twentieth century used "energy models" of motivation. They postulated that the bases of an animal's activities lay in an internal source of energy which was expended in action. Actually the origin of this idea goes back a very long way: the Greek dramatists clearly believed that a display of anger would reduce a man's tendency to behave aggressively, and a similar belief is behind such everyday expressions as "letting off steam". The models used by psychologists differ considerably in detail: Freud used a concept of "libido", Lorenz (1950) of "action-specific energy".

Though neither Freud nor Lorenz went about it in quite this way, this procedure amounts to (1) postulating an intervening variable and (2) reifying it as an entity with properties appropriate to physical energy but possibly irrelevant to the behaviour it is supposed to explain. We can see the difficulties into which this runs by considering how behaviour comes to an end. If behaviour depends on an internal source of energy, it can come to an end only through the expenditure of that energy in action. Thus we should expect every sequence of behaviour to come to an end by the discharge of energy in the performance of behaviour. But if we are tired enough we make seek for comfort, quiet, and darkness, and when we find them, fall asleep. Indeed, as noted elsewhere (pages 10–11, 31–33) behaviour is often brought to an end by new stimuli perceived as a result of that behaviour—a fact not easily compatible with energy theories (Hinde, 1960).

With increasing understanding of the nature of the nervous system, the problem of spontaneity has changed its nature. In the early days of instinct theories, the nervous system was regarded as essentially passive, activity being imposed by stimulation from outside. This picture is now known to be far from correct: the nervous system shows continuous electrical activity, even in sleep. The problem of motivation is thus not, "Why does the animal behave?", but "Why does it do this rather than that?". If we are to tackle such questions analytically, we must first attempt to isolate factors which either elicit particular patterns of behaviour, or predispose the animal to behave in one way rather than another.

### External factors—eliciting and motivating stimuli

A sufficient number of animals have now been studied for us to know a fair amount about the stimuli which elicit a variety of types of behaviour: for example, certain worms may elicit feeding behaviour from a three-spined stickleback, vaguely fish-like objects coloured red underneath may elicit aggressive behaviour (Fig. 4.1), and similar objects not painted red but with a swollen underside and held at a certain attitude in the water may provoke courtship (Fig. 6.1). In these cases, the stimuli produce an almost immediate response, but in others they act more gradually. For example, rat pups can elicit immediate maternal responses from female rats with litters, but with virgin females such responses may appear only after prolonged exposure to the pup (Rosenblatt, 1967). In such a case, the continued exposure apparently produced a change in the internal state of the responding animal—in other words, it had a motivational effect. In yet other cases, external stimuli maintain a state of readiness to respond: at a certain stage in the spring a great tit sings and attacks rivals only when on his territory: stimuli from the territory must predispose the bird to behave in particular ways. It will be apparent that the distinction between stimuli that elicit responses immediately and stimuli that have a motivating effect is, for most purposes at any rate, only one of degree.

### Internal factors

The effectiveness of eliciting stimuli changes with time, and something is known about the bases for this. In the case of feeding behaviour, the effectiveness of stimuli from food varies with, amongst other things, the time since the animal last fed, indicating that progressive internal changes render it more responsive. With the territorial behaviour of a fish or bird, the effectiveness of another individual in eliciting aggression varies with the time of year: we can show that this is related to hormonal changes which occur with the progression of the seasons. Sexual behaviour is similarly influenced by hormonal factors. Thus, responsiveness depends on a variety of factors internal to the animal, including the cumulative effect of past stimulation, the hormonal state, and others to be mentioned shortly.

For a number of types of behaviour, it has been shown that there is a relationship between the strength of the stimulus needed to elicit a response and the strength of the internal factors predisposing the animal to give that response. For instance, if we inject a low level of hormones into a rat it will attempt copulation only with a receptive female, but with a higher dose it will mount a crude dummy. In general, the greater the internal state, the less the stimulus necessary to elicit the response. The relative importance of changes in internal state and of external stimuli in influencing changes in responsiveness varies between responses. As we have seen, a canary may sing without any change in the external situation. This is even more true of various types of searching behaviour: when it has not eaten for a while, an animal may spontaneously (i.e., without any change in the external situation) go and look for food.

In studies of animals, the internal factors most frequently studied result from food or water deprivation, painful stimuli, or manipulations of the endocrine state. But it is usually necessary to ensure that the animals used in an experiment have had comparable previous experience, for experience also affects the behaviour shown in a given situation: two rats equally deprived of food may differ markedly in behaviour if their previous experience differs. The ways in which experience affects behaviour are of course more diverse and complex in primates and in man than in non-primate species.

## Negative factors and consummatory stimuli

So far the changes in what an animal does have been discussed only in terms of the changing incidence of internal and external factors promoting particular types of behaviour—with the implication that behavioural changes occur because those for one type of behaviour gain preponderance over those for another. But this is only half the picture, for we must also consider the factors that bring each type of behaviour to an end. Apart from interruption by another type of behaviour whose causal factors gain preponderance, these are of three main types. First and most obviously, behaviour may cease because the causal factors which elicited it in the first instance disappear: for example, an animal fleeing from a predator will soon cease to do so if the predator disappears.

Second, behaviour may cease because, as a consequence of the behaviour, the animal encounters new factors which switch it off. As we have already seen, this is true of all searching behaviour: the particular behaviour involved in, say, searching for food ceases when food is found, migratory behaviour ceases when (among other things) a suitable habitat is encountered, and so on. A similar principle applies to many types of behaviour that do not involve searching. For instance, the bout of eating behaviour which constitutes a meal is brought to an end long before the food has been absorbed from the stomach and the tissue needs replenished. The cessation is due to stimuli in the mouth, throat, and stomach from the ingested food. If a hole is made in the oesophagus of a dog, so that the food that it eats drops out, the animal will go on eating for much longer because of the absence of consummatory stimuli in the stomach. If food is inserted directly into the stomach, the animal's responsiveness to food is reduced.

Another well-analyzed case concerns the courtship of the three-spined stickleback (Fig. 3.2). As described in Chap. 6, in this species the male builds a nest and then courts any egg-laden female who enters his territory. He leads the female to his nest, where the female deposits her eggs. After he has fertilized them, the male's behaviour toward females entering his territory changes.

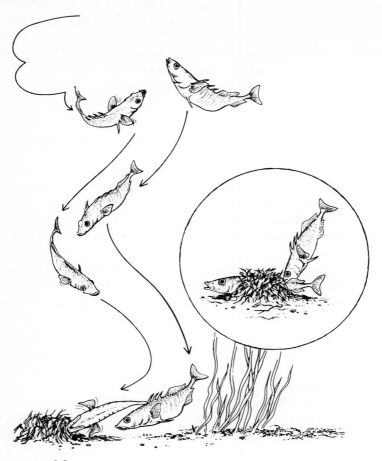

FIGURE 3.2

*Schematic representation of the sexual behaviour of the three-spined stickleback. (From Tinbergen, 1951.) The female, with swollen belly (top right) enters the territory of the male, swimming in a special posture. The male courts her, and when she responds he leads her to the nest. If she follows, he adopts a special posture by the nest entrance. When she enters (inset), a trembling movement by the male elicits spawning. Subsequently the male enters the nest and fertilizes the eggs (not shown).*

Instead of courting them, he attacks them and attempts to drive them out. This change is not a consequence of the act of ejaculation, as might be thought, but of the smell of fresh eggs in the nest: these act as "consummatory stimuli" for courtship (Sevenster-Bol, 1962).[2]

Third, behaviour may come to an end through internal changes resulting from the activity itself or from the continuing presence of the stimuli that elicited it. One issue here is muscular fatigue. Another is habituation, as when we cease to respond to the sound of aeroplanes if we live moderately near an airport. In practice most cases of the waning or cessation of a response involve multiple processes. In simple organisms these can be studied directly. For example, if an earthworm lying outside its burrow is touched lightly, it rapidly withdraws. After a while, if nothing further happens, it emerges again. If it is then touched, it withdraws again. After a few repetitions, however, the withdrawal becomes less rapid, and after a while the stimulus becomes quite ineffective. In this case the neural pathways involved are quite simple, and it is known that the changes in behaviour depend on changes at two synapses.[3] Comparable cases of the waning or cessation of responses have been studied at all levels in the animal kingdom. In higher organisms the changes are of course much more complex: at the behavioural level, they can often be analysed into a number of distinct processes, some leading to an increase and some to a decrease in response strength, some decaying rapidly and some being much more permanent, some specific to the particular stimulus which elicited the response and some less so (Horn and Hinde, 1970).

## Mechanisms

Having thus identified the variables which influence the relative probabilities that the individual will show the types of behaviour in its repertoire, the next stage is to examine the mechanisms by which they exert their effects.

A considerable amount is now known about the neural mechanisms underlying various types of behaviour, but that is the province of physiological psychology and neurophysiology, and would take us too far afield here. However, two points must be made. First, it is much easier to study the mechanisms

[2] It will be noted that consummatory stimuli, defined as stimuli which bring a particular sequence of behaviour to an end, may yet have incentive properties leading to a repetition of the sequence.

[3] A synapse is the region in which two nerve fibres come into close proximity so that a nerve impulse in one fibre can produce an impulse in the second, or a change in the probability that it will fire.

underlying a particular type of behaviour if that behaviour can be readily identified. For example, artificial electrical stimulation of the brain has revealed a great
deal about the mechanisms controlling those types of behaviour that can be
identified by characteristic stereotyped movements, such as eating and fighting,
but much less about those that are less easily identified, such as exploratory and
some forms of social behaviour. Second, progress in understanding the neurophysiological mechanisms underlying changes in responsiveness is much more
rapid if extra-neural factors which affect it can be identified. Once we know that
a given type of behaviour is affected by certain hormones and certain external
stimuli, for instance, we have tools with which to manipulate the intra-neural
state and can thus study it more easily. But in the absence of such tools, many
neurophysiological methods are of little value. Again, it is partly for this reason
that the mechanisms underlying eating and drinking behaviour are relatively
easy to study but the bases of some forms of social behaviour are much more
difficult.

### Animal and human motivation

This discussion has been concerned primarily with non-human species, mainly
lower mammals and birds. It hardly needs saying that the factors determining
changes in behaviour in our own species are very much more complex. Consider
just one issue. As we have seen, a sequence of behaviour may involve searching
for a consummatory situation: the central nervous state underlying that behaviour must therefore involve mechanisms ready to respond to the stimuli and
thus to bring the behaviour to an end. Where the searching behaviour is guided
by the discrepancy between the present situation and a goal situation (see pages
89–90), the central nervous state must involve mechanisms responsive to such
discrepancies. Thus the internal state may include reference to the situation
toward which the behaviour is directed. It is possible without too much difficulty
to conceptualize this for much of the behaviour of animals, but human behaviour, especially human social behaviour, involves goals of much greater complexity, and also much more devious means of reaching them, than will ever be
found in animals. In the human case the neural mechanisms employed in
reaching a goal may involve those associated with language, introspection, and
planning—all processes which, insofar as they exist at all in animals, are
extremely difficult to investigate.

    For such reasons, the account of the problem of motivation just given, derived primarily from studies of animals, can take us only some of the way toward the much more complex problems of motivation in man. However, here, as elsewhere, the very fact that animals are simpler than man helps us to segregate the issues, clarify the problems, and formulate a method of approach.

## The causal networks

One final point must be made. The procedure of identifying the variables that influence the types of behaviour in an animal's repertoire soon reveals the complexity of the mechanisms controlling behaviour in higher organisms. Though it is often relatively easy to identify a few factors of prime importance in any one case, it also becomes clear that a wide variety of other factors also operates. To give an everyday example, how much we eat is determined primarily by how long we have been without food and the nature of the food available to us, but it is also affected by the time of day, the company we are in, the attractiveness of our surroundings, our expectations of what we will be doing next, and so on. Each of these other factors will affect also other activities besides eating.

Similar principles apply to animals. Thus in many birds territorial aggression, song, and courtship are all influenced by male sex hormones and can thus be classed together on a causal basis. But aggression and song are more influenced by stimuli from a familiar territory than courtship, and the presence of a female augments courtship but decreases song. Furthermore male sex hormones also influence sleeping rhythms, activity, feeding behaviour, and many other aspects of behaviour, each of which may be primarily in the control of yet other factors.

Thus, while it is often convenient for some purposes to use causal categories in classifying behaviour—e.g., all behaviour influenced by male sex hormones, or by food deprivation—we must constantly bear in mind that the categories overlap extensively, and that while some of the causal factors we study influence only a few activities, others may affect nearly all those in the species' repertoire. The old view that it would be possible to list the various "instincts" that each species possessed, and to pigeonhole each type of behaviour under one or other intinct, is quite misleading.

Yet some of the controversies in the study of non-human primates rest on just such a misapprehension. Discussions as to whether various sorts of aggression (page 252) are "really" different from one another, whether a male who carries a baby (pages 231–000) is "really" behaving maternally, whether male-male mounting (page 305) is "really" sexual behaviour, miss the point. Our task here is to identify the factors which affect each type of behaviour, and to assess the extent of their overlap in influencing the several kinds of behaviour under discussion. We shall find that some factors may be common to aggression in all contexts, and some may be quite specific; that male-male mounting is influenced by some of the factors that affect male-female mounting, and has some factors specific to it. Such matters are likely to be ones of degree, and the classificatory categories have a certain but limited range of usefulness.

## Summary

We see, then, that to explain the changes in behaviour that an animal shows by postulating "instincts" is not useful. Having recognized motivation as a group of problems, we have seen that some understanding can be gained by the use of intervening variables. The range of usefulness of this approach is, however, limited, and the temptation to reify the variables carries immediate dangers. To understand the mechanisms involved, we must adopt an analytical approach, breaking down the problem by identifying the internal changes on which changes in responsiveness depend. We have seen that we can identify internal and external stimuli and hormonal changes as exerting a positive influence on particular types of behaviour, and stimuli (again internal or external) and intra-neural changes as exerting negative effects. But the more intangible the external factors influencing the behaviour in question, the more difficult is the problem of motivation. Finally, though it is often useful to classify items of behaviour into causal categories, those categories have limited ranges of validity.

# 4

# THE PROBLEM
# OF
# DEVELOPMENT

In the last chapter we saw that the concept of "instinct" has fallen into disrepute because it has been used with reference to two different properties of behaviour, for both of which it is valid at only a rather superficial level of analysis, and which are not necessarily correlated with each other. One of these properties—changes in responsiveness with a constant stimulus situation —has been considered. The second, which relates to the problem of development, is our present concern.

The study of development has run into trouble at the theoretical level for two reasons. It has been bedevilled by dichotomies, and it has been plagued by disputes between workers who adopted different theoretical approaches and did not see that they differed primarily because they were interested in different questions.[1]

The dichotomies concerned are familiar enough and involve oppositions such as human intelligence versus animal instinct, or learned versus innate. In the first place, all such dichotomies run into difficulties if they imply that the

---

[1] For more detailed discussion, see Hinde (1968, 1970), Lehrman (1970).

factors influencing the development of behaviour are of two types only—genetic and those associated with learning. Such a view is misleading because environmental factors can affect the development of behaviour in a number of ways, only some of which come within any generally accepted meaning of "learning". For example, various aspects of behaviour in adult life may be influenced by nutrition during development (Lát et al., 1960). Again, how an adult rat behaves when placed in an empty arena may be profoundly affected by a few minutes of daily handling by an experimenter for about 10 days in early life (see pages 230–234). If we are to stretch the concept of "learning" to encompass such effects of experience, it becomes so broad as to be valueless.

Accepting that changes in the external world can affect subsequent behaviour in a variety of ways, investigators frequently use four types of dichotomy. The first, a dichotomy of "sources of information", is useful when the investigator is interested in the adaptedness of behaviour (Lorenz, 1965). Most of the behaviour of animals (and our own is another issue) is adaptive in the sense that it tends to ensure that the individual showing it will survive and leave offspring. For this to be the case, the behaviour must "fit" the environment in which the animal lives. It is therefore proper to ask how this comes about. Lorenz (1965) points out that there are only two ways in which a developing organism can acquire information about the environment in which it develops—from its genes, and by learning. That Lorenz overlooks the fact that behaviour may be modified by the environment through mechanisms other than learning is not relevant here. His point is that behaviour can ultimately be modified only through changes in the genes or by experience in the environment in the individual's lifetime: its adaptedness must be achieved in one (or both) of these ways. For example, in spring, male three-spined sticklebacks develop a red belly. When behaving territorially, they will attack crude wooden models, provided they are coloured red underneath, as though they were intruding males (Fig. 4.1). This is true even if the sticklebacks have been reared in isolation and have never seen another stickleback. Clearly, that sticklebacks with red bellies should be attacked and sticklebacks without red bellies should not is something which cannot have been learned by a stickleback reared in isolation. The information, Lorenz argues, must have come from an "innate source". On the other hand, when the stickleback swims to a particular place in the stream to gather weed for its nest, it must have learned that that was a profitable place in which to search.

This dichotomy between sources of information throws into relief an important point often overlooked in studies of development. Since behaviour is on the whole biologically adaptive, it is necessary to explain why the environ-

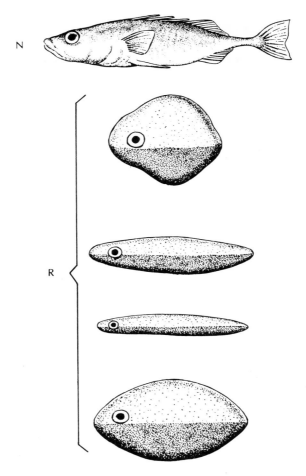

FIGURE 4.1
*Models used for assessing the stimuli eliciting aggressive behaviour from three-spined sticklebacks.*
(From Tinbergen, 1951.)

mental factors which operate in the development of behaviour produce results favourable to the organism, and not deleterious ones. We would take it for granted if we learned that the fur of a mammal grew thicker if it was moved to a colder environment, but why should it be that the processes of hair development should be affected by cold in this way, rather than the reverse? Again, we take it for granted that animals learn to go to a signal which heralds a supply of food, and not to avoid it, but it *could* happen the other way round. In each case, natural selection, acting through the genes, has operated to ensure that individuals respond appropriately to the environmental change. Thus the appropriate use even of environmental information is influenced by natural selection.[1]

This dichotomy of "sources of information" (and "information" is of course being used in a crude everyday sense) may be useful if we are interested in the origins of adaptedness. However, it helps us not at all in understanding the interaction between organism and environment which occurs in development.

A second dichotomy, and the one found most frequently in the older literature, is between types of behaviour—intelligent versus instinctive, or learned versus innate behaviour. Such a dichotomy runs into a number of difficulties:

1 Instinctive or innate behaviour is defined solely in negative terms—it is behaviour whose development is not affected by learning. Any category defined solely in negative terms is likely to be heterogeneous.

2 The distinction is often based upon a deprivation experiment. Thus in the case cited above, the behaviour of the stickleback reared in isolation toward dummies coloured red underneath would be said to be innate. But in a deprivation experiment the animal is deprived only of certain types of experience—namely those which the experimenter considers likely to be relevant to the behaviour in question. There is no doubt that experience of other sorts enters into the development of the behaviour—for instance, most animals must be exposed to light for their eyes to function normally. To cite another example, all tits of the genus *Parus* (e.g., chickadees) open seeds by placing them under one foot and hammering at them with their beaks (Fig. 4.2). Even tits reared in isolation do this, showing that they do not have to learn it by imitation. However, this isolation experiment does not show that the behaviour is independent of all experience. Learning does enter into the perfection of the pattern: when about three weeks old, tits can be seen to be making clumsy attempts to place things under a foot, and these gradually become perfected. If they are not given small objects suitable for placing under the foot, the development of the behaviour is delayed (Vince, 1964).

3 Even worse, behaviour is sometimes labelled as innate merely because it

[1] See Seligman and Hager, 1972; Hinde and Stevenson-Hinde, 1973.

FIGURE 4.2
*Great tit holding mealworm under one foot.*
(Drawing by Priscilla Edwards from photograph
by Margaret Vince.)

occurs in all members of a species. The tit example just quoted shows that
a pattern found in all individuals may yet depend on learning. To cite
another case, the various finch species vary in beak size and feed on seeds
of different sizes (Fig. 4.3). Since it was known that in some species variations in beak size were correlated with the size of the seeds taken, it used
to be assumed that the size of the beak was adapted to the size of seeds the
birds "instinctively" took. In fact, the opposite seems to be the case—the
birds learn to specialize on seeds of a size which their beaks are efficient at
opening. Thus the species-characteristic choice of seeds is in fact based on
individual learning, though the similarities in beak size among the individuals of a species ensure that learning will follow a similar course in all
of them (Hinde, 1959; Kear, 1962).

4 In any case, it does not need to be said that the development of all characters, including those of behaviour, depends on both nature and nurture.
No character depends only on genes or only on the environment. It is,
however, sometimes useful to recognize that there is a continuum between
stable and labile patterns. Some, such as the extensor reflex of the legs of
the human newborn, appear under practically any environmental conditions in which development is possible at all; while others, such as the
acquisition of a particular human language, depend on particular types of
experience. Note, however, that in both cases the character depends on

FIGURE 4.3

*Some European finches, showing differences in beak size. From left to right, hawfinch, greenfinch, goldfinch.* (Drawing by Priscilla Edwards.)

both genes and environment; the knee jerk is influenced by the position of the foetus in the womb (Prechtl, 1965), and chimpanzees cannot in any real sense learn human language even if reared in a human family.

Another type of dichotomy is one of processes, the usual distinction being between maturational processes and those determined by experience. In fact, maturational processes turn out to be another negative category—those not influenced by factors external to the organism. In any case, the relative constancy which they are supposed to have is due merely to the fact that they take place in a homeostatically controlled environment. The constancy of the path followed by a developing nerve trunk, say, is partly due to the fact that the environment within which it develops is always the same within narrow limits, and does not indicate that its development is any the less dependent on the environment in which it occurs.

We see, then, that dichotomies of sources of information, of behaviour, and of processes do not help us very much in teazing apart the complex interplay between organism and environment which is the very substance of development. What we can do, however, is to search for sources of differences in behaviour. We can take organisms of identical genetic background (or groups of organisms which on average have the same genetic constitution) and rear them in different environments. If differences emerge, these must ultimately be due to the differences between the environments. Alternatively, we can take organisms of differing genetic constitution and rear them in identical environments. If differences emerge, they must be due to the genetic differences. Such experiments lead us to a dichotomy of sources of differences. Rather than attempting to categorize types of behaviour or processes of development, we can attempt to identify the sources of differences between characters.

That such experiments do not lead to a distinction between two categories of behaviour cannot be too strongly emphasized. For example, a chaffinch reared in a tit's nest by tits does not develop the ability to place seeds under its foot. However much we do to make the environment in which development occurs identical to that in which tits develop (and of course there are inevitably differences in the intra-egg environment), the species difference remains, and so it must have a genetic basis. However, this does not mean that learning does not enter into the development of the behaviour in tits—we have seen that it does.

Similarly, if we rear genetically similar animals in different environments and find no difference in their behaviour, we cannot conclude that the environment does not affect behaviour, but only that the difference between the two sets of conditions used produces no detectable difference in behaviour.

With these reservations, we can thus identify the sources of some of the differences in behaviour that we observe. Having identified the source as either genetic or environmental, we can then proceed to ask how differences in genetic constitution come to influence the behaviour of the adult, what environmental factors are involved, and how they produce their effects.

Since the organism is an integrated system, any change in its heredity may have diverse consequences. Thus, most behavioural characters are influenced by more than one gene substitution, and most genes influence more than one character. Whether a genetic difference involves one or many genes, its effect may be mediated in diverse ways—by changes in sense organs, effectors, body proportions, the endocrine system, and so on, as well as by changes in the nervous system itself. We have already seen how the seed preferences of European finches are affected by genetic factors determining beak size. As another example, the brown and rufous-sided towhees (*Pipilio*) forage in different places, a difference which appears to be related to the size and musculature of the legs (Davis, 1957; see also Newton, 1967).

Where the young are dependent on maternal care, the route by which genetic differences produce behavioural ones may be very indirect. In one experiment, two strains of mice were reared by foster-parents of the same two strains in all possible combinations. Offspring of both strains showed more visual exploration when 60 days old, weighed more, and had a longer life expectancy, if reared by parents of one strain than if reared by the other (Ressler, 1963). The differences were presumably due to differences in some aspects of maternal care between strains. Maternal care was, however, influenced by the strain of the offspring, as well as that of the parents: thus even this cross-fostering technique did not completely separate genetic from post-natal parental influences. Ressler (1966) also showed that a difference in the environment in which young rodents were reared could, by affecting their maternal behaviour, influence the behaviour of their offspring. Thus, the environmental influence was transmitted across a generation. More recently, Denenberg and Rosenberg (1967) showed that such an influence could be transmitted across two generations. Thus, one must not be too hasty in concluding that strain differences are due to genetic factors.

Just as genetic factors may affect behaviour in diverse ways, so also may experiential ones. When we find that genetically similar individuals reared in different environments behave differently, the latter difference may be due to environmentally induced differences in their sensory equipment, their bodily proportions and effectors, their responsiveness to environmental changes consequent upon differences in the functioning of their pituitary-adrenal systems, or to differences in many other factors as well as to effects of learning in a conventional sense. The identification of a difference as environmentally induced is but the first stage in discovering its bases.

Finally, it must be emphasized that development always involves an interaction between genetic and environmental factors. The finding of a certain relationship between a particular aspect of early experience and exploratory behaviour in adulthood for one genotype does not imply that the same relationship would hold for another genetic strain. Similarly the finding that a given genetic substitution results in a certain difference in behaviour in animals reared in one environment does not necessarily mean that it would result in the same difference if the animals were reared in different circumstances. Development involves a continuing interaction between the organism at each stage and its environment, and the teazing apart of the processes involved in any species demands that we take cognisance of its course in each of a range of genotypes in each of a range of environments. The identification of sources of difference is only the first stage.

### Conclusion

The problem of the development of behaviour is not helped by the use of simple conceptual dichotomies. If we are interested in how behaviour comes to be adapted to its environment, it may be helpful to distinguish between genetic and experiential "sources of information" about that environment. But if our aim is to teaze apart the subtle interplay between organism and environment which is the very essence of development, dichotomies of sources of information, of behaviour, or of developmental processes are of little use. The only profitable course is to attempt to isolate the sources of differences between characters, and then to determine how the factors concerned produce their effects.

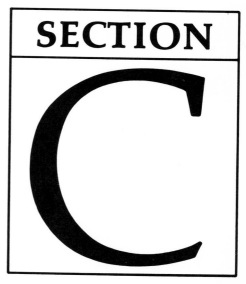

SECTION

C

COMMUNICATION

# 5

# WHAT IS
# COMMUNICATION?

When a number of individuals are brought together through similar responses to a localized stimulus, such as moths to a candle or sharks to a blood meal, the resulting concentration can be described as an aggregation, but not usefully as a social group (page 9). Social behaviour implies that the individuals influence each other's behaviour. This section is concerned with the means whereby such influences are exerted.

We must first come to terms with another semantic issue—the use of the term "communication". Consider three examples:

1  You are sitting at the table and want some salt with your food. You turn to your neighbour and ask politely, "Please pass the salt". If he does so, there is an end to the matter. If he takes no notice you will repeat your request. If he still does not respond you may try again, asking more loudly and perhaps less politely, and you may even try nudging or kicking him under the table. If on the other hand he responds by passing the mustard, you may say, perhaps with an edge to your voice, "Thank you, but it is the salt that I want".

2 You see someone in the street whom you think you met at a party, and are not sure whether to approach him. As soon as he sees you his face lights up into a smile, and you then approach.

3 You are talking to your professor. You notice he is beginning unconsciously to tap with his little finger on his desk. From past experience you know that the movement will soon spread to his other fingers, and then to his fist, so that he will soon be pounding on his desk and shouting angrily at you. You leave quickly.

In all three cases the behaviour of one individual influences that of another, but they clearly differ greatly in nature. The relations between them can be specified in terms of two properties:

1 Whether the sender of the signals "intended" to influence the behaviour of the other individual. Intentions are difficult enough to assess in our own species, and when it comes to animals the difficulties are much greater (see pages 89–90). But a working criterion might depend on assessing whether the sender monitors the behaviour of the recipient and alters his signalling behaviour to maximize his chances of conveying the message. By this criterion "intended" becomes equivalent to "goal-directed"—the sender is responding to a discrepancy between what the receiver is actually doing and what he wants him to do. The latter may involve carrying out a command, answering a question, merely indicating that the message has been received, or what have you (MacKay, 1972).

2 Whether there is reason to think that the signal used has been adapted in evolution to influence others. A number of lines of evidence (Chap. 6) suggest that the threat posture of the robin (Fig. 2.2) or great tit (Fig. 6.6) has been adapted in evolution for a signal function: apart from anything else, it would be difficult to find another explanation for its bizarre form. But many of the mannerisms of one's friends, though conveying a great deal of information about their present state, are individually idiosyncratic and not the immediate product of evolutionary forces. We shall see later that the evidence used to distinguish adapted from non-adapted signals is often indirect, and that the distinction is often not clear-cut: however for present purposes we are concerned only with the ends of the continuum.

In the first example, the request is intended to make your neighbour pass the salt: the words used and the way in which they are spoken are varied in accordance with the apparent difficulty of obtaining it—i.e., with the discrepancy between present and required situation. In so far as verbal language is used, you are using a system adapted for signalling. There is, however, no reason to suppose that the kick you give your neighbour when he fails to respond is a movement which has been adapted in evolution for signalling (see pages 73–75), though it is goal-directed.

TABLE 5.1 *Classification of signals used in examples in text according to the extent that they are directed and adapted for influencing the signalee*

|  | Directed | Adapted |
|---|---|---|
| {"Pass the salt" | ✓ | ✓ |
| {Kick | ✓ | ✓ |
| Smile | ✓ |  |
| Finger-tapping |  | ✓ |

In the second example, the smile used by your acquaintance is, as we shall see, a movement common to all human cultures, and is indeed similar to expressive movements used by other primates (see pages 126–132): there are good reasons for believing it to have been adapted for a signal function. But although he was expressing his feelings by smiling, his smile was not directed toward influencing you in the sense that, in the first example, your request was directed toward obtaining the salt. You might say, "He smiled spontaneously"—though note that this use of "spontaneous" to mean "without deliberation" is different from the "without external stimulus" discussed on page 28. Here, then, the interchange involved a signal adapted for signalling but not directed toward influencing you.

The tapping of your professor's finger influenced your behaviour, but he did not intend that you should leave the room, indeed he was probably not aware of what he was doing. Furthermore, his finger-tapping was an individually idiosyncratic movement, not adapted in evolution for signalling.

Thus, as shown in Table 5.1, our examples differ in the extent to which the signals used are directed toward and are adapted for influencing the behaviour of the signalee. These distinctions are important in part because they have formed the foci of interest of different groups of investigators. If you are a socio-biologist interested in how the structure of a social group arises from the manner in which the individuals composing it influence one another, then clearly you must study *all* the ways in which they influence one another. If you are an evolutionary biologist, interested in the evolution of signalling systems, you will be concerned primarily with those adapted to that end. If you are interested in the communicatory process itself, you are likely to focus only on directed signals. In the past, misunderstandings have arisen because some authors prefer to restrict the term "communication" to cases where directed signals are used (e.g., MacKay, 1972), while others use it more broadly. And to some the character of evolutionary adaptedness is central, while to others it is irrelevant. Two sets of investigators gave figures, for the number of visual signals in the repertoire of the rhesus monkey, that differed considerably—Altmann (1962) listed about 50, while the present author and his colleague Thelma Rowell listed only about 22 (Hinde and Rowell, 1962): the discrepancy was due in part to the difference between Altmann's socio-biological interest in all signals that influence the behaviour of others, and our more restricted interest in those likely to have been adapted in evolution for signalling. Once such differences in ranges of interests are recognized, the semantic issue is no longer a problem.

# 6

# SOCIAL
# RELEASERS

### Stimulus selection and social releasers

In this chapter, we shall be concerned primarily with signals adapted for communication with other members of the species. Each species has a repertoire of such signals, and they are of major importance in its social life. The precise size of the repertoire is always difficult to assess, in part because the presence of intergrading signals and intermediates makes it impossible to specify what is "a signal". But as a very rough indication, Moynihan (1970) found that a variety of species of mammals and birds had from fifteen to thirty-five "major" signals,[1] "major" signals being regarded as those that are qualitatively distinct, with parts of inter-grading continua omitted. Such signals are usually referred to as social releasers, and sometimes as displays.

Before we consider them, a slight digression is necessary.

Our sense organs are continuously being bombarbed by physical and chemical stimuli. To this barrage we respond selectively: some configurations of energy change influence us, others do not. To take an everyday example, we notice circular shapes more readily than shapes with irregular outlines, and patterns with regularly arranged elements more readily than those with irregular ones. This selectivity in responsiveness to the world around us is partly a consequence of the nature of our sense organs: thus we are not markedly affected by changes in the electric field surrounding us, though some fish which have suitable receptors are. Amongst the energy changes to which our sense organs do respond, we respond more to some configurations than to others, the conspicuousness of circles being a case in point: the manner in which this results from the inter-connections of the cells in the retinae and visual pathways is beginning to be understood (e.g., Hubel, 1963), but cannot be considered here. Beyond that, some stimulus patterns are relevant to one type of behaviour, some to another, so that when we are in one physiological state we may be especially responsive to (say) food, in another to water, and in yet another to a member of the opposite sex. Thus selectivity in responsiveness is partly a consequence of properties of the sensory-perceptual apparatus, and thus independent of the particular stimulus or type of behaviour in progress, and partly specific to the current motivational state.

This selectivity in responsiveness is crucial for the understanding of social communication, for it implies that in responding to another individual some stimulus characters are much more important than others. An example is provided by Tinbergen's classic work on the stimuli eliciting certain reproductive responses from male three-spined sticklebacks. In this species the male defends a territory and builds a nest within it. He attacks males who intrude on his territory, but courts egg-laden females (Fig. 3.2). Ter Pelkwijk and Tinbergen (1937) conducted experiments with models to identify the characters important in the elicitation of these responses. Now in spring the male stickleback has a red belly, while the female has not. Experiments with models showed that, in attacking a rival, a territory owner is responding primarily to its red belly. Of the models in Fig. 4.1, the lower four had the character "red belly underneath" and were effective in eliciting attack from a territory owner, while the upper model, although in other respects much more like a real stickleback, was relatively ineffective. By contrast, the courtship response of a territory owner is elicited primarily by the swollen belly of the female and by the rather upright position in which she swims in the water (Fig. 6.1).

[1] A representative bibliography is given in Moynihan's paper: the following papers on sub-human primates may be added—chimpanzee, van Lawick-Goodall, 1968; gorilla, Schaller, 1963; Fossey, 1972; Nilgiri langur, Poirier, 1970a, b; black mangabey, Chalmers, 1968; stump-tailed macaque, Bertrand, 1969; and Japanese macaque, Green, in press. See also Andrew, 1963a b, for important reviews.

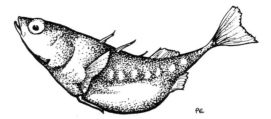

FIGURE 6.1
*Egg-laden female three-spined stickleback.*
(Drawing by Priscilla Edwards from Tin-
bergen, 1951.)

These experiments show that in each case the male is responding primarily
to certain characters of the other individual, and that other characters are of less
importance. Similar selective responsiveness occurs in all sensory modalities. For
example, the song of the white-throated sparrow consists of a series of clear
notes (Fig. 6.2). Falls (1969) was able to make artificial songs differing in defined
ways from normal ones. These were played to wild individuals, and their effectiveness in eliciting approach, attack, or song was assessed. The results showed
that the song had to contain unvarying pure tones without harmonics or other
overtones. The notes also had to be within certain limits of length, and the intervals between them below a certain maximum. The pitch changes between successive notes were of less importance; and other characters, such as the broken
nature of some notes and the slurs which occur in the natural song, of no apparent significance.

In other cases, the number of effective characters is greater, but similar
principles apply. We may consider another example analysed by Tinbergen
(Tinbergen and Perdeck, 1950). After hatching, gull chicks peck at the tip of the
parent's bill. The parent regurgitates food and holds some of it in its bill near
the young. In the course of pecking at the bill tip, the young gets some of this
food and swallows it (Fig. 6.3). In the herring gull, which Tinbergen and Perdeck
used for their experiments, the bill is yellow with a red patch near the end of the
lower mandible. The importance of the various stimulus characters of the adult's
bill for eliciting pecking was assessed by using series of cardboard models;
within each series the models differed in only one stimulus character. An example is shown in Fig. 6.4. The greatest response was obtained from models which

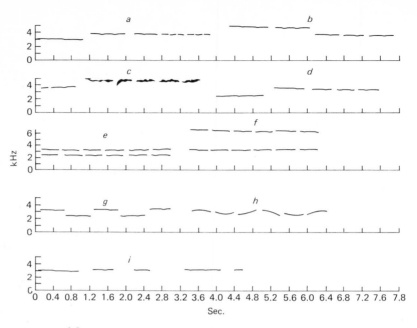

FIGURE 6.2

*Normal white-throated sparrow's songs: (a) ascending; (b) descending; (c) female's song. Artificial songs: (d) normal; (e) two unrelated tones; (f) with first harmonic; (g) alternating pitch; (h) varying pitch; (i) random timing. (From Falls, 1969.)*

were fairly low, near the chick, moving, long and thin, and pointing downwards, and which had a red patch contrasting with the bill near the tip. Thus a number of stimulus characters are important in the elicitation of this response. Other characters, such as the colour of the bill itself or the shape of the head, seemed not to influence the response. In the laughing gull the most effective stimulus for pecking is (1) an oblong shape or rod, (2) of about 9-mm width, (3) held vertically, (4) moved (5) horizontally (6) about eighty times per minute. It must (7) contrast with its background and (8) is more effective if darker than the background than if not coloured. If coloured, (9) red and blue colours are more effective than intermediate wavelengths. The object is more effective (10) at eye level and (11) when seen by both eyes (Hailman, 1967).

Now some of the stimulus characters found to be important in these

FIGURE 6.3
*Herring gull chick pecking at food held in tip of parent's bill.* (Drawing by Priscilla Edwards, from Tinbergen, 1953.)

studies are likely to be effective in a wide variety of contexts. Thus the stimulus objects for many other responses in the repertoire of herring gulls are likely to be more effective if presented moving and at eye level than if stationary elsewhere. Others, like the contrasting red spot on the adult herring gull's bill, may be effective for the feeding response only (though see Baerends and Kruijt, 1973). When a response depends much more on some characters than on others, those characters are often referred to as "sign stimuli", though the term is usually reserved for characters whose effectiveness is also more or less specific to one response.

In the case of species-characteristic behaviour directed toward prey or elicited by objects other than members of the species, natural selection can, either by affecting the course of learning or else more directly, influence responsiveness to the sign stimuli. Pike which respond to a flash in the water, or small birds which respond to almost any stimuli possibly indicative of a hunting falcon, will be more likely to survive and to leave offspring than those with a more specific responsiveness; while birds which do not eat poisonous insects are at an

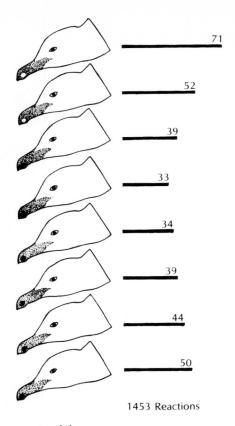

71

52

39

33

34

39

44

50

1453 Reactions

FIGURE 6.4

*Cardboard models of herring gull's beak used in experiments to assess stimuli eliciting pecking by the chick. The lengths of the bars indicate the number of responses elicited by each model in a standardized series of tests.* (From Tinbergen, 1951.)

advantage over those with a less specific responsiveness to potential food. But in the case of interactions between members of a species, natural selection not only can affect responsiveness to the signal, it can also increase the effectiveness of the signal itself. The processes involved are referred to as "ritualization" (see

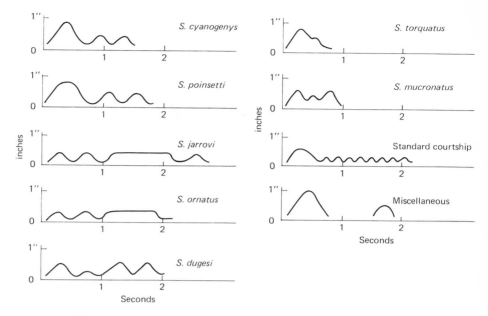

FIGURE 6.5

*Head-bobbing patterns of* Scleropus *lizards. The last two patterns are not species-specific.* (From Hunsaker, 1962.)

pages 73–75). Many of the colours, movements, sounds, smells, and tactile stimuli used by animals in social communication show signs of having been evolved for a signal function. Thus, the redness of the male stickleback's belly is a character which, so far as we know, serves no function other than that of social communication. It has apparently been evolved solely to that end. The swollen nature of the female's belly, on the other hand, is a by-product of the presence of eggs, though even here it may have been enhanced in evolution to make it more effective as a signal, as has certainly been the case with the posture she uses.

Though the cases considered so far have emphasized the importance of special structures in communication, signals often depend primarily on movements. For instance, in winter the dunnock is one of the most inconspicuous of birds, scarcely noticeable as it skulks amongst bushes: in the spring it suddenly becomes remarkably conspicuous as it displays with flicking wings and tail.

The communicative significance of movements is difficult to investigate experimentally, since they are usually difficult to simulate in model experiments (Cullen, 1972). Hunsaker (1962), however, has studied the head-nodding movements used by the males of various species of *Scleropus* lizards. Using a model with a head activated by a cam, he was able to show that the females of the several species studied preferred different rhythms of head-bobbing (Fig. 6.5). Most often, as we shall see, there is a combination of movement and special structure, the one enhancing the effectiveness of the other.

The preceding discussion has mentioned only social releasers operating in the visual and auditory modalities, but of course communication between individuals may utilize any sensory modality available to the species. In general, the principles which have been discussed for visual releasers apply also to other modalities—selectivity in responsiveness, adaptedness for the specific signal function, ritualization in the course of evolution. Most species have several modalities potentially available to them for communication, but there is often advantage in using one rather than another. This subject is discussed by various authors in Sebeok (1968), and will not be pursued here.

Though it is convenient to study communicative systems according to the modality used, in practice there is a high proportion of signals that are composite, so that information is passed through several modalities simultaneously. This is especially the case with signals used over a short range, and presumably augments the subtlety and diversity of the information that can be conveyed.

It is worth stressing here that man's sensory capacities are in many ways more like those of birds than those of most other mammals. Thus in most mammals olfactory stimuli are of considerable importance in social communication (Gleason and Reynierse, 1969). They are important also in the more primitive primates, where many species have elaborate marking patterns to disseminate odours. In monkeys and apes olfactory communication is less important, but plays some role. Thus the sexual behaviour of rhesus monkeys is partly under olfactory control: a pheromone is produced in the vagina and acts as a powerful attractant to the male (Herbert and Trimble, 1967; Michael and Keverne, 1968). As another example, gorillas release an odour when alarmed (Fossey, 1972). In man olfactory stimuli play at most a small role, and that perhaps at an unconscious level. The tendency of women living together to menstruate simultaneously (McClintock, 1971) may be mediated by olfactory stimuli. A male pheromone is detected most easily by women of reproductive age, but men can smell it if given oestrogen (e.g., Comfort, 1971). But man's powers of olfactory discrimination are relatively poor, and he resembles birds rather than other mammals in the over-riding importance of the visual and auditory modalities in social communication. However tactile communication, perhaps underestimated in many Western societies (Benthall and Polhemus, 1974), is important in many cultures, and in this man resembles his primate relatives more than birds.

## Social releasers and conflict

Under natural conditions, factors predisposing an animal to two or more incompatible types of behaviour are often simultaneously present. Thus in a flock of birds feeding on the ground the distance between individuals is governed by a balance between tendencies to remain in proximity with other individuals and to behave agonistically (see page 250) if another individual comes too close. As the birds feed, their behaviour is often interrupted as they look around for potential predators or rivals. When the flock starts to move many individuals have conflicting tendencies to continue feeding and to remain with the flock.

Recognition of the ubiquity of conflict helps a great deal in understanding the complexity of the display behaviour of some species (e.g., Tinbergen, 1952). For example, during the spring great tits settle in pairs on territories which they defend against other pairs. Prolonged skirmishes between neighbours occur along the boundaries. Actual combat is rare, but each bird attacks and flees in turn, and in between shows a bewildering sequence of postures and movements. Among these is the "head-up" posture illustrated in Fig. 6.6. This posture may be followed by a flight away from the rival, it may just subside, or it may lead to a rather hesitant flight toward the rival.

Now when on its own territory, a great tit attacks intruding males immediately; when outside its boundaries, it flees; and only across a boundary do prolonged skirmishes occur. Strictly speaking, this is true only after the boundaries have been established. Earlier the probability that a male will attack a rival decreases with distance from certain preferred stations: the boundary is a region in which the aggressiveness of two neighbours is more or less equal. It is thus also a region in which each bird's tendencies to attack and to flee are more or less in balance. During the skirmishes, the head-up threat posture seems to be given when there is an even finer balance: as we have seen, it is sometimes followed by a rather hesitant flight toward the rival, and sometimes by a flight away. Similar arguments indicate that many of the other varied postures and movements used in the skirmish are also associated with conflicting tendencies to attack and to flee. Once the skirmish is seen to be associated with two incompatible tendencies, it becomes comprehensible (Hinde, 1952).

FIGURE 6.6
*Threat postures of tits. (a) Head-up posture of great tit. (b) Head-forward posture of blue tit.* (Drawing by Yvette Spencer-Booth.)

Similar principles apply to courtship behaviour, though here three or more conflicting incompatible tendencies may be involved. For instance the male chaffinch establishes a territory early in the season and threatens all intruders. An unpaired female will evade the male's attacks but stays around. Slowly his behaviour changes from attack to courtship: he uses a posture which resembles the head-forward threat but is oriented laterally to the female. Often his body is tilted somewhat to display his conspicuous wing marks (Fig. 6.7). At this time the female becomes dominant to the male, and she may drive him away from food sources. Later still the female starts to solicit for copulation, and the male approaches her hesitantly in an upright posture with a curious pattering walk. Many attempts at copulation are unsuccessful because the male flees at the last moment. After copulation the male often flies off suddenly and gives a call more usually elicited by a flying predator.

FIGURE 6.7

(a) *Early courtship display of male chaffinch.* (b) *Male chaffinch showing precopulatory display approaching a soliciting female.* (Drawings by Priscilla Edwards.)

Thus the female may elicit attack, fleeing, or sexual behaviour from the male: what he does depends on the stimuli she presents and on his own internal state. Early in the season his behaviour is primarily aggressive. Later, as his tendency to behave sexually increases, the balance between attacking and fleeing shifts in favour of fleeing. At the time of copulation the main conflict is between tendencies to approach the female and to flee from her. Correlated with these changes, the nature of the postures used by the male changes from primarily aggressive to primarily sexual (Hinde, 1953; Marler, 1956a).

Such analyses in terms of conflicting tendencies provide some understanding of the nature of much complex display behaviour. Whenever a new species is being studied, the richness of its display behaviour is often at first bewildering, but realization that factors for mutually incompatible types of behaviour are

FIGURE 6.8

(a) *Sitting threat of rhesus macaque. The head is lunged forward (left-hand figure) and back (right-hand). (b) Standing threat of rhesus macaques. Note in each case the ambivalence revealed by the positions.* (Drawings by Priscilla Edwards.)

present, and that movements may have become ritualized in evolution for a signal function, usually brings sense to the data. The critical reader will have noted that the "tendencies" postulated in the preceding paragraphs have the nature of intervening variables (see pages 25–28): as such, they are useful only so long as they do make sense of the data, and it would be a logical blunder to look for "tendencies" inside the skull. It is, therefore, as well to list the sorts of evidence on which particular tendencies are postulated.

1 **The situation** Often the situation in which the display is given provides good evidence. As we have seen, passerine birds use threat postures primarily on the boundaries between territories, where it is postulated that tendencies to attack and flee are more or less in balance.

2 **The behaviour which accompanies the display** A threat posture is often accompanied by edging toward or away from the rival: this can be described in terms of the predominance of one tendency. Thus a threatening rhesus monkey usually alternately lunges toward and withdraws from his rival, and his stance may clearly indicate his ambivalence (Fig. 6.8).

3 **Sequential and temporal correlations** The assumption here is that the internal state associated with a display is more likely to have something in common with the internal state associated with an activity that frequently occurs close in time to the display than with that of an activity which does not. Thus the relative strengths of the conflicting tendencies associated with a display can be assessed by counting the relative frequency with which, for example, attacking and fleeing movements follow it. This was first used by Moynihan (1955) to substantiate his view that the various threat postures of the black-headed gull were associated with different absolute and relative strengths of tendencies to attack and flee from the rival: some of his results are summarized in Fig. 6.9. There are a number of difficulties with this sort of evidence, not the least of which is that activities may be associated together in time not because they are associated specifically with particular causal factors, but because they share a low priority amongst the organism's activities and can occur only in the absence of other types of behaviour: it may be for this reason that the different toilet or comfort activities often occur together. Nevertheless this method is one of the most powerful tools available.

Sometimes it is taken one step further by the use of the techniques of

FIGURE 6.9

*Threat postures of the black-headed gull, showing (centre) the approximate frequency with which each is followed by attack (black column) or escape (white columns). The probability that one or other will be shown increases up the diagram, but attack is more likely than escape after the oblique or the aggressive upright (left), and escape more likely than attack after the forward and anxiety upright (right). (Drawings by Priscilla Edwards from Moynihan, 1955.)*

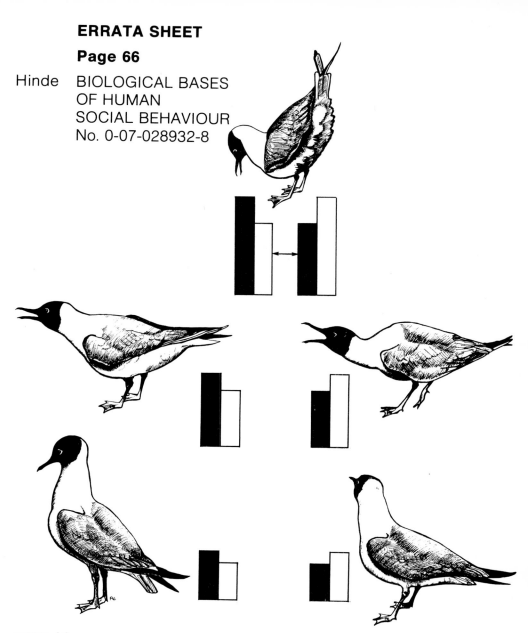

FIGURE 6.9

*Threat postures of the black-headed gull, with the histograms showing the approximate frequency with which each is followed by attack (black columns) or escape (white columns). The probability that one or the other will be shown increases up the diagram, but attack is more likely than escape after the aggressive upright or oblique (left), and escape is more likely than attack after the anxiety upright or forward (right). (Drawings by Priscilla Edwards from Moynihan, 1955.)*

factor analysis. From the frequencies with which different types of behaviour are associated in time it is possible to calculate correlation coefficients between them. Factor analysis consists in determining whether these correlations could be deduced from relations between the elements and a smaller number of hypothetical variables. If they can, then these new variables can be regarded as factors associated with two or more of the behavioural elements and can be said to explain the original correlation. This method has one special value. Just because a display is given in a conflict situation, it may only very rarely be followed by the full expression of one of the conflicting tendencies (e.g., actual attack or actual fleeing). Thus simple correlational evidence might provide little indication of its nature. However because the factor analysis takes account of all relationships between all the items considered, it can reveal relationships between two items which, though themselves uncorrelated, are similarly related to other items (Wiepkema, 1961; Blurton Jones, 1972b). It can thus provide useful leads: we shall mention an example later (see pages 128–129). Factor analysis also has its own dangers (Overall, 1964), and the results must be interpreted in the light of other types of evidence.

4 **The nature of the display itself** Each display posture can be analysed into components, and a variety of types of evidence may indicate that these components are associated with one or other of the conflicting tendencies. Indeed this is sometimes clear from the mere form of the components. For example the upright threat posture of the herring gull varies considerably in form (Fig. 6.10). Sometimes the wings are slightly open and the beak points downward: these are components of attacking by wing-beating and pecking from above. At other times, the body is more oblique to the rival, the beak is pointed slightly upward and the neck is drawn somewhat backward: these are intention movements of escape (Tinbergen, 1953, 1959). Sometimes evidence concerning the significance of the components can be obtained by a sequential analysis: we shall discuss an example of this later (pages 80–82).

5 **Independent manipulation of the separate factors controlling the displays** Sometimes it is possible, by varying the external situation, to alter the relative strengths of the tendencies associated with the displays. This approach has so far been little exploited, but Blurton Jones (1968) has used it to obtain valuable evidence on the bases of the display movements of great tits.

FIGURE 6.10

*Aggressive (upper) and anxiety (lower) threat postures of the herring gull.* (Drawings by Priscilla Edwards from Tinbergen, 1959.)

But it must be remembered that the "tendencies" said to be associated with the displays are not hard entities: they are hypothetical variables postulated to make sense of complex behavioural data (see page 65). It is thus redundant to add that none of the sources of evidence mentioned above is conclusive: their use often involves a modicum of circular argument. If and only if one is clear-headed about this, the methods are useful in bringing order to the data.

The examples discussed so far have been limited mainly to threat and courtship in birds. The principles are applicable to a much wider range of species (fish, reptiles, mammals, and perhaps some invertebrates and amphibians), and in birds they apply also in many other contexts besides threat and courtship. The distraction and mobbing displays given to predators, nest-relief ceremonies, and many other kinds of behaviour have been shown to depend on ambivalence. Furthermore, even in threat and courtship, the tendencies usefully postulated to account for the complexity of the behaviour are not limited to attacking, fleeing, and sexual ones—many other types of behaviour, including nest-building, singing, looking around, and simply staying put, may be involved (Andrew, 1961).

Such an analysis assumes a degree of incompatibility amongst tendencies as assessed by groups of responses—for instance, amongst all attacking patterns, all fleeing patterns, and all sexual patterns. Andrew (1956, 1972), however, has argued that it is "more accurate and more useful in predicting behaviour to say that tendencies to give two groups of responses are present, and that some of the responses of each group are incompatible with each other". In other words, he emphasizes incompatibility between responses, rather than between more global (and abstract) tendencies. He bases this view on evidence that the same display component may occur when two responses are in conflict, no matter which tendencies they are associated with. For instance, tail-flicking is common in small birds in a variety of situations, some of which might be described as involving conflicts between tendencies to attack and to flee, or to copulate and flee. In fact, the tail movements are elaborations of intention movements for take-off (see Fig. 6.11), given when the animal is likely to fly but is inhibited from moving far. Such an approach makes sense of a number of cases which had previously proved puzzling. For instance Tinbergen (1959) made a similar point in relation to the "facing-away" display of the kittiwake, which is given when fleeing is opposed by a tendency to attack, to stay put on a cliff ledge which it owns, or to stay put during pair formation with another bird (see also page 83).

The relative usefulness of the two approaches is a matter of dispute (see Hinde, 1972a, pages 204–206). Though examples of the type just given show the usefulness of thinking in terms of conflict between specific responses, there are other cases in which the more global approach remains more economical. To some extent this is an empirical matter. For example, from a detailed study of the threat displays of great tits, Blurton Jones (1968) concluded that some depend on conflicts between tendencies to flee, stay, or attack, others merely on conflicting tendencies for locomotion in different directions, and yet others on conflict between one major tendency and any other that blocks it. For example, the head-forward threat posture (Fig. 6.6) occurs whenever full attack is prevented, whether by a physical barrier or through inhibition by fleeing; another, the head-up, involves specifically a tendency to flee.

Finally, in this section on the relations between conflict and signal movements, it must be emphasized that only some signal movements depend on conflict. When a bird sings, or calls its young to food, conflict is of minor importance. That conflict is often involved can be understood in functional terms, at least in the case of threat postures. If an individual is going to attack or going to flee, its behaviour is most likely to be effective if it does so directly, without signalling its intention. But if it may do either the one or the other, and which it

FIGURE 6.11

*Schematic representation of movements of take-off in a bird, and some display move-ments of goldeneye* (a) *and* (b) *and turkey* (c) *elaborated from them.* (Redrawn from Daanje, 1950.)

will do depends on the behaviour of the other individual, signalling is essential. Similar types of functional explanation may apply in other contexts: for instance, whether or not a bird takes off may depend on whether its flock com-panions do likewise.

### The evolution of social releasers

Some movements that act as signals also serve another function. The wing-beat frequency used in flight by female *Aedes* mosquitoes also attracts the male. More usually signal movements resemble yet differ somewhat from movements with a different function in another context. Thus in certain Braconid wasps the female's wing-beat frequency alters when the animal is ready to mate (cited by Cullen, 1972). By comparing display movements with other movements of the same species which have no signal function, and by comparing also the display movements of closely related species, it is possible to form hypotheses both about the evolutionary origin of many signal movements and about the changes they have undergone in evolution. Three main evolutionary sources of displays have been recognized:

1  **Intention movements** These are the incomplete or preparatory movements which often appear at the beginning of an activity. For instance the take-off leap of a bird before flying consists of two phases: first it crouches, withdraws its head and raises its tail, and then reverses these movements as it springs off. Many avian displays are derived from these movements, though the relative extent and coordination of the various elements have usually been altered considerably in the course of evolution (Fig. 6.11). Intention movements of biting and striking are a common source of the components of threat postures: the upright threat posture of the herring gull, shown in Fig. 6.10, provides two examples, for the bill is pointing downward, preparatory to striking, and the wings are raised out of the supporting feathers, preparatory to beating the opponent. In other cases, intention movements of preening, nesting, copulation, and many other types of behaviour have given rise to display movements.

   In an important discussion of the evolution of facial expression in mammals, Andrew (1963a, b) emphasizes the importance of self-protective responses as evolutionary precursors of signal movements. In a wide range of species startling, strange or noxious stimulation may induce flattening the ears, closing the eyes, and even a checking of respiration, accompanied by closure of the glottis, followed by a vigorous expiration which clears air from the upper parts of the respiratory tract. These components appear in many situations—when an animal is likely to be attacked, or approaching a possibly hostile female, for example; and have become ritualized as part of many facial expressions. Andrew also points out that the evolution of facial expression and that of vocalizations are closely linked (see also Rowell, 1962).

2  **Displacement activities** Animals which have tendencies to behave in more than one way at the same time sometimes show behaviour which is related

FIGURE 6.12
*Display movements ritualized from preening of the wing in various ducks.* (Drawings by Priscilla Edwards from Tinbergen, 1951.)

to neither tendency and which appears, to the human observer at least, to be functionally irrelevant to the context. For instance in many aggressive and sexual situations, where there are factors making for an approach toward the other individual as well as factors for a retreat (see pages 61–70), passerine birds may wipe their beaks or preen their feathers, show drinking or feeding behaviour, or engage in some other activity that appears to be unrelated to the current situation. Such apparently irrelevant activities, although their causal bases are undoubtedly heterogeneous, are referred to as displacement activities. Some of them have become elaborated in evolution as signal movements. For example, many ducks preen their wings during courtship. A conspicuous structure on the wing which enhances the effectiveness of the movement as a signal is usually present, and in some species the movement itself has changed in form so that the wing is no longer actually touched (Fig. 6.12).

3 **Autonomic responses** Many signal movements are derived directly or indirectly not from movements of the skeletal musculature but from responses controlled by the autonomic nervous system. This includes movements of the hair or feathers, movements of urination and defaecation, and changes in skin colouration due to changes in the surface vessels. In addition, many movements of the limbs or head, such as those involved in grooming or preening, may be responses to stimuli resulting from activity of the autonomic system, being elicited by stimuli produced by thermoregulatory movements of the hair or feathers.

Since there can be no fossil record of the evolutionary history of signal movements, it is not possible to "prove" that a signal movement has been derived in evolution from one of these sources. Nevertheless, by carefully comparing the displays of closely related species, it is possible to obtain evidence that actions are homologous from one species to another on the grounds of formal similarity and other considerations (Tinbergen, 1952; Baerends, 1950; Wickler, 1968; Cullen, 1972).

When the evolutionary source of a display movement has been identified, the changes which it has undergone in the course of evolution can be described. The changes involved are usually described collectively as "ritualization"[2] (Blest, 1961). They include:

1 Changes in the frequency of occurrence, intensity, or speed of performance of a display

2  Changes in rhythmicity of performance

3  Changes in the coordination and/or relative intensity of components

4  Changes in orientation

In addition to changes in the movement itself, conspicuous structures by which it is enhanced have often been evolved. The two processes usually proceed in parallel, so that there is a correlation between the evolutionary elaboration of the movement and that of the structure. For instance, among tits of the genus *Parus* the head-up threat posture is elaborated most in those species that have a conspicuous throat and breast colouration (Fig. 6.13). In the male great tit, which has a conspicuous broad black ventral stripe, the posture is dramatic and may be held for several seconds at a time. The female great tit displays less and has a somewhat thinner stripe. In the coal and marsh tits, which have relatively brief black bibs, the display is much briefer and is usually held only momentarily. The blue tit, in which the head-up posture is very inconspicuous, makes much use of a head-forward posture in fighting over territories: unlike many other species it can raise the cheek feathers in a special way to make this conspicuous (Fig. 6.6) (Hinde, 1952).

Another type of change which has occurred in evolution to enhance the effectiveness of signal movements involves the development of "typical intensity". Most movements which do not have a signal function change continuously in amplitude or in some other dimension as the causal factors change in strength. In many signal movements, however, the form or frequency of the movement remains relatively constant over a wide range of intensities of the eliciting factors. This presumably enhances the signal value of the movement by making it

---

[2] The terms "ritual" and "ritualization" have come to have different meanings in biology and in the social sciences, though there is a connecting strand. When J. S. Huxley used the term "ritual" to describe the complex courtship display of the great crested grebe, it was evocative because the formal and stereotyped nature of the bird's behaviour is reminiscent of a human ceremony. When biologists started to investigate how such signal movements had evolved, the term "ritualization" was applied to the evolutionary changes whereby a movement became biologically adapted for a signal function. As we shall see in Chap. 10, some human expressive movements, such as smiling and crying, have been ritualized in this biological sense as man evolved. Even these, however, are influenced by experience in each individual's lifetime. The forms of other expressive movements are dictated primarily by cultural convention, so that their biological bases are almost lost: the stylized movements made by Japanese actors are extreme cases. Furthermore such movements may have a symbolic meaning divorced from the actual emotional state of the individual concerned. Now human rituals involving a number of individuals may resemble some signal movements of animals in that they are stereotyped and in that they have a communicatory function—communication either amongst those involved or to outsiders. But in most cases their symbolic content is their most important characteristic. In this respect, therefore, the processes that give rise to human ritual are quite different from the evolutionary processes of ritualization in the signal movements of animals.

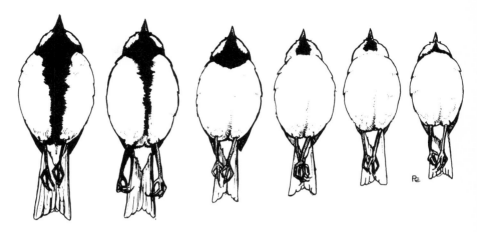

FIGURE 6.13

*Ventral markings of various species of the genus* Parus. *From left to right great* *(male and female), coal, willow, marsh, and blue tits.* (Drawings by Priscilla Edwards.)

more distinctive. Of course, this carries with it the concomitant disadvantage that the signal is less able to convey small changes in the internal state of the signaller: comparative study suggests that for some signals distinctiveness is more important, while for others a graded signal is advantageous.

This raises another issue which can be discussed only briefly here—the adaptedness of signals. In the first place, they are effective. As we have seen, experimental studies have shown that the red breast of a robin or the red belly of a stickleback does elicit attack, threat, or fleeing responses from other individuals (Lack, 1939; Tinbergen, 1951). Correlational studies have shown that those threat postures of blue tits that are most likely to be followed by an attack by the displaying bird are also most effective in eliciting fleeing from others. For example, a bird which faces its rival is more likely to attack than is a bird which does not: the rival is more likely to flee from a displaying bird which faces it than from one which does not (Stokes, 1962; see pages 94–95).

When such signals are effective between naive individuals it indicates that the behaviour of both the signaller and the responding individual has been affected by natural selection. But selection for efficiency in communication has not led to the evolution of a few simple signals, for a number of reasons. For

FIGURE 6.14
*Submissive posture of great tit.* (Drawing by Priscilla Edwards.)

one thing, each species has a repertoire of signals which must be distinct from each other: thus the submissive postures of passerine birds, which involve raising the feathers, a rather hunched position of the body, and a generally rounded appearance, are in many respects the opposite of the threat postures (Fig. 6.14; compare Fig. 6.6). Furthermore, some signals, such as the songs of some birds, serve as individual recognition marks, and there is evidence that selection has operated to produce limited inter-individual variability around species-specific characteristics (Nottebohm, 1972b).

In addition, selection has operated on some signals, such as those involved in pair formation, to produce species distinctiveness—hence the diversity of bird song—and on others, such as warning calls, to produce similarity between species. It has operated to make many signals adequately conspicuous in the contexts in which they are used, but not to the extent that the advantages are outweighed by enhanced vulnerability to predators (e.g., Marler, 1959). Thus, in marmosets the contact calls between individuals become progressively easier to locate as the individuals move further apart—becoming more frequent, longer, and louder, with greater frequency modulation and a wider frequency spectrum. The warning call, however, has characteristics which make it difficult to locate (Epple, 1968).

In these and other ways selection has produced in every social species a repertoire of signals adapted to the contexts in which they are used. But it will be apparent from the preceding discussion that all intermediates may exist between movements that have undergone elaborate evolutionary processes of ritualization in adaptation to a signal function, and movements as yet unchanged by such processes. Similarly, there are structures that are responded to by other individuals of the species though not specialized in any way as signals; there are others which, while still performing their original function, have been modified to some extent as signals—the female stickleback's swollen belly may be and the human female breast is an example; and there are yet others which serve only a signal function. In short, the class of "social releasers" has no sharp edges.

## The information carried by social releasers

This section is concerned with two issues: (1) the extent to which even a quite stereotyped signal may carry diverse types of information (using "information" in its everyday sense); and (2) the nature of the signal and its ability to carry graded information.

The first point can be made most easily with a human analogy. If we hear someone speaking but cannot distinguish the words, we may still be able to tell the sex and mood of the speaker, and perhaps even where he comes from. The speech carries several types of information in addition to that in the words, different aspects of the auditory signals being involved. The same is true of many animal signals: not unexpectedly, the question has been studied particularly in the case of bird song. Songs may carry many types of information—the singer's species, sex, individual identity, territorial status, and so on. There is some evidence that these are encoded in different aspects of the signal (Marler, 1960). Thus species recognition may depend on the overall pattern of notes and the broad features of the note structure, individual recognition on the details of the note structure, the intensity of the internal state of the singer on the frequency of song repetition, and so on (see, for example, Brémond, 1967; Falls, 1969; Stevenson et al., 1970; Beer, 1970).

The information conveyed by changes in frequency of repetition brings us to the second issue. We have seen that the ritualization of signal movements may lead to their becoming stereotyped in that their form is not changed although the causal factors on which they depend vary considerably: they become, in fact, in some degree all-or-nothing movements. This, however, carries with it the disadvantage that, except through frequency of repetition, the signal is less able to convey small changes in the internal state of the signaller—as though a cross face could indicate only, "I'm cross", and not how cross. There is thus also a need for limited variability such that the display can signal

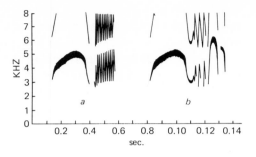

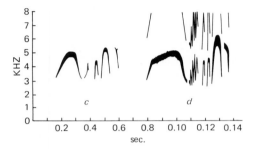

FIGURE 6.15
Sayornis phoebe, *regularly repeated vocalizations (RRV)*: (a) *form RR₁*; (b, c) *two forms of RR₂, the second from a female;* (d) *an RR₁/RR₂ intermediate.* (From Smith, 1969a.)

gradations along one or more than one continuum. This can happen in various ways.

1 **Intensity differences** As we have seen, signals may vary in repetition rate. In addition, many displays vary along a continuum, more components being added and those already present increasing in their expression as the causal factors increase. A case which approximates this condition is the soliciting posture of the female chaffinch, shown in Fig. 2.1.

2 **Related forms** A relatively simple example is provided by the song of the Eastern phoebe, as studied by Smith (1969a). This species has two "regularly repeated vocalizations" (RRV) which are rather similar in form,

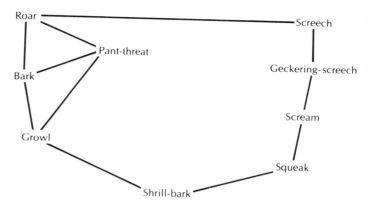

FIGURE 6.16

*Relationships of certain noises made in agonistic situations by rhesus monkeys. The lines indicate named noises, between which intermediates have been recorded. (After Rowell, 1962.)*

*The noises are made in the following situations. Roar, made by a very confident animal, when threatening another of inferior rank; pant-threat, made by a less confident animal wanting the support of the rest of the group in its attack; bark, given by a mildly alarmed animal; shrill bark, the alarm call of the species, probably given to predators in the wild; screech, typically with an abrupt pitch change up and then down, made when threatening a higher-ranking animal and when excited or highly alarmed; geckering screech, made by an animal being threatened by another; scream, made by a losing monkey in a fight while being bitten; squeaks, made by a defeated and exhausted monkey at the end of a fight.*

sometimes occur as intermediates (Fig. 6.15), and are uttered in pure or mixed bouts. Both are given when the bird's behaviour indicates that it has a tendency to associate with another individual and that this tendency is thwarted in some way. One of these songs (RR$_1$) is given in the absence of aggressive tendencies, when the tendency to associate is thwarted by absence of the other individual or is in conflict with tendencies to behave in other ways, such as avoidance or preening. The other (RR$_2$) is given when there is also a tendency for defensively aggressive behaviour, and in the absence of non-social tendencies. Thus the proportion of $RR_1$ and $RR_2$ in mixed bouts provides some measure of the extent to which social tendencies are conflicting with defensively aggressive ones.

3 **Intergradations between forms** This combines the above two principles. An example is provided by the vocalizations given by rhesus monkeys in agonistic situations (Rowell, 1962). These form a number of recognizable types connected by intermediates, as shown in Fig. 6.16. It has been suggested that graded signals are more likely in highly social species than in less social ones (Fox, 1970), but it is clear that other factors, including the nature of the information carried, are also important here.

4 **Interrelations between components** We have already seen that many displays are in fact combinations of more elemental components (page 67). The relations between these components can provide information about the associated internal state along a number of dimensions. In a detailed study of the threat behaviour of blue tits at a winter feeding station, Stokes (1962) recorded nine behavioural components (e.g., crest up or down, wings raised or lowered, etc.) and the subsequent action of the displaying bird. The latter was classified as attacking, fleeing, or staying. The components tended to occur in particular combinations indicating, presumably, similar relations to particular causal factors. The associations between individual components and subsequent behaviour were not large: although birds which raised the crest or body feathers were subsequently highly likely to flee, for other individual components the probability of subsequently attacking, fleeing, or staying was 52 percent or less (Table 6.1).

TABLE 6.1 *Blue tit agonistic display: Single components which provided the best indication of the outcome of an encounter, and the subsequent action as a percent of total occurrences.*

| Best single indicator of outcome | Subsequent action, % of total occurrences | | |
|---|---|---|---|
| | Attack | Escape | Stay |
| Body horizontal | 40 | | |
| Crest erect | | 90 | |
| Crest normal | | | 52 |

SOURCE: From Stokes, 1962.

This poor predictability from individual components was due in part to interactions between the components. For instance, raised nape feathers in an otherwise non-aggressive posture indicated that the bird was *more* likely to attack than a bird in a similar posture without raised nape feathers. But raising of the nape feathers in an otherwise aggressive posture was associated with, if anything, some reduction in the probability of aggression, but a (non-significantly) increased probability of staying (Table 6.2).

However, the combinations of components showed more reliable relationships with subsequent behaviour. One combination led to escape on 94 percent of occasions, another to staying on 79 percent, and another to attack on 48 percent—considerably better than the best predictions which could be made from single components (Table 6.3).

Stokes emphasizes that no combination of components was a perfect predictor of the bird's next action, and suggests that this was because of the crudeness of the categories which it was possible for him to record. However, in agonistic interactions what the bird does depends not only on its own internal state but also on the behaviour of the bird to which it is displaying. Furthermore, as we have seen (pages 69–70), in such contexts it is only when there is

TABLE 6.2 *Blue tit agonistic display: The relation of nape position, when combined with various other types of behavior, to subsequent action.*

| First element, nape erect | Second element | Resultant behaviour, % of total occurrences | | | |
|:---:|---|:---:|:---:|:---:|:---:|
| | | ATTACK | ESCAPE | STAY | PROBABILITY |
| + | Body horizontal | 39 | 15 | 46 | |
| − | (aggressive) | 39 | 26 | 35 | NS‡ |
| + | Wings raised | 27 | 13 | 60 | |
| − | (aggressive) | 35 | 21 | 44 | NS‡ |
| + | Body normal | 32 | 16 | 52 | |
| − | (non-aggressive) | 6 | 47 | 47 | † |
| + | Wings normal | 43 | 15 | 42 | |
| − | (non-aggressive) | 12 | 45 | 43 | † |
| + | Body feathers normal | 41 | 12 | 47 | |
| − | (non-aggressive) | 17 | 34 | 49 | † |

† P < 0.01.
‡ NS—not significant at 0.05 level.
SOURCE: From Stokes, 1962.

uncertainty over what to do next that it will be advantageous to the bird to display: if it is definitely going to attack or flee, it would do best to do so quickly. Where the subsequent behaviour of the signaller depends in part on the behaviour of the signallee, it will not be precisely predictable from the signal.

## The importance of context

Stokes's study of threat display in blue tits shows that the significance of a display component may vary with the context of the other components with which it occurs. The same principle applies when we consider a relatively invariant signal movement, such as a bird's call, or when we consider the display as a whole, though here the context concerns not other aspects of the bird's behaviour, but the environment. In isolating the signal movement, we are singling out only one of the sources of information available to a recipient. Each signal is made in a context, and that context is essential for the interpretation of the message.

Some of the best examples of the role of context come from Smith's studies (1965, 1969a) of tyrannid flycatchers, which have already been cited in another context. The "locomotory hesitance vocalization" is given in a wide variety of situations which have in common the occurrence of a conflict between locomotion and either locomotion in a different direction or some other form of behaviour. Among these situations are the following: (1) One bird of a pair may give

TABLE 6.3 *Blue tit agonistic display: The use of five behaviour elements to predict the outcome of an encounter.*

| Initial behaviour elements | | | | | Subsequent action, % of total occurrences | | | Total occur-rences |
|---|---|---|---|---|---|---|---|---|
| CREST ERECT | NAPE ERECT | FACING RIVAL | BODY HORIZONTAL | WINGS RAISED | ATTACK | ESCAPE | STAY | |
| + | − | + | − | − | 0 | 94 | 6 | 34 |
| + | − | − | − | − | 0 | 89 | 11 | 83 |
| − | − | − | − | + | 7 | 14 | 79 | 14 |
| − | − | − | − | − | 0 | 35 | 66 | 240 |
| − | + | + | + | + | 28 | 16 | 56 | 25 |
| − | + | + | + | − | 48 | 10 | 42 | 48 |
| − | − | + | + | + | 44 | 20 | 37 | 46 |
| − | − | + | + | − | 43 | 21 | 36 | 89 |
| | | | | | | | | 576 |

SOURCE: From Stokes, 1962.

this call whenever it approaches its mate. (2) A male patrolling his territory gives this call every time he ceases flying or approaches a perch without landing. (3) A young bird may use the call when approaching a parent who may respond aggressively. The response to the call varies in a way appropriate to the context. Thus a single call which occurs in a wide variety of situations can induce diverse responses depending on the context and on the motivational state of the recipient.

Such observations require us to make a clear distinction between the "message" and the "meaning" of a signal (Smith, 1965). The message is an encoded description of an aspect of the state of the central nervous system of the signalling individual—namely, that aspect which is common to all situations in which the signal is given. The meaning to a recipient varies with the context: objectively it may be identified with those responses (including covert responses) selected by the recipient from all the responses open to him. The meaning to a recipient thus both depends on the context (including often the individual identity of the signaller) and may be peculiar to that recipient: in a sense, therefore, the meaning is more than the message. This principle is at least equally true of non-verbal communication in primates (Marler, 1965). It will be apparent that, in emphasizing the association between signals and particular internal states, such as thwarted locomotion, Smith has reached a conclusion very similar to that of Andrew (see page 69)—namely, that signal movements are better regarded as associated with particular responses, such as "biting" or "flying", which may be common to a variety of functional categories of behaviour, than with the categories themselves, such as "attacking" or "fleeing".

## Summary

The studies discussed in this chapter show that much communication in animals depends on social releasers which have been specialized in evolution for a communicatory role. Comparative study of closely related species permits reasonable hypotheses about the evolutionary origins of such movements, and about the changes that specialization for a signal function has entailed. Although the signal repertoire of each species is not particularly large, a surprising wealth of information can be conveyed—in part because signals can be combined in a variety of ways, and in part because the context in which a signal is given often affects its interpretation. In the next chapter we shall consider to what extent all communication in animals depends on such specialized signals.

$\boxed{7}$

# LIMITATIONS
# OF THE
# SOCIAL-RELEASER
# APPROACH

The work of Lorenz (e.g., 1935), Tinbergen (e.g., 1952, 1959), Marler (e.g., 1959, 1965) and others on social releasers has led to great advances in our understanding of animal communication. The way has been opened for a causal analysis of signal movements which seem bizarre and incomprehensible at first sight, and comparative studies have yielded insights into their evolution. However, not all communication involves social releasers, and other aspects of communication processes must be studied. In this chapter some limitations of the social-releaser approach to the study of animal communication will be mentioned.

The first, already discussed in Chap. 6, is the tendency to concentrate the analysis on the signals, rather than on the behaviour of the responding individual. Here Smith's distinction between message and meaning has proved a powerful corrective (see pages 82–83). In higher organisms, at least, contextual information provides an important part of the meaning to the recipient (see also Tinbergen, 1959).

Second, the category of social releasers is not clearly defined, for the distinction between movements or structures adapted for a signal function and

FIGURE 7.1

*Male rhesus macaques:* (a) *subordinate,* (b) *dominant.* (Drawings by Priscilla Edwards.)

those not so adapted is by no means sharp. Indeed, the very fact that intention movements have been ritualized implies that the non-ritualized movements must have had some communicatory potential: only in this way could the ritualization process have been given a start. The social-releaser concept has in fact been so powerful that it is easy to focus on the extreme cases, disregarding the fact that many trivial movements, even individually idiosyncratic ones, also serve as signals. For example, much information is conveyed by a monkey's posture as it sits or walks about. A subordinate female in a caged group of rhesus sits with rounded back and head withdrawn. It moves with curved spine, tail stiff but below the horizontal, constantly alert for a potential attacker. A confident rhesus sits or lies in a relaxed way, and walks with its tail hanging loosely. A dominant male strides with tail arched over his back (Fig. 7.1). These postures must affect the behaviour of other individuals: which of their components should be classed as social releasers is a moot point.

A third and related issue is that the social-releaser approach easily leads to the view that communication involves the simple elicitation of responses in the recipient of the signal. Most experimental studies of social releasers have involved the use of models whose effectiveness in eliciting a fairly immediate response can be assessed (e.g., Figs. 4.1 and 6.4). It is, however, recognized that the effects of some social releasers are sometimes cumulative: for instance, a male bird's courtship may produce a gradual change in the endocrine state of the female (e.g., Lehrman, 1965; Hinde, 1965). Such cases are investigated because the male's display is conspicuous, and it is presumed that it must be there for something. But if neither the signal nor the response is immediate or conspicuous, the whole communication process may be overlooked. In practice insignificant signals producing cumulative effects may be of great importance. For instance in non-human primates postures and slight intention movements provide a continuous low-key signalling which maintains dominance status or paves the way for a change, and is crucial for social integration (see detailed discussion by Simpson, 1973b; Menzel, in press). Again, tactile communication, in addition to apparently ritualised signals such as grooming and various copulatory and greeting gestures, may involve more subtle signals which nevertheless have profound effects on the individuals concerned (e.g., Weber, 1973).

A further issue is raised by the finding that some signals, while perhaps eliciting an immediate response, have the effect of assessing the probable behaviour of another individual. This view comes from Simpson's (1968) work on the Siamese fighting fish. This species, and especially the domesticated varieties whose conflicts form a traditional subject for wagers in parts of the Far East, has an elaborate threat display (Fig. 7.2). A skirmish involves each fish alternately facing and turning broadside to the opponent. Facing is nearly always accompanied by erection of the gill covers, and while broadside the fish may flicker their pelvic fins and beat and flash their tails. When two males display through a transparent screen they spend most of their time with one fish facing and the other broadside, continually alternating their positions. While one fish is facing and the other broadside the frequency of the latter's tail-beating tends to increase over the time that the rival's gill covers are held erect, the peak fre-

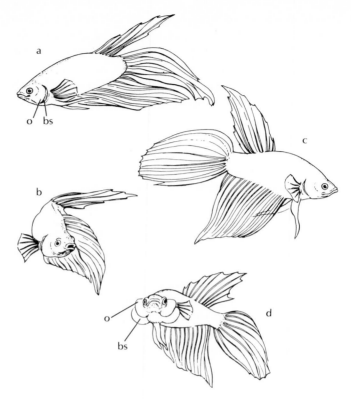

FIGURE 7.2

*Siamese fighting fish* (Betta): *non-displaying* (a, b) *and displaying* (c, d); o-*operculum*; bs-*branchiostegal membrane.* (From Simpson, 1968.)

quency often coming at the moment the rival's gill covers are lowered. This suggests that each fish responds to the other's tail-beating by lowering its gill covers and itself turning broadside.

As the skirmish proceeds there is a gradual increase in gill-cover erection, tail-beating, and biting. At first the proportions of time that each individual spends with its gill covers erect increase in parallel, each fish in some way matching the duration of its gill-cover erections to those of its partner. Only toward the end of the fight does one outstrip the other, which soon then capitulates. Simpson suggests that each fish must alter its subsequent readiness to lower its gill covers in accordance with the duration of its rival's gill-raising bout. Readiness to lower the gill covers may also alter in accordance with the rival's readiness to lower its gills in response to the broadside display. Thus if the fish which is broadside has to beat its tail twice before the rival lowers its gill covers, whereas earlier it had only to beat its tail once, then the fish now broadside may become more resistant to lowering its gill covers when the rival is broadside and beating his tail. It thus seems as though the skirmish involves a gradual escalation, with each fish testing out the other, until one gives up.

Simpson's analysis reveals the complexity of the duels of the Siamese fighting fish but also shows that, so far as we at present understand them, they do not require us to postulate a very complex level of functioning. Although the fish are in effect "testing out" each other, this is the result of sequences which can be described without implying that that is their goal.

Can the communicatory behaviour of animals ever usefully be described as goal-directed? When a robin broadcasts its song from the top of a tree, or when a female moth deposits a scent which will attract males, the behaviour influences other individuals because its performance has been adapted in evolution to that end. There may be no adjustment of individual performance in accordance with a changing stimulus situation to maximize the chances of another individual's being affected.

Thus the signals of sub-human forms need not be used in a goal-directed manner. The question arises, are they ever? The criteria for goal-directed behaviour might seem straightforward: as we have seen, signalling would be considered goal-directed if the effect of the sender's behaviour on the receiver was monitored by the sender in such a way as to promote corrective action by the sender to maximize the signal's effectiveness (MacKay, 1972). While this seems reasonably straightforward, goal-directed behaviour is not really such a hard-and-fast category (Hinde and Stevenson, 1969).

For instance, goal-directed behaviour implies a repertoire of courses of action from which that most appropriate for reaching the goal in the present situation is selected. But how do we know if the sender of the signal has alternative methods of signalling if he never uses them? And what do we mean by alternative? The fighting fish certainly has other signals: if it always behaves in a fixed way with respect to its rival's display, is this because the most appropriate signal is always selected, or because it cannot do otherwise?

Again, if signalling behaviour were governed by the discrepancy between the present situation and the goal situation, we should expect its intensity to decrease with increased proximity to the goal. In fact the opposite is often the case, as when (to take a rather literal example) the cheering of the crowd rises to a crescendo just before a goal is scored (see also MacKay, 1972; Hinde, 1972a, pages 86–88).

Because of such difficulties, it is preferable not to attempt to divide signalling into goal-directed and non-goal-directed categories, but to recognize gradations in complexity of directedness. For example, when a threatening robin turns his body so that his breast is directed toward his rival, or when an incubating plover approached by a potential predator flops along the ground simulating a wounded bird and increasing the vigour of her display the nearer the intruder comes to her nest, the behaviour is clearly directed in a simple sense. However the directedness involves primarily the orientation and intensity of the signaller's behaviour. More sophisticated directedness also occurs in animals, though perhaps only in higher mammals. When a chimpanzee takes its human keeper by the hand and leads him to an inaccessible food source, we are concerned with the meshing of a sequence of perhaps two types of behaviour in the chimpanzee (walking; stopping and looking at the food) with two types of behaviour in the keeper (walking; opening the container). This is of a degree of complexity comparable to the behaviour used to get a neighbour to pass the salt, described on page 49.

Taking the matter one step further, much human conversation not only involves directed signalling, but requires that each participant perceive himself as the target of the other's signalling: indeed establishing that each participant is in fact performing a communicative role is an essential preliminary to any conversation (Lyons, 1972; MacKay, 1972).

The last example must not be taken to imply that human verbal language is always used in a goal-directed way. Simple expletives are not. In other cases the criteria for assessing directedness may have to be rather special. For instance, with informative statements criteria for reaching the goal would depend on assessing a change in the "internal organization" of the recipient. And what about performative statements, such as, "I name this ship. . ." (Austin, 1962)? Or near-automatic responses, such as the Italian *prego* following *grazie* (Lyons, 1972; Hinde, 1972a, page 87)? "Goal-directed" communication is yet another category that is shady at the edges—but none the less useful for that.

**Summary**

In summary, though social releasers, ritualized in evolution for a signal function, form the most conspicuous elements used in communication by many species, not all communication (in a broad sense) depends on them. The influence of one individual on the behaviour of others is often mediated by posture, mien, and subtle movements whose effects may be cumulative rather than immediate. Indeed in non-human primates much communication by social releasers of the classical type is concerned with dramatic episodes; the continuity of social relations, and gradual changes in them, are mediated by more intangible nuances. Unfortunately these have so far been little studied. A further issue concerns the goal-directedness of communication: whilst in lower vertebrates much communication can be described reasonably satisfactorily in stimulus-response terms, some primate communication meets the criteria of goal-directedness.

# 8

# MOVEMENTS NOT ADAPTED FOR A SIGNAL FUNCTION

### Sequential analysis

We have seen that much communication between animals does not involve signals adapted in evolution to that end. Indeed, the distinction between signals that are so adapted and those that are not is far from clear. How are we to identify all the ways in which the behaviour of one individual influences that of others? The use of model experiments, so fertile in the study of social releasers, is less feasible here. Another approach, also used in the study of social releasers, depends on the analysis of sequences of behaviour, and involves two issues. First, if an item of behaviour is a potential signal, it must have some predictive value about what the animal might do next. Thus activity $A$ could be interpreted as a signal that activity $B$ may follow, if the animal shows $B$ after $A$ more frequently than it would by chance. We must note that what the actor does after $A$ may depend on what the other individual does, so that $A$ may be a signal that $B$ will follow only if the other individual shows activity $C$: in such a case, $B$ may actually follow $A$ quite rarely, yet $A$ is still a signal that $B$ may follow.

Second, given that a particular activity could act as a signal, we must next ask whether it actually does so. This involves the analysis of inter-individual sequences: given that the actor shows activity $A$, does the other individual show activity $C$ more (or less) often than would be expected by chance?

As a first example, we may consider K. Nelson's (1964) study of the courtship of the male *Corynopoma riisei*. In this fish, the male performs a number of courtship actions over and over again in no particular order, with few responses from the female. Nelson first divided the male's behaviour into sequences as follows. Two activities can be defined as independent if the probability of the second, given that the first has occurred, is equal to its probability regardless of what has preceded it. In practice, the extent to which two successive activities were independent was found to vary with the time interval between them—the longer the interval before the next courtship action, the less predictable what it would be. The length of the interval at which predictions were possible varied with the nature of the first action: at the 5 percent level of statistical significance, events following the activities "quivering" and "shaking" were independent of it after 10 sec but, in one fish at least, events following "twitching" were still dependent on it after 40 sec. Thus Nelson was able to divide the courtship into *sequences* of statistically dependent activities separated by *inter-sequence intervals*, which themselves separated statistically independent events. Within the sequences, each activity was dependent upon the nature of the immediately preceding action, but upon no other. In this case, therefore, the performance of one courtship activity gave some measure of prediction of what the next one would be.

Another slightly more complicated example has already been discussed: whether blue tits at a winter feeding station will attack or flee from a rival, or merely stay put, can be predicted with significant reliability from the combination of display components they showed previously. Both these examples concern activities describable as social releasers, but the method is equally applicable to other types of behaviour. It established, in effect, that the different items of behaviour in an animal's repertoire do not occur at random, but with some degree of sequential ordering. This regularity could form a basis for communication if other individuals come to respond to $A$ in a manner appropriate to the subsequent appearance of $B$.

We must now consider inter-individual sequences: does activity $A$ by one individual increase the probability of activity $C$ in another? Again Stokes's study (1962) of blue tits provides us with an example. In addition to recording what the displaying bird did after showing various combinations of display components, he recorded also the behaviour of the bird displayed at. Table 8.1 shows the effect of mere posturing by one bird on the behaviour of another, all cases involving an actual attack being eliminated. It will be apparent that the presence of some display components affected the subsequent behaviour of the rival. Erecting the nape feathers, raising the wings, and facing the rival, all indicative of aggression in the displaying bird, reduced the probability of attack from the second bird. By contrast, raising the crest or body feathers, indicating that the displaying bird would not attack (see pages 80–82), did not affect the probability of attack in the other, but was associated with an increased probability that it would stay. The open beak reduced both attack and retreat in the rival, and seemed to convey, "I am aggressive, but at present more interested in feeding than in fighting".

A more complex example is provided by the work of Altmann (e.g., 1962, 1965) on the sociobiology of free-living rhesus monkeys, which we shall discuss in some detail. His first step was to compile a catalogue of socially significant behaviour patterns: this of course could not properly be done until the study

TABLE 8.1 *The signal values of the blue tit postures: The figures show the percentage of occasions on which the responding individual showed attack, escape, or neither when the signaller did or did not show the patterns on the left.*

| Behaviour of first bird | | Reaction of second bird, % of total occurrences | | | |
|---|---|---|---|---|---|
| | | ATTACK | ESCAPE | STAY | PROBABILITY |
| Crest erect | + | 21 | 3 | 76 | † |
| | − | 18 | 37 | 45 | |
| Body feathers fluffed | + | 20 | 5 | 75 | † |
| | − | 19 | 34 | 47 | |
| Body horizontal | + | 20 | 35 | 45 | ‡ |
| | − | 20 | 29 | 51 | |
| Facing rival | + | 15 | 33 | 52 | † |
| | − | 21 | 25 | 54 | |
| Nape erect | + | 5 | 49 | 46 | † |
| | − | 21 | 27 | 52 | |
| Wings raised | + | 13 | 48 | 39 | † |
| | − | 21 | 27 | 52 | |
| Tail fanned | + | 16 | 51 | 33 | † |
| | − | 20 | 27 | 53 | |
| Beak open | + | 10 | 20 | 70 | † |
| | − | 21 | 30 | 49 | |

† $P < 0.01$.
‡ NS = not significant at 0.05 level.
SOURCE: From Stokes, 1962.

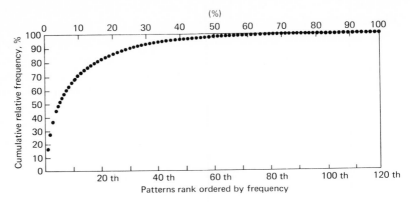

FIGURE 8.1

*Rhesus monkey social behaviour. Frequency distribution of behaviour patterns. The ordinate gives the cumulative relative frequency of the behaviour patterns, which are ranked in order of frequency along the abscissa. (From Altmann, 1965.)*

was completed, but Altmann kept his list open and extended it from 36 to 123 items as the study evolved. Many but not all of these would be classified as social releasers, but that does not affect the present argument.

Data collection consisted of recording sequences of these socially significant behavioural events in the form "who did what to whom". Counts were then made of the number of each class of monad (single events), of each possible class of dyad (two events in succession, e.g., *A* followed by *B*, *A* followed by *C*, *A* followed by *D*, *B* followed by *C*, etc.), of each possible class of triad (*A* followed by *B* followed by *C*), and so on. These were compared with a series of mathematical models, each consisting of a set of probabilities specifying the likelihood of the behavioural events on a particular hypothesis. The simplest model, that all the patterns of behaviour were equally probable and independent of one another, was clearly unacceptable. The second involved calculating the probabilities of each item ("monad probabilities") and showed the extent to which some activities occurred more often than others: more than half the observed events were accounted for by the six most frequent behaviour patterns (Fig. 8.1).

The next model was concerned with the extent to which each event was contingent upon the immediately preceding event. The observed frequency of

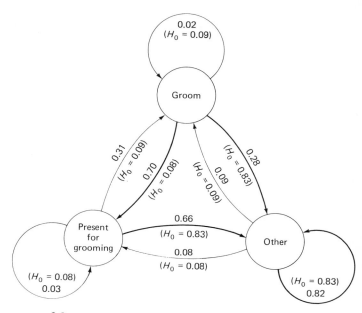

FIGURE 8.2

*Rhesus monkey social behaviour. Transition probabilities for grooming, presenting for grooming, and the sum of all other patterns. The thickness of the arrows is proportional to the probabilities that they represent. (From Altmann, 1965.)*

each dyad was compared with the frequency expected on the null hypothesis that behaviour was independent of the preceding event. This quickly revealed that much behaviour was in fact contingent upon the immediately preceding event. Since it is impossible to discuss all probabilities linking the 120 behavioural items simultaneously, Fig. 8.2 shows the transition probabilities between two patterns, grooming and presenting for grooming, and the remaining 118 patterns. Each arrow shows the observed transition probability and that calculated on the null hypothesis of sequential independence ($H_0$).

The next step was to work with triads, comparing the behaviour which would occur if the behaviour depended on the immediately antecedent behaviour and the item preceding it, but not on the item preceding that, with the actual frequency of occurrence of each triad. Similarly, sequences of four or more

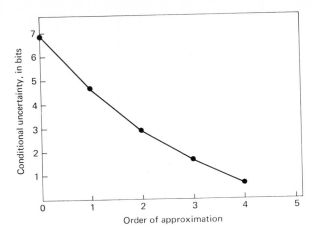

FIGURE 8.3

*Rhesus monkey social behaviour. Relation between the order of approximation and the conditional uncertainty of any behavioural event. (From Altmann, 1965.)*

items could be examined. As sequences of more items were used, the model came to predict the observed behaviour more precisely. This is illustrated in Fig. 8.3 which shows the reduction in "uncertainty", which can be measured in "bits", as more items were considered.

This method is potentially able to tell us quite a lot about which items of individual behaviour are related to the subsequent appearance of others, and how closely. Clearly, the social significance revealed does not depend at all upon whether or not there is evidence that the item has been adapted as a signal in the course of evolution, or upon whether its use is goal-directed, in the sense described earlier, toward influencing the behaviour of others. But the method does reveal something of the complexity of the interactions in that it shows to what extent each behavioural item is influenced by only one, or by more than one, preceding item.

There are, however, a number of difficulties, many of which were pointed out by Altmann himself. Some of these arise from the initial selection of the items of behaviour to be recorded. Clearly, the initial catalogue must have a profound influence on subsequent data collection and analysis, and yet there is bound to be an element of arbitrariness in its selection. For instance, Altmann points out that he included the *assumption* of postures as behavioural items, but not the continuation of the postures—yet a posture may continue to affect other animals long after it is adopted. Indeed the analysis was concerned only with what follows what: the duration of behavioural items was not considered. Second, Altmann's technique involved counting two events as successive whether or not they were performed by the same individual. Thus the sequential probabilities reflect partly communicatory processes, and partly constraints upon an individual's behaviour arising from his own preceding behaviour. Third, there are inevitably practical difficulties in the collection of data on rapid social interactions within a group. Fourth, the conclusions will relate to the sample studied: this may or may not be representative of the species as a whole. On general grounds one would expect differences between individuals of different age and sex, and even between individuals of the same sex and similar age (e.g., Møller et al., 1968; Durham, 1969): a given pattern of behaviour from one individual may produce different responses in different individuals, and in any one individual it may produce different responses from those produced by the same behaviour from another monkey. Furthermore, sequential probabilities may change with time. These are all matters which the method could in theory be used to investigate: for instance, in data collection the behaviour of each individual could be recorded separately. But in practice there are great difficulties in obtaining adequate samples and in analysing the data. The more items in the catalogue, and the longer the sequences of behavioural items considered, the greater the sample size required. With Altmann's 120 items and sequences of four items, analysis was a massive computer-based operation. Some will feel that the mathematical tools used were disproportionate in a study where the variables of age, sex, individual differences, and fluctuations in motivation, all of prime importance in behaviour sequences, have been neglected; to which Altmann replies, "The variability, predictability, and stereotypy of behaviour sequences can now be measured, thus providing a firm basis for the use of these properties in intraspecific and interspecific comparisons" (Altmann, 1965, page 522).

Finally, there is the danger that correlations between events be taken to imply that one caused the other. If event $A$ frequently precedes $B$, this does not necessarily mean that $A$ causes $B$. Many other possibilities are open—for instance, $A$ and $B$ may have a common cause, but $B$ has a longer latency; or $A$ causes $A'$, which causes $B$. To resolve this difficulty, experimental interference is in theory necessary. The difficulty is, however, less pressing in studies of equal precision but more limited scope, such as that of Stokes (see pages 80–82 and 94–95), for then other sources of evidence in addition to the mathematical analysis can be used to support the conclusions of the latter.

One final point must be made. Sequential analysis is suitable for assessing whether activity A of one individual influences the probable subsequent appearance of activity C in another. It is most easily applicable where the effect is immediate, and relatively useless when it is long-term. In the courtship of *Corynopoma riisei* (page 94) the effect of the male's actions on the female was of the latter type: responses by the female were rare and appeared to depend on the cumulative effect of male courtship activities. When they did occur, however, female responses had an immediate effect on the next activity of the male.

### Communication about the environment

Many social releasers convey information about the environment, signalling, for instance, the availability of food or the presence of predators. Anecdotal evidence indicates that some of these cases involve a fairly complex level of functioning. For instance, during attempts to trap baboons in Kenya, some adults sat near the trap and threatened away juveniles who were attempting to take the bait (Maxim and Buettner-Janisch, 1963).

Laboratory experiments under restricted conditions provide further information, mostly involving signals other than social releasers. For example, Mason and Hollis (1962) assessed the extent to which an "informer" monkey could indicate to an "operator" monkey which of four handles the latter should pull in order that both should get a food reward. A high level of success was achieved, the proportion of correct responses increasing from the chance level of 25 percent to over 80 percent. The signals used were apparently arbitrary, differing between each dyad. Communication seemed to occur more rapidly if the monkeys were previously acquainted with each other.

In this experiment, the information conveyed concerned the acquisition of a desirable object Stephenson (1967) carried out a similar study concerned with the avoidance of potentially dangerous ones. He first conditioned individual rhesus monkeys to avoid a novel object by punishing them with an air blast if they attempted to manipulate it. A naive and similarly sexed monkey was then introduced to the object in the presence of the previously trained one. Such experiments led to one of two types of outcome. In the case of three female pairs the naive monkey handled the object and the previously trained one subsequently also did so in spite of its previous training. With three male pairs the opposite happened: the potential responsiveness of the naive monkey toward the object was inhibited by the trained monkey, so that both avoided it. In one case the trained animal actually pulled the naive one away from proximity to the object. Stephenson regards this as a form of admonition. (In view of the small sample size, the sex difference was probably of no significance.)

Menzel et al. (1972) investigated whether such an acquired pattern of behaviour could be transferred across successive groupings of animals. The "task" in this case was simply to play with strange objects. First a group of three chimpanzees (A, B, and C) was exposed to the two objects, then two of these with a newcomer (B, C, and D), then a third trio (C, D, and E), and so on. Initially, both objects were treated with caution. However, in the third trio, individual E habituated to one object and in the fifth individual F habituated to the other. An enduring tradition of boldness and play then ensued for both objects separately. What is of interest here is not that the response of one individual to an object was affected by the behaviour he saw others showing in its presence, for that was known before (e.g., birds, Klopfer, 1959; rhesus monkeys, R. E. Miller et al., 1967), but that the effect was transmitted across successive groupings. By an analogy between the successive groupings and generations, Menzel refers to the transmission as "protocultural".

In other experiments, Menzel (1971, 1972, in press) has shown the value of concentrating on what animals can communicate rather than, or before, examining how communication is achieved. In one experiment he examined the extent to which one of a group of chimpanzees living in a large enclosure (30.5 × 122 m) communicated the location of a source of food or a fear-provoking object to the others. In each test the animals were confined in a cage whilst one of their number was shown the stimulus object in a location hidden from the others. This "leader" was then returned to the group, and a minute or so later all were released. The tests were accompanied by appropriate controls in which no object was hidden.

In the great majority of tests, the group went immediately to the hidden object. Although the leader usually arrived first, the behaviour of the rest of the group could not be described merely as following the leader. Indeed one animal would often run on in front, glancing back at the leader's direction of travel, and then running on to search possible hiding places. The focus of attention was not the leader per se or any particular signals that he emitted, "but 'that something out there, ahead of the group' which was the environmental source of the leader's excitement and the end point of his travel". If the others failed to follow or were prevented from doing so, the leader would try to coerce them with

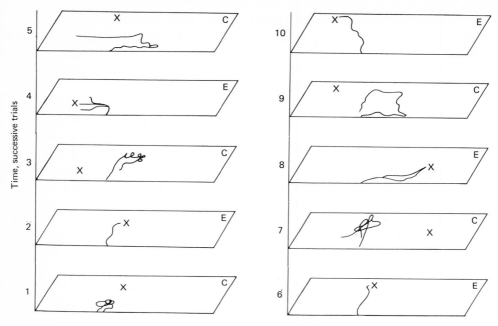

FIGURE 8.4

*Communication about the environment in chimpanzees. Maps showing the travel routes taken by the group as a whole on each of 10 successive trials. E = experimental condition, with one animal shown the food location. C = control condition, with no animal shown the location of the hidden food. X = hidden food. (From Menzel, 1971.)*

whimpers and other expressive movements, or even try to pull them toward the food; such observations indicate that communication was intentional (see pages 49, 89). The other animals went with the leader to food in preference to going to food displayed conspicuously elsewhere; and when two leaders were each separately shown one of two piles of food differing in size, the group usually subsequently went first to the larger of the two piles. When fear-provoking objects were used instead of food, the followers showed almost as much caution in approaching them as did the leaders. Menzel stresses that "no highly specialized vocalizations, hand or limb gestures, or facial expressions were detectable even to highly trained observers". The most effective leadership behaviour was for an individual simply to "get up, orient, and move out 'independently' in a consistent direction, 'as if he knew exactly where he was going, and why'. An occasional glance, directed first to followers and then to goal, seemed to facilitate matters even further, as did the pace and style of locomotion". Menzel points out that information about the food source was probably conveyed by the position of the leader with respect to the others, and by the position of the group in the enclosure, as well as by the leader's bodily movements.

The intentionality of the communicatory process is of particular interest since, as we have seen, clear evidence of goal-directedness in non-verbal communication is hard to come by. Particularly striking evidence was provided by one female who, when she was leader, usually failed to get the food because she was supplanted at the last moment by a male. This female gradually came to employ various devices in order *not* to communicate the location of the food to the male—sitting down at a distance from it; waiting until the male was looking in the opposite direction before going to it; and even deliberately leading the group off in the wrong direction and then doubling back smartly to get the food (see also van Lawick-Goodall, 1971a).

## Summary

Communication about the environment may depend upon a whole spectrum of signals. At one extreme are the social releasers, adapted for a signal function and responded to by others independently of specific experience of them. But these form only part of the range of signals on which communication actually depends. At the other extreme are postures and movements, often less conspicuous and sometimes individually idiosyncratic, of part of the body or of the whole, to which others may come to respond as a consequence of experience. These can be studied by sequential analysis. It is profitable to study not only *how* animals communicate but also *what*: Menzel's experiments with chimpanzees have opened up possibilities for studying subtleties of communication processes that were previously hardly suspected.

# 9
# DEVELOPMENT OF NON-VERBAL COMMUNICATION

In considering the development of signal systems in the individual, we must consider three questions—the development of the motor pattern, developmental factors that lead to the signal's being given appropriately, and the development of appropriate responsiveness.

## The development of signal motor patterns

Most, but not all, social releasers do not require example from other members of the species for their development. If great tits are reared in social isolation, they exhibit most of the display movements and vocalizations in the repertoire of wild-reared birds. Rhesus monkeys reared in social isolation show many of the facial expressions and vocalizations that are characteristic of the species. Although differences in the signals used in communication between wild and caged monkeys have been described, it is not certain that they were due to learning (Kummer and Kurt, 1965).

FIGURE 9.1

*Lip-smacking of female rhesus during grooming.* (Drawing by Priscilla Edwards.)

As might be expected, the various social releasers in the species' repertoire tend to appear in development in a fairly fixed sequence. In part this can be understood in functional terms: those expressive movements important for communication with mother or siblings are likely to appear before those used with a sex partner. Fox (1970) has suggested that a phylogenetic factor may also be involved. The foxes, which lack any complex social organization, have a repertoire of discrete facial expressions. The wolf, coyote, and domestic dog, which are more social, each also has a fairly wide range of intermediates involving simultaneous combinations of various facial expressions. This may indicate an evolutionary advance in the more social species. In ontogeny, the expressions that they have in common with foxes appear first, the combinations later. In her studies of the stump-tailed macaque, Chevalier-Skolnikoff (1971) similarly suggested that ontogenetic development follows a course descriptively and functionally similar to evolutionary ritualization.

In some cases it is possible to trace the ontogenetic development of adult expressive movements from behaviour patterns of the juvenile or infant. Anthoney (1968) discussed several examples as a result of his study of captive baboons. "Lip-smacking", a conciliatory gesture used in greeting and sexual situations by many higher primates (Fig. 9.1), seems to develop from movements of sucking. It actually involves pulling the tongue away from the dento-palatal

FIGURE 9.2

*Lip smacking of juvenile to female's nipple and of female baboon to male's erect penis.* (Drawing by Priscilla Edwards from Anthoney, 1968.)

surface while the mouth is slightly open, and Anthoney assumes the movement to be identical with that of sucking. He suggests that lip-smacking becomes a motor pattern of greeting and sexual behaviour by processes of generalization and association. There are numerous contexts in which these could occur. Thus females other than the mother frequently lip-smack to the infant, sometimes directing the movement to or performing it on the infant's genital area: with male infants this often produces an erection (Fig. 9.2). Lip-smacking to older infants by adult females is often followed by an embrace or by presentation and mounting. The infant sometimes lip-smacks to one of the female's nipples during greeting, and lip-smacking may be elicited by other part-cylindrical objects. In the stump-tailed macaque, Chevalier-Skolnikoff (1971) similarly traced the development of lip-smacking from the sucking and rooting responses of the infant.

Anthoney also suggests that the embrace used in greeting and the mounting pattern used in copulation are derived from the grasping reflex of the infant (see also Ransom and Ransom, 1971; Hanby, 1972); and that grooming patterns are derived from movements made by the infant at the nipple, grooming the mother developing as a substitute for sucking when the mother rejects the infant's attempts to gain the nipple.

Some communicatory movements develop in adulthood. Thus a mother monkey often signals her intention to move off by glancing at her infant, by lowering her hind quarters, or by a touch on the infant's back (e.g., De Vore, 1963; Hinde et al., 1964). Chevalier-Skolnikoff has shown that the latter is derived by abbreviation from the hugging movement with which the female earlier holds her infant to her.

Of course, even when signal movements characteristic of the species do develop gradually in the individual, the course of development could hardly be determined solely by learning during the course of a series of more or less random events: such a mechanism could not lead to the constancy of form that is seen in practice. Whether or not ontogeny repeats phylogeny, it would seem that phylogeny must have bequeathed a strong predisposition to learn along lines which lead to the development of patterns which are characteristic of the species or at least of a high proportion of its members.

The learning of signal movements by imitation is extremely rare. That it can occur in higher primates is suggested by the painstaking experiments of Gardner and Gardner (1971). They taught a captive chimpanzee to communicate with its human fosterers by establishing a relationship with the animal and using signs based on the American sign language for the deaf. But in other species imitation seems to be unknown, except for the case of bird vocalizations.

The development of avian vocalizations is in fact of special interest. Here, too, some signals develop in the absence of any possibility for imitation. The vocal repertoires of domestic fowl and of ring doves develop normally even in birds deafened soon after hatching (Konishi, 1963; Nottebohm and Nottebohm, 1971). In such cases, genetic determinants must be adequate to ensure the development of the species-characteristic pattern in the absence of example and, indeed, in spite of considerable diversity in experience (Lade and Thorpe, 1964; Nottebohm and Nottebohm, 1971).

Even though developing normally in the absence of any opportunity for imitation, vocalizations may still have a complex ontogeny. The songs of many birds (see below) seem to develop out of call-notes which themselves have a developmental history (e.g., Nottebohm, 1970).

Experiments, in fact, show that even where imitation of other individuals is not essential for the development of a vocalization, certain types of experience may still be of importance. The call-notes of the chaffinch, though not the song (see below), develop fairly normally in birds reared alone in auditory isolation (Thorpe, 1961). However, their development is abnormal in birds deafened when three months old (Nottebohm, 1970). Similarly, song sparrows, hatched and reared by canaries in isolation from their own species, sing the normal song of their species when adult; but if deafened before they start to sing they produce quite aberrant songs (Mulligan, 1966; Nottebohm, 1970, 1972b). Such observations suggest that feedback through the ear plays a part in development. Whether feedback plays a similar role in the development of any non-vocal signals has not been investigated but seems less likely (Hinde, 1970).

In the development of some vocalizations, imitation does play a major role. For example, males of the Indian hill mynah learn their calls from other males living in the same area, and females imitate females (Bertram, 1970). Male bullfinches and zebra finches imitate the song of the male that reared them, whether father or foster-parent (Nicolai, 1964; Immelmann, 1969). One male bullfinch foster-reared by canaries passed on his canary-like song to his son, grandson, and greatgrandson!

But evidence that a vocalization is learned by imitation does not imply that the bird will learn any sound that it hears. The young bullfinch is almost restricted to learning the song of its foster-parent, and learns it in preference to that of conspecifics singing nearby. We shall see shortly that what a chaffinch will learn is restricted in a different way. Such restrictions on what is learned

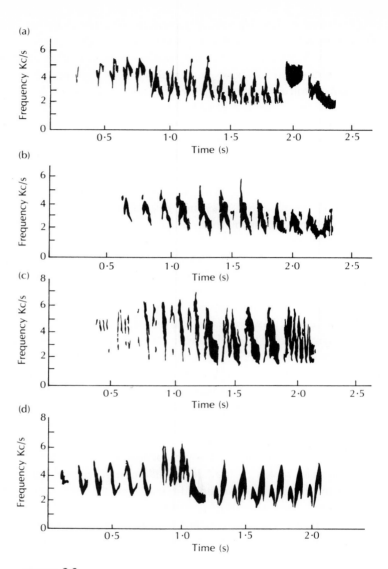

FIGURE 9.3

*Chaffinch song:* (a) *characteristic normal song;* (b) *song of an individual reared in isolation;* (c) *song of an individual from a group reared in isolation;* (d) *song produced by a bird reared in isolation, after tutoring with a rearticulated chaffinch song with the ending in the middle.* (After Thorpe, 1961.)

provide further examples of the close interaction of genetic and experiential factors in development (Hinde and Stevenson-Hinde, 1973).

A case which demonstrates how complex the development of signal movements may be, and at the same time incorporates the principles just mentioned, is that of the song of the chaffinch (Thorpe, 1961). The experimental findings can be briefly summarized as follows:

1 The normal adult song lasts about 2.5 sec and is divided into three phrases followed by a terminal flourish (Fig. 9.3a). It develops in the bird's first spring from a rambling subsong which has no definite duration and a wide range of notes. The development seems to consist of the progressive omission of extreme frequencies and gradual approximation toward the normal pattern (Fig. 9.4). The subsong itself seems to develop from call-notes which appear earlier in development.

2 Chaffinches hand-reared in auditory isolation from all other individuals from a few days of age develop only a simple song which, though recognizably a chaffinch song, is not divided into phrases and lacks a terminal flourish (Fig. 9.3b). This indicates that imitation of the normal song is essential for its development.

3 Chaffinches hand-reared in isolation from normal song but kept in groups each sing a song which is unlike normal song, is characteristic of the group, but differs between groups (Fig. 9.3c). This indicates that learning during counter-singing occurs within each group.

4 Chaffinches caught in their first autumn and subsequently kept in isolation, and chaffinches hand-reared in auditory isolation but exposed to recordings of chaffinch song during their first autumn, subsequently develop near-normal songs. Thus some learning occurs during the first few months, long before the bird itself starts to sing.

5 Chaffinches reared in isolation will not subsequently produce any song to which they are exposed. For instance, an artificial chaffinch song in which the notes had a pure tonal quality and were thus unlike those of normal chaffinch song was not imitated, but chaffinch songs played backward, or with the terminal flourish placed in the middle, were (Fig. 9.3d). Thus there is a restriction on what a chaffinch will learn, and the criterion seems to be a note structure resembling that of normal chaffinch song.

6 Chaffinches isolated only from their first autumn are even more restricted in what they will learn.

Since the final song pattern develops gradually from the subsong, and since its form is influenced by experience of hearing songs long before the bird itself

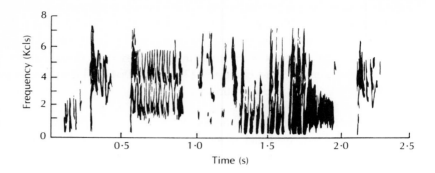

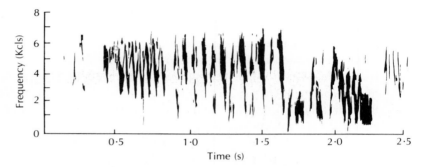

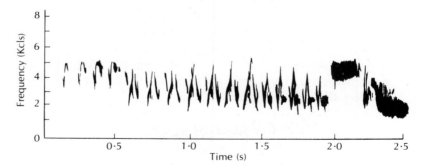

FIGURE 9.4

*Three stages in the subsong of the chaffinch: (a) chirps and rattles having a large range of frequencies; (b) transition to full song; (c) spring song, still looser and longer than normal full song. The full song of same individual is shown in the upper diagram of Fig. 9.3. (After Thorpe, 1961.)*

starts to sing, one possibility is that the effect of that experience is to increase the reinforcing effectiveness of hearing the full song. On this view, the development of the full song from the subsong would be due to the reinforcing value to the bird of hearing itself sing the full song.

Two predictions from this view have received experimental support:

7 Deafening the bird after it had experienced song, but before it started to sing itself, would make it impossible for the bird to monitor its own output and thus would nullify the effects of the early experience. This is in fact the case (Konishi and Nottebohm, 1969; Nottebohm, 1970).

8 Since reinforcers (defined as stimuli that increase the frequency of responses emitted immediately previously) are usually effective for a range of responses, any reinforcing effect of hearing song on singing should operate also for other responses. This is the case (Stevenson, 1967; Stevenson-Hinde, 1972).

One way of relating all these findings is to suppose that the naive bird has a crude "model" or "template" of the species-characteristic song, which is improved by experience of that song. On this view, sounds that approximate to that model are reinforcing. This postulation of a "template" is of course merely a heuristic device for tying the various experiments together.

9 Each bronchus with its tympanic membrane and hypoglossus nerve constitutes an independent sound source. During ontogeny the chaffinch comes to produce most of its vocal repertoire from one side, the other one producing only minor contributions (Nottebohm, 1972a).

10 Operations on adult chaffinches involving unilateral and bilateral denervation of the syrinx show that there is neural lateralization of the control of song production: section of the left hypoglossal nerve results in the loss of most of the song's components, while section of the right has relatively minor effects. These losses are irreversible. However the same operation at an earlier stage reveals considerable plasticity (Nottebohm, 1972b).

It will be clear even from this much simplified account that song learning is complex, depending on interactions between the organism as it is at each stage and its auditory experience. Indeed, Nottebohm (1972a, b) believes that it involves much more even than trial-and-error attempts to match a template, and represents a series of non-communicatory exercises, each of which prepares the way for succeeding stages. The early subsong serves to establish efferent-proprioceptive-auditory associations which make the subsequent imitation of an auditory model much easier.

A further quite different type of observation is compatible with the postulation of a model or template. This concerns antiphonal singing—i.e., cases in which two individuals sing different parts in alternation. Usually each bird sings its own particular note or song, and never that of the other bird. However, there are a few records of one bird singing both parts in the absence of its partner (see, for example, Thorpe, 1972), as though it knew what should be sung and completed the missing parts.

Just why it is that the development of some vocalizations depends on experience while that of others does not is far from clear. Nottebohm (1972b) suggests that two factors may be important. First, the effectiveness of a song in stimulating a female may increase with its complexity, and complexity can be achieved more readily by an increased ability to learn song repertoires within genetically determined limits than by the evolution of a more complex genetic determination. Second, the formation of local dialects may be important in speciation. It is perhaps because the use of vocal signals to attract females is much less common in mammals that they rarely show vocal learning.

In summary, many social releasers and other movements of potential communicatory significance appear in individuals reared in isolation. This indicates that imitation cannot be necessary for their development. However, many signal movements have quite complex developmental histories, and experience other than imitation, including perception of the individual's own movements or vocalizations, may play an important part. Imitation is involved in the development of some bird vocalizations, and these are of special interest in demonstrating the operation of constraints on what can be learned.

### The use of signal movements

Relatively little is known about developmental factors influencing the use of signal movements. In the case of social releasers, all the evidence indicates that their appropriate use is initially independent of experience—though, of course, experience may affect the frequency with which the individual's internal state is such that the signal is given.

However, the frequency with which social releasers are emitted may also be altered by appropriate reinforcement. For instance, the frequency with which a budgerigar gives a certain call can be increased by food reinforcement (Ginsburg, 1960), and the frequency with which a chick gives distress calls increases if calling leads to the presentation of a stimulus object that it has learned to respond to as a parent (see Chap. 11). Whether the frequency of any signal movement in the species' repertoire could be similarly affected by any reinforcer is, however, an open issue (see Hinde and Stevenson-Hinde, 1973).

Similar experiments have been conducted with primates. In one experiment an experimenter stood with her back to a young chimpanzee in a cage, until the chimpanzee made a "low guttural bark". Then she reinforced the vocalization by turning and playing with the animal. The frequency of the vocalization increased. Subsequently, the observer deliberately failed to provide the reinforcement, and the vocalizations became less frequent (Randolph and Brooks, 1967).

Another type of evidence perhaps suggesting the importance of social reinforcement comes from a comparison of captive wild-born chimpanzees with animals that had been kept under conditions of social deprivation. The former vocalized much more than the deprived animals in a variety of stressful situations. The difference could not be accounted for in terms of a difference in the extent to which animals in the two groups were distressed, and thus was apparently due to a difference in the tendency to vocalize. The authors suggest two possibilities: either the deprived animals had received no social reinforcement for vocalizing, which had therefore suffered extinction, or they did not vocalize because they rocked and showed other stereotypes instead (Randolph and Mason, 1969). The two explanations are not of course incompatible.

There is thus plenty of evidence that experience may affect the incidence of species-characteristic signal movements. In the case of human signal movements, such as crying and smiling, experience affects their occurrence within a few days of birth (e.g., Bernal, 1972): as discussed in Chap. 15 however, the nature of the effect is by no means always simple. Further effects of experience on social releasers in adults are discussed on pages 135–138.

Signal movements not characteristic of the species must of course acquire their initial effectiveness because of their association with a particular internal state in the signalling animal. Learning processes may enter subsequently to enhance or diminish their use in the context in question, or to modify their form.

## Development of appropriate responsiveness

Once again, many species-characteristic signal movements are responded to appropriately even in the absence of any experience indicating their significance. For example, nestling great tits respond with immobility to the parents' alarm calls shortly after, and even perhaps before, hatching.

There is some disagreement as to whether individual primates brought up under conditions of social deprivation respond appropriately to social releasers. Miller et al. (1967) linked two restrained monkeys by closed-circuit television. One animal was presented with a stimulus indicating either an impending food reward or an electric shock. The other monkey, by observing the image of the other's face, had to pull one of two levers for both to avoid shock or receive food. Monkeys reared normally could perform this task, but individuals reared in social isolation for their first year could not (see also Sackett and Ruppenthal, 1973).

Such experiments are, however, difficult to interpret: socially deprived monkeys are emotionally disturbed in many ways, and it is difficult to know whether the inadequacy was due to an inappropriate response to the signal or due to some other abnormality (e.g., hyper- or hypo-aggressiveness). Furthermore, experiments with restricted animals eliminate many of the cues available in a natural situation: comparable experiments in a free environment might have given quite different results (see Menzel, in press). Evidence pointing in the opposite direction comes from some experiments by Sackett (1966) with rhesus monkeys reared in isolation from social stimuli. Until they were ninety days of age, such infants showed little response to pictures of monkeys with threatening faces projected onto the walls of their cages, but when older they gave full fear responses.

Whether or not social experience is necessary for basically appropriate responses to social releasers, there can be no doubt that it is essential for the subtle nuances. The role of experience in the development of responsiveness to signals other than social releasers is obvious.

### Summary

In summary, most species-characteristic signal movements can develop independently of example by other members of the species, are used appropriately, and are responded to by other individuals irrespective of previous experience of them. However, many have a quite complicated developmental history, and in the case of some birds' songs, imitation is involved. The development of other signal movements, their appropriate use, and responsiveness to them must depend on learning. Such cases have not yet been studied in any detail, but it seems likely that, in some at least, the course of learning is constrained by other aspects of the species' structure or behaviour.

# 10

# HUMAN
# NON-VERBAL
# COMMUNICATION

### The diversity of human non-verbal communication

So far most of the examples of non-verbal communication have been drawn from animals. As clearly recognized by Darwin (1872), however, man has a comparable system, which plays an essential part in his social life. This involves postures, gestures, and facial expressions, only some of which have been adapted in evolution for a signal function. Before considering these signal movements, it is necessary to emphasize some characteristics which make their study peculiarly difficult.

First, just because human non-verbal communication is used as an integral part of verbal interchanges, as well as independently of them (see pages 123–124), its study demands special precautions against over-generalizations. For example there are some who believe that verbal language is so much part of man's nature that non-verbal communication can hardly be studied in its own right (e.g., Leach, 1972)—a view which provides a valuable corrective to over-

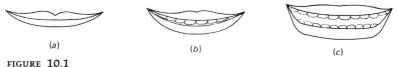

(a)                      (b)                    (c)

FIGURE **10.1**

*Three common smiles:* (a) *simple smile;* (b) *upper smile;* (c) *broad smile.* (From Brannigan and Humphries, 1972.)

enthusiastic biologists but, as we shall see, is itself an over-statement (see pages 138–139).

Second, context is perhaps even more important in the interpretation of many human expressive movements than it is in lower forms. This means that model experiments, of such value in studying social releasers in animals, are of limited value in the human case. Even photographs of expressive movements have proved to be useful in only a few instances (e.g., Ekman et al., 1969). The importance of context is indicated in another way by studies of the varied roles of direction of gaze and eye contact. Eye engagement is important in establishing and defining the nature of a relationship, in obtaining information about the responses of others, in controlling who speaks in a conversation, in reducing distraction, and so on (Argyle, 1969). It would be meaningless to study gaze isolated from its context—it is the nature of eye movements in the context in which they occur that is important in communication. As we have seen, context is often crucial in animals. Whether it is more important in man, or whether it is only that in man we are able to study more subtle nuances for which it is essential, hardly matters (see also page 138).

Third, the richness of the material in itself poses a tremendous problem. At the extremes, two approaches are open. Either one can study fairly global categories of expressive movement, such as laughing, smiling, or crying. These are, after all, the categories of expression to which we think that we respond, and thus the most likely to be relevant. Or, at the other extreme, one can analyse expressive movements into their elements—some examples are shown in Figs. 10.1 and 10.2. Such an approach soon shows that, as in birds (see pages 80–82), the elements may be combined in different ways to give different shades and even qualities of meaning. For example, smiling may be modified by elements normally indicating threat, doubt, or refusal to respond. A tendency to square the mouth corners and expose and protrude the lower teeth can indicate threat: when combined with smiling this can produce the oblong smile shown

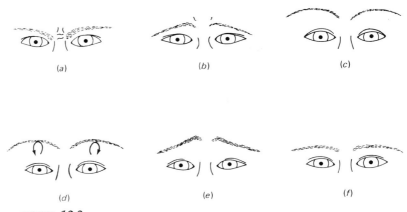

FIGURE 10.2

*Eyebrow units:* (a) *angry frown;* (b) *sad frown;* (c) *raise;* (d) *flash;*
(e) *sad raise;* (f) *neutral.* (From Brannigan and Humphries, 1972.)

in Fig. 10.3*b*. Similarly, mouth corners down (Fig. 10.3*c*), indicating doubt, can
be combined with a smile to produce a wry smile (Fig. 10.3*d*); and tight lips
(Fig. 10.3*e*), indicating no verbal response, may give a compressed smile (Fig.
10.3*f*) (Brannigan and Humphries, 1972).

Such an approach soon shows that such categories as "smile" or "cry" are
in fact heterogeneous, containing variants indicative of a considerable range of
internal states. These may be describable in terms of two dimensions, as the
threat movements of the herring gull (Fig. 6.10) can be understood in terms of
tendencies to attack and withdraw, but are usually even more complex (see pages
126–132). Indeed, one's intuitive knowledge of the multi-dimensional variability
of human expressive movements leads one to wonder just how much of an
over-simplification some of the work on animals involves. On the other hand,
this sort of approach requires the isolation of a large number of elements—
Grant (1969) listed 118, over half of which concerned the face, and Brannigan
and Humphries (1972) described even more. These elements may overlap and
combine in an almost infinite variety of ways with which it is difficult to cope
even with the most sophisticated computer-based methods. Furthermore, the
same element may convey different meanings according to the context in which
it is used (see, for example, Smith and Connolly, 1972).

A fourth issue, related to the last, is that many common terms for expres-

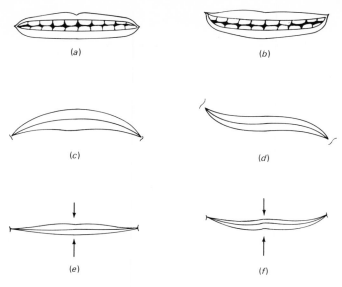

FIGURE 10.3

*Interactions in the form of units:* (a) *oblong mouth;* (b) *oblong smile,* (c) *mouth corners down;* (d) *wry smile;* (e) *tight lips;* (f) *compressed smile.* (From Brannigan and Humphries, 1972.)

sive movements are misleading. Thus Brannigan and Humphries (1972) point out that crying covers at least two objectively distinct patterns: one is characterized by sobs, tears, sad frown, mouth corners back, etc., and is indicative of "genuine distress", while the other involves an angry frown and few or no tears and (in adult group psychotherapy) may reveal an attempt at group manipulation. Smiling involves at least seven distinct patterns. The objective study of human non-verbal communication thus demands the shedding of a fair number of everyday assumptions.

### Classification of human non-verbal communication

The diversity of human non-verbal communication is so great that it demands some system of categorization. Several have been proposed, each of which reflects the interests of its author, but none is wholly satisfactory—either the categories are too limited, or they overlap. This is not necessarily a reflection on the system: as we have seen in other contexts, man-made pigeonholes almost inevitably constrain nature. And even though not perfect, classificatory systems form a useful aid to thinking. Some of them are based primarily on the physical characteristics of the movements (e.g., Grant, 1969; Brannigan and Humphries, 1972; McGrew, 1972), and space does not permit their further consideration here. We shall consider two with functional implications, and one which emphasizes the relations between verbal and non-verbal communication.

The first is based on that of Ekman and Friesen (1969; Ekman, 1971) and of earlier writers, and depends on criteria of usage (i.e., the circumstances in which the act is used); origin (how it was acquired); and coding (the degree of resemblance between the act and its message). In what follows only the bare outline of the scheme can be summarized. The order of the categories has been changed to clarify the relations with the work on sub-human species discussed in earlier pages.

1 **Affect displays** At first sight, this is the category of human expressive movements most closely related to those studied in non-human forms. In everyday speech, the movements referred to are expressions of emotional states—of happiness, fear, and so on (though in some cases the state may be simulated—Ekman, personal communication).

However, two features of this category in the scheme of Ekman and Friesen require comment. First, they limit the term "affect" to momentary feeling states, and give a "tentative, perhaps partial, list of primary affects: happiness, surprise, fear, sadness, anger, disgust and interest". Their list is based primarily on their finding that these effective states are distinguished in photographs by observers of facial displays in several cultures. This category of affect displays is more restricted than that of the expressive movements studied by students of animal behaviour, and the latter are bound to have reservations about the list. First, is it too limited? Insofar as it is based on responses to photographs, could it not represent a list of expressions whose "message" (see pages 82–83) is relatively independent of context, rather than affects that are primary in any other sense? And on the other hand, is it not possible that some of these "primary" affects are themselves complex (see, for example, pages 61–76, 133–135)? This however does not affect the validity of the classificatory system as a whole.

Second, Ekman and Friesen regard the face as the primary site of affect displays, believing that most bodily movements accompanying emotional states are responses to those states rather than direct consequences of them. There seems, however, to be little evidence to support this distinction. In animals facial expressions become more important in higher mammals that have an elaborate facial musculature, and are used more in short-range contacts than are postures and gestures, but otherwise they perform similar roles. Furthermore, many of the expressive bodily postures and movements used by man are found also in sub-human primates (see pages 134–139). It may be, however, that postures and gestures are more affected by cultural influences than are facial expressions.

2 **Adaptors** These are movements, often fragmentary, which when completed have also a functional content unrelated to communication. They may be directed toward the body (e.g., hand-to-face movements, auto-erotic movements, grooming movements), other people (e.g., begging gestures, movements involved in aggression, flight, or establishing affection or intimacy), or objects (e.g., the movements used in driving a car or wielding a tool). Ekman and Friesen believe that all these movements were first learned as adaptive efforts to satisfy needs, perform bodily actions, and so on, and are emitted in adulthood as fragments, maintained by habit, and triggered by something in the current situation. But the category is clearly heterogeneous. Some cases, such as incipient movements of aggression or flight, could be classed as species-characteristic intention movements, and are clearly comparable to the displays used in threat, etc., by non-human forms. Their use as communicatory gestures could be ascribed in part to phylogenetic influences, though the extent to which they have been ritualized in evolution for a signal function is variable and in any case a matter for further enquiry. Some of these could be classed also as affect displays. Some, such as grooming, could be described also as displacement activities: grooming occurs also in conflict situations in chimpanzees and monkeys (e.g., van Lawick-Goodall, 1968), though in man its occurrence and form are heavily influenced by cultural factors. Yet others are culturally elaborated movements, like the movements originally learned in the context of smoking or wielding a tool.

3 **Emblems** These are non-verbal acts which have a direct verbal translation, usually of a word or two. Examples are making a fist, obscene gestures, and deaf-and-dumb languages. They are used most frequently when verbal exchange is impossible, or must be emphasized. Emblematic expressions may resemble affect displays but, unlike simulated emotions, differ suf-

ficiently from the actual emotional expression to make it evident to the beholder that the emotion is not being actually experienced, but only referred to (Ekman, 1973). Where emblems are closely related to affect displays or to intention movements, they may have considerable cross-cultural generality. Often, however, they are culture-specific.

4 **Illustrators** These are movements directly tied to speech, serving to illustrate what is said verbally. They include movements which emphasize words or phrases, point to objects, depict spatial relationships or movements, and so on.

5 **Regulators** These regulate the back-and-forth nature of a conversation between two interactants. The most common is the head nod, but eye contacts, slight postural shifts, and so on are also important.

Space does not permit a more detailed discussion of Ekman's classificatory scheme, which has gone a long way toward bringing order to a complex range of phenomena. Another, somewhat simpler scheme is proposed by Argyle (1972), who recognizes three categories defined solely in terms of consequence.

1 **Managing the immediate social situation** This includes the conveying of interpersonal attitudes (superior-inferior, like-dislike) and emotional states, and indicating the individual's status, group membership, sexual availability, and so on.

2 **Sustaining verbal communication** These may affect the meaning of utterances, determine who is to speak, provide feedback, and so on. Here we have the prosodic and paralinguistic components mentioned later.

3 **Replacing verbal communication** Sign languages of many degrees of complexity are to be found in different cultures throughout the world.

It will be seen that these categories cut across the system proposed by Ekman and Friesen (see above). For instance, signals used to manage the social situation may or may not be affect signals.

Another classificatory scheme, shown in Fig. 10.4, reflects the point of view of a linguist (see Lyons, 1972; Hinde, 1972a). Lyons regards the several categories as having different degrees of "linguisticness", i.e., as differing in the extent to which they are specific to human language as opposed to non-verbal communication and the signalling systems of other species. The verbal com-

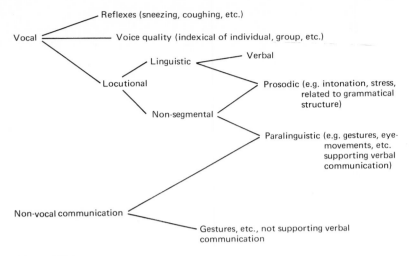

FIGURE 10.4

*Relations between verbal and non-verbal communication.* (From Hinde, 1972a.)

ponent is the most linguistic. Next come prosodic features which are intimately related to grammatical structure. Less linguistic are the paralinguistic features, which include such characters as the loudness of the speech, and also gestures and facial expressions that support the verbal interchange. Finally, vocal reflexes and non-vocal gestures that do not support verbal communication are at most distantly related to human language.

This scheme demonstrates the difficulty of defining "language". Either the term "language" may be applied to all communication (however that is defined —see pages 49–52), in which case it becomes too broad to be useful, or it is limited to some subset of communicatory acts. In the latter case, however, it is difficult to know where to draw the line. On the one hand, the strictly verbal component may or may not involve directed communication in the sense defined previously (see pages 89–90); while, on the other, reflexes such as sneezing could be said to be communicative in a general sense. More to the point, the verbal component is intimately related to changes in voice quality and gestures which support the verbal message. The paralinguistic category clearly overlaps with the categories of illustrators, regulators, and to a lesser extent adaptors, discussed above.

None of these schemes is comprehensive (see also Duncan, 1969; Mehrabian, 1969). In addition to the categories of communication already considered, man communicates by using objects and customs whose meaning depends on language, such as clothing (Barthes, 1967), cooking (Lévi-Strauss, 1966), and rituals (Leach, 1972), and also by systems which do not necessarily imply any particular linguistic code, such as music and painting (e.g., Gombrich, 1972).

### Origins of human communicatory movements

The richness and diversity of the expressions, postures, and gestures used in human non-verbal communication provide a formidable obstacle to any attempt at understanding their evolutionary or cultural history. So far few cases have been studied in any detail, and they serve only to illustrate the complexity of the problems. But one thing is certain—any simple-minded attempt to divide them into those that are part of man's phylogenetic heritage and thus constant among cultures, and those that are culturally determined, is bound to fail.

We are concerned here with a developmental problem, but one that it is seldom possible to tackle with experimental techniques. We must therefore start with a comparative approach. If we find similarities in expressive movements across human cultures, it is probable that the development of those movements does not depend on aspects of experience peculiar to particular cultures.

Many expressive movements, such as those of smiling, laughing, and crying, are in fact common to all cultures so far investigated. Indeed sometimes whole syndromes of behaviour, such as those associated with anger or flirting, are qualitatively though not quantitatively similar between cultures (Eibl-Eibesfeldt, 1972). Though the motivational bases of the movements and their interpretation by other individuals are more labile than the movement patterns themselves (see pages 105–116), there is good evidence that at least the "primary affects" (happiness, sadness, anger, surprise, disgust, and fear, see page 122) are associated with similar facial expressions in various literate and pre-literate cultures (Ekman and Friesen, 1969; Ekman, 1971). Thus culture-specific aspects of experience are unlikely to be important in their development.

Of course, just as lack of variation among individuals does not mean that experience per se has no influence on development (Chap. 4), so also expressive movements that are similar across cultures could depend on aspects of experience common to those cultures. Constancy in development could result from constancy in experience. One possibility might be that children in all cultures learn to use similar expressive movements by imitation, so that the cross-cultural similarities are due to the enduring effects of tradition. Apart from the general implausibility of this view, the finding that many expressive movements appear in children born blind and deaf make it extremely unlikely that any form of imitation is involved in their development (Eibl-Eibesfeldt, 1972). This source of evidence does not rule out the possibility that they are synthesized by operant conditioning of their elements, though that seems even more unlikely.

Yet another possibility is that expressive movements develop from reflex movements elicited by stimuli which are almost inevitably encountered during development. For example, Ekman and Friesen (1969) suggested that the disgust affect display might develop from the movements of the mouth and nose involved in rejecting a bad taste or smell: on this view, the development of the movement pattern depends on an experience which, at some time or other, all human beings must surely have. Somewhat more plausibly Eibl-Eibesfeldt (1972), pointing out that people react adversely to being stared at or to eye-patterns resembling a stare, suggested that this could result in the independent learning of patterns of shifting the glance, and of lowering the lids and briefly looking away, during friendly social contact. These suggestions may eventually find empirical support.

However, in many of the cases under consideration there seems to be no need to invoke such mechanisms. It is known that some quite complicated movement patterns of lower forms, such as the swimming movements of anuran larvae (Carmichael, 1927), can develop in the normal way even though input from the periphery varies within wide limits. In such cases development is determined by genetic factors so that it is stable in spite of gross differences in experience between individuals. There is no reason why many of the expressive movements of higher animals and man should not develop in a similar way. Thus it is now accepted that the development of some expressive movements may be comparable to that of those fixed action patterns in lower species which appear in near-perfect form on the first occasion that the appropriate stimuli are present (Tomkins and McCarter, 1964; Ekman and Friesen, 1969; Eibl-Eibesfeldt, 1972). This is, of course, most clearly the case with expressive movements which have been adapted for a signal function (i.e., ritualized), such as the smile or frown.

On this view, resemblances between affect displays and movements of biting, withdrawal, disgust, and so on are to be regarded as indicators of their evolutionary origin, rather than, or as well as, their development in the individual (e.g., Andrew, 1963a and b). We may consider two examples for which a considerable amount of comparative evidence is available. In the first, the smile-laugh complex, similarities in form and context are apparent not only

FIGURE 10.5

*Bared-teeth display or fear grin of rhesus macaque.*
(Drawing by Priscilla Edwards.)

across human cultures but also, though to a lesser degree, between animals and man. It has been studied with a number of techniques by van Hooff (1972).

Among the possible sub-human homologues of smiling and laughing are the "bared-teeth display" and the "relaxed open-mouth display". The bared-teeth display (Fig. 10.5) is often accompanied by vocalizations such as screams, squeals, and geckers, and is found in a wide range of mammals. It is usually accompanied by a tendency to flee, the display occurring especially when this is thwarted—for instance, in a cornered animal. A number of hypotheses have been advanced for the derivation of the display—for instance, that it evolved from elements evoked by strong aversive stimulation of the face (e.g., strong expiration, lip retraction) or as a secondary consequence of vocalizations (Andrew, 1963a), or from movements of defensive aggression (biting) (van Hooff, 1962).

In higher primates the bared-teeth display accompanied by vocalizations

FIGURE 10.6
*Relaxed open-mouth display in crab-eating monkey.* (Drawing by Priscilla Edwards from van Hooff, 1972.)

occurs primarily in situations where the animal has a thwarted tendency to flee, and is thus submissive or on the defensive, but the display also occurs where other strong tendencies are thwarted, and the animal is frustrated. And in some genera of primates the *silent* bared-teeth display, though normally given as a submissive gesture, is sometimes given by a dominant animal to a subordinate: it then appears to have a reassuring function. In yet other genera it is associated with lip-smacking in contexts which suggest that it is being used as an expression of attachment. There are thus reasonable grounds for believing that, in the course of primate evolutionary history, the silent bared-teeth display, originally a defensive or protective pattern, came to signify submission, non-hostility, and finally friendliness.

The relaxed open-mouth display resembles a staring open-mouth display given in aggressive contexts, but differs in that the mouth corners are not pulled forward and eye and body movements are lacking in tension. It is found in some monkeys and baboons, and in chimpanzees, and typically accompanies boisterous mock-fighting and chasing. It is often accompanied by an "ohh-ahh" vocalization (Fig. 10.6).

van Hooff has made a special study of the expressive movements used by chimpanzees. His technique involved a form of factor analysis (see page 67).

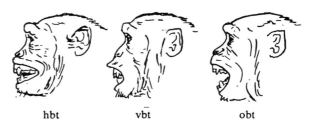

FIGURE 10.7

*Three types of silent bared-teeth display of the chimpanzee. From left to right: horizontal, vertical, and open-mouth bared-teeth display. (From van Hooff, 1972.)*

The occurrence of the fifty-three most frequent behavioural elements appeared to be explicable in terms of five main causal categories which he designated "affinitive", "play", "aggressive", "submissive", and "excitement" systems. The silent bared-teeth display was closely related to the affinitive category, the relaxed open-mouth display to the play category. Furthermore, three types of silent bared-teeth display could be distinguished—horizontal, vertical, and open-mouth (Fig. 10.7): various lines of evidence indicated the former to be primarily submissive, the other two primarily affinitive.

van Hooff thus suggests that the chimpanzee silent bared-teeth display encompasses not only the phylogenetically old appeasing type, but also the more recently evolved "friendly" types. He further suggests that the silent bared-teeth display is phylogenetically related to our smiling, and the relaxed open-mouth display to our laughing. In man, however, as in a few sub-human primates such as *Mandrillus*, the two displays have become closely related and often merge. On this view, human laughter is regarded as most closely related to the relaxed open-mouth display though somewhat akin to the open-mouth from of the silent bared-teeth face, with the smile as a less intense form of the latter, the two originally independent phylogenetic sources having merged.

That this is not the whole story is, however, indicated by the fact that there are situations in which only smiling is appropriate (expressions of sympathy, appeasement) and laughter would be definitely out-of-place and even offensive, while in other situations laughter is more appropriate. Furthermore, a number of investigators have emphasized not only that there are differences in form between smiling and laughter, but also that each may vary in form in

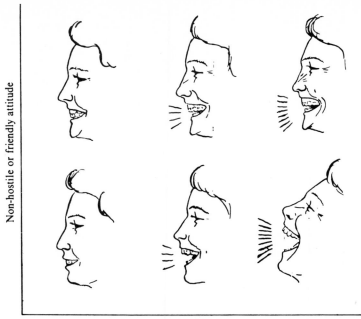

'Playfulness'

FIGURE 10.8

*Two dimensions of variation of the smile-laugh continuum. From bottom to top there is increased baring of the teeth. From left to right there is increased mouth opening and vocalization. (From van Hooff, 1972.)*

ways which are interpreted differently by an observer (Grant, 1969; Blurton Jones, 1972b; Brannigan and Humphries, 1972).

van Hooff points out that this variation cannot be described along a single continuum, but demands are least two dimensions. One leads in its most intense form to the "cheese", or broad smile, which is often seen in greeting and is associated with the manifestation of a non-hostile, friendly attitude. The other dimension leads to the wide-mouth laugh accompanied by "ha-ha" vocalizations, which is especially characteristic of children's play. Figure 10.8 shows how many of the variants in the smile-laugh continuum can be understood in terms of two dimensions, one of "friendliness", involving, among other things, baring of the

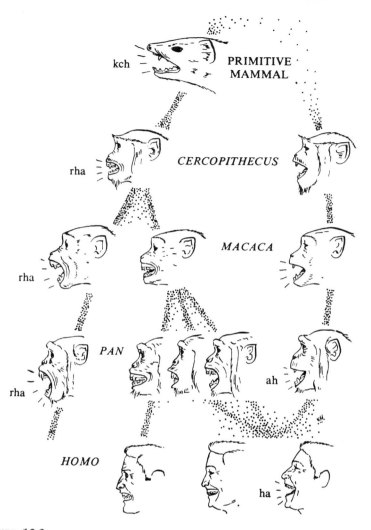

FIGURE 10.9

*A hypothesis for the phylogenetic development of laughter and smiling suggested by homologues in existing species related to man's ancestors. On the left is shown the evolution of the silent bared-teeth display and the bared-teeth scream. The former, initially a submissive and later also a friendly response, seems to converge with the relaxed open-mouth display (on the right), a signal of play. (From van Hooff, 1972.)*

teeth; and the other of "playfulness", involving increased mouth opening and vocalization: whether other dimensions are also necessary to account for the whole range of variation is an open issue.

van Hooff found this interpretation also to be in harmony with studies in which human subjects were asked to place a list of adjectives and participles (e.g., jovial, roguish, meek, affable) into various "motivational" categories (aggressive, submissive or fearful, affinitive, and playful), while other subjects were asked whether the words indicate an attitude that is accompanied by smiling or laughing. Those words which were assessed as describing affinitive moods were the ones describing a state most likely to be accompanied by a smile, while those assessed as describing a playful mood were assessed as most likely to be accompanied by a laugh.

Thus van Hooff believes that laughter and smiling involve a continuum of intergrading signals whose variation can be described in at least two dimensions. The extreme forms, the broad smile and the wide-mouth laugh, show formal and functional relationships to the silent bared-teeth display and the relaxed open-mouth display of lower forms. The forms of smiling and laughing most used in social interaction can be regarded as intermediates. Figure 10.9 represents the sort of way in which evolution could have occurred, though of course it is not to be interpreted too literally: there is, for instance, no suggestion that man has evolved from chimpanzees—only that in terms of this character man's ancestors passed through a stage not too different from that seen in modern chimpanzees.

There is a good deal of circumstantial evidence in support of this scheme. For instance, Krebs (cited in Blurton Jones, 1972b) found that children low in dominance status at a nursery school smiled more when initiating an interaction with high-ranking children than did high-rankers when initiating interactions with low: this suggests that perhaps the use of the human smile in appeasing situations is still not so very far from that of the sub-human primate's fear grin. However, van Hooff's scheme must not be regarded as more than a working hypothesis (see, for example, discussion in Hinde, 1972a, pages 238–241), and there is urgent need for more refined studies of the human smile in which finer categories are distinguished (Grant, 1969; Brannigan and Humphries, 1972). Indeed, when we find that laughter is normal behaviour at funerals in some cultures (Ekman and Friesen, 1969; La Barre, 1947, 1964), it becomes clear that, while we may be able to trace the phylogenetic origin of an expressive movement, we must consider many subsequent influences to gain understanding of its current use.

Another case of some interest is the eyebrow flash, which has been dis-

FIGURE 10.10

*The eyebrow flash.* (Drawing by Priscilla Edwards from a photograph in Eibl-Eibesfeldt, 1972.)

cussed in some detail by Eibl-Eibesfeldt (1972). When greeting, people of many cultures smile, nod, and raise their eyebrows with a rapid movement, keeping the eyebrows raised for about one-sixth of a second (Fig. 10.10). Eibl-Eibesfeldt has filmed this eyebrow flash in greeting in Europeans, Balinese, Papuans, South American Indians, and Bushmen, and has seen it in other cultures.

There is, however, some cultural variation: in central Europe reserved individuals do not use it, and in Japan it is considered indecent and suppressed. In some cultures it is used also in other contexts—for instance, we often use it as a general sign of approval or agreement, when seeking confirmation, when beginning a statement in dialogue, when flirting, strongly approving, thanking, and calling for attention during discussions. Eibl-Eibesfeldt suggests that the common denominator in these situations is a "yes" to social contact, the eyebrow flash being used either for requesting or for approving a request for contact. It is in fact used for a factual "yes" in Polynesia.

By looking at other contexts in which it occurs, Eibl-Eibesfeldt was able to make a suggestion as to the nature of its origin. It occurs in surprise, and in other situations associated with attention, including those involving disapproval and indignation. Eibl-Eibesfeldt suggests that the eyebrow lift of surprise was the starting point for the ritualization of several attention signals, as shown in Fig. 10.11. This scheme is of course purely speculative. It would be difficult to support it with comparative evidence, since among those non-human primates which move their eyebrows there is considerable variation in the manner in which they do so. (It is, however, the case that eyebrow raising in non-human

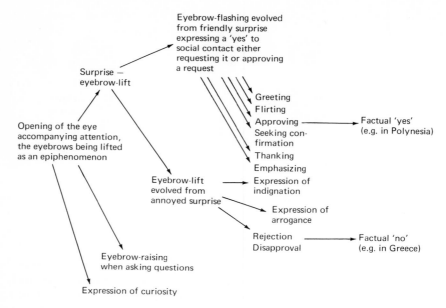

FIGURE 10.11

*Hypothesis for the evolution of eyebrow movements into signals in man.* (From Eibl-Eibesfeldt, 1972.)

forms is often associated with an alert face: it is sometimes accentuated by colour contrast between the upper eyelids and the surrounding skin.) Furthermore, it is not clear which of the changes in Eibl-Eibesfeldt's scheme are supposed to be evolutionary changes now common to all cultures, and which are culture-specific. Once again, however, it provides a reasonable framework for synthesizing diverse observations.

In the two examples just considered, the central element appears to be a movement pattern whose form is more or less predetermined, and which is related to a certain range of internal states. However, not all cross-cultural or cross-specific similarities involve the form of a movement pattern. Sometimes they concern general muscle tonus: a dominant rhesus monkey and one that is subordinate and dejected are readily distinguished by a naive human observer on the basis of his knowledge of comparable differences in his own species (Fig. 7.1). Another type of case concerns the quality of vocalizations. The shrillness of many vocalizations is related to the extent to which the lips are drawn back. Since drawing back the lips is associated with fear (page 127), shrill vocalizations tend to be associated with fear in both monkey (Andrew, 1963a, b; Rowell, 1962) and man. In such cases the similarities between cultures or species depend not on genetically determined stability in the development of a specific movement pattern, but in the similar determination of other aspects of behaviour (e.g., relation between muscle tonus and internal state) which lead to similarities in expressive movements.

Even where similarities do involve the form of the movement, we must remember, as noted earlier, that this does not necessarily imply the genetic determination of a movement pattern independently of environmental influences —the similarities may be due partly to common factors inherent in the situation predisposing individuals to develop a particular type of movement pattern. This is even more true where more complex sequences of movements are involved. The complex patterns expressing coyness, embarrassment, and flirting are a case in point. In many cultures these patterns involve bringing the hands in front of the face, mouth, or eyes. This seems to be related to hiding, for a similar movement is seen in children wanting to hide (Eibl-Eibesfeldt, 1972) and also in chimpanzees startled by a sudden noise or movement nearby (van Lawick-Goodall, 1968). However, the precise way in which the hands are brought up varies markedly, and the constant feature is not the movement pattern itself, but its end result. Thus the similarities are presumably a consequence of individuals learning to bring about a commonly acceptable situation—a barrier in front of the eyes. Additional complexities may be superimposed: thus in flirting the movements are often associated with ambivalence between flight and approach, and may be accompanied by patterns inviting contact.

Many other examples could be cited. For instance, greeting behaviour involves, of course, much more than the eyebrow flash. In chimpanzees, greeting by males is often preceded by some ritualized aggressive behaviour, swaggering, stamping, and so on. The actual greeting involves a variety of postures and gestures including bobbing, bowing and crouching, touching, kissing, embracing, grooming, presenting the genital region, mounting, and occasionally hand-holding (Fig. 10.12). Many of these patterns occur also in human greetings. Indeed some of them seem to be pan-cultural; for instance, Eibl-Eibesfeldt (1971) has shown that they can provide a basis for mutual understanding between Europeans and the as yet unacculturized Waika Indians of the Orinoco region in South America. However, it is an open question to what extent the similarities in movement patterns involve genetically determined stability in spite of wide differences in experience, or similar transferences from infantile or parental

FIGURE 10.12

(a) *Chimpanzees greeting by touching hands.* (Drawing by Priscilla Edwards from a photograph in van Lawick-Goodall, 1968.) (b) *Chimpanzees touching lips.* (Drawing by Priscilla Edwards.)

patterns, or similar responses to common factors in the greeting situation—for instance, differences in status leading to submissive gestures, and physical contact bringing reassurance. In any case the complexities of the greeting situation must not be forgotten. In both chimpanzee and man it not only involves minimizing the fear or expressing the pleasure that an encounter may induce, but also permits the individuals concerned to place each other in the social hierarchy. And in man greeting rituals may permit individuals to manipulate each other in a variety of ways (Goody, 1972). Such uses must be taken into account in considering its origins (see also Kendon, 1973).

We have so far been concerned primarily with the form of human expressive movements. We have seen that in many cases, though not of course all, movements of characteristic form develop independently of social experience, and that in some such cases it is possible to formulate hypotheses about their evolution. But to be effective as a signal within any particular culture, the movement must be linked to a particular internal state of the signaller. The relationship of expressive movement to internal state is in fact more labile than the form of the movement itself. In some cases—for instance, smiling, crying, and the expression of disgust—there is a basic relationship to an internal state which is independent of social experience. However, the extent to which that state is induced by external factors may be closely affected by social learning: what we find amusing or sad is much influenced by the culture in which we live. And social experience affects also the extent to which the internal state may be expressed—for instance the degree to which anger or sexual interest is allowed to become apparent. In addition, emotional states may elicit further emotional states, as when we are angered by our own fear or frightened by our own anger; and these secondary emotional states may be culturally influenced and their expression superimposed to a varying degree on the primary expression. Also, when we are aware of our expressive movements we may inhibit or dissimulate them because of their known social consequences (see Ekman, 1971).

Of course not all signal movements are common to all individuals. Individually idiosyncratic movements or modifications of movements, provided they are linked to specific internal states, may acquire signal function if other individuals learn to respond appropriately: much of our interaction with those with whom we are most intimate depends on signals of this type. And the effectiveness or ineffectiveness of each potential signal will lead to further modifications in its form and frequency: our non-verbal repertoire is constantly being modified in social intercourse.

Amongst movements that have acquired a signal function are those that take the place of verbal communication, and these are inevitably affected by social learning. Even here, however, there may be some cases in which movement patterns are common across cultures. "Yes" and "No" are expressed by head-nodding and head-shaking in most cultures. Nodding as a positive gesture may be related to the eyebrow flash as discussed above (Eibl-Eibesfeldt, 1972), and there could be a predisposition to use head-shaking in negative contexts as a consequence of turning the head away to refuse the breast (Darwin, 1872) or to shake off foreign objects (Eibl-Eibesfeldt, 1972). However there are some variants: for example, in Greece, "No" is expressed by a strong backward jerk of the head. A movement similar to this backward jerk is used in a number of other cultures for an emphatic "No", and even more widely to express refusal or disagreement. It may therefore be an intention movement of withdrawal.

While the preceding discussion has aimed to show that many of the differences between the development of the communication systems of animals and that of non-verbal communication in man are differences of degree, it hardly needs to be said that there are also differences of kind which arise from the fact that so much of man's non-verbal communication takes place within a context which includes language and cultural conventions (Lyons, 1972; Leach, 1972). Indeed, as Leach points out, much human non-verbal communication, especially that which is involved in ritual, is concerned with abstractions and metaphysical ideas not in the immediate context. Though the hand movements of a Catholic as he crosses himself may depend on some of the same principles as determine the behaviour of animals (e.g., superstitious learning in the sense of Skinner, 1948; Herrnstein, 1966), they are also embedded in a frame of reference which has no animal counterpart. This frame of reference depends on words.

Though both the ceremonies involved in our everyday relations with one another and those occurring in public ritual are dependent on language, this does not necessarily mean that at all levels they are peculiar to particular cultures. Are there universals in non-verbal symbolic codes? Leach (1972) argues that actions involving use of the body or parts of the body, or objects related to the body, are widely distributed as constituents of human ritual sequences, and that this is because man himself is a cultural universal. But Leach goes further than this, suggesting that "human beings have an innate, but very general, tendency to organize their expressive behaviour grammatically in the manner of a language system". On his view, gesture elements such as raising the eyebrows are equivalent to single phonemes, such as $p$ or $k$, which occur in all natural human languages but do not themselves have any meaning. Their meaning depends rather on the context in which they occur. Some evidence for this view is provided by the limited success which human subjects have in interpreting photographs of gestures and facial expressions: the meaning of many elements depends on the presence of other elements, on changes in the elements with time, and on other contextual factors (see also pages, 82–83; also Gombrich, 1972, for a discussion of the importance of contextual factors in interpreting expressive movements in paintings). But even still photographs can be interpreted with *some* success, and in any case the fact that the meaning of expressive elements depends on the others with which they are associated is not a human peculiarity: Stokes's analysis (pages 80–82) of aggressive behaviour in blue tits demonstrates exactly the same point. What is peculiar to man is that the variations depend on a language-dependent cultural context.

Leach's view appears to conflict with that of most students of animal behaviour and others influenced by them. While the latter tend to emphasize the fixity across cultures of the messages (see page 133) carried by signals, Leach and many other anthropologists emphasize their cultural dependence. Both views involve over-generalization. Some signals are almost culture-independent. Others have a culture-independent core but may be more or less affected by the influences of particular cultures: the smile/laugh continuum and the eyebrow flash and its derivatives are cases in point. Others may have a degree of cultural universality which depends on the use of parts of the body or objects inevitably associated with particular contexts by the very nature of man or of the world in which he lives. And of course yet others are culture-specific. But even those symbolic codes that seem most culture-dependent, and we must include here most public ceremonials, may rest at a deeper level of analysis on cross-cultural universals. To take a simple example, whatever the symbol used for "yes", that for "no" is likely to be in some sense opposite to it. There may be factors in the nature of man which predispose him to use certain signs for one or the other, but in addition, the signals are also likely to be in some way opposed to each other. To take a more complex example, Lévi-Strauss (1966) has argued that differences in styles of food preparation and table manners involve elements of a universal code demonstrating our status with respect to society and nature. In his view, however, the universality concerns not the particulars but the relations between them and the way in which they are used. This view is, however, not easy to validate.

## Non-verbal communication and human language

As knowledge of the complexity attained by the communicatory systems of animals has increased, it is natural that speculations should arise on their relationships with those of man. Unfortunately, there is as yet no wholly satisfactory framework to form a basis for comparison. The most complete scheme so far developed is that of Hockett and Altmann (Hockett, 1960; Hockett and Altmann, 1968; Altmann, 1967b). This depends on the isolation of sixteen "design features" present in human verbal communication, and the assessment of whether these are or are not present in those of animals. These design features are concerned with the capabilities and properties of the communication systems, not with their mechanisms.

To exemplify this method of approach, we may consider four of these design features. Human language employs symbols which are abstract or

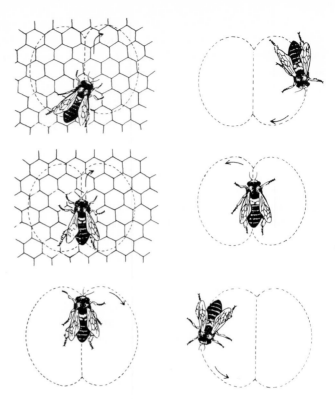

FIGURE 10.13a
*Communication of the distance and direction of a food source by the honey-bee. The waggle dance.* (From Von Frisch, 1954).

arbitrary in that they do not resemble in physical contours that which they represent; it is based on discrete signals; it can refer to events remote in time and space; and it is "open" in that new messages can be coined freely and easily. Let us ask whether these properties are shared by the dance of the honey-bee (von Frisch, 1954). There is considerable evidence that the worker bee can convey to other workers the distance and direction of a new food source by signals related to a particular pattern of movement which it performs in or near the hive. Direction appears to be related to the direction of the bee's movement during the waggle phase of the dance: when the dance is performed on a vertical surface, the angle between this run and the vertical represents the direction of

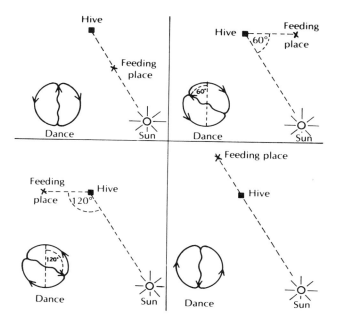

FIGURE 10.13b

*Communication of the distance and direction of a food source by the honey-bee. Indication of sun's bearing on a vertical comb surface. (From Von Frisch, 1954). The small diagrams on the left show the dance as it appears on the vertical comb.*

the food source with respect to the sun. Distance is related to the speed of movements during the same phase (Fig. 10.13b)[1]. Now, since the symbols (e.g., direction of dance) are physically related to the direction of the food source, and vary continuously, they cannot be said to be either arbitrary or discrete. In only a very limited sense can it be said that the dance permits the coining of new messages, since such messages can refer only to hive or food locations, but it can refer to a food source remote in space. By contrast, to take another example, the auditory communication system of doves does involve discrete and arbitrary signals, but is not open and cannot refer to things remote in time and space. In

[1] This account has been criticized by Wenner (1967), Johnson (1967), and Michener (1969); the points relevant here seem to be satisfactorily answered by von Frisch (1968) and by Gould et al. (1970), but the matter is still uncertain.

this way, the extent to which different species share design features with one another and with human language can be compared.

As Hockett and Altmann themselves point out, one of the difficulties with this system is that the design features tend to be defined in an all-or-none fashion, when many of them are in fact matters of degree. There is thus considerable room for differences of opinion as to whether a feature is or is not present. We have already seen one such difficulty with "openness". Another concerns the property of "semanticity", which in this context is taken to mean associative ties between signal elements and features in the outside world (but see Lyons, 1972). Some hold that man is unique in his ability to communicate information about his environment, as opposed to information about his own internal state, but some students of animal behaviour would argue that the possession of different calls for different types of predators by many passerine birds (Marler, 1959) and some monkeys (Struhsaker, 1967) is evidence for semanticity (see also Menzel, in press, cited pages 100–103). But when the argument is pressed it becomes hard to draw a line anywhere in the series, "There is a predator behind that tree"; "I believe there is a predator behind that tree"; "I am afraid because I believe there is a predator behind that tree"; "I am afraid". Which, if any, conveys information only about the signaller and which, if any, only about the environment?

In spite of the difficulties involved in applying them precisely, such methods show that no non-human system of communication approaches the complexity of human language. Verbal language has properties of grammatical and conceptual complexity which are peculiar to it (e.g., Lyons, 1972). Nevertheless, verbal language must have originated from something, and it seems not unreasonable to seek its origin in pre-linguistic utterances of some sort. Support for such a view has recently come from parallels between the sign stimuli (see page 57) used in communication by lower forms, and the so-called "speech cues" in human speech. These are characteristic acoustic patterns which permit important phonetic distinctions. For instance, speech cues enable us to distinguish between the back rounded vowel (as in "boot") and the front unrounded vowel (as in "but"), or between sounds with labial articulation (b, p, m) and those with alveolar (d, t, n) or velar articulation (g, k). There is some evidence, as yet only suggestive, that responsiveness to some of these speech cues may be independent of experience of them, and they also share other properties with social releasers. Mattingly (1972) thus suggests that pre-linguistic speech functioned as a set of social releasers (see also Eimas et al., 1971). In his view, evolution of language depended both on this primitive communication system and on man's intellectual development permitting him to make a semantic representation of the world of experience. It required also the development of grammar—i.e., of complex but rule-governed relationships between semantic and phonetic representations.

There are also some interesting parallels between human speech and some communication systems of lower species employing acoustic signals. Thus Marler (1970) points out that in both bird song (pages 109–114) and human speech,

1 Learning by the young from adults plays a major role in development.
2 Dialects arise as a consequence of that learning.
3 There is a sensitive period during which the ability for vocal learning is at a maximum.
4 There are predispositions emerging during this sensitive period which have the effect of guiding the learning in certain directions.
5 Hearing plays a role not only in allowing the young organism to hear the sounds of other adults, but also to hear its own voice, as a vital factor in normal development.
6 There is an early stage of somewhat amorphous sound production (babbling in infants, subsong in birds).
7 One side of the brain tends to assume dominant control of sound production.

Marler is of course careful to point out that these parallels do not indicate any direct relationship between bird song and human speech, though they may indicate that natural selection has acted similarly on both—a fact not so surprising since both are concerned with long-range communication (see also Hall-Craggs, 1969). But Marler uses the parallels to make an important point: any species whose biology depends in a fundamental way on learning processes can ill afford to leave the direction in which learning will take place to chance. Song learning must be guided by a set of well-defined constraints in order that the young bird does not learn the songs of alien species. In the same way it is inevitable that human language should be subject to constraints in what is learned (Sinclair, 1973; Ryan, 1973).

There is in fact much evidence that man is specialized in a number of ways, anatomically and physiologically, for using verbal language; and children will learn to speak, even in the face of considerable handicaps, according to a fairly definite "developmental schedule" (Lenneberg, 1967). By contrast chimpanzees, even when brought up in a human home and subjected to intensive training, make at most only limited progress toward acquiring any form of human language. Just how much progress they make is still not fully clear (Brown, 1970; Gardner and Gardner, 1971; Premack, 1971; Lyons, 1972): what is abundantly evident is that the chimpanzee has no *motivation* to learn a language in the sense that a human child has.

However the precise nature of the differences between man and ape which permit the former to acquire verbal language is extremely difficult to pinpoint. Since so many human abilities depend on language, it is by no means easy to separate the extent to which man is able to acquire language because of his highly developed abilities for learning, from the extent to which his abilities for learning depend on language. Does his language ability depend on a special competence peculiar to language? Chomsky (1968) has pleaded for a non-dogmatic approach to this problem: if the same learning strategies were used in a number of different domains, including that of language, there would be no need to postulate a special language ability; but if different strategies or predispositions are involved, we must.

Now some writers (e.g., Chomsky, 1959, 1968), impressed with the finding that all human languages are based on similar principles of semantics, syntax, and phonology [though there is in fact little general agreement as to precisely what those universal principles are (Lyons, 1972)], suggest that children must be genetically endowed with a "knowledge" of the structural principles common to all human languages. In support of this view is the fact that children learn the language of the community in which they live in a very short time and after hearing only a limited sample of utterances from others, themselves often grammatically inadequate (but see Ryan, 1973). However, we have already seen (Chap. 4) that attempts to divide behaviour into innate and learned categories can be sterile, and similar arguments must apply to a category of genetically endowed knowledge. The basis of Chomsky's view must thus be considered in the light of the earlier conclusion that the study of development must first involve the study of *differences*.

We have seen that the higher apes can go only a little way toward acquiring human language—this indicates that man *differs* innately from non-man in his ability to acquire language. This is often (and dangerously) abbreviated to the statement that the ability to acquire language is "innate" (compare Chap. 4). This in turn is often taken to mean that knowledge of the basic structure common to all language is "innate". Just because the structure is common to all language, it is presumed that knowledge of it is independent of learning any particular one, and that it is that knowledge which enables the child to "make sense" of the ungrammatical sentences that it hears, to construct sentences itself, and subsequently to differentiate between grammatical and ungrammatical ones.

However, such a view begs important questions. First, even if "knowledge" of the basic structure of language is independent of learning any particular one, that in itself does not mean it is independent of learning a language. More important, the ability to acquire language develops gradually and may depend on all sorts of non-verbal and even non-auditory experience. It may be that similarities in the deep structures of languages are related to constant features of the physical and social world. Interaction with the physical world at an earlier age is certainly essential for the child to acquire language. And language acquisition depends on verbal input in relation to contextual events in the physical and social world: it is inconceivable that a child merely exposed to conversation on a tape recorder would learn to speak (Hinde, 1972a). Indeed Bruner (1968) has pointed out the similarity between manipulative hand skills and some aspects of language, such as the notion of subject and predicate, and has suggested that some of the formal aspects of language may have their precursors in the infant's interactions with objects (see also Hebb et al., 1971; Sinclair, 1973; Ryan, 1973). Such problems are extremely difficult to investigate: environmental factors in the development of language universals cannot be assessed because, for obvious ethical reasons, the non-linguistic environment cannot be varied experimentally in such a way as to produce differences in language development.

Whether human verbal communication depends on a generally high level of cognitive and intellectual ability or on a special faculty for language must remain *sub judice*, but it is quite clear that verbal language in its fully developed form is unique to man. Although biologists may argue as an article of faith that human verbal languages must have evolved, and must therefore have evolutionary origins, linguists find few signs of evolutionary change among languages themselves, and must therefore remain agnostic on this issue (Lyons, 1972). Human affect displays can be related to those of animals, and perhaps so also can some of the intention movements and other gestures used by man in communication. Other aspects of human non-verbal communication are closely tied to verbal language, and have no counterpart in lower forms. And no relation is to be discerned between non-human displays and human verbal language, even though human language sometimes performs a similar function to such displays.

**Summary**

Communication in our own species depends to a not inconsiderable extent on non-verbal signals comparable to those found in non-human forms. The diversity and complexity of these signals pose considerable problems for their study, and various classificatory schemes have been proposed. For some human expressive movements it is possible to erect reasonable hypotheses about probable evolutionary relationships with movements found in other primates. Even in these cases, the use of the movement may be markedly influenced by experience, and there are, of course, many human non-verbal signals that are specific to particular cultures and even particular individuals. The relationships between verbal and non-verbal communication are rather tenuous.

# SECTION

# D

# THE DEVELOPMENT OF SOCIAL BEHAVIOUR

# 11

# THE DEVELOPMENT OF SOCIAL BEHAVIOUR IN BIRDS

The general problem of the nature-nurture issue in development was considered in Chap. 4. In this section we shall turn specifically to the development of social behaviour. Although our main concern is with the development of social behaviour in primates, some of the issues have been studied in more detail in birds.

A young moorhen normally begs from its mother, obtains warmth from its mother, and once a few days old, follows its mother when she moves about. Thus a number of different filial responses are all directed to the mother. If moorhen eggs are hatched in an incubator and the birds are reared by hand, they can readily learn to beg from a pair of forceps, to obtain warmth from an infra-red lamp, and to follow a wooden box. Thus under these artificial conditions each of the responses normally directed to the mother comes to be directed toward a different object: with experience the artificial stimuli become increasingly effective. Presumably each of the objects possesses some stimulus characters in common with those aspects of the mother that normally elicit the response in question. However, if a young moorhen is taken from the nest when a few days old, it can be reared only with difficulty: at first those artificial stimuli that would have been effective with a newly hatched bird merely elicit avoidance responses. This implies that during the first few days of life the ranges of stimuli effective for the several filial responses become narrowed to those actually encountered during that period (Hinde et al., 1956; Hinde, 1961).

The learning process involved is known as "imprinting" (Lorenz, 1935). Although Lorenz's earlier claim that imprinting is a special form of learning with unique properties cannot be sustained, it is clearly of great importance in development. It has been studied especially in chickens, ducks, and geese: since these species do not feed from their parents, nearly all studies have been concerned with the response of following the parent.

A young chick, duckling, or gosling will follow a wide range of moving objects if first exposed to them during a fairly brief period beginning soon after hatching. With continued exposure the young bird follows the object more and more readily and persistently, and after a while will not follow other moving objects—and indeed will flee from them. This following response lends itself to experimental study in an apparatus of the type shown in Fig. 11.1, where the bird's readiness to follow objects suspended from a rotating arm can be assessed. The newly hatched bird has an initial tendency to approach conspicuous objects within fairly wide limits of size, shape, and colour, though for each species some objects are more effective than others. Within limits, the effectiveness of an object tends to increase with its conspicuousness to the human eye: chicks reared in isolation respond more readily to a flashing light than to a mother hen (Reese et al., 1972). The tendency to approach is markedly enhanced if the object emits intermittent sounds resembling the maternal calls of the species (Gottlieb, 1971): the relative importance of auditory and visual stimuli varies between species. Thus while conspicuousness is an important characteristic of effective objects, effectiveness is not defined by conspicuousness alone.

After a certain period new objects cease to be effective in eliciting the following response, and the range of adequate objects is restricted to ones similar to those already experienced. This period is known as the "sensitive period". Some authors have claimed that it is only a few hours in duration, but most workers find it to be rather longer than that (e.g., Bateson, 1966): its duration depends on the conditions of experimentation and varies between species.

Under natural conditions the only conspicuous moving objects with the appropriate properties that the young bird sees repeatedly are its parents and peers. During the sensitive period it becomes imprinted on them: this ensures that it subsequently follows them and them only. Even so, this might seem a rather chancy way for the bond between mother and offspring to be established —especially in a bird capable of locomotion from hatching. In other contexts we know that birds can respond appropriately to stimuli from another member of the species independently of experience: for example, young great tits respond appropriately to the species-characteristic alarm call of their parents the first time they hear it. Why, then, is not the following response organized in a similar way? A possible answer comes from consideration of the diversity of stimulus characteristics which the mother must present to the chicks. We recognize a mother hen as such from whatever angle we see her, however far away she is, whatever the lighting conditions—in each case within limits, of course. Our ability to do this is termed "object constancy", and is acquired gradually: we have learnt the ways in which the stimuli from objects alter as we change our angle of regard, or as the lighting conditions change. The young bird is unlikely to possess this faculty, yet its survival depends on its following its parent unfailingly. Perhaps the best solution is an initial responsiveness to a wide range of objects which becomes limited to those that are familiar as object constancy is acquired (Hinde, 1961).

What is it that sets the limits to the sensitive period? If chicks will follow a moving object when one day old, why will they not do so when one hour or one week? The earlier limit seems to be related to the development of locomotor ability: Hess (1959) found that the curve of increase of speed of locomotion of chicks with age corresponded closely with that showing the onset of the sensitive period. This, of course, does not demonstrate that locomotor ability is itself the operative factor: many other changes are also going on at this age—for instance there are marked changes in RNA (ribonucleic acid) synthesis (Bateson et al., 1972), in the organization of the visual system (Sackett, 1963), and in the general excitability of the nervous system (Kovach, 1964). To some extent these changes depend on experience: chicks exposed to white light for 30 min imprint to a flashing light more readily than chicks kept in the dark, perhaps through activation of their visual pathways (Bateson and Wainwright, 1972).

The end of the sensitive period depends even more closely on the conditions of rearing. In chicks the sensitive period can be extended by rearing them in isolation (Guiton, 1961; Sluckin, 1962), and in ducks by rearing them in diffuse light (Moltz and Stettner, 1961). Since the decline in the tendency to follow the test object at the end of the sensitive period is correlated with an increased tendency to flee from it, this influence of the environment on the duration of the sensitive period could be mediated by the development of fear

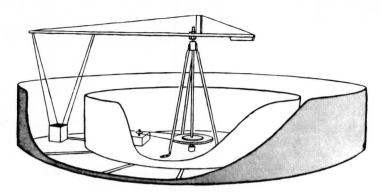

FIGURE 11.1

*Apparatus used for studying the following response of young chicks. The arm rotates, carrying the box round the circular runway.* (From a drawing by P. Bateson.)

responses (Hinde et al., 1956; Hess, 1959). Now objects that are strange to an animal are likely to elicit fear responses. "Strangeness", however, implies a previous learning of the familiar. It seems probable, therefore, that the sensitive period is one in which the bird learns the details of objects in its immediate environment. During this period it is likely to approach conspicuous and especially moving objects that it encounters. Only as it becomes familiar with this environment are strange objects responded to as such, and only then do they elicit fleeing. After the end of the sensitive period the learning of the properties of new objects can still go on, but only if they do not first elicit fleeing (Bateson, 1966; Sluckin, 1962; Sluckin and Salzen, 1961; Hinde, 1962).

Strong support for this view comes from an experiment by Bateson (1964a). Chicks were reared in individual pens, the sides of which were painted with conspicuous horizontal or vertical stripes. They were then tested in an apparatus of the type shown in Fig. 11.1. In each test, chicks tended first to avoid the moving model, and then to follow it. Avoidance persisted for a shorter time if the object was painted in a manner similar to the walls of the pen in which the chick had been reared than if it was painted differently (Fig. 11.2). Thus in the first days after hatching the chicks learn the characteristics of the environment in which they are reared and discriminate objects sufficiently dissimilar from those to which they are accustomed. The ability of the chicks to discriminate was shown to be related to the conspicuousness (as judged by a human observer) of the pattern with which the walls of the home pen were painted: with

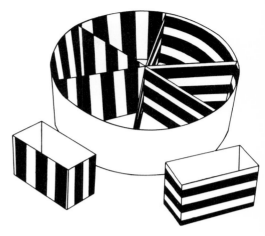

FIGURE 11.2a

*Rearing pens and models used to test following response of domestic chicks.* (Drawn by L. Barden.)

a more conspicuous (and therefore presumably more readily learnt) home environment, avoidance of differently painted models in the test pen persisted for longer, and thus following was more delayed.

On this view imprinting consists largely of the development of familiarity with the conspicuous object. This suggests that it resembles "perceptual learning"—a process previously studied with other species in quite different contexts. In a classic study Gibson (Gibson and Walk, 1956; Gibson et al., 1959) kept rats in cages with shapes cut out of metal stuck on the walls. The ability of the animals to learn to go to one of two shapes for a food reward was subsequently tested. Rats previously exposed to one of the shapes used in the test learned the discrimination more easily than did rats that had not been so exposed. The effect was more easily obtained the greater the "attention-getting" properties of the stimulus, but it did not matter whether the shape to which the rat had been exposed was the reinforced or the non-reinforced one in the subsequent discrimination test. Thus familiarity with an object in one context increased the ease with which that object was discriminated in another.

Bateson (1964b) carried out a comparable experiment with chicks reared in the pens with patterned sides (Fig. 11.2). Their ability to learn to approach one of two cards in a discrimination apparatus (Fig. 11.3) was assessed. The dis-

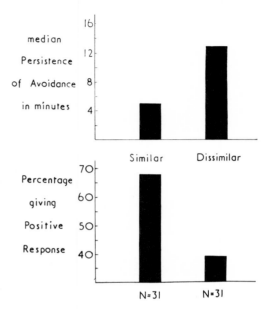

FIGURE 11.2b
*Persistence of avoidance of model and per-
centage of chicks following model when
reared in pens and tested on models in Fig.
11.2a. (By permission of P. P. G. Bateson.)*

crimination was learned more readily if either the reinforced or the non-reinforced card was painted like the home pen than if both were painted in some
different fashion (see also Chantrey, 1972, and references cited). The similarity
between this experiment and the classic perceptual learning one suggests that
similar processes operate in the two cases. The finding that the acquisition of
familiarity affects both discrimination learning and imprinting confirms the
suggestion that there is a close relationship between imprinting and perceptual
learning. It also implies that imprinting is not limited to the following response.
It can be presumed that, in the natural situation, the increasing familiarity of the
mother facilitates discrimination by the chick between stimuli from the mother
and other stimuli that might elicit each of the filial responses, and thus the
attachment of all filial responses to her.

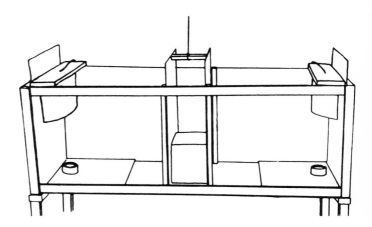

FIGURE 11.3

*Apparatus for testing discrimination learning in chicks. The chick is released from the centre. The two food cups are initially concealed under the covers, and have patterned cards behind them. (Drawn by L. Barden, by permission of P. P. G. Bateson.)*

Laboratory experiments on learning tend to involve series of training or test sessions—in other words, a series of episodes. It is easy to assume that learning is episodic, occurring at special moments in the lifetime of an animal. In the case of perceptual learning this is a misleading implication. The learning of the properties of the object which is studied in imprinting experiments can be regarded as an artificially isolated part of a process of learning about the environment which was started before hatching. On this view, the early distress calls of the chick would be related to the loss of contact and warmth which became familiar in the egg (Collias, 1952).

However the young does not wait passively until exposed to a conspicuous object, but shows behaviour which is likely to bring it into contact with one. During the few days after hatching, chicks are more active in a grey environment than in one painted with black and white stripes which reflect the same total amount of light: this suggests that a chick is more likely to be active in the absence of conspicuous objects than in their presence, behaviour which would be likely to bring the chick into the presence of an object suitable for it to imprint on, and to keep it there (Bateson, 1964c).

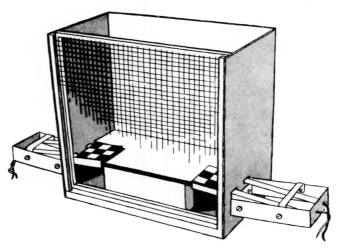

FIGURE 11.4

*Apparatus used for assessing the reinforcing effectiveness of a flashing light for young chicks. (From a drawing by P. Bateson.)*

*The light, which was placed outside the box and in front of the mesh side, was switched on when the chicks stood on one of the two chequered pedals. The other chequered pedal was used as a control.*

That chicks do in fact tend to repeat responses which bring them into the presence of a conspicuous object has been shown by Bateson and Reese (1969), who found that chicks and mallard ducklings would learn a response that produced a conspicuous stimulus on which they had not previously been imprinted. The chick was placed in the apparatus shown in Fig. 11.4. While the chick stood on one of the chequered areas a rotating light in front of the cage was turned on, but when it stood on the other the response was merely recorded. Chicks soon learned to depress the area that switched on the flashing light. Furthermore there was a sensitive period, during which the light acted as a reinforcer in this way, which corresponded with the sensitive period for the following response and was similarly influenced by rearing conditions. Thus operant conditioning may play an important part in the development of following (Bateson and Reese, 1969).

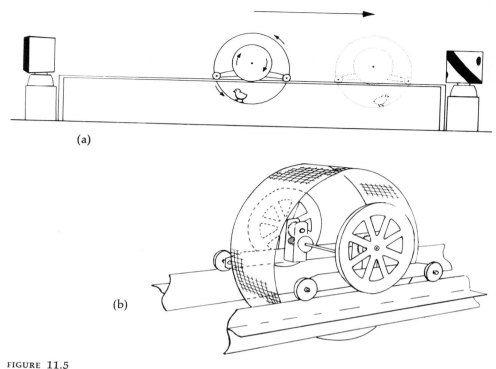

FIGURE 11.5

(a) *Running wheel used to test relative attractiveness of two stimuli. When the chick attempts to run in one direction the wheel moves in the other.* (b) *Detail of running wheel.* (By permission of P. P. G. Bateson.)

This experiment indicates that the learning which leads to attachment to the mother is by no means simple. The chick learns about its mother through perceptual learning, and at the same time learns responses that bring it into her presence through operant conditioning. Perceptual learning and operant conditioning proceed hand in hand, with the former narrowing the range of stimuli with reinforcing properties for the latter. At the same time the reinforcing properties of those objects with which the chick does become familiar are augmented: this also has been shown experimentally, for a chick will learn to run a T maze or will peck a key to establish contact with an object on which it has been imprinted (Campbell and Pickleman, 1961; Hoffman and Kozma, 1967; see also Hoffman et al., 1966). Furthermore, as following becomes limited to the mother the chick probably becomes conditioned to features in addition to those which originally elicited the response.

Meanwhile the chick sees objects from different angles and distances, and probably thereby acquires object constancy—anyway, it comes to respond to its mother as an individual, no matter from what angle or distance it sees her. This is probably assisted by two other properties of the chick's perceptual development. First, as the chick becomes familiar with a stimulus, it comes to respond preferentially to a stimulus slightly different from it. This has been demonstrated by Bateson (e.g., 1973; Bateson and Wainwright, 1972) in an apparatus in which the chick is placed in a running wheel which can move along a railway (Fig. 11.5). The wheel is geared in such a way that if the chick tries to run in one direction, it will be carried in the other. If conspicuous stimuli (e.g., flashing lights) are placed at either end of the runway, the chick will first try to approach one, but will be carried toward the other. Proximity enhances the attractiveness of a stimulus, so at a certain point the chick will turn and try to approach the stimulus toward which it has been carried: its efforts will, of course, have the opposite effect. The chick will thus tend to approach first one stimulus and then the other, and its movements will indicate the relative attractiveness of the two stimuli. Bateson found that the chick's behaviour could be explained on the supposition that it first had a mild tendency to approach stimuli that differed considerably from that on which it had been trained (e.g., a flashing light), but as familarity with the training stimulus increased, it came to have an increasingly strong preference for stimuli that differed only slightly from the familiar one (Fig. 11.6). This tendency to prefer objects slightly different from the familiar one would, in the natural situation, have the effect of familiarizing the chick with different aspects of the mother (see also Wünschmann, 1963).

A second process concerns the manner in which these different aspects of the mother come to be classed together. We have seen that rats and chicks go to one of two stimuli for a food reward more readily if one of the stimuli is familiar. But, in the case of chicks and also monkeys, animals pre-exposed to two stimuli more or less simultaneously found a discrimination task involving those two stimuli more difficult than did animals for whom the stimuli were novel. Bateson and Chantrey (1972) suggest that this is because the animal "classifies together" stimuli seen in the same context. Chantrey (1972) showed that chicks pre-exposed to two stimuli at different times found their subsequent discrimination easier than did animals to whom they were novel: in this case, presumably, the stimuli are not classified together. Rats differ from monkeys

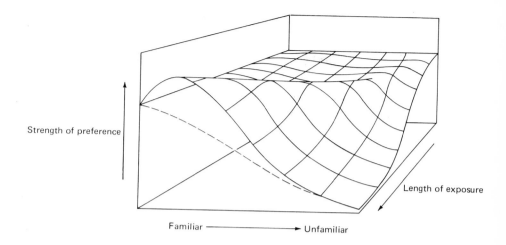

Strength of preference

Length of exposure

Familiar ⟶ Unfamiliar

FIGURE 11.6

*Theoretical model showing how strength of preference of chicks for an unfamiliar model varies with its difference from a familar model and the chicks' length of exposure to the familiar model. (From Bateson, 1973.)*

and chicks in that simultaneous pre-exposure to two stimuli does facilitate their subsequent discrimination (Gibson et al., 1959): Chantrey suggests that this is because rats, who are not such primarily visual animals as chicks or monkeys, do not in fact examine the stimuli simultaneously. This process of classifying together will clearly aid the chick in responding to the varying stimulus configurations presented by the mother as though they belonged to one object.

As stressed earlier, the following response is not the only part of filial behaviour addressed by the chick to its parent. Similar processes are associated with obtaining food, warmth, tacticle comfort, and so on from the mother, the relative importance of these various types of behaviour differing among species. Since each response becomes associated with characteristics of the mother in addition to those that elicited it initially, some aspects of the mother will become associated with more than one filial response. Thus the mother comes to embrace both stimulus characters specific to particular filial responses and other characters common to most or all of them.

Thus the factors contributing to the development of a chick's attachment to its mother are (1) the chick's initial responsiveness to rather ill-defined stimulus characters of the mother, and its tendency to seek out conspicuous stimulus configurations, (2) the mother's increasing familiarity, (3) the chick's learning further features of the mother, (4) its tendency to respond to aspects differing sligthly from those with which it is familiar, (5) its tendency to classify together aspects which it sees in rapid succession, and finally (6) the fact that the mother elicits several different types of behaviour from the chick. At this point we may recall some of the characters of an affectionate relationship mentioned in Chap. 2, and especially that it is multiplex, involving several types of behaviour.

The mother also soon comes to have another of the properties present in affectionate relationships. We have seen that as the young chick becomes familiar with its environment, strange objects elicit fear responses. Conversely, in a strange environment, familiar objects can provide comfort. For example, a chick which has been reared in a group of chicks for 7 days gives frequent distress calls if placed alone in a strange pen, but its distress calling is reduced if a mirror is present, presumably because the mirror provides some of the visual stimuli with which it has become familiar. With a chick reared in isolation for 7 days the mirror tends to have the reverse effect, presumably because it provides additional strange stimuli (Kaufman and Hinde, 1961). In natural conditions the mother becomes the epitome of familiarity, and her presence is sufficient to ameliorate the fear-provoking effects of a strange environment. She becomes in effect a comforter, sought the more vigorously the greater the distress experienced. The mother's role in providing security becomes so important that "proximity to mother" becomes a sine qua non for all maintenance activities, and in her absence the chick shows a special type of searching behaviour likely to restore contact. The biological advantage of this is obvious, since the mother provides warning of and protection from predators, warmth, guidance, and so on, and the chick's survival depends on her proximity.

This brief survey of the development of affiliative responses has been biassed in two ways. First, we have been concerned primarily with the young bird's increasing attachment to its mother or mother-figure. Similar processes of course operate in its attachment to other individuals, especially to peers, and even to aspects of the physical environment. Second, we have seen how the parent affects the development of the young bird, but have said little about how the young affects the parent's behaviour. However, at this phyletic level at any rate, parental care always involves an interaction between parent and young. This interactional nature of the relationship will be discussed further in the following chapters.

**Summary**

The development of parent-offspring relationships in birds involves a complex of learning processes, including perceptual learning, operant conditioning, and classical conditioning. As a result, responses by the young bird to particular aspects of the parent give rise to a relationship having some of the properties of an affectionate relationship in man.

# 12

# THE EARLY DEVELOPMENT OF PRIMATE SOCIAL BEHAVIOUR

## Introduction

The previous chapter was concerned with the development of social behaviour in birds; the next four chapters are concerned with primates. In moving from one to the other it is important to remember that (1) the synapsid and diapsid reptiles, from which mammals and birds arose, have been distinct since the Permian period—that is for about 250 million years; (2) parental care has evolved independently in the two groups; and (3) the basic structure of the forebrain differs markedly between birds and mammals. On the face of it, therefore, similarities in behaviour are not very likely to indicate similarities in underlying mechanisms. Nevertheless birds and mammals are faced with many of the same problems in their development, and we may expect evolutionary convergence to have produced some of the same characteristics of behaviour. We shall in fact find that a number of the principles which emerged from studying the development of social behaviour in birds will be found to apply also to primates (see also Salzen, 1967). In what follows, material will be drawn from studies of a variety of primate species to illustrate the various problems that arise, and the usual cautions concerning cross-species generalizations are essential (see page 4). Furthermore, since the slow rate at which primates breed makes them unsuitable subjects for studying many aspects of early development, we shall consider some data from other mammals, in particular from rodents. It will therefore be necessary for the reader to bear constantly in mind that species differ: even when the principles are generally valid, the details may not be.

In non-human primates the early development of social behaviour occurs in interaction with the mother. In some species infants are handled by other females from soon after birth, but the contribution of such females is always subsidiary to that of the mother (pages 219–221). In only a few species does the father play an important role (pages 221–225). As the infant matures he interacts to a considerable extent with his peers, but these interactions are largely controlled by the mother. Thus it is with mother-infant interaction that we shall first be concerned. In this chapter the establishment of the mother-infant relationship is discussed: some data on its gradual dissolution are presented in Chaps. 13 to 15.

It is necessary to add that study of the development of social behaviour involves many inter-related themes: it simply is not possible to sort out the material into a series of neatly compartmentalised problems. These inter-relations will become abundantly apparent in the sections that follow.

### Early movement patterns and the development of motor skills

Newborn primates,[1] like newly hatched birds, have a repertoire of simple movement patterns which mediate interaction with their social environment. These include movements of clinging, finding the nipple, and so on, as well as a variety of facial expressions, vocalizations, and other social signals.

Monkeys spend most of their early months, and apes much of their early years, clinging to their mothers in a ventro-ventral position (Fig. 12.1) or riding on their backs (Fig. 12.2), and when moving about most mothers give little if any support to their infants. It is thus essential for the infant to be able to cling to his mother as she runs or leaps about. The infant's ability to cling depends on basic reflex patterns. Sudden movement of the mother produces movements of the arms which serve to bring them into contact with the mother's body: this response is still present in the human baby as the Moro reflex, given on stimulation of the vestibular organs or of the muscles in the neck (Prechtl, 1965).

[1] More detailed and sophisticated analyses of the early interactions between infant and mother have been made in other mammals—see, for example, Rosenblatt, 1965, 1972; Schneirla et al., 1963.

FIGURE 12.1

*Rhesus macaque. Ventro-ventral position of infant on mother.* (Drawing by Priscilla Edwards.)

Grasping itself is associated with flexion of wrist and elbow, and in the human baby can be elicited by stretching the flexor and adductor muscles of the shoulder: it is intensified if the finger flexors are stretched (Twitchell, 1970). In addition to clinging with hands and feet, an infant monkey also holds on to its mother's nipple with its mouth: the nipple thus provides a fifth point of support.

FIGURE 12.2
*Stump-tailed macaque: dorsal riding.*
(Drawing by Priscilla Edwards after
Bertrand, 1969.)

The neonatal monkey's strong grasp enables it not only to cling to its mother as she moves about, but also to climb up its mother's ventrum—a response important in helping it to find the nipple.

Neonatal gorillas (Fossey, personal communication) and chimpanzees (van Lawick-Goodall, 1968) also can cling unaided, though the mother often gives additional support with her arms and thighs. In man, this ability is absent: although it is said that some human neonates can support their own weight, the power is soon lost. However, as we have seen, remnants of the grasping pattern are still present: its reduction, and the fact that human mothers of many societies normally carry their babies, are of course related.

The means whereby the baby finds the nipple provides another example of an early movement pattern important for early social development. The young primate, and this includes the human baby, has a "rooting reflex". It moves its head from side to side, thereby increasing the probability that the nipple will contact a sensitive area around the mouth which includes the upper and lower lips and parts of the cheeks. If this region is stimulated the head is turned in such a way that the mouth moves toward the point with which contact was made (Fig. 12.3). The nipple is then grasped with the lips and, if the nipple touches the soft palate, sucking is induced (Prechtl, 1958; Gunther, 1955). The

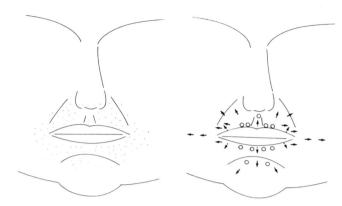

FIGURE 12.3

*Schematic drawing of the reflexogenous zone of directed head movements. Full arrows symbolize the direction of head-turning, dotted arrows the lip movement and opening response of the mouth. (From Prechtl, 1958.)*

act of sucking is itself highly organized, occurring in a complex pattern of bursts (Kron et al., 1963): it has a soothing effect on the baby, even though it obtains no milk thereby and even if it has never previously been fed from breast or bottle (Kessen and Mandler, 1961).

The responses that contribute to clinging and sucking are of course only part of the infant's equipment of movement patterns: some others will be discussed in the context of communication. Though it is convenient in each case to characterize the pattern by its most conspicuous elements, this can be misleading. Each apparently local movement pattern involves restrictions on or requirements for activities in other parts of the body: for example, sucking a nipple is associated with a diminution in diffuse activity (Wolff and Simmons, 1967). Thus a description in terms of local activity in isolated parts of the neuromuscular machinery may be only part of the picture.

## Early responsiveness to stimuli and the development of perceptual abilities

The young infant's repertoire of movement patterns would be of little use if they were not reliably elicited by appropriate stimulation. Some of the responses just mentioned, elicited by non-visual stimuli, appear on the first occasion that

FIGURE 12.4
*Surrogate mothers as used by Harlow.* (Drawing by Priscilla Edwards.)

the naturally appropriate objects are encountered. The stimuli which elicit the responses of grasping and sucking have already been indicated (pages 164–167). Another example is provided by Harlow's classic experiments demonstrating the importance of "contact comfort" to a rhesus monkey infant. He provided infants with surrogate mothers consisting of a wire framework which might or might not be covered in terry cloth, might or might not have a nipple providing milk, might or might not have a head, and so on (Fig. 12.4). One of the most important characters turned out to be the terry cloth covering. When rhesus monkey infants were given two artificial mother surrogates of which one was covered with terry cloth and one was not, they spent nearly all their time on the cloth mother even though they could obtain milk only from the wire one. This responsiveness to "contact comfort" is of course related to the ventro-ventral position in which the infant spends most of its time (Fig. 12.1; Harlow and

Zimmerman, 1959). However textural stimuli are not the only ones determining an infants' clinging preferences: mother surrogates that provide milk, are warm, or that rock, are preferred to ones that are without milk, cold, or stationary (Harlow and Suomi, 1970). Parallels with human infants are obvious: they also can be soothed by contact, warmth, or being rocked, as well as by the opportunity to suck.

Visual stimuli from the mother probably do not become of major importance in mother-infant interaction until the infant has had considerable visual experience—and this even though, contrary to earlier opinion, the visual system shows quite a degree of organization from the early days of life. Much of our knowledge here concerns our own species. The eye movements of human newborns show evidence of endogenous organization (Prechtl and Lenard, 1967). Newborns direct their attentive responses more to some visual stimuli than to others, indicating that they are already able to select from amongst the stimuli available to them (Fantz, 1966; Wolff, 1963). Some degree of perceptual constancy seems to be present at a surprisingly early age: Bower (1966, 1969) found size and shape constancy in two-week-old infants. Learning can be demonstrated experimentally in the first few days of life (Lipsitt, 1966).

Exploration of the further development of perceptual abilities depends in part on studying the stimulus characteristics that catch the infant's attention. At first it is directed especially toward stimuli that move, have contrasting contours, and contain a number of discrete elements. But during the first month increasing familiarity with frequently encountered stimulus configurations paves the way for a new phase—the direction of attention toward stimulus configurations that resemble ones with which the infant is familiar, but differ somewhat from them (Kagan, 1970). The operation of this "discrepancy principle" is illustrated by experiments on the attentiveness of young infants to stimuli resembling a human face. With very young infants cards painted to resemble a face are no more attractive than comparable cards with the same features rearranged in an irregular manner (Fig. 12.5), but after a few months cards with the features arranged in a face-like way are preferred (Fantz, 1965; Fantz and Nevis, 1967; McCall and Kagan, 1969; Kagan, 1970). Still later, around eight months of age, fixation times to both regular and irregular faces become low and similar.

These changes can be understood as follows. The early development of responsiveness to face-like stimuli is presumably a consequence of the infant's frequent experience of the relatively invariant face or faces of his caretakers. The preference of a four-month-old for a regular facial stimulus can be interpreted as resulting from the moderate degree of discrepancy between the stimu-

FIGURE **12.5**
*Representations of face-like stimuli presented to infants.* (From Kagan 1970.)

lus and the faces with which he has become familiar. With a disarranged face
the discrepancy is too marked, and attentiveness is less. Fantz and Nevis (1967)
found that home-reared infants of five or six months of age showed a more
marked discrimination in favour of the face-like stimulus than did institution-
raised infants: this could be due to the greater familiarity of the former with
particular faces and their responsiveness to discrepancy from them. With still
older children, it is suggested, the normal face is so familiar that photographs
and models are readily assimilated. Marked discrepancy may, however, produce
fear (cf. Hebb, 1949). These interpretations are of course speculative, and
require more detailed longitudinal study, but the parallels to Bateson's model
(see pages 158–159), devised as a result of experiments with chicks, are clear. The
difficulty here is that the discrepancy hypothesis used *post hoc* seems almost
irrefutable.

The development of sensori-motor skills depends on the concurrent development of the perceptual and motor mechanisms. For example, the visuo-
motor coordination of a newborn rhesus infant is poorly developed, and for
several days it is unable to grasp an object that it sees without trial and error.
Not until it is between sixteen and twenty-eight days old can it pick up pieces

of food and transfer them to its mouth (Mason and Harlow, 1959; Hinde et al., 1964). Experiments have shown that practice plays an important role here: voluntary movements of the limbs under visual guidance are essential for normal progress (Held and Bauer, 1967). Of course the time scale of development differs considerably among species: the grasping response of the human infant develops gradually through a series of stages (Twitchell, 1970; Connolly, 1970a and b, 1973), and hand-eye-mouth coordination is achieved even more slowly by the human infant than by monkeys. However in both monkey and man, development is similarly affected by experience, especially by opportunities for the voluntary manipulation of objects (White, 1970).

The further development of perceptual abilities and the closely related questions of the development of motor and cognitive skills are beyond the scope of this book. It hardly needs to be emphasized that they do not involve an inevitable unfolding of patterns of increasing complexity: rather each advance depends on previous ones, on the synthesis of abilities achieved in previous stages in interaction with the environment. In the development of both perception and motor skills the early stages of development include the differentiation of component and finer patterns from gross and cruder ones, while later stages include the acquisition of the ability to combine components into higher-order schemes (e.g., Piaget, 1953; Bruner, 1968, 1969a and b, 1970; Connolly), 1973). In neither case can development be understood without the postulation of intervening cognitive structure, and as knowledge of the capacities of infant animals grows it becomes necessary to postulate such structure at earlier and earlier stages.

In summary, the primate infant is at birth already responsive to certain simple stimulus patterns mediating interaction with its mother. Though its sensory-perceptual systems have a considerable degree of organization, further development in interaction with the environment increases its ability to respond to more complex patterns, especially in the visual modality.

## Early maternal behaviour

With its armoury of motor patterns and responsiveness to stimuli, the young monkey is able to secure its immediate needs with some help from its mother. The mother[2] must give it some physical support, provide it with milk, keep it clean, and protect it.

[2] In all non-human primates, care of the infant devolves principally on the mother, though in some species the father makes a substantial contribution (pages 221–225). In those species for which data are

Adequate maternal behaviour depends in part on the conditions in which the mother herself was reared. Monkey mothers which have been reared in a severely deprived social environment are often incapable of rearing infants. The deficiencies seem to involve not so much specific responses as more general motivational abnormalities, including hyper-aggressiveness to the infants (Harlow and Harlow, 1965, see also pages 234–238). The role of earlier experience in the development of specific maternal responses is discussed briefly below.

The immediate motivational determinants of maternal behaviour are little understood. In some species stimuli from the young, as well as eliciting maternal behaviour, appear also to affect the internal state of the female, as shown by her tendency to behave maternally later on. For example, the maternal behaviour of female mice is "primed" by the ultrasonic calls of the young (Noirot, 1972), and in man sophisticated obstetrical practice involves giving the newborn to the mother to hold immediately after delivery (Klaus and Kennell, 1970): the mechanisms involved in the two cases are no doubt different. Hormonal changes also play a role: blood transfused from lactating female rats into virgin females increases the tendency of the latter to behave maternally (Terkel and Rosenblatt, 1968; Rosenblatt, 1970).

The inter-relations between maternal behaviour, lactation, and stimulation from the infant are complex (e.g., Findlay, 1970), and the evidence at present available comes from diverse species. During pregnancy female rats direct more and more of their self-licking to the nipple line and genitalia: this appears to contribute to mammary gland development, and perhaps to the secretion of anterior pituitary hormones (Rosenblatt and Lehrman, 1963; Roth and Rosenblatt, 1967). In both rodents and primates the initiation and maintenance of lactation depend on suckling by the infant. Thus rats continue to lactate for longer if their litters are frequently replaced, and female monkeys without infants have been made to lactate by stimulation from an infant (Harlow and Harlow, 1965). Stimuli from the young other than those consequent upon suck-

available, immediately pre- and post-adolescent females show more tendency to interact with infants than do males (pages 219–221); it is likely that this sex difference in behavior is influenced prenatally by hormonal factors (pages 307–309). However, virtually all patterns of maternal behaviour are shown at least sometimes by males (pages 221–225); no doubt the tendency of males to behave maternally is influenced by experiential and immediate environmental factors, as well as by internal ones (pages 310–313). Similar principles appear to operate in man (pages 308–309), though the relative importance of experiential factors is probably greater, and the potential overlap between the sexes more extensive. When the human case is under consideration the term "mother" is convenient both to facilitate biological comparisons and because most human babies are in fact at present cared for primarily by their natural mothers, but no value judgements about the potential roles of non-maternal females or males are intended.

ing can produce milk ejection: some human mothers secrete milk when their baby cries.

Maternal behaviour, other than nursing, can occur in the absence of lactation in a wide range of species (Wiesner and Sheard, 1933; Spencer-Booth, 1970). But while lactation is not essential for maternal behaviour, it probably augments it: mice are more ready to cross barriers or overcome obstacles to reach pups when they are lactating than when they are not.

The consequences of nursing may affect subsequent nursing behaviour independently of its effects on milk production. Some of the most precise work here has been carried out with rabbits, which normally nurse their young only once a day (Zarrow et al., 1965). Cross (1952) found that rabbits could be induced to nurse more than once a day if loss of milk were prevented at the first nursing by sealing the teats with collodion. He therefore concluded that mammary distension was the chief factor in the motivation of nursing. However, Findlay (e.g., 1970; Findlay and Roth, 1970; Findlay and Tallal, 1971) found that rabbits would nurse their litter normally even if the mammary glands had previously been emptied by a foster-litter while the mother was anaesthetised. From this and other experiments he concluded that mammary gland distension is a sufficient condition for nursing behaviour, but not a necessary one. He also showed that distension is not essential for the long-term maintenance of nursing behaviour: females whose glands were emptied daily by a foster-litter while they were unconscious would still continue to nurse their own each day when they came round. This suggests that suckling acts as a consummatory stimulus to the mother, for the stimulation received during nursing reduces the mother's tendency to nurse: the suckling bouts of rabbits are in fact longer if the teats are treated with a local anaesthetic. Thus the nursing situation is itself complex, with the behaviour of the infant having interacting positive and negative effects on its repetition.

Other types of maternal behaviour depend, like nursing, on a delicate interaction between mother and infant. Thus how much physical support the mother provides depends in part on the infant: healthy newborn monkeys cling to their mothers unaided for most of the time, but mothers may carry dead babies for days. Chimpanzee and gorilla mothers give more support than do monkey mothers. The amount of support given by the mother decreases with time: as it grows older the baby is cradled more loosely between the mother's arms and legs, and later still the mother sits without enclosing the baby at all (Fig. 12.6).

Under normal conditions most monkeys have at least plenty of opportunity

FIGURE 12.6
*Stump-tailed macaque: loose cradling of infant.*
(Drawing by Priscilla Edwards after Bertrand,
1969).

to learn how to hold an infant by observing mothers in the troop: as we shall
see later, they spend much time close to their own mother, and may "help" with
younger siblings (pages 217–221). It is therefore not surprising that they show
considerable competence even with their first infants. However, there is some
evidence that a good deal of learning may go on during the first few hours of
the infant's life. For instance, one captive rhesus mother for some time after the
birth of her infant held him too tightly, so that his head was fixed in the crook
of her arm and he could not possibly gain the nipple (Fig. 12.7). She even held
him upside down for 16 min, but after the first hour or two she held him normally and reared him successfully (Hinde et al., 1964). This mother was unusual
in that she did not eat the placenta, which dragged along by the cord for several
hours. However, a degree of ineptness with the neonate has been recorded in
other monkey mothers (Bertrand, 1969). In our own species also prior observational learning and practice both play a role: it is difficult to know how effective
verbal instruction on how to look after a baby would be without them.

In addition to supporting and feeding the infant, the mother must clean
and protect it. She removes the birth fluids from the infant after birth and continues to groom it frequently for months or years. The increased aggressiveness
which mothers show in defence of their offspring is probably hormonally
mediated: this is discussed again later (pages 255–256). Just how the more general
protectiveness of a mother toward her infant arises is quite unknown, but it
determines much of her behaviour. In most species the mother is constantly

FIGURE 12.7
*Primiparous rhesus mother holding baby so that it cannot reach nipple. The cord is still attached to baby and also to the placenta (not shown).* (Drawing by Priscilla Edwards.)

aware of the position of her infant when it starts to leave her, and goes to it at once if danger threatens (see Chap. 13).

Thus at the time of birth of her infant, the primate mother, whether or not she has previously had access to babies, is equipped with some patterns of behaviour which will form part of her interaction with her infant, and also with predispositions to learn to increase her competence. She has usually also already had considerable experience of babies, and perhaps even practice with holding them. In the development of maternal responsiveness physiological and behavioural issues are inter-related, and the interaction between mother and baby forms the forum in which each improves skills and adjusts to the other.

### Limitation of the range of effective stimuli and establishment of preferences

We saw earlier (Chap. 11) how the chick's following behaviour can initially be elicited by a wide range of stimuli, that this is later narrowed by experience, and that stimuli which become familiar also thereby become more effective. We have also seen how, partly as a consequence of its perceptual development in proximity to the mother and partly as a consequence of the several responses which it comes to direct to her, the chick forms with its mother a relationship which has some of the properties of a multiplex affectionate relationship in man. Similar processes occur in the newborn primate. He, too, does not initially respond to his mother as an individual, but shows a number of separate responses directed toward different aspects of her body. Initially each of these responses can be elicited by a wider range of stimuli than those that she offers, the range of effective stimuli becoming narrowed in development. At the same time, by processes probably similar to those occurring in the chick, he comes to respond to her as an individual.

The narrowing of the range of stimuli effective for a filial response is clearly seen in the nursing situation. The newborn monkey or human baby can learn to suck from the breast fairly easily, but it is often difficult to teach it to suck from the breast if it has previously sucked solely on a bottle. Indeed in rhesus monkeys this early learning soon leads to a marked preference for one nipple rather than the other, at least for non-nutritive sucking (Hinde et al., 1964). In one of the rare cases of twins in rhesus monkeys, side preferences seemed more important than nipple preferences: sometimes if disturbed the twins would knock into each other in their attempts to get to their "own" sides, but when there they sometimes attached to the wrong nipple, so that the nipples were crossed (Spencer-Booth, 1968a; see also Deets and Harlow, 1970).

In association with this establishment of preferences, learning occurs at many stages in the sequence of responses leading up to sucking. That young rhesus monkeys will learn to approach a situation in which they are able to suck from a bottle was shown by Mason and Harlow (1958). Learning was apparent in infants that were only a few days old: indeed the age at which clear evidence of learning could be obtained seemed to be determined primarily by the development of the ability to show the locomotor activity demanded by the test situation. In the human baby, at least, learning extends also to the sucking response itself. At first, though patterned, it is relatively stereotyped; but the rhythm of sucking and the precise character of the sucking movements are quickly adjusted to improve the yield of milk (Bruner, 1969a). Furthermore, learning extends to contextual factors, which may come to play an important part in supporting the feeding response (Cairns, 1972a).

It is thus apparent that even the basic response of sucking involves learning processes by the infant whose complexity is only gradually being revealed.

FIGURE 12.8

*Breast feeding, showing how the baby's nares may become occluded by his upper lip.* (Drawing by Priscilla Edwards, after Gunther, 1955.)

These processes are often most conspicuous when they go wrong. For instance the nipple-finding sequence can be markedly affected by experience on the early occasions on which the baby is put to the breast. If the areolar tissue of the mother's breast is insufficiently extensible, the baby's soft palate may be inadequately stimulated and sucking is not properly elicited: such babies easily become "lazy suckers" in the course of a few experiences. If the breast shape is such that the baby's upper lip is pressed against its nose (Fig. 12.8), it may give an anoxia response, beating with its fists against its mother's breast. This can be rapidly conditioned, so that after a few experiences the infant may give this response before it is actually put to the breast. This, incidentally, is very traumatic for the mother, who feels rejected by her infant, and the seeds of difficulty in the relationship may be sown (Gunther, 1955).

Just as the sucking response used in feeding becomes more or less limited and adapted to the mother's breast, so also do the stimuli effective for other responses become restricted. As we shall see (pages 182–184), a baby's smiles can first be elicited by a wide range of stimuli, including sounds and a variety of visual stimuli (Wolff, 1963; Ahrens, 1954). By one to three months of age, however, smiling is largely restricted to the human face, and later to particular human faces (Ambrose, 1961). A wide range of objects in addition to those from the mother's body can initially provide contact comfort, and the human infant usually becomes attached to certain particular ones, such as a blanket or soft toy: his learned responsiveness to and familiarity with the object of his choice leads to its retaining a greater effectiveness than novel, and apparently equally suitable, comforters. It is because of this narrowing of the range of effective stimuli that the earlier an infant monkey or chimpanzee is separated from its mother, the more readily it adapts to a human fosterer (Lemmon, 1971).

As in birds, under conditions of artificial rearing the various infantile responses may become attached to different objects. Rowell (1965) reared an infant baboon by hand. The baboon received contact comfort by clinging to her or to her clothing, and also received reassurance from a dummy teat. He obtained milk from a bottle and would choose bottle or teat according to whether he was hungry or in need of reassurance.

Although the range of effective stimuli is normally narrowed by experience, there is some evidence for a degree of appropriate selectivity in responsiveness in animals reared in isolation. This was obtained by Sackett (1970), using the choice chamber shown in Fig. 12.9. The infant monkey was placed in the centre compartment, and two or more stimulus animals were placed in carrying cages hooked to the outside of the choice compartments. The experimenter then scored entries into the choice compartments or orientation toward the stimulus animals. Infant monkeys which had been separated from their mothers at birth and had had no access to animals other than age-mates preferred an adult of their own rather than of related macaque species, and preferred an adult female to an adult male. Furthermore infants of both sexes initially preferred a female adult to a male, but the preference of males changed with age, so that individuals one to two years old came to prefer a male. The number of test animals used in these experiments was, however, small, and repetition would be desirable.

How soon does the infant come to recognize his mother individually? This is a question that is often asked but requires more rigid formulation before it can be answered. During the period in which the mother is gradually being transformed from a collection of stimuli for more or less unrelated responses into an individual, the infant may respond so strongly to some of her features that differences in others are of minor importance. As a result, the infant may

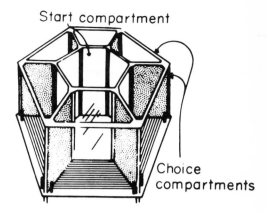

FIGURE 12.9
*Apparatus used to study social preferences in monkeys. The animal under test was placed in the centre. Two or more stimulus animals were placed in transparent travelling cages on the outside of the choice compartments. The experimenter recorded which choice compartment the animal entered or oriented toward. (After Sackett, 1970.)*

respond individually to her in terms of some of her characteristics or in some contexts, but not in others. Thus as assessed by attentive responses, some human infants discriminate their mother from a stranger by one month of age, and most do by three months (Yarrow, 1967), but on the basis of evidence from a study of smiling, Ambrose (1961) believed that mothers' and strangers' faces were not discriminated before thirteen weeks of age. As another example, in a study in Uganda Ainsworth (1967) found differential smiling from at least ten weeks of age, but no difference in frequency of infant vocalization between interactions with a stranger and with the mother until about twenty weeks. Thus if the question, "When does the infant recognize his mother?" is posed operationally as, "When does he behave differently to his mother and to a stranger?", the answer depends on the response (and no doubt also the measure of that response) used in the test and probably also on many aspects of the testing situation, such as the alternatives presented to the infant.

On the reciprocal question of how soon a mother learns to recognize her own infant, few hard data exist for non-human primates. In galagos several days seem to be necessary (Klopfer, 1970). Stump-tailed monkey mothers are very upset by the removal of their infant even in its first few days of life. For about 10 days after the birth such distress can be alleviated by the sight of any infant of approximately the right age, but after that only their own infants are effective (Jensen, 1965).

Thus the filial responses, initially elicited by a wide range of stimuli, gradually become restricted to those presented by the mother. At the same time the infant's perceptual and cognitive abilities are developing, and he comes to respond to his mother as an individual. It is difficult to escape the conclusion that the processes involved are similar to, though of course more complex than, those in the chick (see Chap. 11).

### Communication between mother and infant

Pregnancy and birth form the beginning of an on-going interaction between mother and infant which continues until the latter becomes independent. Communication (in a broad sense) between them depends on the growing and inter-related perceptual, cognitive, and motor capacities of the infant.

The early post-natal development of most non-human primates occurs in an environment formed in large part by the mother's body. Closely attached to her, the infant must become closely acquainted with the tactual, kinaesthetic, auditory, visual, and olfactory stimuli that she provides. As we have seen, to some of these stimuli he responds as soon as he is born. As he develops further, his mother's body is his first toy, and many of his waking hours are spent in its exploration.

From immediately after the birth, both mother and infant have characteristics which are particularly likely to catch the attention of the other. On his part, the infant provides physical stimuli to which the mother is especially attuned: the fact that mother monkeys may carry still-born babies for days suggests that the infant provides contact stimulation for the mother as well as vice versa. In most species of monkeys the infants have a distinctive coat colour or some other characteristic which elicits maternal responses from adults, and it has been suggested that the head shape of the human baby has similar properties (Lorenz, 1943; Gardner and Wallach, 1965).

On the reciprocal issue of whether the newborn is especially sensitive to any of the stimuli presented by the mother, there is strong evidence that the human face possesses characteristics that are especially likely to catch the infant's attention—characteristics of contrast, movement, three-dimensionality, and so on (see pages 155–156 and Kagan and Lewis, 1965). In addition, the manner in which the mother holds the baby makes it easier for the baby to learn her features. She likes to look into the baby's face, and tries to get the baby to look at her. Being held and rocked may not only soothe a crying baby, but also alert it (Korner and Thoman, 1970), and when the infant is at the breast, its mother's face is at about the distance at which it can focus most clearly (Haynes et al., 1965). As we have seen, the configuration of the human face soon becomes familiar.

In the auditory modality, there is evidence that infants exposed to the sound of the human heartbeat gain weight better than do infants not so exposed: the tendency of parents to carry babies against the left breast rather than the right may be related to this (Salk, 1973; Weiland and Sperber, 1970). Again, infants are more likely to respond positively to sounds having some characteristics of the human voice at an even younger age than that at which he becomes responsive to faces (e.g., Hutt et al., 1968; Eisenberg, R. A., 1969; Eimas et al., 1971).

In addition to features that tend to make mother and infant catch each other's attention, there are of course a number of species-characteristic signals adapted specifically for communication. The infant monkey has a repertoire of vocal signals (e.g., Chevalier-Skolnikoff, 1971): for instance he gives frequent "whoo" calls if separated from his mother for a while, and a series of geckering screams which may escalate into a tantrum if the mother will not take him on the nipple. The distress calls of the infant have a profound effect on the mother, though how she responds depends both on her own state, determined perhaps in part by how recently the infant has been on her, and on the context—for instance if the infant is losing his grip on a branch she will go to him immediately. Physical contact with the mother reduces the frequency of the infant's distress calls almost immediately—indeed it has been shown experimentally that a higher magnitude of electric shock is necessary to evoke distress vocalizations from young chimpanzees when they are being held than when they are not (Mason and Berkson, 1962).

In the human infant the analogue of these distress calls is crying. This is more complex than appears at first sight: from quite early on cries are differentiated into at least three distinct patterns—a basic form occurring, for instance, in hunger, progressing from an arrhythmical low-intensity cry to a louder and rhythmical form; a "mad" cry, somewhat similar in form but with the components of the sequence differently emphasized; and a pain cry with a sudden onset, a pause, and then a series of gasping cries. Mothers respond to these patterns appropriately (Wolff, 1969; Bernal, 1972), and can also learn quickly to respond discriminatively to the cries of their own infant and not to the cries of other infants (Formby, 1967).

Crying may have a variety of causes—hunger, cold, pain, and so on. When a specific cause is apparent, its removal is of course the best way of stopping the crying. The response induced in the mother is in fact not specific, but is goal-directed toward seeking out the cause and removing it. Often the crying is not due to a specific organic cause. Sometimes it ceases if the general level of stimulation is reduced. More often a variety of consummatory stimuli, such as those provided by non-nutritive sucking (even on a dummy), gentle human voices, contact and cuddling, rocking (Kessen and Mandler, 1961), or even continuous stimulation through a variety of modalities (Brackbill, 1971) may reduce the crying. The efficacy of such stimuli suggests that, for the human baby, as for chicks (page 160), monkeys, and apes (page 181), absence of stimulation normally provided by the parent is an important cause of crying. Observation supports this view: even five-week-old human babies may start to cry if a person they are looking at disappears (Wolff, 1969). At this age the disappearance of any person will induce the response, but later of course the range of effective persons becomes narrowed.

The neonatal monkey also has a number of distinct facial expressions (e.g., Chevalier-Skolnikoff, 1971). One of the most easily recognizable by the human observer is the grin (Fig. 10.5), given in situations of fear or distress, whose nature is discussed on page 127.

The subtleties of the facial expressions shown by human infants soon after birth have so far defied adequate description and classification, in part because they lack the discreteness of the later forms. However they produce marked effects on the mother. Of special effectiveness are the more stereotyped patterns shown in distress or, slightly later, in greeting, and of those one of the most interesting is the smile. This is, as we have seen (pages 126–132), a nearly uniquely human pattern, though its origins from a grin can be traced in non-human forms. At first smiling occurs spontaneously, or in response to a high-pitched voice, but it is not linked to any particular visual stimulus (Wolff, 1963). A few weeks after birth visual stimuli become effective, but the infant will smile at an oval stimulus card with a pair of black dots almost as readily as at a human face. Furthermore, an experimenter's face with the nose and mouth covered is effective, but a face with the eyes covered, or a whole face in profile, is not. It thus seems that at this age the essential element in the visual stimulus situation eliciting a smile is the eyes; and the response appears to be comparable with social responses in other species, where one part of the stimulus situation is more important than others (pages 53–61). It must be stressed, however, that it is not yet known how much the peculiar effectiveness of the eyes depends on previous visual experience in general, or on experience of the human face in particular (cf. page 181). With increasing age the probability of smiling to a wide range of objects first increases. Soon, however, the optimal stimulus situation comes to require more and more facial features, and the range of objects that will elicit smiling becomes narrower. This subsequently involves a limitation not merely to faces, but to faces with which the infant is familiar: this of course occurs gradually but is usually apparent at about seven months of age (Ahrens, 1954; Ambrose, 1961).

However even at this age the smile is not elicited only by the human face. Kagan (1970) cites a number of studies showing that smiles can be elicited by events marginally discrepant from the expected, even events involving inanimate objects (cf. pages 169–170). Kagan suggests that the infant is likely to smile as he assimilates an initially discrepant event. Whether smiling in such circumstances is different in kind from social smiling, or whether social smiling is also to be interpreted in terms of discrepancy—after all it occurs especially when a familiar face is first seen after an interval during which its "image" may have faded somewhat—remains to be seen. In any case, it is clear that smiling undergoes a fairly complex developmental history (see also Gewirtz, 1965). The ages at which these changes occur vary with the conditions of rearing (Ambrose, 1961; Gewirtz, 1965).

Although ritualized signals, including facial expressions and vocalizations, play a crucial role in communication between mother and infant in both man and non-human forms, it cannot be too strongly emphasized that the bulk of interaction depends on subtle and often individually variable signals. As we have seen, the distinction between ritualized and non-ritualized signals is in any case far from clear (pages 85–91); and we must not get an over-simple view of the communication between primate mother and baby from the fact that some of the signals seem to have been ritualized in evolution according to principles which can be studied also in fishes and birds.

For example, at first the infant monkey's grasping response depends on reflexes initiated by stimulation of the flexor muscles in his arms (pages 164–165). When the infant starts to leave his mother, she will pick him up before moving off, but later the picking up becomes abbreviated, in a way that differs between individuals, to a touch or even a slight extension of the mother's arm toward the infant, as though beckoning. Later still the mother simply leaves, and the infant responds to her movement.

In the human case responsiveness by either partner to small movements by the other is of course even more diverse and idiosyncratic. The delicacy of the communication that occurs is demonstrated by Kulka's (1968) study of the behaviour of human mothers and their babies in the feeding situation. Records of heart rate and muscle tension from infant and mother gave clear evidence that tension was transmitted to or created in the infant when the mother held it uncomfortably or felt tense herself.

At a later age even the ritualized signals, such as smiling and crying, are accompanied by many other expressive movements, such as waving of the arms and legs, which carry an important part of the message. Other (relatively) non-ritualized signals are diverse and play a very large role in the interactions between mother and infant; for instance, babbling, gurgling, arm-waving, back-arching, fist-beating, and a host of other movements have profound effects on the mother. The "meaning" of each gesture or vocalization depends, as in non-primate species (see pages 82–83), on the context in which it is given. This context includes accompanying signals from the infant, other contextual factors, and even the time of day: for instance, the manner in which a mother responds to her infant's cry varies with the time since it was fed (Bernal, 1972).

But communication does not depend only on simple stimulus-response sequences. From birth on the mother tries to interpret nearly every movement the infant makes (Bernal, personal communication), often using contextual cues to supply meaning. The baby gradually learns new ways of extending his range of communication with his mother. Only a small part of the communication between them is related to the satisfaction of basic physiological needs, and both seem to enjoy communication for communication's sake. From an early age infant and mother come to engage in quite complex idiosyncratic communicatory sequences, involving mutual gazing, hand movements, vocalizations, smiling, looking away, and so on. The interactions are often described as "playing", but there is no clear line between communication and games: a delicate interplay between pleasure in the expected and pleasure in the slightly novel is part of both. At the same time the mother's delight in her baby's simple achievements helps to cement the bond between them. Although mutual gazing and quite complicated interactional sequences occur also in chimpanzees, and sometimes even in monkeys, the richness and diversity of the communication between human mother and infant represent an almost qualitative advance over non-human forms.

In both monkey and man the infant's cognitive and affectional development proceed hand in hand (cf. Piaget and Inhelder, 1948). Social interactions depend on prior cognitive and affectional development, and augment their subsequent growth. The relationships are probably complex. For example, babbling interchanges between the human infant and its caretaker may lead to increased babbling as a consequence of social reinforcement, and provide the infant with opportunity to monitor the sounds he makes and thus gain control over his own voice. In the course of development the infant comes to be able to use its signals in a goal-directed way to influence its mother's behaviour. Much later still the interaction between them becomes such that the behaviour of each is regulated in relation to the on-going behaviour of the other (see page 202).

In non-human species, compliance with the mother's signals may be a matter of life and death. Stayton et al. (1971) believe that in human infants also there is an early disposition to comply with maternal commands and prohibitions, and that this is independent of efforts to train or discipline the baby. They suggest that it forms the earliest manifestation of obedience. Infant obedience appears to be related to the sensitivity of the mother's responsiveness to the infant's signals (see also pages 238–242).

In the human case the development of verbal language is of special interest for communication. We shall not discuss this here, but we may note that it seems to be possible to identify in the vocalizations of infants some features that appear to be precursors of the language system which will develop later—for instance, the "innate breath group" which will later be used in the segmentation of speech into sentences, and the ability to differentiate consonants (Eimas et al., 1971). In the very early stages of speech, context is crucial in giving meaning to utterances of both mother and infant (Bloom, 1970), and the mother speaks in a manner that facilitates the acquisition of language by her child (Ryan, 1973).

## Further experience in the mother-infant relationship

The establishment of the relationship between mother and infant depends primarily on sequences of interaction between them in the course of nursing, maintenance activities, play, and just being together. That engaging in such activities must be reinforcing for both partners is almost self-evident to the observer of mother-infant interaction: each individual develops ways of behaving that enable it to engage in the various types of interaction with the partner. It has also been tested experimentally. In rodents, for instance, a number of studies have shown that mothers will cross electric grids or learn mazes if doing so brings them into proximity with their young. More precise experiments to determine which aspects of the interaction are reinforcing are usually impracticable because of the difficulty of arranging that one of the partners should interact in some ways but not others, though some progress has been made. Thus, as we have seen, a monkey mother may carry a dead baby for days: she also shows temporary distress if it is removed, suggesting that contact even with a dead baby provides some reinforcement. With chimpanzees of a somewhat older age it has been possible to use human experimenters to take the mother's role. In this way Mason (1967) showed that opportunities to play, to be petted and groomed, and to a lesser extent to groom, were all rewarding to young chimpanzees.

In human children, the frequency with which infants smile can be increased if smiling is reinforced by picking up and petting the infant (Brackbill, 1958; Brossard and Decarie, 1968). Gewirtz (1961) has pointed out that smiling, laughter, reaching, manipulating, vocalizing, and many other infant activities can all cause the mother or other caretaker to approach, and that the activities are thereby reinforced. Vocalizations of the infant can also be reinforced by smiling and petting: in the laboratory infants who receive such stimulation on vocalizing one day, vocalize more on the next (Rheingold et al., 1959). Yarrow et al. (1972), working in the home environment, found that how much an infant vocalized while exploring an object was related to its mother's responsiveness to its vocalizations: this strongly suggests that the laboratory data of Rheingold et al. can be generalized to real life.

However the course of development cannot always be predicted on straightforward reinforcement lines. Bell and Ainsworth (1972) have found that infants whose mothers most readily pick them up when they cry in any one quarter of the first year of life tend to be the ones that cry least in the next quarter, and that a low frequency of crying at the end of the first year tends to be associated with a high frequency of other communicative behaviour. Of course those mothers who respond quickly to their infant's cries may also differ in many other respects from mothers who are less responsive, so that the effect on crying may be indirect (see pages 239–241). Furthermore, latency is only one characteristic of the mother's response: many other features of her behaviour may affect the baby's subsequent crying behaviour (Sander et al., 1970; Bernal, 1972).

The experience which the infant primate acquires is not limited to mother-infant interaction. As he crawls over his mother's body, as he is carried about, handled, and groomed, he is constantly meeting new patterns of stimulation: as he gazes about and even more as he starts to make exploratory forays, he is actively seeking new experiences. Exploratory behaviour (another admittedly loose category) comes to occupy more and more of his time as he develops: its complexity and diversity have been emphasized by Hutt (1970). Exploratory behaviour is at first made possible by the fact that, like birds, young primates do not show fear of strange objects or situations for a while after birth: there seems little doubt that processes comparable to the perceptual learning that occurs in chicks are important also in the acquisition of the response to strangeness in young primates. Fear of the unfamiliar requires a previous base line of the familiar, and that must be acquired by experience.

Whether the relations between the attractiveness of familiar and novel stimulus objects suggested by Bateson's model (pages 158–159) apply also to the primate infant is still not tested. A number of authors have stressed the importance for cognitive development of an optimal balance between discrepancy from and match with the models of the external world already formed by the child. Too little incongruity may produce boredom, too much may be stressful, and only a moderate degree of incongruity can lead to cognitive growth (e.g., Hunt, 1964, 1967). Although there have been a number of studies of the relative attractiveness, to infants of particular ages, of familiar and unfamiliar objects (e.g., McCall and Melson, 1969; McCall and Kagan, 1969; Weizman et al., 1971; Schaffer, 1973), more studies in which the effects of age and experience are controlled, with stimuli that differ in both familiarity and degree of difference, will be necessary to bring order to this important area (see Kagan et al., 1966).

We have seen that fear of the unfamiliar leads to an ending of the period during which chicks will follow novel objects (pages 151–154), and a comparable fear of strangers develops in young primates. Most human infants, after successively failing to discriminate strangers, responding positively to them, and behaving somewhat apprehensively in their presence, begin to show positive fear and attempt to withdraw from them: the age at which this occurs is variable but is between seven and fourteen months in most infants (Freedman, 1961; Ainsworth, 1967; Bronson, 1971; Schaffer et al., 1972). No doubt some of the individual variation in the onset of fear of strangers depends on experience: Schaffer (1966) believes that it starts later if the infant has previously had much social experience, and Robson et al. (1969) found a relationship between mother-infant gazing in the early months and the infant's response to strangers at eight to nine and one-half months. The complexity of the factors influencing the onset of stranger anxiety is emphasized by Brody and Axelrad (1971).

In this context the wide species differences in the amount of social experi-

FIGURE 12.10
*Rhesus infant showing intense fear.* (Drawing by Priscilla Edwards.)

ence that infant monkeys have before apprehension of strangers develops is of interest. In some monkeys, such as the langurs and bonnet macaques, the infant is held by a number of different individuals from soon after birth (Jay, 1965; Kaufman and Rosenblum, 1969b; Rosenblum, 1971a and b). Even in these species the infant sometimes struggles to return to his own mother, but the familiarity with a number of different individuals which the mother's permissiveness allows would seem likely to produce less stranger anxiety later. In other species, such as the rhesus macaque, many mothers do not permit their infants to be handled by other females, and their experience is consequently restricted.

Fear of novelty and of strangers could in principle bring an end to the infant's exploratory behaviour. If he was afraid of all situations with which he was not familiar, he could remain locked in his familiar environment for life. In chicks there appears to be an endogenously controlled reversal of the increasing tendency to avoid strange objects and situations: the persistence with which chicks reared in isolation avoid novel objects declines after the third day. Whether any comparable change occurs in primates is not known: monkeys reared in isolation show intense fear of novelty on release.

But of far greater importance here is the influence of the mother's proximity. In her presence strange objects and environments lose their terror and can be explored, touched, and manipulated before joining "the familiar". This has been demonstrated experimentally in monkeys. Young rhesus exposed to strange objects in the presence of a mother surrogate could explore them visually from the security of close contact with the surrogate, then make brief exploratory sallies toward them, and thus gradually achieve familiarity. In the absence of the mother surrogate they showed only intense fear (Fig. 12.10; Harlow and Harlow, 1965).

Not only can the mother's presence ameliorate the effects of strange and potentially frightening situations, it becomes increasingly necessary for the occurrence of all normal behaviour (e.g., Cairns, 1972a). Just as the chick ceases feeding and exploring if it loses visual contact with its mother, and shows instead distress calling and searching, so also does the young primate. Similarly the mother's proximity can help the human infant to come to terms with strange objects or strange situations. Whether a baby does in fact explore more in the mother's presence depends in part on the nature of their relationship and the personality of the baby (e.g., Escalona, 1969): indeed Ainsworth et al. (1971) have used the behaviour of year-old infants in a strange situation, with and without their mothers, as a means of assessing the quality of the mother-infant relationship (see page 240).

However, the mother does not act solely to reduce fear and enhance exploration. The mothers of young monkey infants at first restrain their exploratory sallies, holding on to a foot or tail, or pursuing them and picking them up. It is in this context that many of the early "conflicts of will" between mother and infant arise, the mother being restrictive of the infant's outgoing behaviour. We shall consider these changes in the next chapter. With older infants, the mother's example may augment the infant's fear in particular situations.

## Conclusion

The account of the formation of the mother-infant relationship given in the preceding pages has been much influenced by the work of Bowlby (1969, 1973): it is in part through his influence that our understanding of the early development of social relationships has been put on a firm footing during the last 20 years.[3]

Bowlby's approach is essentially biological. Pointing to the fact that in nature maintenance of proximity between mother and infant is necessary for the infant's survival, he regards the development of the mother-infant relationship as due to a number of response systems evolved specifically to that end. These are often collectively referred to as "attachment behaviour" (see also Ainsworth, 1967, 1969), though the use of a global term must be allowed to obscure neither

[3] A very valuable recent introduction to the development of social behaviour, combining a number of different approaches, is given by Schaffer (1971b).

the great diversity and complexity of the types of behaviour involved, nor the fact that they are not always closely correlated with one another (Cairns, 1972a; Coates et al., 1972a and b). In the young infant, Bowlby emphasizes especially sucking, clinging, following, crying, and smiling: these become incorporated into sophisticated "goal-corrected" systems which serve to maintain mutual proximity between mother and infant. The satisfaction by the mother of the infant's physiological needs also plays a role, but not a major one. An important corollary of Bowlby's approach is that the infant's social development is channelled by the repertoire of movement patterns, of responsiveness to stimuli, of perceptual and cognitive abilities with which he is equipped. Thus the infant is not passive clay upon which the effects of experience are imprinted. Just because he shows particular responses, just because his perceptual abilities are organized in particular ways, just because he actively explores his environment, he selects some forms of experience and bypasses others, thereby constructing his own environment: what he learns is constrained and directed by what he is (Hinde and Stevenson-Hinde, 1973). As the infant grows up, not only does the security he derives from his attachment to his mother-figure permit him to explore his environment and expand his cognitive skills, but his increasing cognitive skills permit him to internalize her image and to recognize that a mother temporarily absent is not a mother lost for ever. As the social bond with his mother becomes more and more able to withstand temporary absences it grows in complexity. Bowlby has stressed that one or more social relationships which provide stability in the infant's changing world but which have the flexibility to grow with him are essential to his development. To what extent it is necessary that there should be an enduring relationship with *one* particular mother or mother-figure is still controversial (see page 239), but there can be no doubt that the child's emotional development, his cognitive development, and his social situation are all closely interwoven.

A final word of caution concerning the cross-species comparisons that have been made is perhaps necessary. It is not suggested that the development of social relationships in man is just like that in chicks. Because certain principles derived from the study of chicks are relevant to and revealing for the human case does not mean that the study of a small number of response systems can give as nearly complete an understanding of the development of human social behaviour as it can of that of the chick. Indeed, as the above account has tried to show, human mother-infant interaction utilizes a great diversity of ritualized and non-ritualized signals; and involves communications for communication's sake to an extent which, in its implications for subsequent social development, differs in kind from that of non-human forms. And the account given in the preceding pages emphasizes those aspects of mother-infant interaction that we are beginning to understand at the expense of those we do not. It is one thing to relate the infant's smile to expressive movements in non-human forms, and smiling in greeting can perhaps be understood in terms of discrepancy between the familiar face and its imperfectly remembered image (page 183); but we are still a long way from understanding, for instance, all facets of the delight a baby can show when a parent returns home at the end of the day.

As a matter of fact the field of social development as a whole provides a wonderful example of the power of the comparative method. Principles emerge from the study of relatively simple animals and can there be studied to advantage. They may then turn out to help in the understanding of more complex animals, or even man. However the understanding that they bring is not complete: its shortcomings reveal further complexities which can then be studied in their own right. Sometimes consideration of these complexities reveals that related phenomena were in fact present in the simpler organisms but had been overlooked—perhaps because generalization so often involves simplification (page 4). Thus comparative studies of this sort can be a two-way process, throwing light both up and down the evolutionary scale.

## Summary

Newborn primates have a repertoire of movement patterns present at birth or developing soon thereafter, considerable perceptual abilities, and responsiveness to certain stimuli, which form the bases for their social behaviour. Adequate maternal behavior depends on previous social experience, but little is known about the mechanisms involved. Maternal motivation is influenced by, but not dependent upon, lactation, itself affected in a number of ways by stimulation from the young. In the course of the interaction with its mother, an infant's initially wide responsiveness becomes narrowed and the various filial responses are elicited preferentially by stimuli from the mother. Communication between mother and infant depends in part on social releasers and in part on less stereotyped and often idiosyncratic sequences of interaction: the latter may involve responsiveness to subtle expressive movements in the partner. With age the infant develops fear of the unfamiliar, but receives reassurance from the presence of the mother.

# 13

# THE COURSE
# OF RHESUS
# MOTHER-INFANT
# INTERACTION

### Introduction

In the last chapter we discussed in qualitative terms the formation of the mother-infant relationship and the processes whereby it begins to acquire its multiplex affectionate nature. Here we shall be concerned with the dynamics of that relationship over the period from infancy to early adolescence. A basic requirement for understanding the dynamics of a relationship is that the questions being asked should be clearly formulated. In what follows we shall discuss three which are often confused, arguing that they must be kept separate if understanding of the course of the relationship is to be achieved. These are:

1 What is the nature of the sequences of mother-infant interaction at any one age, and to what extent is each of the partners responsible for their initiation?

2 Are the age changes in the relationship primarily due to changes in the mother, to changes in the infant, or to both?

3 At any one age, are the differences observed between mother-infant pairs due to differences between mothers, differences between infants, or both?

In an interaction as complex as that between mother and infant primate, comprehensive answers to these questions are quite out of our reach. In this chapter we shall therefore focus primarily on one series of studies of rhesus monkeys, using them to illustrate one approach to the questions posed above. In doing so, we shall select data concerned with only two aspects of behaviour— that involved in ventro-ventral contact between mother and infant, and that involved in the maintenance of mutual proximity when the infant is off the mother. Data from other species, and the relevance to man of the principles that emerge, will be considered only briefly.

### Changes in the rhesus mother-infant relationship with age of infant

The newborn rhesus monkey remains in physical contact with his mother for 24 hr a day and is totally dependent on her. By the time he is two and one-half years old he may often sit near or even in contact with her, but for much of the time his behaviour is oriented toward his peers. We shall discuss data concerning these changes obtained from small captive groups of rhesus monkeys, each consisting of a male, two to four females, and their young. Each group lived in a 6-m-long outside pen connecting with an inside room. These conditions were of course far from natural, but at least the developing infants had a more complex social environment to grow up in than is often the case in laboratory studies, and yet reasonably precise observations were possible. The data were obtained by recording techniques which, though of only moderate precision, permitted simultaneous qualitative observation of the nature of the interactional sequences: although not so fine-grained as that which computer-based recording techniques are beginning to provide, they illustrate some important basic principles.

Figure 13.1 shows how five measures of mother-infant interaction change with age. There are two measures of mother-infant proximity—the *time that the infant spends off its mother,* and the *proportion of that time that it spends more than about 60 cm from her,* that is, out of arm's reach. For the first few days of its life the infant stays on its mother, clasping her in the ventro-ventral position, and usually attached to the nipple. Gradually it begins to move about a little on her body, and after a week or so it may leave her for the first time. At first the mother does not let it go far, but over the ensuing weeks it spends more and more time off her, and a higher and higher proportion of that time at a distance from her.

Two of the other measures in Fig. 13.1 are concerned with the relative roles of mother and infant in determining the amount of time that the infant spends on its mother. They are derived from counts of the number of occasions when the infant attempts to make ventro-ventral contact (see Fig. 12.1) and is accepted $Mk_I$ or rejected $R$ by the mother, the number of times contact is made on the mother's initiative $Mk_M$, and the number of ventro-ventral contacts that are broken by the mother $Bk_M$ or baby $Bk_I$. These are combined in two ways. First, the *relative frequency of rejections* is given by the ratio of the number of times that the infant attempts to get on its mother and is rejected $R$ to the total number of times it is accepted $Mk_I$, goes on on the mother's initiative $Mk_M$, or attempts unsuccessfully to get on $R$—i.e., $R/(Mk_I + Mk_M + R)$. Since the frequency with which the infant gains contact on the mother's initiative decreases rapidly over the first few months, the relative frequency of rejections soon approximates to the failure rate of the infant's attempts.

A related measure is the difference between the percentage of ventro-ventral contacts made on the infant's initiative and the percentage of contacts broken by the infant, i.e.,

$$\frac{Mk_I \times 100}{Mk_I + Mk_M} - \frac{Bk_I \times 100}{Bk_I + Bk_M} \text{ , abbreviated to } \% \, Mk_I - \% \, Bk_I$$

This is a measure of the *infant's role in ventro-ventral contact*—if the infant were responsible for all makes and no breaks it would have a value of +100 percent, and if the mother were responsible for all makes and no breaks it would be −100 percent (Hinde and White, 1974).

Figure 13.1 shows that, for young infants, this measure of the infant's role in ventro-ventral contacts is negative. This means that the proportion of contacts broken on the infant's initiative is higher than the proportion made by the infant. At this age, therefore, the mother is primarily responsible for ventro-ventral contacts. Later, however, this measure becomes positive, indicating that the infant becomes primarily responsible. This change is accompanied by an increase in the relative frequency of rejections—i.e., the mother rejects a higher proportion of the infant's attempts to gain ventro-ventral contact.

The last measure tells a similar story about the maintenance of proximity between mother and infant. The infant's role in maintaining proximity is assessed by counting the number of approaches (distance between mother and infant changes from more than 60 cm to less) and leavings (distance changes from less than 60 cm to more), and calculating the difference between the per-

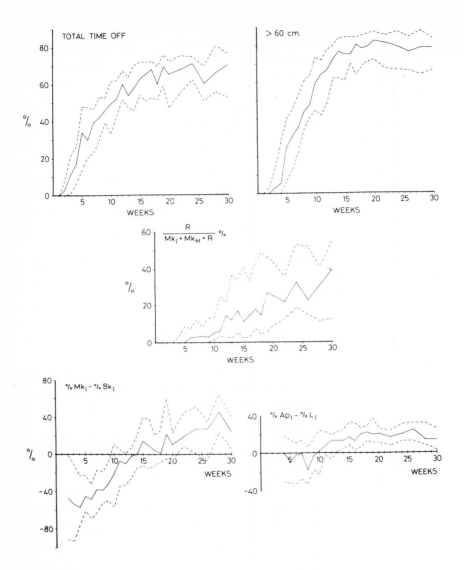

FIGURE 13.1

*The course of mother–infant interaction in small captive groups of rhesus monkeys. Top left: total time off mother (number of half-minutes in which infant was off mother as proportion of number watched). Top right: time out of arm's reach of mother (number of half-minutes in which infant was more than 60 cm from mother as proportion of number for which it was* centage of approaches due to movement by the infant and the percentage of leavings due to movement by the infant, i.e.,

$$\frac{Ap_I \times 100}{Ap_I - Ap_M} - \frac{L_I \times 100}{L_I + L_M} \text{ , abbreviated to } \% \ Ap_I - \% \ L_I$$

This measure of the *infant's role in maintaining proximity* also changes from negative to positive, indicating that in the early weeks the maintenance of proximity is mostly due to the mother, but later it is due to the infant (Hinde and Atkinson, 1970).

From data of this sort the following general picture emerges. During the first few days the infant is constantly on the mother. It starts to leave her when a week or two old, and during the next few months it leaves its mother more and more often in the course of exploring its environment or, when a few months old, playing with its peers. At first the mother often restricts the infant's movements by holding on to it when it attempts to leave: often the infant's tail or leg provides a convenient handle. At this stage the mother is primarily responsible for ventro-ventral contact (i.e., $\% \ Mk_I - \% \ Bk_I$ negative) and also for maintaining proximity (i.e., $\% \ Ap_I - \% \ L_I$ negative). Later the mother rejects more and more of the infant's attempts to gain contact and shows less concern if he goes to a distance from her. The infant then becomes primarily responsible for contact and for the maintenance of proximity (Hinde and Spencer-Booth, 1967a).

These data are concerned with only limited aspects of mother-infant interaction and must be interpreted with caution. For instance, although the mother

*off her). Centre: Relative frequency of rejections (ratio of number of occasions on which infant attempted to gain ventro-ventral contact and was rejected by mother (R) to number of occasions on which it made contact on mother's initiative (Mk$_M$), made contact on its own initiative (Mk$_I$), or attempted unsuccessfully to gain contact (R). Bottom left: Infant's role in ventro-ventral contacts (number of contacts made on infant's initiative, as a percentage of total number made, minus number of contacts broken by infant, as percentage of total number broken). Bottom right: Infant's role in maintenance of proximity (number of approaches, i.e., distance decreases from > 60 cm to < 60 cm, made by infant, as percentage of total number made, minus number of leavings made by infant, as percentage of total number made. Each point is based on data from 14 to 20 mother-infant pairs. Observations were made between 0900 and 1,300 hr over the first 30 weeks of life. Medians and inter-quartile ranges are shown.*

is primarily responsible for contact and proximity during the early weeks, stimuli from the infant are clearly important both in initiating many sequences of behaviour and for the mother's long-term maternal state. And again, the finding that after a few months the infant is primarily responsible for maintaining proximity when 60 cm distance is used as a criterion does not necessarily mean that the same would be true at longer distances (vanderStoep, personal communication). Studying free-living baboons, Owens (1973) found that the mothers played a greater relative role in maintaining proximity within 5 m than they did in maintaining it within 60 cm: the mother's behaviour tended to keep the infant out of arm's reach but within communicating distance. Furthermore, as distance communication becomes more important and as the infant becomes more sophisticated, the mere crossing of an arbitrary boundary could become potentially misleading as a guide to who was responsible for the change in the proximity.

Nevertheless the data are relevant to a current discussion over human mother-infant relations. For a long time it was customary to regard the child as passively moulded by the activities of his mother and other caretakers. Perhaps this was natural enough in that it is possible for pediatricians to instruct the mother but not the child. But it is an attitude that totally neglects the infant's repertoire of behaviour, the stimuli that he offers to his caretakers, and the extent to which he influences their behaviour. It neglects indeed the fact that mother and infant form a miniature social system, with each influencing the behaviour of the other. This point has recently been emphasized forcibly by Bell (1968, 1971), who contrasts the emphasis on the mother in studies of human development with the findings for other mammals, where the influence of the offspring on the mother is clearly recognized (Harper, 1970). We have already seen how the infant's smiles, cries, and other signals play a crucial part in determining the parents' behaviour. They act as elicitors of parental responses, as reinforcers determining the frequency and manner with which the parent interacts with the child, and on a longer term determine the parents' attitude toward the child (e.g., Ainsworth, 1963; Rheingold, 1968). Bell (1971) cites data showing that many interaction sequences are started by the child as often as by the mother. Such data have led to a general acceptance of the importance of the child's role, and of the need for the parent not merely to attempt to mould the child, but to order his or her behaviour in response to the child's changing nature. The need now would seem to be to add the age dimension by attempting to specify the relative roles of parent and child in interactions of different types at various ages.

## The relative importance of changes in mother and in infant in producing the age-changes observed

Each of the five measures of mother-infant interaction shown in Fig. 13.1 depends upon the behaviour of both mother and infant. Thus the age-changes shown could depend on changes in the infant's behaviour, changes in the mother's behaviour, or both. To understand the social development of the infant, it is necessary to teaze apart the role of changes in mother and infant in causing the age-changes observed.

A convenient starting point is to consider how far observed changes in the measures can be understood as the effects of one or more of four simple types of change in the participants, namely an increase or a decrease in the tendency of the mother or the infant to respond positively (i.e., other than by avoidance or aggression) to the other. The hypothesis that changes in the relationship depend on only four types of basic change will of course prove too simple, but it provides a convenient starting point.

The predicted directions of the effects of these simple basic changes on five measures of the mother-infant relationship are shown in Table 13.1. To take one example, an increase in the infant's positive responsiveness to its mother would lead to a decrease in the time it spent off her and in the time it spent at a distance from her, an increase in the relative frequency of rejections, and an increase in the infant's roles in both ventro-ventral contacts and maintaining proximity to its mother. Predictions can similarly be made for each of the other types of change. Now examination of the table shows that a *decrease* in the time the infant spends off its mother due to a change in the *infant's* behaviour will be accompanied by an *increase* in the infant's role in ventro-ventral contacts and in the relative frequency of rejections, whereas with a *decrease* in time off due to a change in the *mother's* behaviour there would also be a *decrease* in the infant's role in ventro-ventral contacts and the relative frequency of rejections. Thus the nature of the correlation between time off and the infant's role in ventro-ventral contacts, and of that between time off and the relative frequency of rejections, will reveal the relative importance of changes in the behaviour of the mother and of changes in the behaviour of the infant in causing the observed changes in time off the mother. If measures are taken at several different ages and time off is positively correlated with the other two measures, the age-changes must be due primarily to changes in the mother. If the correlations are negative, the age-changes must be due primarily to changes in the infant. If the correlations are low, changes in both mother and infant may be involved. By a similar argument, a positive correlation between the time spent at a distance from the mother and the infant's role in maintaining proximity indicates that changes in the mother's behaviour are primarily involved, and a negative correlation that changes in the infant's behaviour are. It will be apparent from the table that if changes in time off the mother and in time at a distance from the mother have the same basis, they will be positively correlated with each other: usually they are, but not always (Hinde, 1969b).

Bearing these principles in mind, we can look again at the data. It is apparent from Fig. 13.1 that as the time off the mother increases, so do the relative frequency of rejections and the infant's role in maintaining proximity. And as the time at a distance increases, so does the infant's role in maintaining proximity. Thus, from Table 13.1, the age-changes in the time that the infant spends off and at a distance from its mother are due more immediately to changes in the mother than to changes in the infant. This was a surprising conclusion, since the increasing independence of the infant is correlated with, and seems at first sight to be due to, its increasing physical stature and capacities, and its increasing interest in its social and physical environment. However, other lines of evidence confirm the importance of the mother's role. Infants reared on surrogates (see Fig. 12.4) showed a slower decrease in the frequency of body contacts than did infants reared by their own mothers (Hansen, 1966): this difference was presumably due to the absence of rejection by the inanimate mother surrogates.

TABLE 13.1 *Mother-infant relationship*\*

| | Total time off | Relative frequency of rejections, $R/(Mk_I + Mk_M + R)$ | Infant's role in ventro-ventral contact, $\% Mk_I - \% BK_I$ | Time at a distance from mother 60 cm | Infant's role in proximity, $\% Ap_I - \% L_I$ |
|---|---|---|---|---|---|
| Infant Mother $\longrightarrow$ | − | + | + | − | + |
| Infant Mother $\longleftarrow$ | + | − | − | + | − |
| Infant Mother $\longleftarrow$ | − | − | − | − | − |
| Infant Mother $\longrightarrow$ | + | + | + | + | + |

\* Predicted directions of change of five measures with four types of simple change in either mother or infant. These changes involve respectively an increase or a decrease in the infant's tendency to respond positively to the mother, or similar changes in the mother's tendency to respond positively to the infant.

Furthermore infants reared in groups of two or four, without mothers or surrogates, clung to each other with remarkable persistence: this also suggests that maternal rejection is important in the gradual decrease in ventro-ventral contact. Whilst it sometimes happens that maternal rejection increases rather than decreases the infant's dependent behaviour (Kaufman and Rosenblum, 1969a), this is likely to be marked only in a poor, homogeneous environment (Jensen et al., 1968), and if the infant is not yet ready for weaning. Rejection of a young infant by its mother may cause the infant to cling more tightly to its mother as the only source of security that it knows: an older infant similarly rejected might go off and feed itself or play with its peers. No doubt the extent to which the mother rejects the infant is determined in part by the infant's response.

This emphasis on the mother's role in the increasing independence of the infant does not imply that the infant would not achieve independence in the end if the mother took no action. That infants reared on inanimate mother surrogates *do* leave them more and more (see above) shows that changes in the infant which facilitate its independence are in fact occurring. Nor is it implied that the changes in the mother's behaviour arise endogenously. They may be initiated by changes in the infant's behaviour, such as its increasing demand for milk or its more vigorous locomotor play. Development involves a constant interaction between infant and mother which must be gradually teazed apart: thus the infant's changing milk consumption and play behaviour depend on prior maternal care, which in turn depends on signals from the infant, and so on. Furthermore at each stage the mother's behaviour to the infant is likely to be regulated by its results: she is less likely to persist with rejections if they lead to tighter clinging or to tantrums. But it is clear that the importance of changes in the mother's behaviour in permitting and promoting the independence of the infant is not to be underestimated; and it appears to be changes in her that immediately regulate the speed with which independence is achieved.

This analysis underlines the necessity, in studies of development, for specifying rather precisely the questions that are being asked. We have seen that during the early weeks it is the mother who is primarily responsible for the maintenance of proximity with the infant (i.e., infant's role, % $Ap$ − % $L$, is negative). We have also seen that during that period it is changes in the mother's behaviour that are primarily responsible for the *decreasing* proximity of the infant. Thus the question of whether mother or baby is mainly responsible for the maintenance of proximity at any one age is a different question from whether it is changes in the mother or changes in the infant that are primarily responsible for changes in mother-infant proximity with age.

Of course any account which attempts to assign responsibility to one or other partner for changes in a social relationship is almost bound to be an over-simplification. Although the above analysis underlines the importance of the mother's role in the age-changes observed, it undervalues changes in other aspects of the relationship. These have already been referred to briefly (Chap. 12), and we may exemplify them here with some further data about rhesus infants. From records of the bouts of continuous ventro-ventral contact between mother and infant it is possible to calculate the probability that the infant will terminate the bout during each successive half minute after its "initiation", and the probability that the mother will. For infants up to eight months old the probability that the infant will terminate the bout in each successive time interval is about the same for bouts that were initiated by the infant and bouts that were initiated by the mother. The same is true for the probability that the mother will terminate the bout. However there are slight differences. With young infants (one to four weeks old) the infant is slightly more likely to terminate the bout in each time interval if the mother initiated it than if he did, and the mother is slightly more likely to terminate it if the infant initiated it than if she did. By twenty-eight to thirty-two weeks this difference has disappeared and even reversed. Approximately the same is true for bouts *not* in ventro-ventral contact (Fig. 13.2). This age-change indicates an increasing integration of the behaviour of mother and infant: while at first each is likely to initiate a bout (in or out of contact) when the other is not ready to reciprocate and thus likely to break it off, later the behaviour of each partner becomes better regulated in relation to the ongoing behaviour of the other. This increasing mutual adjustment, which takes place during a period when the behaviour of each partner is itself changing, seems at first to be out of harmony with the decreasing intimacy of the relationship, but the two must not be confused: intimacy here is inferred from measures of time spent together, mutual adjustment from the manner in which the time spent together is determined.

Whether the conclusions that have been drawn about the mother's role in the increasing independence of the infant are applicable also to the human case is not yet clear. Just as with the rhesus monkey, the distance that a human child will go from its mother increases with age. In a study of mothers and children placed on an unfamiliar unfenced lawn, Rheingold and Eckerman (1971) found that the mean farthest distance that the infant travelled from the mother increased from 6.9 m by one-year-olds to 20.6 m by four-year-olds (see also Anderson, 1972). Furthermore, the readiness with which infants would leave their mothers could be increased by attractive toys. However this does not necessarily mean that the age-changes in the relationship are due to changes in the infant. Rheingold and Eckerman's discussion of the "process by which the infant separates from his mother" suffers from a failure to distinguish between questions concerning the distribution of responsibility for the nature of the relationship at any one age, and the questions concerning the way in which changes in the partners contribute to changes in the relationship: the subtlety and complexity of the relationship are thereby underestimated.

## Mother-infant interaction and gene survival

In the last section evidence that the mother plays a considerable part in promoting the independence of her infant was presented. Here we shall turn briefly to a quite different type of argument, considering not the immediate dynamics of the mother-infant relationship but its nature from the point of view of evolution. In an important paper Trivers (in press) has shown how the mother's role in promoting the independence of her infant makes sense from the point of view of natural selection.

It is in theory possible to assess, for any behavioural interaction, the benefit and cost to each participant in terms of the effects on their eventual reproductive success. But in computing the selective value of a genetic change affecting an interaction, one must consider the effect of that change not only on the individual involved but also on the reproductive success of all related individuals, appropriately devalued by the relevant degrees of relationship. The degree of relationship can be calculated in terms of the number of genes shared by common descent. Thus an infant shares half its genes with each parent and, assuming that he had both parents in common with his siblings, half his genes with each sibling: if the mother was sired by a different male for each birth, each infant would share on average only one-fourth its genes with each sibling. By allowing in this way for effects on the reproductive success of related individuals one can obtain a measure of the "inclusive fitness" (Hamilton, 1964) of a genetic change.

Now the mother-infant relationship can be considered in terms of the benefit and cost to each member of the dyad. Benefit to the mother is to be measured in terms of the eventual reproductive success of the current offspring, cost in terms of any reduction in the probable reproductive success of future offspring consequent upon her investment in the current one. (Possible effects on other related individuals, e.g., cousins, are for present purposes neglected.) Bene-

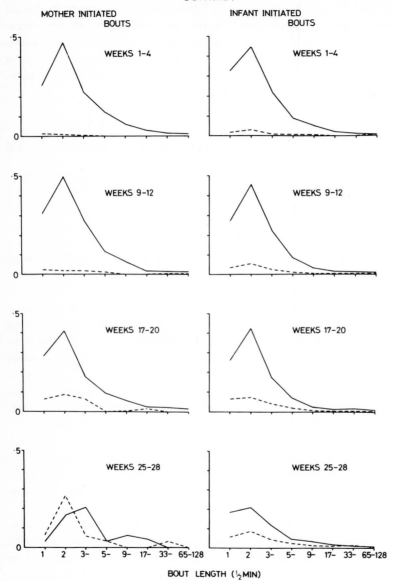

## (a) BOUTS IN VENTRO-VENTRAL CONTACT

MOTHER INITIATED BOUTS    INFANT INITIATED BOUTS

WEEKS 1–4    WEEKS 1–4

WEEKS 9–12    WEEKS 9–12

WEEKS 17–20    WEEKS 17–20

WEEKS 25–28    WEEKS 25–28

BOUT LENGTH (½ MIN)

FIGURE 13.2

(a) *Probability that bouts of ventro-ventral contact between mother and infant would be terminated by infant (continuous line) or mother*

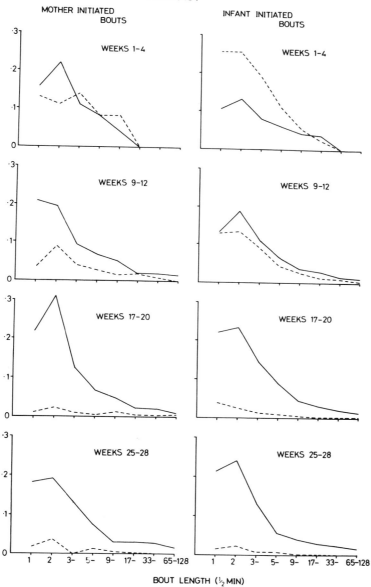

(b) BOUTS OUT OF VENTRO-VENTRAL CONTACT

*(discontinuous line) in successive time intervals after their initiation. Bouts initiated by mother (left) and infant (right) are shown separately. (Hinde and White, 1973.) (b) The same as in (a) but for bouts out of ventro-ventral contact.*

fit to the infant lies in his own reproductive success, cost in any reduction in the reproductive success of his (unborn) siblings. Now when the infant is small, he is absolutely dependent on nursing, and the cost of nursing to the mother is relatively small. But as the infant becomes increasingly able to feed itself, the benefit it derives from nursing decreases. At the same time, since the infant is growing and thus presumably requires more milk, the cost to the mother increases. If cost and benefit are measured in the same units, the cost to the mother will eventually come to exceed the benefit to the young, so that the mother's long-term reproductive success will decrease if she continues to nurse. However, the infant will continue to benefit from the nursing in his own right, and the cost to the mother will affect his inclusive fitness only half as much as it affects the mother's, since only half their genes are shared. Thus until the cost to the mother is more than twice the benefit to the infant, the infant's overall fitness will continue to be higher than if he did not nurse. Thus between the time when the benefit and cost to the mother are equal, and when the cost becomes twice the benefit, continued nursing will reduce the mother's inclusive fitness but still enhance that of the infant. During this period natural selection will favour the mother's halting maternal behaviour and the infant's eliciting it.

On this argument the period during which natural selection will operate in opposite ways on mother and infant will depend on whether future offspring of the mother will also share the same father, and on the rate of change of benefit and cost to the organism in question. However we have so far been concerned only with the question of whether *any* parental investment should be made. Trivers has extended his argument to consider also *how much*. At any point in the period of parental care the mother is selected to invest that amount of care which maximizes the difference between the associated cost and benefit, but the infant is selected to elicit that investment which maximizes the difference between the benefit and half the cost. On any reasonable assumptions about the rate of change of benefit and cost curves with age, the infant must be selected to elicit more parental investment than the parent is selected to provide. Hence throughout the whole period of dependency the infant will be tending to demand more than it is in the parent's interest (from the point of view of natural selection) to give. It will be apparent that Trivers's argument is in harmony with the observation that the mother plays an important role in promoting the independence of the infant, as demonstrated by the data in the preceding section.

Trivers has extended this interesting line of argument to consider other aspects of social relations within families of various sorts, and his conclusions provide a new perspective from which to view early social behaviour.

## Contributions of differences between mothers and between infants to differences between relationships

We may now consider briefly the third question—to what extent are differences between the relationships of different mother-infant pairs at any one age due to differences between mothers and to what extent to differences between infants? A moment's consideration will show that this is not the same as asking who initiates interactions at the age in question: when most interactions are initiated by the infant, differences in the responsiveness of mothers could be primarily responsible for observed differences between relationships.

The model in Table 13.1, used earlier for age-changes in the mother-infant relationship, can be applied also to differences between relationships at one age. From data for a number of mother-infant pairs at any one age we can calculate the (rank-order) correlation coefficients between the various measures of mother-infant interaction. If the coefficients between time off the mother and the infant's role in ventro-ventral contact were +1.0, differences between mothers would be entirely responsible for the differences in time off observed, and similarly for time at a distance. If the coefficients were −1.0, then differences between infants would be responsible. Intermediate figures indicate the relative importance of differences between mothers and differences between infants.

Some data for rhesus monkeys, selected to illustrate the sort of conclusion that can be reached, are shown in Table 13.2. They show that

1 In all age ranges considered, the infants that play a large role in ventro-ventral contacts also play a large role in maintaining proximity when off their mothers.

TABLE 13.2 *Mother-infant relationship: data for 19 rhesus pairs\*: Spearman (rank-order) correlation cofficients between individual mean scores over the periods indicated.*

| Correlation between | Period, in weeks | | | |
|---|---|---|---|---|
| | 1–4 | 9–12 | 17–20 | 25–28 |
| % $Mk_I$ − % $Bk_I$ and % $Ap_I$ − % $L_I$ | 0.65‡ | 0.79‡ | 0.67‡ | 0.55† |
| Total time off and $R/Mk_I + Mk_M + R)$ | 0.61‡ | 0.22 | 0.46† | 0.35 |
| % $Mk_I$ − % $Bk_I$ and $R/(Mk_I + Mk_M + R)$ | 0.48† | 0.62‡ | 0.67‡ | 0.09 |

*A correlation coefficient of 1.0 would mean that the mother-infant pair highest on one measure was also highest on the other, the second highest on one measure was also second highest on the other, and so on. A correlation of −1.0 would mean that the highest on one measure was the lowest on the other, and so on. A correlation of 0 would mean no relation between the scores on the two measures.
† $<0.05$.
‡ $<0.01$.

2 Differences between mother-infant pairs in the time that the infant spends off the mother are primarily due to differences between mothers (cf. Table 13.1). The decrease (rather irregular, according to these data) in the correlations with age indicate a decrease in the relative importance of differences between mothers as compared with differences between infants.

3 Up to week 20 those infants who play the largest part in ventro-ventral contacts are rejected in the highest proportion of their attempts to gain contact. Later, however, this relationship disappears. The latter finding is an indication of smoother mother-infant relations (cf. page 202), with the infant's approaches being determined by distance signals from the mother.

### Temporary mother-infant separation

In its early weeks of life, the mother is the only social companion of any importance to the rhesus monkey infant. Once it is a few months old, it spends much time playing with other infants, and may form relationships with other adults, as we shall see in Chap. 14. But over the first year or so, all social interactions depend on the presence of the mother as a secure base. The infant goes out from her, and returns to her. He continues to sleep on or with her at night. If he temporarily loses sight of his mother, he gives distress calls and shows clear signs of disturbance. What, one may ask, is the effect of a somewhat longer period of separation? Does development return immediately to its original course on reunion, or is it temporarily or permanently diverted? Experiments involving temporary separation of mother and infant monkeys have been carried out in several laboratories, and have provided further insight into the nature of the mother-infant relationship.

If the mother of a six-month-old rhesus infant is removed from the group in which they were living for a few days, the infant remaining otherwise in the same environment as it had been in previously, its initial response involves frequent distress calls (Fig. 13.3). It may show a brief period of hyperactivity during which it appears to be searching for its mother, but very soon it becomes depressed. Its locomotor activity falls to a low level, and it shuffles about in a hunched depressed posture (Fig. 13.4). The frequency of distress calling falls off considerably but remains well above pre-separation levels. If the separation period is prolonged, there may be some recovery of locomotor activity, but this varies considerably between individuals. These effects of separation from the mother presumably result not only because the infant can no longer interact

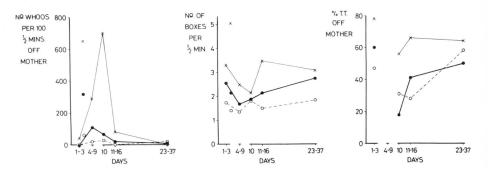

FIGURE 13.3

*The effects of a 6-day-separation experience on rhesus monkey infants. From left to right, frequency of distress calls, a measure of locomotor activity, and the time off the mother (see Fig. 12.1). The mother was removed on day 4 and returned on day 10. The thick line connects the medians (16 infants) for data in the pre-separation period (days 1 to 3), the separation period (days 4 to 9), the day of reunion (day 10), and two later periods. The thin lines show individual data for the two infants with the most extreme pre-separation scores. The points off the lines are for the first day of separation: these data are included in the separation median. Infants were twenty-one to thirty-two weeks old at the time of the separation experience. (From Spencer-Booth and Hinde, 1971.)*

with her, but also because of the disappearance of the support which her presence provides for all aspects of his behaviour (Cairns, 1972a). We have seen that proximity to the mother is a sine qua non for all normal behaviour: she forms the most important feature in his world, and with her disappearance his behaviour is inevitably disrupted.

When the mother is returned to the group, mother and infant usually come together immediately. The infant's hunched posture disappears fairly quickly, and in a week or two he may return to his pre-separation level of locomotor activity. The infant is often first very clinging, and the mother usually first accedes to the infant's demands, then rejects them, and then there is a slow period of readjustment. The severity of the effect is increased, and the rate of recovery after reunion decreased, with longer periods of separation.

Although all rhesus infants separated from their mothers show these responses to some degree, there are startling individual differences. No doubt

FIGURE 13.4
*Rhesus infant showing depressed posture frequently adopted during separation from mother.* (Drawing by Priscilla Edwards.)

many factors influence the infant's response to separation, but an important issue seems to be the nature of the relationship he had with his mother beforehand. Those infants whose attempts to gain ventro-ventral contact have been rejected most by their mothers, and which have had to play the greatest role in maintaining mutual proximity, tend to be most distressed during and after separation. Speaking colloquially, the more secure the infant beforehand, the less he is distressed on reunion after a temporary period of separation (Spencer-Booth and Hinde, 1971a; Hinde and Spencer-Booth, 1970, 1971).[1]

   This fits with another, at first sight rather surprising, finding. If separation experiments are performed the other way round—that is, if the mother is left in her home pen and the infant is temporarily removed—the infant suffers both separation from his mother and the trauma of exposure to strange surroundings. We might thus expect the distress to be greater than when the separation is effected by leaving the infant in his home pen, the mother being removed. During the period of separation this may be the case, though the evidence suggests that the difference is one of kind rather than degree: infants whose mothers are

[1] Trivers (in press) points out that these results are in keeping with his views on parent-offspring conflict (see pages 203–206). Thus the increase in infant initiative in staying near the mother after reunion is consistent with the assumption that the infant has been selected to respond to its mother's disappearance as an event whose recurrence it can help to prevent by devoting more of its energies to staying close to her. Similarly, the fact that the infant of a relatively rejecting mother responds more strongly after reunion than the infant of a less rejecting mother supports the view that the infant has been selected to adjust its behaviour to a mother who temporarily disappears in a logical way, treating a previously rejecting mother as more likely to disappear again than a less rejecting one.

removed soon become depressed, while infants removed to a strange place often show considerable hyperactivity. Be that as it may, after reunion the infants who had themselves been removed show less distress than those whose mothers had been temporarily placed elsewhere: their locomotor activity soon rises to pre-separation levels, and their distress calling remains low (Fig. 13.5). The key seems to be in the trauma suffered by the mothers. Mothers who have been in the home pen during the separation period are ready to accede to the infant's demands as soon as he is returned. The infant is rejected little and has to play a smaller relative role in the maintenance of proximity. The infant is thus comforted, and his behaviour soon becomes relatively normal. But if the mothers have themselves been disturbed by removal, and must also re-establish their social relations with group companions on their return, they are less able to cope with their infants, who continue to manifest considerable distress.

These results point to the importance of the mother's behaviour in re-establishing the infant's security after the reunion. They also indicate that it is not only the prior experience of separation itself that leads to the infant's continuing distress after reunion, but the disruption of the mother-infant bond that results from the separation period. Further experiments showed that mere exposure of mother and infant to a strange environment, without separation, does not produce continuing distress in the infant after return to the home cage. If both mother and infant are removed from the home situation to a distant cage for a few days and then returned, the infant shows little distress and begins to play with his group companions almost immediately after he gets back. Although the mother must re-establish relations with her group companions, the infant is not particularly demanding as he has not been separated from her. But if mother and infant are removed from the group and separated from each other, the infant shows considerable distress after their reunion within the home group, and plays little (L. McGinnis, in preparation).

Another factor which may be important here must be mentioned. If the infant remains in the home pen while its mother is away it may become adversely conditioned to it, while if it has itself been removed, it will have suffered no aversive experiences there (see Gewirtz, 1961): this again could lead to infants whose mothers had been removed showing more distress after reunion (Hinde and Davies, 1972a and b). Thus a separation experience has a number of aspects, each of which may affect the subsequent behaviour of the infant: further experiments will be necessary before these aspects can be fully assessed.

A brief period of separation from the mother can have long-term effects on rhesus monkeys. Infants whose mothers were removed for one or two periods

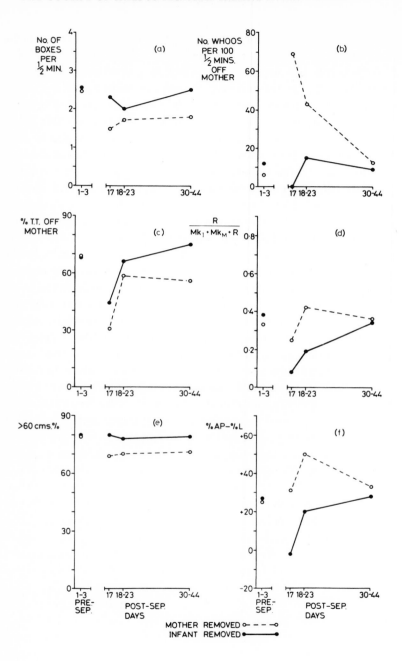

of 6 days when they were six to eight months old behaved differently from controls in tests given when they were twelve and thirty months old. The differences can be roughly characterized as involving greater disturbance by strange objects, and were apparent only when the infants were tested in a strange pen (Spencer-Booth and Hinde, 1971b). In another study, Sackett (1968) found that infants which had been frequently separated from their mothers in early life were lower in social dominance than controls at three years of age.

Other experiments on the effects of brief periods of separation in rhesus, in other macaques, and in other species of monkeys have produced results broadly similar to these.[2] In squirrel monkeys, infants who receive maternal care from other females during the separation period are less affected (Rosenblum, 1971b). Comparable symptoms are shown also by infants or juveniles separated from peers with whom they have been brought up (Suomi et al., 1970; Erwin et al., 1971). Furthermore, field data show that young wild-living chimpanzees which lose their mothers also show symptoms of depression generally similar to those described here: one, fourteen months of age, died of malnutrition; two, each three to four years old, were adopted by older siblings, but one died after about 18 months; and another three-year-old disappeared, and presumably died, after about 2 months (van Lawick-Goodall, 1971a and b). Another rather exceptional case, documented in detail by Thorndahl (personal communication), concerns an eight-year-old male chimpanzee who was still dependent upon his mother. When she died he left her body only briefly for the first 3 days, made only brief interactions with other chimpanzees during the next few days, became steadily more depressed and withdrawn, showed severe anorexia, and eventually died 26

[2] See, for example, Jensen and Tolman, 1962; Seay et al., 1962; Seay and Harlow, 1965; Kaufman and Rosenblum, 1969a; Kaplan, 1970; Preston et al., 1970. Data on various forms of deprivation in a variety of species are reviewed by Brofenbrenner, 1968, and Scott, 1971.

---

FIGURE 13.5

*Comparison of the effects of separating mother and infant rhesus monkeys when the separation involved removing the mother, leaving the infant in the home pen (i.e., "mother removed"), and removing the infant, leaving the mother in the home pen (i.e., "infant removed"). The separations were made on day 4, and mother and baby were re-united on day 17. Group medians are shown (N = 5 or 6). For further description of measures used, see legends to Figs. 13.1 and 13.3.*

days after his mother. Although a post-mortem showed considerable parasitic infection, the course of events suggested that the death of his mother was an important factor in causing his own.

Most of the experimental work on this subject was undertaken with the specific intention of tackling a problem in human behaviour. Spitz (e.g., 1946, 1950) described a syndrome of "anaclitic depression" shown by children living in a nursery. The symptoms included apprehension, sadness, withdrawal, crying, insomnia, anorexia, and so on. The best therapeutic measure was the return of the mother. About the same time Bowlby (1951, 1969, 1973) found that children undergoing temporary separation from their mothers often showed acute symptoms of stress, and suggested that such an experience could have long-term effects on personality development. At the time such ideas were met with profound scepticism: indeed in many hospitals it was accepted practice not to allow parents to visit their children on the grounds that the children were "upset" when they went away again.

But since Bowlby's early papers a great deal of clinical evidence has shown conclusively that, under certain circumstances, an inadequate relationship with or separation from the mother-figure (and of course this does not necessarily mean the natural mother) can have profound effects (Ainsworth, 1962; Bowlby, 1969, 1973; Rutter, 1972). While diverse consequences have thus been traced to "maternal deprivation", the present need is to sort out the various factors involved, the various symptoms to which they give rise, and the relations among them. Much confusion has arisen from the lumping together of cases in which the child failed to form adequate bonds[3] in early life, cases in which bonds were formed but were later disrupted, and various other forms of stress and deprivation in the early years (see, for example, Howells, 1970). In an important review Rutter (1972) writes as follows:

*. . . the syndrome of acute distress is probably due in part to a disruption of the bonding process (not necessarily with the mother); developmental retardation and intellectual impairment are both a consequence of privation of perceptual and linguistic experience; dwarfism is usually due to nutritional privation; enuresis is sometimes a result of stressful experiences in the first five years; delinquency follows family discord; and psychopathy may be the end product of a failure to develop bonds or attachments in the first three years of life. None of*

[3] "Bond" is used for an affectionate relationship (see pages 18–19).

*these suggestions has yet got firm and unequivocal empirical support and it is important to remember that they remain hypotheses which require rigorous testing.*

Of these, of course, it is the disruption of bonds to which the monkey work is most relevant, and in the context of this book it is of some interest to examine just how the monkey data relate to those obtained with children in Western European and North American cultures. The fact that the symptoms are similar is in itself of interest, for rhesus monkeys presumably operate at a simpler cognitive level than do human children. Thus, *insofar as* the symptoms are similar, they *require* no more complex explanation for the human case than is necessary for monkeys. This implies no lack of appreciation of the importance of cognitive factors in separation anxiety in either monkey or man (Littenberg et al., 1971). Second, the distress of rhesus monkeys after their mothers had been removed was related to the frequency with which their attempts to gain contact had been rejected and the role they had had to play in keeping near their mothers before separation. These are the inverse of the qualities of maternal responsiveness and initiative that Schaffer and Emerson (1964) found to be important in the formation of human mother-child relationships—namely the readiness with which a mother responded to her infant's crying and the extent to which she took the initiative in interactions with it. In neither the study of mother-infant separation in monkeys, nor that of mother-infant affection in man, was the actual amount of time that mother and infant spent together a factor of major importance within the range of variation encountered.

Third, the finding that infants showed more distress on reunion if their mothers had been removed from them than if they had been removed from their mothers seems unlikely to be parallelled in the human case. We would expect children taken away to a strange place to be more upset afterwards than children left at home while their mothers went away for awhile. But at a deeper level of analysis the monkey findings are suggestive. They indicate that in a separation experience, while the trauma of separation may itself be important, the mother's behaviour on reunion and the disturbance of the mother-infant relationship may also be important issues. This is likely also to be true of man.

This question of the level of analysis at which generalizations should be made is relevant also to another issue. The comparisons being made are between rhesus monkeys and children in Western European and North American cultures. The effects of separation may well be much less in cultures where an extended family situation is usual. The importance of the nature of the relationship or relationships between the child and its caretaker(s) is however likely to be equally great.

Finally, the finding that long-term effects of a short period of maternal deprivation occur in rhesus monkeys strengthens the evidence that such effects occur also in man. While there is plenty of evidence that separation from the mother can cause immediate acute distress in human children, the evidence that separation experiences alone can cause long-term deleterious consequences has rested largely on clinical material (Bowlby, 1969, 1973), and has not always been supported by survey data (e.g. Howells, 1970, Rutter, 1972). However Douglas (in press), using data from a large sample, has recently shown that children who have spent more than a week in hospital, or who have been admitted on more than one occasion, before the age of five, are more likely to be adversely rated in adolescence than those who have not been so admitted. The variables concerned involved reading ability, teachers' assessments of troublesome behaviour out of class, delinquency, and instability in jobs immediately after leaving school. In the latter two cases the association with hospital experience before the age of five was found only for children who experienced further hospital admissions between five and fifteen. While the objection that a stay in hospital involves other unpleasant experiences in addition to separation from the mother can not be answered from these data, it now seems almost certain that a separation experience may have a long term effect on behaviour development.

Of course the responses shown on the loss of a loved one are not precisely the same in monkey and man. For reasons which are not fully understood, children often reject their mothers for a while after reunion, ignoring them or behaving to them as though they were strangers: this pattern of behaviour persists for longer, the longer the separation has lasted. Such behaviour is less common in monkeys (but see Rosenblum, 1971b). As just mentioned, in children temporary separation does not necessarily involve disruption of the bond with a loved one, for a bond can be maintained in the absence of physical presence: it is unknown how far similar processes operate in monkeys. And the distinction between "grief", the "biological" response to separation or bereavement shown by both animals and man, and human "mourning", the conventional behaviour dictated by the mores and customs of the society, is clearly of great importance (Averill, 1968). In any case, the types of separation experience which humans undergo are more diverse and more severe than any yet studied experimentally in monkeys (see Yarrow, 1964).

It remains to emphasize that the trend of the evidence is to indicate that an important aspect of a separation is the bond disruption which accompanies it.

This implies that the effects of separation will vary with age. They are likely to be less severe with children too young to form a bond, and with children old enough either to sustain a relationship without physical presence or to be independent, than with children of intermediate age. The consequences of the disruption of any one bond will also be influenced by the alternatives available: the effects of mother-infant separation may be much ameliorated if the child has strong bonds with his father and siblings, and especially if he lives in some form of extended family.

Just because so many factors may influence the effects of separation, the evidence that separation can be damaging must not be over-interpreted to suggest that it must necessarily be so. The happiness of the child depends on that of the mother, and in some cases too rigid a sense of maternal duty may not be conducive to relaxed and happy motherhood. In any case some separations are almost inevitable for every child, and in some distressing circumstances it may even be better for a child to be away from its mother. But the relationships that a child forms are crucial for its subsequent social development.

### Summary and conclusion

Most of the material in this chapter has been concerned with limited aspects of the developing relationship between the infant rhesus monkey and its mother. Several questions about the dynamics of the relationship were first distinguished. These questions concerned the effects of *changes* or *differences* in mother or infant, and the observant reader may have noted that similar principles determine the questions that can most profitably be asked about both the development of patterns of behaviour (Chap. 4) and the development of relationships—in the former case *differences* in genetic constitution or environment, in the latter *differences* in the nature of one or other partner.

An approach toward answering the questions posed, dependent on the examination of correlations between measures, has been outlined. Experimental interference, such as temporary separation between mother and infant, can also illuminate the nature of the interaction. Although the measures used are crude, they demonstrate the complexity and subtlety of the relationship. Appreciation of complexity brings scepticism of many of the global qualities often used to describe the mother-infant relationship, such as "attachment" and "maternal sensitivity". Yet we use such qualities every day in describing relationships. Herein lies the challenge of studying interpersonal relationships. Relationships depend on, and indeed *are*, sequences of detailed interactions: the qualities by which we habitually distinguish them too often turn out to apply to a narrower range of phenomena than we had hoped. Clearly one of the most urgent tasks at the present time is to define the limits of usefulness of some of the concepts which, at any rate in day-to-day dealings, we are bound to use in describing relationships.

# 14

# SOCIAL COMPANIONS OTHER THAN THE MOTHER

### Introduction

In its early weeks of life, the mother is the only social companion of any importance to the non-human primate infant. Soon, however, it starts to interact with other members of its species. In this chapter we shall consider briefly the nature of its relationships with them.

### Aunts

Older females, referred to here as "aunts" though without any implication of blood relationship, are of special importance in many group-living species. In a study of captive rhesus macaques, Spencer-Booth (1968b) found that, as in man (Brindley et al., 1973), older females interacted with infants much more than did older males; and that, amongst the females, it was those not yet quite adult that were most attracted to the infants. Nulliparous adult females tended to interact with infants more than females who had had young of their own. The behaviour

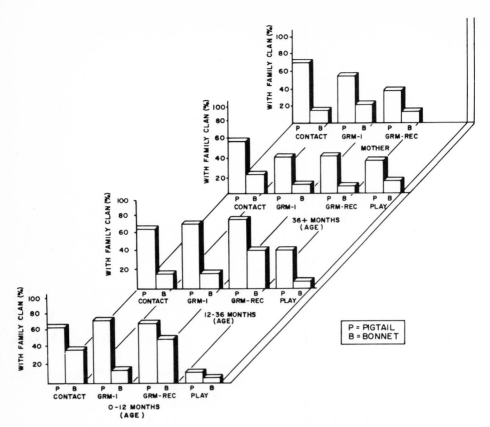

FIGURE 14.1

*The relative involvement with family-clan members in bonnet and pig-tailed macaques as a function of age. The four types of behaviour depicted are physical contact, initiating grooming, receiving grooming, and social play. (From Rosenblum, 1971.)*

shown toward the infants included investigation, grooming, protection, cuddling and carrying, play, and aggression. Its nature and extent appeared to depend on a number of factors—the age of the infant, young ones being more likely to elicit maternal behaviour and older ones social and aggressive responses; the behaviour of the infants, who might either avoid or seek the aunts' attention; and the mother, who restricts her infant's interactions. In the case of orphans, it may proceed to the point of adoption (Sade, 1965).

Though rhesus mothers do not permit their infants to interact much with other females during the early weeks of life, other species are more permissive.

Langur mothers, for instance, allow their infants to be passed around from hand to hand amongst adult females within a few hours of birth (Jay, 1965; Poirier, 1968). Black-and-white colobus monkey infants are often held by other members of the troop when 3–5 months old (Leskes and Acheson, 1971). The same holds for Douc langurs (Hill, 1972) and for vervets (Lancaster, 1971).

In a few cases the effects of such interspecies differences in maternal temperament on the development of the young have been studied under controlled conditions. Thus Kaufman and Rosenblum (1969a, b) compared the course of mother-infant relations in the pig-tailed and bonnet macaques. In the pig-tailed macaque the course of mother-infant relations is similar to that described earlier for the rhesus. The bonnet mothers, however, have a generally more relaxed attitude: they restrain, guard, and retrieve their young less than do pig-tailed mothers. The bonnet infant thus spends more time at a distance from its mother, interacts much more with other females, and plays more with other young. Later, the pig-tailed mothers continue their relatively coercive maternal pattern by rejecting and punishing their infants at the time of weaning much more than do bonnets. These differences between bonnet and pig-tailed macaques have far-reaching effects. Under laboratory conditions Rosenblum (1971a) has shown that pig-tailed macaques direct more of their social behaviour toward other members of the same clan (i.e., their mother and her other offspring) than do bonnets (Fig. 14.1). Rosenblum suggests that this is because the pig-tailed infants interact less with individuals other than their mother, and therefore establish a more enduring and selective relationship with her, than is the case with bonnets. This strong relationship with the mother facilitates the growth of attachments to siblings older and younger.

Since females who relate closely with one another within a troop are thus likely to be related, care for another's offspring may be adaptive (see page 203). It may also provide practice which will aid the aunt when she bears an infant herself (see page 172). However care by an aunt does not always aid survival. Hunkeler et al. (1972) describes a case in Lowe's guenon where a mother who became ill after parturition allowed her infant to be adopted by another female. After a few days the infant died, apparently of starvation, while the mother survived.

## Males

The extent to which young monkeys interact with adult males varies greatly among species. At one extreme lie certain New World monkeys, among which the infant is carried for much of the time by the male (e.g., marmosets, Hampton

FIGURE 14.2
*Rhesus male and infant.* (Drawing by Priscilla Edwards.)

et al., 1966; Epple, 1967; titi monkey, Mason, 1968; *Callimico goeldii*, Heltne et al., 1973). At the other extreme are species such as the patas monkey, whose males normally stay somewhat aloof from the troop and even in captivity show little interest in infants (Hall, 1965; Hall et al., 1965).

Most species lie between these extremes. The males protect the infants from predators and intruders, show some interest and considerable tolerance of them, sometimes interfere actively in disputes on their behalf, but rarely show anything approaching maternal behaviour.

In the rhesus monkey the males are tolerant and protective of infants, but only occasional individual adult males initiate interaction and play with them (Fig. 14.2), though under certain captive conditions males seem to play with infants more regularly (Harlow et al., 1971; Redican and Mitchell, 1973). In some other group-living species, however—even species closely related to the rhesus—the males interact freely with the infants and often carry them about. In the Japanese macaque the males in some (but not all) troops care for infants during the birth season, while the mothers are preoccupied with the newborns (Itani, 1963; Alexander, 1970). In the Barbary macaque the males show a marked tendency to interact with infants. They may carry them when the group is in a dangerous situation, and play with them when the group is relaxed. Sometimes a male seems to use an infant as a "passport" for approaching another animal in a situation in which tension is potentially present: possession of the infant may protect him from attack (Deag, 1973; Deag and Crook, 1971).

In baboons (*Papio anubis*) at the Gombe National Park, Tanzania, Ransom and Ransom (1971) observed a number of types of special relationships between adult males and infants:

1 Some adult males had long-lasting relationships with females which did not depend on the oestrous cycle of the female. When the female gave birth, this relationship might be widened to include her offspring. The male would remain with the infant in the mother's absence, grooming it and sometimes carrying it. This sort of relationship was most marked in the case of multiparous mothers, and in one case a female would regularly leave her three- to four-month-old infant with the male for periods of up to 30 min several times a day. Such relationships persisted well beyond weaning.

2 Sometimes the males would be protective to infants, especially if danger threatened, or if the mother was relatively slow to respond to the infant. This could lead to the growth of a relationship between male and infant.

3 Some sub-adult or young adult males took an interest in the infants of young low-ranking females. Sometimes such a male would take the infant for 30 min or more. The infants formed relationships with the males, and would turn to them for comfort in the absence of their mothers. Such relationships could form the basis of later pair-bondings (cf. hamadryas baboon, page 224).

4 If an individual was carrying an infant, it increased the readiness of adult males to permit him to approach (cf. Barbary macaque, cited above). Some males sought proximity to infants in order to further their own ends in male-male interactions in this way, especially at times of social stress within the troop. If such a situation persisted, the infant might begin to initiate the interaction itself. Ransom and Ransom suggest that such early interactions could form the basis for the mutually supportive relationships that occur among older animals.

In the hamadryas baboon male-infant relationships provide the raw material from which troop organization develops. In this species the basic social unit consists of one male and one or more females, sometimes accompanied by sub-

FIGURE 14.3

*Hamadryas male holds the first of two quarreling females to approach him and stares at her opponent, while two other females cooperate in his threat.* (Drawing by Priscilla Edwards from Kummer, 1967.)

adult males. The sub-adult males sometimes kidnap temporarily, and may even adopt, infants. They also often form the centre of play groups of juveniles. The juveniles will run to the male and may clasp him if frightened, and he may then threaten the aggressor (Fig. 14.3). The male thus acts as a protective mother for each infant in turn. Since he protects sometimes one infant and sometimes another he becomes an ambivalent figure, and the infants compete for proximity to him. The male comes to adopt particular infants for progressively longer periods, and this may ameliorate the process of weaning. Soon after the females are one year old they enter into a consort relationship with a particular young adult male. This male then takes on the maternal role toward the female, but also ensures her continued proximity by attacking or threatening her if she strays. From such relationships the one-male unit develops, the male-female bond seeming to arise from a transferred mother-infant relationship (Kummer, 1967, 1968).

Finally, in monogamous species (see page 297) the males may play a large role in the care of the infants, carrying them about for much or even most of the time.

In a review paper written before some of these data were available, Mitchell (1969) drew conclusions which in fact largely summarize and extend them. As factors affecting paternal behaviour he listed:

1 Kinship—increasing paternal behaviour.
2 Familiarity with the mother—increasing paternal behaviour.
3 Crowding—decreasing paternal behaviour.
4 Social change. When a new langur male takes over a troop he sometimes kills the young infants within it. This has the result that the mothers soon come into oestrous again (see page 334).
5 Sex of the infant. Females evoke more paternal behaviour than males.
6 Dominance of mother—increasing paternal behaviour.
7 Age of infant—paternal behaviour decreasing with age.
8 Consort relations—increasing paternal behaviour.
9 Cultural propagation. Paternal behaviour is more marked in some troops of the Japanese macaque than in others.
10 Time of year. Paternal behaviour in the Japanese macaque is more prevalent in the birth season.
11 Interest in the centre of the troop or in achieving proximity to dominant individuals (see above).
12 Death of infant's mother—increasing paternal behaviour.
13 One-male groups. Paternal behaviour is more common in some but not all cases.
14 Hormonal factors. In free-ranging rhesus macaques, where paternal behaviour is rare, Wilson and Vessey (1968) observed it in two out of eight castrate males.
15 Early experience. Mitchell suggests that, for instance, differential behaviour of the mother toward male and female infants could affect their subsequent aggressive and affiliative behaviour.

## Peers

Apart from the mother the most important social companions for most young monkeys are the other young in the group. Most young primates are born into a group where there are a number of contemporaries available as play-companions: the only exceptions are species which live in small family groups (e.g., gibbons) and those in which the group size is so small that it is unusual for two infants to be present.

Play is a category of behaviour that is impossible to define but inescapable in practice. Social play develops from exploratory responses directed preferentially toward moving objects and is of course dependent on confidence and a readiness to make bodily contact with other individuals: these are derived from the relationship with the mother. In rhesus monkeys under laboratory conditions there is first a stage of "parallel play", in which infants manipulate objects in the physical environment in close proximity to one another, but do not actually play with each other. This develops into social play, including "approach-withdrawal" play, which involves chasing but minimal physical contact, and "rough-and-tumble" play which merges into aggressive play. These are associated with incomplete sexual, grooming, maternal, and other patterns (Harlow and Harlow, 1965). As with human children (Blurton Jones, 1972b), rough-and-tumble play is more common in males than in females, maternal patterns more common in females than in males.

The most detailed study of social play under natural conditions concerned baboons in the Gombe Stream National Park, Tanzania (Owens, 1973). Play started at two to six weeks of age, the play-face (see page 128) being seen in an infant only seventeen days old. Amongst males it increased to a mean of about 300 sec per hr at fourteen months, and then gradually decreased to about 30 sec per hr in five-year-old animals. The levels for females were somewhat lower. Play-partners tended to be of the same sex and similar age, though there was also a considerable amount of play between animals of markedly different age. The selection of play-partners was related to the amount of time individuals spent in proximity to each other, and infants whose mothers spent much time together were especially likely to play together (see also Fady, 1969). It seems possible that affectional ties established during play in infancy may persist into adulthood and affect the social structure of the group.

Comparative data suggest that the sorts of play patterns that are shown bear some relation to the adult behaviour of the species. For instance, fast running and other locomotor activities, in addition to play-biting and wrestling, are important in the ground-living patas monkey (Hall, 1965), while in tree-living species climbing and swinging may predominate. Field studies indicate that some play activities may be quite complex. For instance, in baboons, although the larger of two play-partners usually takes the more active role and vocalizes less than its partner, the reverse is sometimes the case with males widely separated in age: apparently the older individuals "hold back" (Owens, 1973). Furthermore baboon play sometimes takes on a tripartite character, with three individuals interacting in essentially different roles with one another (cf. Kummer, 1967). For instance one individual may protect another (perhaps a sibling) from rough play by carrying it away or playing with its play-partner itself (Owens, 1973). Sometimes play resembles "king-of-the-castle" or "follow-the-leader" (e.g., stump-tailed macaque and review of other species, Bertrand, 1969; gorilla, Schaller, 1963; and Fossey, personal communication). Chimpanzee play involves tickling and poking as well as other patterns (van Lawick-Goodall, 1968). In all these and many other species play consumes so much time and energy that it must be of crucial adaptive importance in development.

## Conclusion

It will be apparent that the infant monkey lives in a complex nexus of social relationships. Although its first and most intense relationship is that with its mother, it soon begins to interact with others, and thereby acquires many social skills. Each category of social companion interacts with the infant in a variety of ways, and these overlap between the categories. For instance, peers normally elicit play behaviour and may act as grooming companions: the mother also interacts with the infant in both these ways, so that either may substitute at least in some degree for the other. To the extent that the different categories of social companion can substitute for each other, the classification of social influences according to the companions that provide them may thus obscure important issues (see pages 235–236). This of course does not imply that the social environment is important only in providing the requisite amount of various types of interaction: development involves also the formation of relationships with individuals (Hinde, 1972b).

Other social companions, in addition to interacting with the infant directly, may also have a profound effect on the nature of the relationship between mother and infant. This has been established experimentally in rhesus monkeys: mothers living alone in large cages tend to be more permissive with their infants than do mothers living in groups. (The complexity of the effects of relationships upon relationships within even a small monkey group is discussed in Chap. 23.) In another species of macaque it has been established that the physical environment also affects the mother-infant relationship (Jensen et al., 1968).

Just why, in functional terms, there are such marked inter-species differences in the extents to which males and females other than the mother interact with the infant is an as yet unanswered question. Presumably the differences depend in part on differences between species in the cost and benefit (see page 203 and Trivers, in press) to mother and infant of interactions with others, and in part on differences in cost and benefit to those other individuals. For example, a male may benefit both immediately (by using the infant as a passport) and reproductively (by increasing the chances of reproductive success of an infant related to him). The benefit in the latter case will of course depend on the degree of relationship between the male and the infant. In some cases males, far from responding positively to infants, show infanticide (page 334). This has been observed when a male langur takes over a new troop: the young in it are probably not closely related to him, and it has been suggested that, as a result of the infanticide, the dead infants' mothers come into oestrous again so that they are able to bear the new male's offspring the sooner. These questions are considered in more detail by Hrdy (in press).

The influence of the social environment on the infant and on the mother-infant relationship hardly needs emphasizing in the human case. The mother's behaviour to her child is markedly influenced by the behaviour of other individuals both within and outside the family. She may have to meet conflicting demands from other children and from her husband, and she may be helped or constrained by grandparents, aunts, and neighbours. The child itself is likely to form warm relationships with a number of other individuals: indeed the relationship with the father or with another caretaker is sometimes stronger than that with the mother. At the same time the child may have to compete for affection or for its material well-being with its peers. Furthermore in man the social nexus has a time dimension: for example the mother-infant relationship is affected by the mother's attitudes in pregnancy and her expectancies for the future, each of which is affected by her present and her expected social situation (Newson and Newson, 1968).

# 15

# SOME SUBSEQUENT EFFECTS OF EARLY SOCIAL EXPERIENCE

### Introduction

As soon as one starts to observe early social development, one is struck by the extent of the differences among individuals. This has already been illustrated in Fig. 13.1: at each point the scores of half the mother-infant pairs lay outside the discontinuous lines. Such differences could arise in many ways—because of intrinsic differences between mothers and between infants, or through factors in the physical or social environment which affect their interaction (see Chap. 13). However they arise, the differences are such as could markedly affect the subsequent course of infant development. We have already seen one example of this in a cross-species comparison: there are relationships between the ways in which bonnet and pig-tailed macaque mothers interact with their infants that are related to the social structure in the groups (page 221). To cite another case, in one group of olive baboons some mothers started to reject their infants repeatedly as early as week 10 and continued to do so for the next 10 or 20 weeks, while others did not start until the infants were thirty-five to forty weeks old, when the mother started to show oestrous cycles again. The early group did not have to reject their infants so severely as the late group. The late-weaned infants would spend several hours a day fighting with their mothers to gain the nipple, and would have prolonged tantrums, even though at this age they were hardly at all dependent on the mother for food (Ransom and Rowell, 1973). Such differences seem likely to affect the infants' subsequent development.

Again, several authors have noted that primiparous monkey mothers tend to be less competent and more anxious during the early days or weeks of their infants' lives than do experienced mothers (e.g., Jay, 1965; Mitchell and Stevens, 1969). It may also be that their nipples are more sensitive, for Ransom found that primiparous baboon mothers reject their infants more. DeVore (1963) recorded that baboon infants with dominant mothers were subject to less insecurity and frustration, while subordinate mothers were shorter tempered and less responsive to their infants. In the squirrel monkey, infants of more protective mothers explore less, and learn more generalized fears (Baldwin, 1969). To cite a human example, primiparous women breast-feeding forty-eight-hour-old infants spend more time in non-feeding activities, change activity more often, talk to the infant more, and smile more at female infants than do multiparous women (Thoman et al., 1972). All such differences *could* affect the subsequent behavioural development of the infants.

In the human case there has indeed been a growing belief, due in large part to Freud's influence, that early experience and especially early social relations play a large part in subsequent personality development. This has led to many attempts to establish relationships between particular types of early experience (e.g., breast versus bottle feeding, regular versus demand schedules, nature of toilet training) and later development. But the results have been disappointing (Caldwell, 1964). Numerous reasons can be suggested: important factors were not controlled, the analysis was made at too global or too fine a level, and so on. The most crucial issue is of course the extreme complexity of development. A particular sort of maternal behaviour may produce different effects in different children, and in the same child at different ages, in different contexts, or in different circumstances. In the next section we shall consider an experiment with mice which demonstrates this complexity.

### Interactions between experiential factors

Here we shall turn briefly to rodents in order to make two important points about the development of behaviour. These are that

1  Apparently insignificant early experiences, or changes in the early environment, can have profound effects on the subsequent behaviour of the organism.

2  The consequences of various types of early experience may depend on interactions between them: to study such interactions, it is necessary to manipulate several factors at once.

These points are exemplified in an experiment by Denenberg (1970): rats were used for the work simply because sufficiently large numbers can be kept and tested in the laboratory.

Four aspects of the animals' experience were varied:

1  Some of the mothers of the experimental animals were "handled" in their infancy, whilst others were not. Many studies have shown that handling rodents for a few minutes daily between birth and weaning has far-reaching effects on their physical and behavioural development, affecting characters from brain chemistry to exploratory behaviour. These effects may result from the disturbance to the mother-infant relationship (Richards, 1967): there is considerable evidence that they are mediated by an endocrine mechanism (Levine, 1969). A common finding is that handled animals are more active and defaecate less if placed in an open arena for a test period in adulthood. Here the aim was to see whether handling in infancy affected maternal behaviour and through that the behaviour of the offspring of the handled animals.

2  Some of the animals were themselves handled in infancy, whilst others were not.

3  Some were born and reared to weaning in an ordinary laboratory maternity cage; others were born into a larger "free-environment" cage of greater complexity.

4  After weaning some animals were reared in small laboratory cages, some in "free-environment" cages.

Each of these variables separately had been shown previously to affect the behaviour of the offspring in an open field in adulthood. In the present experiment they were combined into an experimental design as shown in Table 15.1. With the additional variable of sex, this resulted in thirty-two groups, and three animals were run in each group. In choosing tests, Denenberg and his colleagues used the fact established previously that various measures of the behaviour of adult rats (namely, activity and defaecation in an open field, running in an activity wheel, amounts of food consumed and water drunk after various sorts of stress, defaecation and activity during habituation to an avoidance conditioning apparatus, and various judgments of timidity) were all well correlated with one another and could be regarded as measurements of a factor termed "emotionality". He also included several tests of exploratory behaviour.

The scores obtained were examined by factor analysis (see pages 66–67). Of the factors which emerged from the analysis, three could be labelled "emotional reactivity", "consumption-elimination", and "field exploration". Table 15.2 shows how these were modified by various treatment factors. Only handling affected emotional reactivity, and the finding of only one significant interaction indicated that the effect of handling did not depend on the other experimental manipulations used. Exploratory behaviour was affected by handling either the pups or their mothers (though the effects were positive in the first case and negative in the second) and, unlike the finding with emotional reactivity, seven interactions were significant. This indicates that the tendency to show exploratory behaviour is affected by a whole range of experiences, including those of

TABLE 15.1 *Experimental design used in a study of rat behaviour*

| *Conception to day 21, experience of natural mothers in their infancy* | *Days 1–20, handling experience of pups* | *Days 1–21, pre-weaning housing* | *Days 21–42, post-weaning housing* |
|---|---|---|---|
| NH | NH | MC | LC |
| NH | NH | MC | FE |
| NH | NH | FE | LC |
| NH | NH | FE | FE |
| NH | H | MC | LC |
| NH | H | MC | FE |
| NH | H | FE | LC |
| NH | H | FE | FE |
| H | NH | MC | LC |
| H | NH | MC | FE |
| H | NH | FE | LC |
| H | NH | FE | FE |
| H | H | MC | LC |
| H | H | MC | FE |
| H | H | FE | LC |
| H | H | FE | FE |

Note: NH = nonhandled controls, H = handled, MC = maternity cage, FE = free environment, LC = laboratory cage.
SOURCE: Denenberg, 1970.

the individual's mother, and that no one event is a prime determiner. The handling experiences of both pup and mother also affected the consumption-elimination factor.

This experiment thus indicates that certain experiences in early life can affect, in various ways, a variety of types of behaviour in adult life. This does not mean that those early experiences *determine* behaviour in later life. In other experiments Denenberg and his colleagues showed that stress or other experiences in adulthood could markedly modify and even reverse the effects of the early experiences in the tests. For example, the offspring of non-handled mothers are more active in the open field than the offspring of handled mothers. However, if the animals are allowed to become pregnant and rear a litter before testing in the open field, the results are reversed: females raised by handled mothers are more active than those raised by non-handled mothers.

While the finding that the behaviour of an adult can be affected by experiences that her mother had in infancy is surprising enough, that is not all. Denenberg and Rosenberg (1967) have taken it one stage farther and found that handling an animal in its infancy can affect the open-field activity of her grand-pups. In the experiments reported by Denenberg this effect was demonstrable only if the mother had an enriched experience before or after weaning.

TABLE 15.2 *Qualitative summary of the results of an analysis of variance of the experiment shown in Table 15.1*

| Factor variable | Significantly modified by | Effect |
|---|---|---|
| Emotional reactivity | Handling pups in infancy (5 of 5)* One interaction | Reduces emotionality |
| Exploratory behaviour | Handling pups in infancy (3 of 5) | Increases exploratory behaviour |
| | Handling mothers during their infancy (3 of 5) Seven interactions | Decreases exploratory behaviour |
| Consumption-elimination | Handling pups in infancy (1 of 3) | Decreases defaecation |
| | Handling mothers during their infancy (1 of 3) | Decreases food intake |
| | Post-weaning housing in free environment (1 of 3) Two interactions | Decreases water intake |

* Numbers in parentheses indicate number of significant effects out of total number possible. For example, five tests defined the factor of emotional reactivity; in all instances the Offspring Handling main effect was found to be significant.
SOURCE: Denenberg, 1970.

These experiments, using relatively simple treatment variables and relatively lowly mammals, show how complex the relations between early treatment and adult behaviour can be. We should expect them to be even more complex in man, and indeed they are. One example must suffice. Moss et al. (1969) found that a rating of the animation of the mother's voice during a pregnancy interview could be used to predict the type of stimulation she provided for her baby when it was one and three months of age. However the stimulation involved primarily behaviour that would soothe and modulate rather than excite with male infants, but primarily behaviour that involved the distance receptors with female infants. Another variable, the educational status of the mothers, also affected the type of stimulation they gave: less-well-educated mothers tended to give more physical stimulation. Increased stimulation by the mother of the distance receptors at three months of age was related to less discomfort in the presence of strangers at eight to nine and one-half months.

In view of such facts, it is hardly surprising that many studies of the long-term effects of particular types of early experience have come up with negative results, especially when the factors assessed were gross ones, such as social class (Richards, 1971). However some such studies have given positive results, and, as we shall see, more detailed studies have provided strong evidence that early experience can affect later behaviour.

### Rearing in conditions of social deprivation

One way to establish that early social experience does affect subsequent behaviour is to assess development under conditions of varying degrees of social isolation. We may consider some work with rhesus monkeys. In a series of studies Mason (1960, 1961a, b, 1962) compared rhesus monkeys captured in the field with animals born in the laboratory, hand-fed for 15 to 20 days, and subsequently reared in cages with no tactile contact with other monkeys. He found considerable differences in social behaviour and in responses to novel environments and to alien species.

Harlow and his co-workers (review Harlow and Harlow, 1965, 1969; Sackett, 1968; Mitchell, 1968; McKinney et al., 1971; see also Missakian, 1969) found that rhesus monkeys brought up under conditions of severe social isolation developed into neurotic and asocial adults. The abnormalities included orality, self-clutching, and deficiencies in sexual and maternal behaviour, with social indifference, hyperaggression, excessive fearfulness, and other symptoms, and diminished responsiveness to noxious stimulation. The severity of the effects varied with the period of isolation. Total isolation for only 3 months produced depression on removal from isolation, but after recovery from this there were no marked permanent abnormalities. Isolation for 6 months produced considerable permanent effects, and isolation for 1 year destroyed all social abilities. The most sensitive period seemed to lie between three and nine months of age, since animals isolated for the first three months of age and then exposed to social interactions developed almost normally.

Total social isolation is of course an extreme condition, and the results of such experiments are far from easy to interpret. However Harlow and his colleagues have also assessed the effectiveness of rearing with either mother or peers in ameliorating the abnormalities produced by the more extreme conditions. Rhesus infants reared by their own mothers but denied access to peers showed deficiencies in affectionate behaviour and were hyperaggressive. The effects were present if access to peers was denied for 4 months and were marked after 8 months. [It must be noted, however, that the small size of the cages in which these animals were kept may also have affected their development. Spencer-Booth (1969) placed infants which had been reared by their mothers with visual but no tactual access to other animals into social groups when they were a year old. Social interactions were qualitatively similar to, though somewhat less frequent than, those of infants reared by their mothers in a group situation].

Rhesus infants raised without mothers but with peers developed physical attachments to one another. The long-term social adjustments of such animals appeared to be not markedly deficient, peer-peer interactions apparently compensating for the lack of mothering. Animals reared with the same individual peer throughout formed strong partner-ties, but with less carryover to peers encountered subsequently, than infants raised with frequently changing peers.

On the basis of such results, Harlow suggests that infant-peer relations are more important for normal development than are infant-mother ones. In harmony with this view are the further findings that infants reared on surrogate mothers with access to peers are only slightly and temporarily retarded in comparison with mother-raised infants with access to peers, and that rhesus infants reared in isolation from other animals can subsequently be rehabilitated by experience with peers. In the expectation that the most effective "therapist" monkey would be one which would make contact with the isolate, would not provide a threat of aggression, and would subsequently provide a medium for the development of an increasingly sophisticated social repertoire, 1 month old

therapists were placed with three- to 4-month old social isolates. The therapists initiated clinging to the isolates, who subsequently clung back, and essentially normal social interactions subsequently developed (Harlow et al, 1971;
Harlow and Suomi, 1971).

However it is necessary to make a number of reservations about Harlow's
view that peer relations are of paramount importance in the development of
normal social behaviour. First, experiments involving a direct comparison
between mother-raised and peer-raised infants must be interpreted with great
caution. Rhesus infants, raised by mothers in the absence of peers, attempt to
play more with their mothers, and this may elicit negative responses from the
mothers (Hinde and Spencer-Booth, 1967b). A mother may thus behave differently if the infant has no peers present from the way in which she would behave if
peers were available.

Second, quite apart from the importance of the mother in providing milk,
she controls the infan't's access to his peers (page 189) and by example teaches
him much about his environment (page 243). And, at any rate in a large cage,
mothers confined alone with their infants may play with them and thus take on
some of the role of peers.

Finally, recent more precise observations by Goy and Goldfoot (1973)
have demonstrated considerable differences between rhesus infants taken from
their mothers at 3 months of age and allowed access to peers for one half hour
each day, and infants reared in social groups with unlimited access to both
mothers and peers. In the first group mature mounting patterns developed in the
2nd and 3rd years of life, and preferences for mating partners of the opposite
sex not until the animals were three or four years old. In the more complex social
environment the ages were respectively three to four months and six months.
Furthermore the infants exposed only to peers showed dominance relations based
on clear aggression—submission behaviour, while those reared by their mothers
rarely showed aggressive or submissive reactions. In the latter case agonistic
interactions were largely limited to the mothers.

These detailed data show that infants reared with only limited exposure to
peers may differ in many subtle aspects of their social behaviour from infants
living also with their mothers. Although exposure to peers alone may be enough
to ensure superficially adequate social behaviour in adulthood, it does not produce behaviour identical with that to be seen in animals which have developed
in a normal social situation. While the give-and-take interactions involved in
playing with peers are, as in human children, no doubt of great importance for
the development of social skills, the importance of the mother as a "secure

base" and in controlling the social interactions of her infant is not to be underestimated.

The Wisconsin experiments have also provided information on the effects of early experience on another aspect of the subsequent selection of social companions. Rhesus monkeys reared in partial isolation (i.e. visual and auditory but no tactile contact with other monkeys), but hand-fed by experimenters during their early weeks, subsequently preferred one of the caretakers to another monkey when tested in the apparatus shown in Fig. 12.9 at three and one-half years of age. A further finding, perhaps less easily understood, is that juvenile and even adult monkeys tend to associate with monkeys reared in similar conditions to themselves (i.e. total isolation, partial isolation, feral) than with monkeys reared differently (Sackett and Ruppenthal, 1973).

In addition to this extensive work on rhesus monkeys reared in various degrees of social isolation, considerable information is also available for chimpanzees. Chimpanzees reared in a restricted environment showed abnormalities in behaviour, including stereotypes (Davenport and Menzel, 1963), and were less able to cope with novel objects and novel situations than were wild reared animals (e.g., Menzel, 1964). Their social behaviour, also, was usually markedly affected, though there is some evidence that later social experience can compensate for early deprivation to a greater extent than in monkeys (reviewed Goy and Goldfoot, 1973). In some cases the effect of environmental restriction may operate quite early: for example Menzel et al. (1970) compared chimpanzees reared in his laboratory with wild-born controls which had been captured before their manipulative skills had developed. The latter were superior in their ability to use sticks to reach objects.

However, it is as well to note that rearing in conditions that are abnormal for the species does not necessarily produce deleterious effects. Lemmon (1971) has reported that chimpanzees separated from their mothers at birth and reared in a human environment showed social, sensori-motor, and vocal behaviour earlier than did chimpanzee-reared infants. He suggests that this was because of the increased immediacy and appropriateness of the responses of the human fosterers. The same was true of a rhesus monkey infant reared by L. E. White and J. Hanby.

Another study with chimpanzees raises the possibility that the development of rather more intangible aspects of adult personality may require early social experience. Gallup (1971) found that chimpanzees, unlike rhesus monkeys, show signs of being able to recognize their own mirror images. After a few days' experience they would use the mirror to inspect and manipulate parts of their body which they could not otherwise see. If their bodies were marked with an odourless dye while they were anaesthetized and they were shown the mirror on recovery, they touched and tried to inspect the marked areas while watching the reflection. Such evidence of self-recognition was absent in laboratory-reared chimps raised in isolation. This might suggest that the concept of self arises out of social interaction with others.

Some data exist on human children found after being brought up under conditions of considerable social isolation (e.g., Köhler, 1952; Davis, K., 1947; Baerends, 1973), though their reliability is often difficult to assess. It is clear that such children are initially very backward and may appear to be congenitally subnormal: how far they can subsequently catch up no doubt depends on the age at which they are discovered. More extensive data are available from studies of institutionalized children. Since institutionalization often involves social interaction which is infrequent and of poor emotional quality, the effects on development are often considerable: a recent review has been given by Rutter (1972). In institutions in which some approximation to family life is attempted, intermediate effects are found (e.g., Tizard and Tizard, 1971).

### Long-term effects of variations in the early social environment

The studies reviewed in the previous section involved rather drastic departures from the normal social environment. We may now consider some in which the conditions used were less extreme.

We have seen that the rhesus monkeys reared at Wisconsin under conditions of social deprivation became very inadequate mothers, behaving brutally or with indifference to their offspring (pages 234–235). When the latter grew up they tended to be inferior to controls reared by more normal mothers in the development of play and sex behaviour, and to be significantly more aggressive (Mitchell, 1968; Harlow, 1969). A major source of difference appeared to lie in the deficient use of signal movements by the infants reared by motherless mothers (Møller et al., 1968).

In another study rhesus infants reared by their own mothers were compared with four infants who were rotated amongst four mothers every 2 weeks for the first 32 weeks of life. The differences were not great, but the latter showed more disturbance behaviours throughout this period, and also more variability in weight gain and in mother-infant interaction. On subsequent isolation the multiple-mothered infants showed more disturbance than control infants (Griffin, 1966). When three years old these animals tended to be higher in social dominance than normally reared animals (Harlow and Harlow, 1969; Sackett, 1968).

This study was concerned with a question arising from Bowlby's work on children (see pages 189–191). Bowlby held that monomatic rearing (i.e., rearing by one mother) is preferred to polymatric rearing even when the quantity of overall interaction is comparable. In Bowlby's view, there is an intrinsic importance in a "monotropic" relationship with a mother-figure, whereas others have argued that, provided the child receives proper maternal care from not too large a number of mother figures, all will be well. The evidence available from studies of human children is inconclusive (Bowlby, 1969; Stevens, 1971), but on general grounds it seems likely that the importance of the age factor has been underestimated here: monomatric rearing may be important at some stages but not at others.

Yet another group of studies has already been mentioned—those in which the long-term effects of a short perior of separation between mother and infant were assessed (pages 208–216). We saw that there is some evidence for long-term effects in monkeys, and that in man the evidence for long-term consequences of brief periods of separation is also substantial.

Of special interest are studies which do not involve experimental interference but rather make use of the natural variation in mothers or in mother-infant interaction, relating it to differences in the subsequent behavioural characteristics of the growing young. Amongst non-human primates the only extensive data concern the influence of the mother's dominance rank on that of her offspring: we shall discuss this later (Chap. 22). More evidence is available in the human case: although of a correlational nature, there are strong indications that cause-effect relations are involved. For example Ainsworth and Bell (in press) offer several types of evidence that the nature of mother-infant interaction affects both cognitive and social development. In one study, which has already been mentioned briefly (page 187), babies were seen every 3 weeks and data on their crying, and the mother's responsiveness to it, collected. Those infants whose mothers *most frequently* ignored their crying in any one-quarter year were likely to be among the most frequent criers in the next quarter. The converse, however, did not hold—the frequency of infants' crying was not strongly related to the proportion of their crying episodes that the mother ignored in the next quarter. These two results suggest that infants become more frequent criers if their mothers are not responsive. Furthermore, the infants who cried more *persistently* were likely to have mothers who were frequently slower to respond. Thus a vicious spiral could be established: babies of mothers who are unresponsive to their crying tend to cry more later on, which in turn further discourages the mother from responding promptly, which results in a further relative increase in the infant's crying. Of course the data show only a *correlation* between relative changes in infants' crying and maternal responsiveness: the effects could be mediated by some other related quality of their interaction. In addition, those infants who cried little at the end of the first year seemed to communicate more with their mothers in other ways: presumably mothers who were responsive to crying were responsive also to the child's other attempts to communicate, and encouraged their development.

A second line of evidence that the nature of mother-infant interaction affects subsequent behavioural development concerned the infant's competence in dealing with the physical environment. Mothers who were rated as sensitive to the baby's signals and permitted the baby freedom to move about and explore the world tended to have babies relatively accelerated in psycho-motor development. Ainsworth and Bell suggest that the mother's sensitivity to the baby's signals builds up his sense of competence, and that this carries over into his transactions with the physical world.

These investigators studied also the nature of the balance between the infant's attachment behaviour to his mother and his tendency to explore his environment (see also Ainsworth et al., 1971). The evidence indicated that infants which have harmonious interactions with their mothers, and whose mothers are generally responsive, tend to explore more (see also Ainsworth and Wittig, 1969). Maternal sensitivity was found also to affect cognitive development during the first 2 years of life: here the effect was presumably indirect, mediated by the interaction with the environment made possible by the more sensitive mothering.

Another study of a somewhat different nature concerned 41 disadvantaged five-month-old infants (Yarrow et al., 1972). Observers made two 3-hour visits to their homes, sampling the infants' behaviour in every third 30-sec period. Data were collected on the range of physical and social stimulation available to or received by the infant. Among the many interesting correlations found, two groups may be mentioned here. First, "goal orientation", a cluster of items including such behaviour as persistent and purposeful attempts to secure objects just out of reach, was correlated with the level, variety, and positive effect of social stimulation received, and the contingency of the caretaker's response to signs of distress in the infant. It would therefore appear that the social environment may affect the manner in which the infant interacts with his physical environment. Second, there were a number of positive correlations between measures of the nature and quantity of infants' responsiveness to the inanimate environment, and the variety and "responsiveness" (i.e., feedback potential) of the objects in that environment. There were, however, no significant relationships between the physical and social environments—indicating that global characterizations of environments as "depriving" or "stimulating" are oversimplified.

When so many studies emphasize the importance of early social relationships for the subsequent development of the offspring, it is easy to forget that the child can have too much of a good thing. For every aspect of maternal behaviour—protectiveness, responsiveness, solicitude, and the many other dimensions which we do not yet know properly how to isolate or assess—there is a "normal" range, with variants in both directions. Since children show variation in every conceivable behavioural characteristic from birth on (e.g., Sander, 1969), and since no two parents are alike, the interaction between mother and child is always delicate. Although in the great majority of cases adequate adjustment occurs, there are bound to be some where the changing characteristics of the growing child fail to mesh with the changing characteristics of its parents, producing strain in their relationships. For example, Tinbergen and Tinbergen (1972) suggest that the development of certain symptoms, characteristic of the various disturbances labelled as autism but to be seen at times also in normal children, is related to disturbance of the delicate balance between bonding and parental intrusion. In encounters with adults, an infant may be in a state of conflict between bonding or social tendencies, and fear. Normally the fear wanes and social behaviour soon predominates, though this takes longer with timid children. In extreme cases the motivational conflict cannot be resolved, and the over-activation of fear in the presence of others becomes progressive. This, the Tinbergens suggest, can lead to symptoms of autism.*

One gross variable shown to be related to the child's behaviour is the socio-economic status of the mother. In a study of ten-month-old girls in the Boston, Massachusetts, area, Kagan and Tulkin (1971) found that middle-class mothers were more likely to entertain their children with objects, encourage them to walk, and reward them for new achievements than lower-middle-class mothers. Middle-class mothers also responded more rapidly to crying and were more likely to respond verbally. In the laboratory the children from the two groups differed in a number of ways. For instance, the middle-class children quietened more to their mother's voice than to a stranger's, and vocalized more

* A more extensive discussion, concerned with a range of conditions in which early social relationships have been inadequate, is given by Clancy and McBride (1974).

when it ceased: they also vacillated more in choosing a toy. In another study more upper than lower-middle-class eight-month-old children were found to respond fearfully to a mask with the features disarranged, and with somewhat older children there was a positive correlation between social class and fixation time to jumbled faces or human forms. Kagan and Tulkin suggest that the differences can be explained in terms of differences in a set to explain discrepancy (cf. pages 169, 183) and in the richness of cognitive structures, assumed to be due to the differences in parental treatment observed. The necessity for coming to terms with the precise factors involved in such global variables as class is emphasized by Richards (1971).

An even more global variable is that of national culture, but careful comparative studies can yield data of considerable interest. For example, Caudill and Weinstein (1969) compared the maternal care received by three- to four-month-old babies in Japan and the United States, and related it to the behaviour of the babies. They found that American mothers showed more vocal interaction with their infants, and stimulated them to greater physical activity and exploration, than did Japanese mothers, while the latter had more bodily contact with their infants and soothed them more than did the Americans. There were parallel differences between the babies: the American babies were more happily vocal, more active, and more exploratory of their bodies and their physical environment than the Japanese babies. Caudill and Weinstein point out that these differences are in line with the differing expectations for later behaviour in the two cultures and believe that they form the bases of important areas of difference in emotional responsiveness.

The relations between child-care practices and the structure of a society must of course operate both ways. On the one hand the broad features of a society—whether it is technologically advanced or backward, whether necessities are scarce or abundant—influence the attitude of parents to children and influence the duration of the child's dependence. The nature of the society's economic structure may also influence the extent to which children are brought up to be obedient or self-assertive. But, as we have seen, child-care practices will also influence adult personality, and thus the structure of the society. In theory, a society could be stable only if its child-care practices produced personalities which perpetuated it. In practice most societies are constantly changing, in part because their circumstances change, either through their own activities or through external agencies. This affects the rising generation both directly and indirectly through the child-care practices of the parents. Their personalities and values are likely to be incompatible in some degree with the old order, and stability is never attained.

## Social learning

A final group of data concerns not the more general effects on the infant's personality or abilities that result from the early social environment, but more specific consequences of associating with other individuals in particular contexts. The distinction from the data considered in the previous section is of course not absolute. The role of example is obvious enough in man (e.g. page 172), but the extent to which social learning occurs in non-human primates is of some interest.

On the whole, monkey mothers seem not to teach their infants. In a number of species mothers sometimes put their infants down, walk a little away, and then look back and wait for their infant to follow (e.g., rhesus, Hinde et al., 1964). Mothers also sometimes pull their infants away from strange objects (Japanese macaques, Menzel, 1966) or snatch from them food items to which they are not accustomed (Itani, 1958; Kawai, 1963).

More important, however, are various forms of observational learning[1] by the young. The potential importance of such learning has been well documented in laboratory studies. Monkeys can learn to accept food that they see other individuals take (Weizkrantz and Cowey, 1960), and to avoid situations that are seen to cause pain to others (Hansen and Mason, 1962; Mason and Hollis, 1962; Stephenson, 1967, cited on pages 100–101).

Comparable learning between the infant and its companions in the contexts of avoidance and food-getting behaviour occurs also in nature. The infant's proximity to its mother ensures that it can learn from her fear responses (e.g., Baldwin, 1969), so that differences in responsiveness to snake-like objects between wild- and hand-reared monkeys may be due to the prior influence of parental example on the former (rhesus, Joslin et al., 1964). Often the young eat fragments that their mothers drop, or feed at the same food source (Japanese macaque, Kawamura, 1958; chimpanzees, van Lawick-Goodall, 1968; gorilla,

---

[1] Social learning has also been studied in birds (e.g., Hinde and Fisher, 1951; Klopfer, 1959; Turner, 1965) and other species. The complexity of the processes involved in imitation is indicated in a review by Flanders (1968). Whether or not observational learning can be understood in conventional stimulus-response reinforcement learning terms (Gewirtz, 1971), or whether it requires cognitive intermediaries (Bandura, 1971), is an issue beyond our present concern.

Schaller, 1963). In squirrel monkeys, food-catching skill is learned by young animals from older juveniles, rather than from their mothers. In the Japanese macaque the plants eaten by each troop are to some extent peculiar to that troop, and selection seems to depend on tradition. Not only do the yearlings tend to eat what their mothers are eating, but as we have seen, the mothers may act as teachers: if a yearling picks up a plant not eaten by the troop, its mother may snatch it away (Itani, 1958; Kawai, 1963; Imanishi, 1965).

While mothers are thus the guardians of tradition, the younger generation are the innovators. One group of Japanese macaques now has the habit of washing the sand from sweet potatoes in the sea. This habit was first seen in an eighteen-month-old female, Imo. From her it spread to her playmates, and her mother also attempted it. Up to 1958 the only adults over five years old who learned to wash sweet potatoes were the mothers of Imo's playmates. But when Imo's playmates became adult, their infants learned "naturally" from their mothers. Later different styles of potato washing developed, roughly along kinship lines (Kawai, 1965a).

The same Imo, when three years old, was responsible for another innovation. The wheat with which the monkeys are fed often blows onto the sand, and it is then necessary for them to comb the wet sand for single grains. Imo was seen to pick a handful of mixed sand and wheat and throw it into the sea, wait until the sand had sunk, and scoop up the wheat. This spread to other young animals, but after 4 years the only animal that had learnt as an adult was Imo's mother. A more controlled study in which the macaques were given wrapped sweets to eat had a similar result—the one-, two-, and three-year-olds picked the sweets up first. One youngster would learn from another. Mothers at first would snatch the candy from the youngsters or prevent them from getting it, but later they also would eat the candy. Thus again the habit spread from infants to adults who cared for them. Propagation to animals of higher rank depended on the existence of a previous relationship—younger to older sibling, or female to male (Itani, 1958; Kawamura, 1963; Imanishi, 1965; Tsumori, 1966, 1967).

In chimpanzees "teaching" is more important than in monkeys, the mother seeming to encourage her infant to walk, follow, climb, and so on. She also has great importance as a model: for instance the infant tends to feed in the same places and on the same foods as his mother (see also Hayes and Hayes, 1952). In the Gombe Stream National Park in Tanzania, but not in all parts of their range, chimpanzees "fish" for termites by inserting probes into the holes in the termites' nests, and then mouthing off the termites that are clinging to the probe when it is withdrawn. Infants spend long periods beside their mothers while fishing in this way, and may go through the motions even though too inept to be successful (van Lawick-Goodall, 1968). Their behaviour resembles that of a human child playing with its mother's saucepans, and at least gives the impression that it is reinforcing "just to do what Mum does". Much learning must go on in this way. Such observations suggest that "identification" (cf. page 291), may play nearly as important a role in some non-human primates as it does in man (e.g., Sears, 1957).

## Summary

Although early social experience differs considerably between individuals in a manner that would be expected to affect development, it is not easy to relate particular characteristics of the early social environment to particular behavioural characteristics of the adult. This difficulty is in part due to the complexity of development, and the interactions between the many factors influencing its course. However, rearing under extreme conditions of social deprivation (not unexpectedly) has marked consequences on the development of behaviour, and there is a growing body of evidence for both monkey and man that variations within the normal range of social experience can have specific effects on subsequent development. In addition, of course, learning in particular social contexts has important consequences for later behaviour.

# AGGRESSION; SOCIO-SEXUAL BEHAVIOUR

# 16
# AGGRESSIVE BEHAVIOUR

### The difficulty of definition

It is a recurrent theme throughout this book that the classificatory categories and explanatory concepts used in science in general, and in the study of behaviour in particular, are seldom either "true" or "false", but rather are devices with a limited range of usefulness. Aggression[1] is yet another case. Before it can be discussed, some indication of what is meant by aggression is clearly essential, yet no definition is wholly satisfactory.

A limitation on subject matter is first necessary. We are primarily concerned here with the behaviour of individuals toward others of their own species, not with that of groups or nations. This eliminates two categories of behaviour that many would class as aggressive. The first is predatory behaviour, directed toward members of other species. This is best distinguished from intra-specific

---

[1] A recent synthesis of the literature is given by Johnson (1972) and a carefully edited book of readings by Megargee and Hokanson (1970).

fighting, since in any one species predatory behaviour and intra-specific fighting are usually elicited by different external stimuli, depend on different internal states, usually involve some different movement patterns, and may involve different neural mechanisms (Hutchinson and Renfrew, 1966). The exclusion of predatory behaviour at this point closes no issues: it may be that there are relationships between it and intraspecific aggression—for instance, individuals with a strong proclivity for one may also have a strong tendency toward the other—but this is an empirical issue, to be settled from the data.

Second, we are not here concerned with inter-group strife or war, though the former is mentioned briefly later (pages 277–278). War has causes quite different from those of aggression between individuals, and even the behaviour of many of those who take part would not fall within some definitions of aggression.

Within what remains, behaviour directed toward causing physical injury to another individual must clearly be labelled as aggressive: here there can be no disagreement. Many authors (e.g., Buss, 1961; Carthy and Ebling, 1964) omit or do not insist on the qualification "directed toward", but it is necessary to exclude accidental injury. Whether injury other than physical should be included is an open issue: in the human case it seems logical to include verbal abuse, and perhaps even teasing, but the question of the extent to which verbal aggression and physical aggression share a common causal basis is an empirical issue, to be settled from the data in particular cases.

Attack on another individual usually involves risk of injury for the attacker: attack is therefore often not single-minded, but associated with elements of self-protective and withdrawal responses. As we have already seen (page 67), this is evident from the study of threat postures, which often consist of a mosaic of elements of attack and withdrawal. It is thus often convenient to lump together attack, threat, fleeing, and submissive behaviour as "agonistic behaviour" (Scott and Fredericson, 1951): within this category the precise limits of aggressive behaviour are hard to specify.

Aggressive behaviour, in the narrow sense of behaviour directed toward causing physical injury, often results in settling status, precedence, or access to some object or space. Whether this is true of all aggressive behaviour is largely a matter of definition: insofar as an individual who causes physical injury to others is subsequently avoided, his aggressive behaviour has determined access to the space around him. But the complementary question, of whether all behaviour that results in settling status, precedence, or access is to be labelled as aggressive, is at the root of much disagreement in discussions about aggression. Just because aggressive behaviour (in the sense of behaviour directed toward causing injury) often has these results, the term "aggressive behaviour" is often used in popular speech in a broader sense to include all sorts of self-assertive or go-getting behaviour, whether or not it is directed toward causing physical injury (e.g., Daniels et al., 1970). For instance we talk about an aggressive sales-man without necessarily meaning that he is a physical danger to others. Psy-chiatrists, too, often use aggressive behaviour in this wider sense.[2] Most students of animal behaviour, on the other hand, use aggression more narrowly, to mean behaviour directed toward causing physical injury to others: for instance, the song of territorial birds keeps intruders at a distance, but is not usually included within the category of aggressive behaviour.

This divergence of view depends in part on whether we are primarily inter-ested in the consequences of the behaviour, or in its causation. If we define aggressive behaviour in terms of its consequences (e.g., settling status, etc.), the question of causation is left open. But if we are interested in causation, we must ask on what evidence we would conclude that violence to others and the self-assertiveness of the salesman share a similar causal basis. One type of evidence would be that salesmen who behave assertively are also likely to be violent; another, that external factors, or internal states, likely to make a salesman go-getting would also be likely to make him violent.[3] Neither of these types of evidence has yet been produced, and common experience denies such correla-tions. Another possible type of argument might be that denial of opportunity for violence leads to increased self-assertiveness, and vice versa. In some circum-stances this may happen, but it is not in itself sufficient evidence that they have a common causal basis: it could be that an inhibitory effect of one on the other is removed when opportunity for the former is denied. Thus the extended sense of aggression sometimes used in common speech can not be taken to imply a common causal basis for violence and go-getting behaviour.

That common parlance does indeed provide shaky ground on which to base scientific enquiry into mechanisms can be illustrated even more vividly from the writings of the psychiatrist Storr (1968). He goes so far as to conclude that the

---

[2] The double entendre, pointed out to me by Judy Bernal, must surely stay.

[3] Some observations bearing on the complexity of such relationships are given by Blurton Jones (1972b). In a factor analysis (pages 66–67) of data obtained from young children in a nursery school he found a moderately consistent factor with high loadings for the items fixate, frown, hit, push, and take-tug-grab. However, the taking of objects seemed to be not so much part of aggressive behaviour, as the context in which it was initiated. This was confirmed by the finding that the readiness of a child to behave aggressively was not correlated with his readiness to take objects from others. This and other lines of evidence indicate that, in two-year-olds, the motivation of taking things is not generally aggressive. Of course taking may later become an aggressive response when the child learns of its effects on others.

basis even of intellectual achievement lies in the aggressive part of human nature, basing his argument on the observation that we describe intellectual effort with "aggressive" words—for instance, we speak of "attacking" and "getting our teeth into" problems. It is unnecessary to emphasize that the implication that violence to others and intellectual endeavour share a common causal basis does not long stand examination by the sort of criteria just discussed.

However the conclusion that go-getting behaviour and aggression (in the sense of behaviour directed toward causing physical injury) may differ in their causal basès must not be taken as indicating that all examples of behaviour in the latter category are similar. Moyer (1968) distinguished six types of aggression (inter-male, fear-induced, irritable, territorial, maternal, and instrumental) and claims that they differ in either the brain structures involved or in their dependence on external factors or hormones. Insofar as they do differ, then from the point of view of causation, aggression is a heterogeneous category. To take a particular example, in one study the aggression scores obtained by different strains of mice varied according to the situation in which they were tested (e.g., defence of pups, free social situation, after isolation), one species or strain being superior in one situation and another in anther (Karczmar and Scudder, 1969): although "aggressive behaviour", even according to the narrow definition, was clearly involved in each case, a strain which fought vigorously in one context did not necessarily do so in another.

Where behaviour directed toward causing harm to another individual also results in settling status, precedence, or access to some object or space, a further distinction is often useful. This depends on whether it is the settling of status, etc., or the infliction of physical harm that is the primary goal of the aggressive individual. Examples of the former can be identified by the fact that the aggressive behaviour is directed toward producing the consequence in question (status, precedence, etc.), in the sense that variations in circumstances lead to variations in the behaviour that maximize the probability of that consequence (see pages 89–90 for discussion of goal-directedness). For example in spring a male great tit may be more likely to attack other individuals when it meets them in some places—perhaps near song-posts or potential nest-sites—than when it meets them in others. The juxtaposition of these places leads to the marking out of a defended area: the bird's aggressiveness varies in such a way that a territory is defended. By contrast a bird in a winter flock may attack any other individual that approaches within a certain distance. If food happens to be nearby, the attack may settle access to the food. But if attacks are no more likely when food is nearby than when it is not, then access to food is only an incidental consequence of the attacks, not their goal.

A moment's reflection will reveal that this distinction is not wholly satisfactory. It could be argued that the aggressiveness of the great tit in the winter flock was directed toward keeping a space around him free of other individuals. Indeed it has been argued that virtually all aggression in animals is "instrumental" (Scott, 1966), but the distinction soon becomes merely verbal.

The same difficulty arises with aggression in our own species: while it is often clear that aggressive behaviour is directed toward the achievement of a goal other than the injury of another individual, it is not clear precisely what evidence is necessary to establish that behaviour that appears to be directed toward harming another individual "really" has some other goal. This does not mean that the distinction between instrumental aggression and "pure" aggression is not useful, but that there are limits to its usefulness.

The converse is, usually, less open to dispute. If behaviour causes physical harm to others but is not directed toward doing so, it is not usefully classed as aggressive behaviour if we are interested in problems of causation. Only if it is the consequences that we are interested in—if, for example, we are investigating all the ways in which certain forms of harm arise—does it make sense to include in one category all behaviour that causes harm to others whether or not directed to that end.

Another category of behaviour which poses difficulties for the definition of aggression is play. In nursery school children factor analysis and other types of evidence suggest that two sets of behaviour elements should be distinguished— punch, hit, glare, low-frown, and red face; and wrestle, roll, chase, laugh, and play-face. The former is labelled aggressive behaviour, while the latter shows clear analogies to the rough-and-tumble play of non-human primates (see page 283) (Blurton Jones, 1972b; Smith and Connolly, 1972). Nevertheless particular instances are often difficult to assign to one or the other category, and in studying baboons Owens (1973) found that "play" fighting merged into "real" fighting (see also Cairns, 1972b).

Finally, if one accepts behaviour directed toward harming another individual as the central core of the concept of aggression, it is necessary, in the human case, to remember that the means used to inflict that harm may be extremely devious. Furthermore, one can frame one's definition to include "psychological harm" as well as physical harm, or to exclude it: if one does include it, the problem of deciding whether the behaviour in question was directed toward causing the psychological harm, or whether the latter was merely an incidental consequence, is likely to be even more tricky than with physical aggression. And finally one can include subjective feelings, fantasies, and dreams, or confine one's attention to behaviour.

It is thus clear that the category of aggressive behaviour, while containing a generally agreed nugget, is shady at the edges. If we define it in terms of its actual or potential consequences—even injury to other individuals—we must remember that behaviour with a common consequence may be causally heterogeneous. Our definition will also then depend on how we define "injuring others", and we must recognize that the means employed may be extremely diverse. All this discussion of a matter of definition may seem excessive: later sections will show that it is not.

### The causes of aggression in animals

In discussing the causal bases of aggression, it is necessary to draw information from studies of a wide range of species. The generalizations made must thus be treated with special caution.

By definition, aggressive behaviour is normally directed toward another individual. In addition, it is normally elicited by stimuli from another individual. These may be visual (e.g., Tinbergen, 1951), auditory (e.g., Thorpe, 1961), or olfactory (e.g., Ropartz, 1968; Mugford and Nowell, 1971): some studies analyzing the stimuli involved are discussed in Chap. 6. Much aggression is thus primarily the consequence of the proximity of another individual. This usually means that aggression between two individuals is more likely to occur the closer together they are.

In harmony with this, studies on a wide range of species show that aggression is more common when population density is high (e.g., rats, Calhoun, 1962; baboons, Kummer, 1968; rhesus monkeys, Southwick, 1969). Of course this does not mean that the increased proximity of other individuals is the only factor leading to an increase in aggression when population density increases. And just to show that there is an exception even to the rule that proximity enhances aggression—male hamadryas baboons (Kummer, 1968) and chimpanzees (McGinnis, 1973) are more likely to attack consort females if they start to wander off.

There has been much dispute over the role of other factors, internal or external to the individual concerned, in the instigation of aggression. Some of the difficulties here have arisen from neglect of the heterogeneity of aggressive behaviour: aggression can arise in more than one way, and generalizations about *the* cause of aggression are inevitably misleading.

In the first place, the degree of proximity necessary for aggression to be elicited may be affected by the internal state of the individual. During the winter many small birds live in flocks and attack other individuals only if they come within a foot or so, but during the breeding season they attack any intruder onto a larger area: the difference is primarily due to a change in endocrine state. Hormonal changes also underlie changes in aggressive behaviour within the breeding season in birds (e.g., doves, Vowles and Harwood, 1966), and comparable changes occur over the oestrous cycle and reproductive cycle in mammals (e.g., rats, Barnett, 1969; mice, Noirot, 1972).

In the laboratory, the male sex hormone testosterone is known to augment aggressiveness in the males of a wide range of species (e.g., doves, Bennett, 1940; mice, Beeman, 1947; various papers in Garattini and Sigg, 1969), and ovarian hormones in the females of some (e.g., hamsters, Kislack and Beach, 1955; Payne and Swanson, 1971). Though hormonal changes normally affect aggressiveness by acting on the central nervous system, they may also act in other ways. For instance the dominance order in bachelor groups of red deer is largely determined by antler size, the immediate hormone level being of minor importance. The shedding and growth of the antlers is, however, under hormonal control, which thus affects aggression indirectly (Lincoln et al., 1970). As another example, in mice aggressive behaviour is influenced by pheromones whose production is under hormonal control. These include an aggression-inducing hormone in males (Ropartz, 1968) and an aggression-inhibiting one in females. Krsiak and Steinberg (1969) have shown that drug treatment of one mouse can affect the aggressive behaviour of another.

The internal factors determining aggressiveness are not solely hormonal. In cold weather, or early in the breeding season, a great tit may fluctuate from territorial to flocking behaviour over a period of a few minutes: at one moment a male may be feeding quietly with a dozen other individuals within a few feet, but at the next he will fly up to a song-post and attack any birds within a hundred yards. Correlated hormonal changes are possible but unlikely, and it is a reasonable supposition that there are temporary central nervous states with some independence of the more enduring hormonal ones. Such states are often initiated by, but outlast, a particular incident of aggressive behaviour, so that an individual which has been fighting shows an enhanced tendency to fight after his rival has disappeared. If such a state is aroused in one individual by the proximity of another which the first does not dare to attack, he may re-direct his aggression onto a third. A courting male gull may re-direct the aggressiveness aroused by his mate toward a passer-by (Moynihan, 1955; Tinbergen, 1959); and a monkey, attacked by a superior, may immediately attack an inferior.

Central nervous states comparable to those that must accompany normal aggressive behaviour can be induced by electrical stimulation of the brain in both birds (e.g., von Holst and von St. Paul, 1963; Brown, 1969) and mammals (e.g., Clemente and Lindsley, 1967; Delgado, 1969; Flynn, 1973). In some cases the electrical stimulus merely elicits aggressive patterns in a reflex-like way: such patterns cannot then be conditioned to a simultaneous stimulus, such as a tone. In other cases electrical stimulation of the brain produces aggressive behaviour which seems normal in all respects: for instance its manifestation may vary with the relative dominance of other animals present. In such cases the electrical stimulation probably affects diverse mechanisms, both producing aggressive activities directly and sensitizing the animal to peripheral input. This last finding is due to MacDonnell and Flynn (1966): electrical stimulation of the brain that causes a cat to behave aggressively sensitizes areas around the mouth and nose so that, if touched there, the cat opens its mouth and orients its head toward the stimulus: these movements are part of biting (see also Flynn, 1973). Stimulation in an appropriate brain locus can also suppress aggressiveness, and in one of Delgado's experiments a subordinate monkey learned to press a lever which caused the brain of the dominant monkey to be stimulated, thereby inhibiting his aggressiveness.

Sometimes the effect of the internal state on aggressive behaviour does not involve a neural mechanism more or less specific to aggression, but is more indirect. Thus fighting in flocks of wild birds tends to be more common when the weather is cold and food is scarce, unless conditions are very severe (Hinde, 1952). However, this does not necessarily mean that aggression is directly enhanced by an internal state correlated with food deprivation. In a study of captive chaffinches Marler (1956b) assessed the "50 percent distance"—i.e., the distance between two individuals at which there was an even chance of their tolerating each other. This distance was 25 cm for males (Fig. 16.1) and 7 cm for females. Marler then watched birds feeding from perches fixed 20 cm apart and subjected to various periods of starvation. The proportion of occasions on which both perches were occupied that led to fights was not affected by food deprivation. However, lack of food did increase the readiness of subordinate birds to approach dominant ones at the food, and thus also the frequency with which the tolerance distance was infringed. The frequency of encounters may

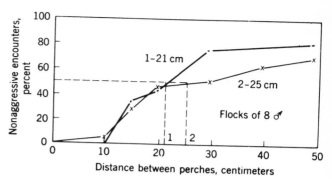

FIGURE 16.1

*Percentage of occasions, on which chaffinches perched at the distance apart shown on the abscissa, that did not involve aggression. Data for two flocks of eight males. (From Marler and Hamilton, 1966.)*

also rise simply because the birds become more active when mildly hungry (Andrew, 1957).

Proximity during feeding may also enhance aggressive behaviour in primates. Chalmers (1968) found that there was more aggression amongst mangabeys when they were feeding on localized food sources than when they were feeding on dispersed food: the increase was primarily a consequence of their greater mutual proximity, not of direct competition over food items. In wild-living chimpanzees the provision of bananas was correlated with an increase in the frequency with which individuals were involved in aggressive interactions (Wrangham, personal communication).

In other species and/or other contexts, hunger may lead to a decrease in aggression. In a captive group of rhesus monkeys Southwick (1969) found that reduction in the space available led to an increase in aggressive interactions, but semi-starvation led to a decrease, caused both by the time spent in food-seeking and by lethargy (see also Loy, 1970a). In rodents hunger is likely to decrease aggression unless food is available only to one animal (Lagerspetz, 1964).

Sometimes the internal state seems to affect aggressiveness by determining the context in which aggression occurs. Thus a territorial bird may ignore a nearby rival outside his territory but attack a more distant one who is within its boundaries. Similarly, late pregnant and lactating mice are more aggressive near their pups than elsewhere: it is significant that lactation is accompanied by a reduction in shock-induced aggression, which is of course assessed in the absence of the pups (Thoman et al., 1970). Furthermore the object of their aggression changes. Whereas non-pregnant females attack strange females and tolerate strange males, females in late pregnancy attack strange males and non-pregnant females but tolerate, and may even cohabit with, other pregnant females (Noirot, 1972).

In the weaver finch *Quelea* Crook and Butterfield (1970) have evidence that dominance rank in non-breeding groups is influenced by the pituitary hormone LH (luteinizing hormone), while the gonadal hormone testosterone affects social status in encounters over a sexually valent commodity such as nest-material. In all these cases the internal state appears to influence the relevance of stimuli rather than, or as well as, the intensity of the behaviour.

So far we have considered the influence (direct or indirect) on fighting of changes in internal state due to food deprivation or hormonal action. Often, however, aggressive behaviour may be affected by situational factors. An obvious case is the territorial song bird: as soon as he crosses the territorial boundary he ceases to attack other individuals and may flee from them. Aggressiveness may also be affected by social stimuli. The aggressive behaviour of mice may be reduced by the presence of a female (Levine, L., et al., 1965), but that of male rats appears to be increased (Calhoun, 1963; Barnett et al., 1968). Male zebra finches show more aggressive behaviour if another individual is present in an adjacent cage, especially if that individual is familiar (Caryl, 1969), and agonistic encounters between males of the African weaver finch *Quelea* are more frequent when females are present (Crook and Butterfield, 1970). Female chimpanzees sometimes appear to encourage males to behave aggressively (van Lawick-Goodall, personal communication).

Aggressive behaviour often occurs in situations which can be described as "frustrating", and some workers have regarded frustration as the primary cause of aggression. This view was worked out in detail by Dollard et al. (1939; see also Miller, 1959; Rozenzweig, 1944) and has been applied especially to the human case, where the frustration may take a number of forms and be either real or imaginary. Many of the experiments on frustration-induced aggression make quaint reading now, particularly because of the lack of clear definition of either frustration or aggression. However, the influence on aggression of a situation which can be described as "frustrating" has been demonstrated experimentally in animals. Pigeons were taught to peck a key by making the delivery of food contingent upon key-pecking. Then the reinforcement condition, when

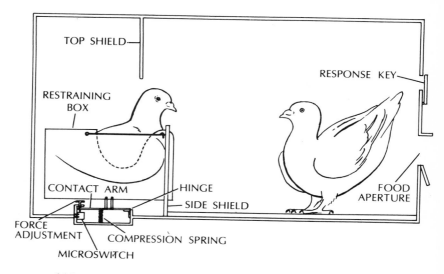

FIGURE 16.2

*Schematic diagram of apparatus for measuring extinction-induced aggression in pigeons. The shields prevent the experimental pigeon from getting behind the target pigeon. (From Azrin et al., 1966.)*

key-pecking yielded food, was alternated with extinction, when it did not (Fig. 16.2). At the beginning of the extinction periods the experimental pigeon would attack a nearby pigeon, or even a stuffed model. The duration of attack varied with a number of measures which could be regarded as related to "frustration", such as the number of preceding reinforcements and the degree of food deprivation (Azrin et al., 1966). As another example, aggression in paired encounters between hens was greater when the birds were food-deprived and food was present but not available (because covered by perspex) than in any of the following conditions: birds not deprived/food available, not deprived/no food, deprived/no food, or deprived/food available (Duncan and Wood-Gush, 1971). There have also been a number of observations of frustration-induced aggression in the field: for instance van Lawick-Goodall (1968) records that chimpanzees may behave aggressively when an artificially provided supply of bananas becomes exhausted. Aggression redirected onto a subordinate after an attack by a dominant animal (see above) can also be regarded as frustration-induced.

There are certainly some circumstances in which frustration does not augment aggression (e.g., Lagerspetz, 1964), and it may reduce it—for instance, when goal-oriented behaviour interferes with the aggression (Lagerspetz, 1964; Ginsburg and Allee, 1942). There is also some evidence that frustration increases aggression only when the animal has previously been reinforced for reacting aggressively to frustrating situations (Scott, 1962). Beyond that, differences of opinion about the importance of frustration in the induction of aggression have been in part due to the looseness of the concept: it would, for instance, be easy to coin a definition of frustration such that a territory-owning great tit was frustrated by an intruder. Furthermore the original frustration-aggression hypothesis has been amended by Miller (e.g., 1959) with the suggestion that frustration instigates a number of responses, of which aggression is only one. Frustration is thus regarded merely as increasing the likelihood of aggressive behaviour, its actual appearance depending on other factors—external stimuli, inhibitory factors, individual characteristics, and so on (see, for example, Berkowitz, 1962).

It has also been shown for a wide range of species that fighting can be elicited by an aversive stimulus, such as an electric shock. If two rats are confined over an electric grid, one or both animals are likely to show attack responses toward the other when the shock is turned on. The extent to which shock-induced aggression resembles naturally occurring aggressive behaviour is controversial. On the one hand, shock-induced aggression is decreased by castration and influenced by previous social experience and other factors in the same way as natural aggression (Azrin et al., 1964; Ulrich, 1966). It may also involve behaviour directed toward obtaining an object suitable to attack: squirrel monkeys can be trained to pull a chain which produces an inanimate object that can be attacked, and the frequency of chain-pulling increases markedly when the shock is turned on (Azrin et al., 1965). On the other hand the attacks do not resemble natural fighting in that they are stereotyped and closely bound to the shock stimulus. Mice induced to fight by means of electric shock show a more defensive type of fighting than mice that are merely placed together after a period of isolation, and the two forms of fighting are affected differently by drugs (Hoffmeister and Wuttke, 1969). However field data suggest that pain-induced aggression is not merely a laboratory phenomenon. For instance van Lawick-Goodall (personal communication) reports that an injured adult male chimpanzee was exceptionally aggressive. Pain-induced aggression, like that induced primarily by proximity, involves a conflict between tendencies to attack and escape. In many natural situations it is slight pain that is likely to induce aggression: more intense pain leads to escape.

Fear[1] also may act as a potent cause of aggression. Wild chimpanzees seeing a previously familiar individual who had become partially paralyzed were at first afraid, and then behaved aggressively (van Lawick-Goodall, 1968). The defensive fighting of a cornered animal may be regarded as due to the augmentation of aggression by fear or by the frustration of escape. Just as fear is often elicited by unfamiliar stimuli, so also is aggression particularly likely to be elicited by unfamiliar individuals. For example, Southwick (1969) found that the removal of two individuals from a captive group of rhesus monkeys, and replacing them by strangers, resulted in a large increase in the frequency of aggressive encounters. Where attacking behaviour is associated with potential harm to the attacker, fear may have the opposite effect and reduce aggression: it is in such circumstances that drugs which reduce fear may enhance aggression (Knight et al., 1963).

This brief survey of research findings shows that aggression in animals may be augmented by a number of factors internal or external to the animal. Clearly it is futile to look for *the* cause of aggression—aggression may have diverse causes, and any one episode may depend on multiple factors.

### Is aggression inevitable?

So far we have spoken as though aggression was always reactive, precipitated by the proximity of another individual, though exacerbated by pain, frustration, and so on. If this were an adequate description, then to control aggression we need look only for means of ameliorating those external factors that give rise to it. While some writers, such as J. P. Scott (1958), have taken this view, others, such as Freud in his earlier writings (S. Freud, 1922; see also A. Freud, 1949), Klein (1948), Lorenz (1966), and Ardrey (1967), regard aggression as arising from forces internal to the individual—endogenous, spontaneous, and therefore inevitable. Seen as opposed alternatives in this way, the problem is clearly of fundamental importance: if aggression is inevitable, we can seek only to minimize its destructiveness. However we shall see that, as so often in biology, the opposition of alternatives is misleading.

We may consider first whether aggression is always imposed by the external situation, or whether animals actively seek fights. That the latter does occur has actually been demonstrated in the laboratory. Thompson (1963) has shown

[1] Fear is used here as an intervening variable—see pages 25–27. Bowlby (1973) gives an important discussion of the use of this term.

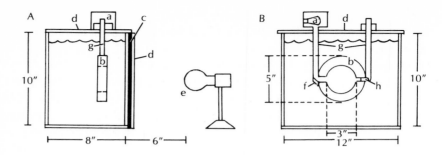

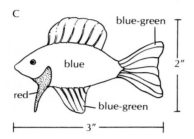

a. 6 watt, 110 v.a.c. lamp

b. response ring

c. one-way glass

d. transluscent lucite

e. 75 watt, 110 v.a.c. lamp

f. 45° front surface mirror

g. 1/2" lucite tubing

h. cl-404 glass photocell

FIGURE 16.3

*Reinforcing effects of visual stimuli for aggression in* Betta *splendens. (From Thompson, 1963). (A) Side view of tank, showing response ring, one-way mirror, and lamp. The mirror was presented by switching off the lamp. (B) Front view of tank facing the mirror. Responses were recorded by the beam of light reflected from the mirror* f *onto the photocell* h. *(C) Model of male.*

that members of at least two species will learn to carry out a simple task if its performance is followed by stimuli eliciting aggressive behaviour. For instance the frequency with which a Siamese fighting fish will swim through a lucite ring placed in its aquarium will increase if swimming through the ring is followed by stimuli which elicit aggressive behaviour (Fig. 7.2), such as a model fish or a mirror. The apparatus used is shown in Fig. 16.3. The frequency with which the fish swam through the ring increased when swimming through led to the presentation of an aggression-eliciting stimulus and decreased when it did not. The more effective the stimulus in eliciting aggression, the more effective it was in enhancing the frequency with which the fish swam through the ring (see also Adler and Hogan, 1963; Hogan, 1967). Not only stimuli which initially elicited aggression, but also stimuli which had come to do so through being paired with an aggression-eliciting model, would reinforce swimming through the ring (T. I. Thompson, 1969). The behaviour of swimming through the ring could properly be described as seeking an opportunity to behave aggressively. Comparable data for three-spined sticklebacks are given by Sevenster (1973).

Similarly juveniles of the coral fish *Microspathodon chrysurus* learn to swim into a glass bottle through which they can display to an antagonist on the other side. The behaviour shows many of the characteristics of responses learned with more conventional reinforcers: for instance it is extinguished by non-reward, and shows long retention after training under conditions of partial reinforcement. Rasa's (1971) interpretation of her findings is that they provide evidence for a "truly endogenous appetitive behaviour for aggression" in this species.

While no comparable experiments have yet been carried out with mammals, the opportunity to kill a mouse can be used to reinforce an operant response in rats (van Hemel and Myer, 1970), and similar principles probably apply (see also Azrin et al., 1965, cited above).

Of course such experiments must not be used lightly as a basis for broad generalizations. For one thing, in both Thompson's and Rasa's experiments the fish was exposed fairly frequently to aggression-eliciting stimuli, which could have been important in maintaining an "aggressive" internal state (see above). Furthermore the situation is more complicated than the experiments just cited indicate. Naive fighting fish with a mirror continuously present may acquire a response to turn the mirror off; and fish which had cohabited with other fish for a long time, and whose aggressive behaviour had therefore habituated, learnt an operant to turn the mirror off more readily than to turn it on (Baenninger, 1970). Thus the experiments with Siamese fighting fish do not show that "aggression" is always reinforcing even in that species, but they do show that it can be.

Now countless field observations have shown that territory-holding animals frequently patrol their territories. Passerine birds, for instance, fly from tree to tree, moving to the attack if an intruder is seen. Such behaviour could be regarded merely as a rather generalized type of appetitive behaviour. But in view of the data cited above from carefully controlled laboratory experiments showing that "aggression" can be reinforcing, and in view of the strong impressions of field observers that patrolling territory owners are especially likely to visit places where fights have recently occurred and that they are especially ready to fight, it seems reasonable to regard such patrolling as a positive seeking for aggression.

Does this mean that aggressive behaviour is "spontaneous"? As we have seen (pages 28–29), the term "spontaneous" can usefully be applied to a change in the output of a system when there is no corresponding change in input. In this sense the behaviour of the Siamese fighting fish, or of a song bird patrolling its territory, can be regarded as spontaneous. "Spontaneity" here does not mean that the behaviour is independent of all previous experience: the fighting fish swam frequently through the ring only because it had learned to do so. Indeed, since a stimulus light associated with mirror presentation acquired the ability to elicit aggressive behaviour, the lucite ring itself may have come to elicit an internal state conducive to aggression. But even if aggressive behaviour can be spontaneous in this sense, this does not necessarily mean that it is inevitable. The emphasis on the inevitability of aggression which is to be found in the recent writings of Lorenz (1966), Ardrey (1967), and others comes from their use of an "energy" model of motivation. We have already seen how misleading such models can be (pages 28–36).

Let us look at the way in which such an energy model has influenced Lorenz's thinking in this context. By causing him to focus on certain characteristics of aggressive behaviour that are compatible with the model, it has led him to suppose that aggressive behaviour is inevitable in the way that such a model would predict. One such characteristic is the manner in which aggressiveness is often increased by a period of isolation. A number of workers have found that mice and rats kept in isolation for a period of days or weeks fight more vigorously when subsequently paired (Fig. 16.4) (e.g., Lagerspetz, 1964; Hatch et al., 1963; Sigg, 1969; Valzelli, 1969; Cairns, 1972b) and the vigour with which they fight decreases with successive, closely spaced encounters (Lagerspetz, 1964). Such findings are compatible with a model postulating the accumulation of aggressive energy while no fighting occurs and its subsequent expenditure in action. However, isolation does not always produce an increase in aggressiveness. For example, Heiligenberg and Kramer (1972) found that isolation decreased rather than increased the aggressive behaviour of males of the cichlid fish *Haplochromis burtoni*. Attack readiness was assessed by the frequency with which the cichlid directed attacks toward small test fish present in its aquarium —a measure highly correlated with the readiness to attack adult males of the same species, but with the advantage that the small fish did not fight back. The attack readiness fell to a low level if the male was isolated from adult conspe-

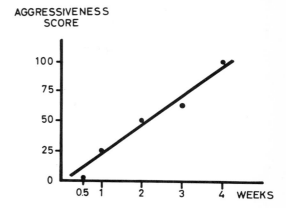

FIGURE 16.4

*Increase in aggressive score obtained by mice when tested after various periods of isolation.* (From Valzelli, 1969.)

cifics for several weeks, but recovered within a few days after repeated exposure to adults or to dummies. Figure 16.5 shows actual data for the increase in attacks on the test fish that resulted from dummy presentations once every 15 min for 8 hr a day over 10 days. The continuous line is derived from a theoretical model of the changes in attack readiness. Heiligenberg and Kramer regard their results as disproving a spontaneous build-up of "aggressiveness", and as indicating that attack readiness needs to be constantly replenished by specific external stimuli causing long-lasting incremental effects (see also van Hemel and Myer, 1970). In mice, too, aggressiveness may be enhanced by recent fighting (Lagerspetz, 1964).

But even where isolation does produce an increase in aggressiveness, there is no evidence that the effect is specific to aggression, or that it can be dissipated only through aggressive behaviour. Social isolation is a very unusual condition for most animals, and may be expected to have diverse effects, many of which may have repercussions on aggressive behaviour. Furthermore, post-isolation tests concern responsiveness to an aggression-eliciting stimulus, not appetitive or operant behaviour: although it is likely that the two are correlated (Premack, 1965), it remains to be proved (see Cairns, cited below). Also the effects vary between strains (Valzelli, 1969) and depend in a complex way on the period of isola-

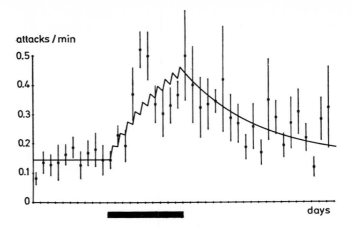

FIGURE 16.5

*Rise in attack rate of* Haplochromis *during 10 days (bar underlining abscissa) of repeated presentation of a fish model. Vertical lines indicate variances. (From Heiligenberg, 1973, by permission of author.)*

tion and the number of post-isolation trials (Kršiak and Janků, 1969) in a manner which cannot be simply explained in terms of an energy model.

That the effect of isolation on subsequent aggressiveness could be mediated in ways not involving the accumulation of aggressive "energy" has in fact been suggested by a number of authors. Thus isolation-induced aggression could be related to the weight gain which occurs during isolation, for in mice there is a correlation between weight and aggressiveness: although this is not likely to provide a full explanation (Daranzo, 1969), it may play some role. Perhaps more likely to be important are the changes in endocrine activity which occur during isolation (Hatch et al., 1963; Sigg, 1969). Though the precise nature of the changes is still not fully understood (Welch and Welch, 1969), isolation produces a general tonic lowering of adrenal activity in rodents, but also a heightened phasic response: such changes in endocrine activity could affect aggressiveness directly, or by more general effects on responsiveness or activity. Isolation produces in the brain a change in the metabolism and rate of turnover of certain neural transmitters (e.g., catecholamines) known to be related to aggressive behaviour, the change being such that there is a more rapid production of such transmitters in the presence of aggression-eliciting stimuli (Welch and Welch, 1969; Vowles, 1970). These changes could lead to a heightened responsiveness to such stimuli.

Recently a series of experiments by Cairns (1972b) has provided firm evidence that the consequences of isolation on fighting are mediated by mechanisms not specific to aggressive behaviour. He found that the behaviour in a social encounter of previously isolated mice differed in two ways from that of mice which had previously been living in a group. First, isolates placed with a test animal were more likely to initiate interactions of all sorts—sniffing, grooming, climbing on the other animal's back, and so on. Second, the previously isolated animals were more reactive, responding with a startle response or by freezing to even mild stimulation from the test animal. This heightened *reactivity* to stimulation was found also in non-social situations. By contrast differences in *activity* were only slight or non-existent. On the basis of these results, Cairns suggested that the effect of isolation on fighting is due not to an enhanced tendency to seek fights per se, but to the more rapid escalation of social contacts into aggressive encounters. This was supported by direct observation and also by data from experiments in which the behaviour of the test animal was manipulated by drug administration: the probability of attack increased with activity. Cairns ascribes the behaviour of the isolates to the high proportion of time normally spent by mice in bodily contact with others: isolates show an increased sensitivity to tactile but not to photic stimuli.

Another type of observation sometimes cited in support of an energy model of aggressive motivation is the temporary reduction in readiness to fight which sometimes occurs after a prolonged encounter. This could be described as the expenditure of fighting "energy" in action and its restoration with time. But it could just as well be ascribed to a self-inhibitory effect of fighting which decays with time: comparable phenomena are well known in many other types of behaviour. On general grounds we should expect an aggressive encounter to have multiple consequences upon subsequent aggressiveness, some positive and some negative, some decaying rapidly and some near-permanent: which predominates would depend on a variety of factors, including the precise circumstances and duration of the initial encounter and the time since it occurred (Hinde, 1970, Chap. 13).

A related type of observation compatible with, but not requiring, an energy model is that an animal deprived of the stimuli normally adequate to elicit aggressive behaviour will attack suboptimal objects. Lorenz describes how a fish kept in an aquarium with fish of a variety of other species, but no members of its own, may sometimes attack individuals of that other species from amongst those present which most resembles its own: this does not happen if one member of its own is available to be attacked. This he ascribes to the accumulation of aggressive energy up to the point at which a normally inadequate object elicits attack: Lorenz further implies that, in the absence of that object, the energy would accumulate still further until an even less adequate object was attacked, or until aggressive behaviour directed toward nothing at all burst forth. But it could also be ascribed to fluctuations in the readiness to show aggressive behaviour with time depending, perhaps, on changing priorities amongst the various activities in the fish's repertoire. On this view any increase in the readiness to behave aggressively could be expected to subside with time, and would not carry the implications of inevitability which accompany an energy model.

Thus the model of accumulating internal energy for aggression is misleading on a number of counts. It implies a unitary cause for aggression, while all the evidence suggests that the causal bases of aggression are much more complex than that (pages 254–261). It implies that a tendency to behave aggressively can be lowered only by discharging the energy in action, a view for which there is no hard evidence (e.g., Berkowitz, 1962): although an aggressive episode is sometimes followed by reduced aggressiveness, in other circumstances aggressive behaviour can enhance the subsequent tendency to aggression (pages 264–266; see also Hokanson, 1970). The energy model also implies that aggressiveness is necessarily enhanced by isolation: this is true in some cases but not in others, and where it is true explanations not involving energy models are more likely (page 267). And finally it implies that increased responsiveness to aggression-eliciting stimuli is necessarily accompanied by an increased tendency to seek out such stimuli. For that there is as yet no evidence, and Cairns's data on mice suggest the opposite: so also do the endocrine changes just mentioned, which involve *lower* tonic adrenal activity. Thus the prediction of the energy model that, if an animal is deprived of aggression-eliciting stimuli, its tendency to show aggressive behaviour would gradually increase up to the point at which it would seek avidly for an object to attack, however grossly inadequate that object may be, is by no means a necessary conclusion from the data, but only from an outdated model of motivation quite inapplicable in this case.

The view that aggression is the consequence of the building up of aggressive energy which is subsequently discharged in action is of course in keeping with the classical doctrine of catharsis, which recurs frequently in our literature and is supported today by many psychiatrists. However the evidence bearing on this question for man has been assessed by Berkowitz (1962), and lends little support to the view. Although a display of anger may bring some tension reduction, such evidence as is available indicates, as we have seen, that any reduction in the probability of further aggressive behaviour is at most temporary.

Thus while animals may spontaneously seek fights, the evidence that the tendency to show aggressive behaviour inexorably increases with time until it suddenly bursts forth is quite inadequate, and the data can be interpreted in other ways which do not imply that aggression is inevitable.

### Violence in nature

It is easy for a chapter on aggression to give the impression that violence is much more common in nature than it actually is. Though there is certainly often intensive competition between individuals, and the outcome of this is often settled by agonistic behaviour, death and injury are less common than might be expected. There is a variety of evolutionary reasons why both the frequency of aggressive episodes, and the violence within them, should be minimized.

1  Both participants in an aggressive encounter are likely to be hurt. An individual up against insuperable odds does better either to accept a submissive status or to try his luck elsewhere (Tinbergen, 1968). But it is also better for the potential winners of aggressive interactions to avoid them if they can, for combat brings risk of injury to both parties.
2  Excessive aggression can lead to the neglect of such activities as courtship, or feeding and rearing the young (Tinbergen, 1956). The deleterious consequences of this "aggressive neglect" have been documented in the gannet (J. B. Nelson, 1964).
3  Excessive aggression may expose the aggressor to predation.
4  Hostility may be diverted toward unrecognized relatives, and thereby affect their reproductive success and thus the replacement of genes held in common by the aggressor and its opponents (Hamilton, 1964; Wilson, 1971; see also page 203).

Of the various ways in which violence is reduced, the most obvious involves the use of threat postures instead of actual combat. It has already been suggested (pages 69–70) that when an individual is definitely going either to attack or flee from another individual, he would do best to do so immediately; but if he is undecided, and what he will do depends in part on the behaviour of the other individual, he may do best first to signal his intention and see how the other responds. Hence the use of threat postures, which are used especially in situations of ambivalence. Submissive postures are also part of the signal repertoire of many species, and serve to turn off the aggressiveness of an attacking individual. Often they are physically the opposite of the species' threat posture (Figs. 6.6 and 6.14). Presumably natural selection has operated to make aggressors responsive to such postures because any fight entails risk of injury. For the same reason, it presumably pays individuals which are likely to win an encounter to use warning signals, and individuals who are likely to lose to sheer off when they receive them: the territorial song of song birds is a case in point, for individuals are likely to win encounters on their own territories.

Most species of birds have a relatively simple repertoire of a song, a few threat postures, and one submissive posture (see Chap. 6), but in the higher primates the diversity of behaviour used in agonistic situations is much greater. van Lawick-Goodall (1968) records how high-ranking male chimpanzees may intimidate rivals by staring, jerking the head, raising an arm, hunching the shoulders, swaggering, stamping, shaking branches, raising hair, throwing rocks, or vocalizing (Fig. 16.6). The threatened animal may present its rump, whimper or scream, bow, bob, crouch, reach out to the aggressor, kiss him, and so on.

Violence is also reduced by various forms of social system. One general issue here is that violence tends to be less between known individuals. Strange individuals introduced into a rhesus troop are almost invariably attacked (Southwick, 1969). Overt aggression is usually less marked between territorial neighbours, or between members of the same flock or group, than it is between strangers. Often, therefore, the ordinary route of development within a group is conducive to the reduction of violence. Abnormal conditions involving the mixing of groups tend to enhance it.

As we have seen, proximity between individuals is associated with increased probability of aggression. If individuals are spaced out on defended territories (see pages 61–62), aggression is likely only on the boundaries, and even there, once the boundaries are established, exchanges between rivals are usually limited to threat.

Another form of social system which has the consequence of reducing actual violence is the "dominance hierarchy". If a number of individuals, initially strangers to one another, are put together, there may initially be a considerable amount of fighting. After a while, however, the outcome of aggressive interactions becomes predictable. Some individuals are consistently dominated by others, while others consistently dominate. The result is a dominance hierarchy, which may involve a linear sequence from the despot to the most subordinate animal, or other variations on this theme. This type of social structure, found in

FIGURE 16.6
*Displaying male chimpanzee.* (Drawing by Priscilla Edwards from a photograph in van Lawick-Goodall, 1968.)

a wide variety of vertebrates up to and including man, will be discussed in more detail later. However one point must be emphasized here. Although the emergence of a stable dominance hierarchy is associated with a reduction in violence, this must not be taken as indicating that hierarchical social systems have been evolved by natural selection acting on the group or species to reduce intra-specific strife. Such systems are more readily to be understood as the result of natural selection acting on the individual: it is clearly in the interests of those at the top of the hierarchy to maintain their precedence without the necessity of continuously fighting for it, and it is better for those at the bottom not to be continuously challenging their superiors.

Finally, the existence of these ways in which actual violence is reduced in nature does not mean that aggressiveness is infrequent. Fights do still occur—the scars and torn ears seen on so many animals in the field bear witness to it. And even where actual blows are not exchanged, agonistic encounters may lead indirectly to the death through starvation or reproductive failure of the less successful individuals. As Lack (1969) points out, the reduction of fighting to a ritual may make the world of birds seem idyllic, but "we could not enjoy a society in which one-third of our adult friends and over four-fifths of the teen-agers die of starvation each year."

### Is aggressiveness a valuable human characteristic?

In a book concerned mostly with the behaviour of animals, discussion of *value judgments* about human aggression might seem out of place. It is, however, justi-fied by the false arguments used in this context in the past.

It is partly because aggression is sometimes used in a broad sense to include all ways in which man asserts himself over his environment and expresses his individuality (pages 250–254) that it is sometimes regarded as a praise-worthy human characteristic. If "aggressive behaviour" is taken to embrace all man's influence over his environment, the world would certainly be a different place without it. But of course judgments about the value of aggression in that broad sense need have no relevance to aggression in the sense of causing harm to others. Even in this narrow sense, however, some authors imply that aggres-sion is not so unpleasant and useless for mankind as it might appear. Their arguments all rest on loose thinking.

Some argue that since aggression arose through natural selection, it must be valuable to the species. Several points must be made here. Natural selection operates primarily through *individuals*: a trait is selected because those indi-viduals that possess it are more likely to survive and reproduce. The question of whether a trait is valuable to the individuals that possess it is an entirely differ-ent one from that of whether the possession of the trait by some individuals is valuable to the group to which they belong. In our own society those who are prepared to use physical violence may be able to achieve their own ends more readily than others, but that is not the same as saying that their behaviour is beneficial for society.

This sort of confusion forms the basis of the interpretations put on many forms of aggressive behaviour by Wynne-Edwards (e.g., 1962, 1972). Holding the view that animals have evolved means to keep their population levels below that at which food shortages become a problem, he believes that aggressive behaviour is one means to that end. For example, red grouse show territorial aggression which results in some individuals claiming territories whilst others are forced to retire to live in flocks in less suitable areas. Wynne-Edwards sees this as a means for ensuring that the breeding habitat is not over-populated, and even regards the behaviour of the losers as "altruistic". But it would be more in keeping with what we know about the way in which natural selection acts to assume that the behaviour of both territorial winners and territorial losers is in their own best interests. The territorial winners secure for themselves an adequate space for the rearing of their young. The chances for the losers of reproducing successfully are small, but they may do better to withdraw from a hopeless fight while there is at least some chance of another opportunity later on, than to expend their energies in attempting to carve out an inadequate territory against insuperable odds (see Lack, 1966, page 299ff. for a critique of Wynne-Edwards's views).

Another point about the argument that aggression must be beneficial because it arose through natural selection is that, when applied to man, it neglects his rapid cultural evolution. This has placed him in circumstances quite different from those in which natural selection operated, so that traits that were selected for in protohominids may be maladaptive now.

It is also suggested that aggression is beneficial to the species because it ensures that the fitter individuals get priority of access to food, mates, and other valuable commodities (e.g., McDougall, 1923; Ulrich and Symannek, 1969). In that "fitter" is equated with "more aggressive", the argument is circular, and also implies that the more aggressive individuals are the ones that society wishes to perpetuate: not all would agree with this view. If "fitter" is not to be equated with "more aggressive" the argument fails through lack of evidence for a correlation between aggressiveness and fitness in other respects. Even where there is a correlation (Lagerspetz, 1964; Karczmar and Scudder, 1969), the nature of the causal link still has to be investigated: for instance, both could be consequences of more efficient metabolism. As applied to animals (e.g., by Boelkins and Heiser, 1970), the view that aggression is beneficial to the species in this way involves the false view of natural selection discussed in the preceding paragraphs. As applied to man, it overlooks the fact that there are other ways of reducing competition.

Yet another argument is that a hierarchical structure in society ensures peace and order within the community and that the aggression involved in its maintenance is therefore in the end beneficial (e.g., Stokes and Cox, 1969). Clearly this would be unnecessary if aggression were not potentially present:

the argument thus has a modicum of circularity. Presumably what is meant is that societies with a hierarchical structure imposed from above are often stable. But that stability, far from being a beneficial consequence of the aggressiveness of individuals, occurs in spite of it. The ordered dominance system gains stability only when the subordinate individuals cease to challenge the more aggressive ones—presumably because it is better for them to accept a subordinate position than struggle against hopeless odds (see above). And whether it is beneficial for the society as a whole depends on the values of those at the top.

Now of course law and order must be maintained, but a social order based on a hierarchical system maintained by force may not be so desirable as it seems: it may conceal untold tensions. And support for such an imposed hierarchy because it ensures government by those fittest to govern implies a positive correlation between strength and wisdom not always borne out by common experience. Such support becomes even more positively objectionable when it is further implied (e.g., by Storr, 1968) that pariah castes, such as the Untouchables of India, "serve a valuable function in human communities for the discharge of aggressive tensions": the Untouchables would be unlikely to share this view.

It is also often said that aggression forms part of many normal and pleasurable human activities. Some, for example, have argued that aggressive male dominance is essential to the relations between the sexes. Not many would nowadays agree with this view as applied to man: amongst animals, while aggressive and fleeing responses are often closely interwoven with sexual ones, they interfere with mating rather than promote it. In fish and birds courtship displays are usually given during a period in which male dominance is reduced to a point at which mating is possible (Tinbergen, 1959; Hinde, 1970); and in fish, birds, and mammals a high tendency to aggression may interfere with mating (King, 1956; Sevenster, 1961; Lagarspetz, 1969). Under certain circumstances the occurrence of aggressive behaviour, in addition to having a short-term negative effect on sexual behaviour, may also be correlated with a longer-term positive one (Sevenster, 1961). However there is no evidence that the long-term effect is specific to aggression, and it may be mediated by a change in general arousal affecting many different activities (Wilz, 1972). Many psychoanalysts hold the view that sex and aggression are closely related, but the fact that words like "screw" and "fuck" are used in both contexts, adduced in support of their view (Solomon, 1970), is another example of the risks entailed in basing scientific conclusions on colloquial speech.

One other argument must be mentioned. Pointing to evidence that only species that show inter-individual aggressiveness show inter-individual bonds, Lorenz (1966) and others have argued that some of the best aspects of social life exist only because of their antitheses. But the evolutionary correlation, insofar as it exists, between aggressiveness and social bonds is of dubious relevance to the quite different question of whether a causal relation exists, i.e., of whether aggression contributes to affectional bonds within the lifetime of any one individual or society. And the height of absurdity is reached when Storr argues that "it is only when intense aggressiveness exists between two individuals that love can arise".

Some time has been spent on these views because they are so dangerous if accepted uncritically. There is of course no dispute that aggressive behaviour has been selected as an adaptive characteristic in the great majority of species of higher animals, and that individuals who show it to a reasonable degree are more likely to survive and leave offspring than individuals who do not. But this is a completely different matter from the implication that aggressiveness in man may be a characteristic valuable for human society. There is no need to emphasize that aggressiveness can be a vice, and our concern must be with means to reduce it. It is sometimes argued that we do not know what repercussions a reduction in individual aggressiveness might have on the structure of human personality, but it seems unlikely that a reduced tendency to injure others could have deleterious effects. In any case, the question can justifiably be postponed in the face of the urgency of the present situation.

### The bases of human aggression

Studies cited in earlier sections (pages 254–261) show that aggression in adult animals has diverse causes. If that were the only finding from animal studies of relevance to man, they would still have been worthwhile, for even in the human case there has been a tendency toward over-simple theorizing. This has sometimes taken the form of ascribing aggressive behaviour to a unitary internal drive or instinct, sometimes to a single type of external factor.

The view that aggression depends on an internal drive comes from two sources. One is the psychoanalytic view (e.g., S. Freud, 1922; A. Freud, 1949; Klein, 1948; Storr, 1968), involving an energy model of motivation. The shortcomings of such models have already been discussed (see above). The other involves observation of the near-ubiquity of aggression in animals (Lorenz, 1966; Ardrey, 1967) and the presumed importance of aggressiveness to our hunter/gatherer forebears (e.g., Tiger and Fox, 1972): as the preceding discussion shows, the occurrence of aggressive behaviour in itself provides no evidence for the nature of its causation. The view that aggression depends solely on external factors stems from attempts to fit the complexity and diversity of human behaviour into the straitjacket of a particular theoretical approach, such as the frustration/aggression hypothesis discussed earlier. The work discussed in the preceding pages shows how aggression depends neither solely on internal nor solely on external factors, and that even in animals aggression has multiple determinants. This is even more likely to be true of man.

In fact many of the principles that can be formulated on the basis of studies of animals—the roles of proximity, various aspects of the internal state (including also hypoglycaemia, Wilder, 1947), frustration, pain, and fear (including strangeness, though not necessarily in young children, McGrew, 1972)—cover also the main factors determining aggression in man, though they must clearly be interpreted more broadly in the human case. For example, the objects and situations that precipitate aggression are much more diverse than in animals (e.g., Berkowitz, 1962); in man pain and frustration may arise from verbal slights, or imagined insults, or may even be entirely illusory; and the likelihood that frustration will induce aggression may depend on whether the frustrated individual thinks he will be able to retaliate (e.g., Worchel, 1957), as well as on many other factors. That frustration can lead to aggression in the long term as well as in the short is suggested by various types of indirect evidence. For example, the number of lynchings in the Southern United States between 1882 and 1930 tended to be high during periods of economic depression, and to fall with the return of prosperity. This has been interpreted as a redirection of the aggression, instigated by frustrations associated with depression, toward victims unable to retaliate (Hovland and Sears, 1940).

Man's learning ability makes possible the use of aggression in an instrumental fashion to gain goals other than harm to the opponent in a wide range of contexts. Thus violence may be used to counter not merely threats to an individual's survival, but also threats to his self-esteem and dignity, or to crucial inter-personal relationships. Indeed one use of aggression common in man but at least rare in sub-primate forms is as a means of communication: much of the aggressiveness shown by young children may be a means for obtaining the attention of peers and adults.

Whatever its source (see Chap. 17), some propensity to aggression is almost inevitable from the earliest years. A crucial issue is thus the means whereby it can be controlled. Socially unacceptable behaviour by a young child is at first restrained primarily through anticipation of reward or punishment from controlling adults. Later, however, the standards of behaviour thus imposed by others come in some degree to be accepted as his own. Once such "internalization" has begun, the individual tends to observe prohibitions at times when transgressions are unlikely to be discovered (e.g., Bandura and Walters, 1959; see also pages 289–292). There are hints that such control of behaviour by "conscience" or "guilt" occurs in chimpanzees (e.g., Kellogg and Kellogg, 1933), but in both complexity and importance it is on quite a different level in the human case. This is an important factor to be taken into consideration in generalizing from animal to man.

Another difference between human and animal aggression lies in the frequency with which men (especially males, Tiger, 1969) show aggressive behaviour as a group. Though there are numerous examples of animals co-operating in defensive aggression toward predators, there are few of co-operation in aggression directed toward individuals of the same species. Cases have been reported in rats (Lorenz, 1966), though their precise bases are not clear, in some birds which hold group territories (e.g., Davis, 1940), and in some mammals which form closed groups or troops (see Chap. 25). However the aggressive behaviour shown by groups of men has few close parallels in the animal kingdom. We are concerned here not with war, but with phenomena such as mob aggression. In such cases the violence often seems so unpredictable and so far removed from the social norms that new types of explanation seem necessary. How far can mob violence be understood in terms of the principles described so far?

First, in many cases the individuals concerned may have been reared in conditions conducive to the development of aggressive potentialities—in poverty, or with affectional deprivation (e.g., Lieberson and Silverman, 1965). Often these potentialities are maintained by a chronic state of stress deriving from real or imagined repression (e.g., Caplan and Paige, 1968; Ransford, 1968). The individuals concerned may feel isolated from and in the power of the society in which they live (Ransford, 1968), or unable to communicate with other groups. In addition other stresses, even though apparently irrelevant, may exacerbate matters. For these reasons, the immediately precipitating factors may be relatively trivial, though often they involve a particular incident which symbolizes the more general issues (Lieberson and Silverman, 1965).

If violence starts, it is likely to spread rapidly. It often appears that all the normal social inhibitions against damage to person and property have vanished. This, however, is a mistaken viewpoint. While some social conventions are abandoned, others are created: mob violence is not generalized but is directed toward particular goals which usually represent some of the initially frustrating factors. This may involve a good deal of rationalization—the damage done to "them" is justified in terms of the damage "they" might do to "us", or even to themselves, if not prevented. And often the goals of mob violence are most accurately described not as destruction, nor even acquisition, but as communication. It is often this aspect which determines the direction of the violence.

This goal of communication operates not only between the mob and outsiders, but also between the individuals composing the mob. In the first place common aggression toward outsiders may increase harmony within the group (Sherif and Sherif, 1953). More important, within the mob, violence not only is socially acceptable but affords hierarchical status. Not only are those initially most insecure and in need of status often most likely to behave aggressively, but their acts of violence are especially prone to being reinforced by the approval of other group members. Furthermore the leaders will tend toward progressively more extreme measures because their status is enhanced to the extent that they are followed, and the initially more passive participants may be drawn along as the norm of behaviour becomes ever more destructive (see also Wheeler and Caggiula, 1966). Violence breeds violence.

Insofar as the aggression is a form of seeking status or security within the group, and insofar as it is a means of communication to those outside, the violence may be only an unfortunate sequel to the threat and bombast which precede it. Threat and bombast, passively received, may die away. But if they evoke a reciprocal reply, violence is the more likely to occur. It is partly for this reason that mob control is so difficult—it may be impossible not to become involved.

Thus even mob violence has its roots in factors similar to those that have been studied in non-human species—though there are of course many additional factors which derive from the additional complexity of the human case. War, of course, is a different issue. Just because it involves behaviour directed toward causing harm to other individuals, it may be said to involve aggressive behaviour. But this merely serves to illustrate that phenomena grouped together by such a definition may have diverse causes and consequences. Although war may sometimes depend on the bypassing, through the use of long-range weapons, of our normal inhibitions against physical aggression (Lorenz, 1966), its causes must surely be sought in other spheres, and at other levels of analysis, than those we have been considering so far. And because we live in an era overshadowed by the bomb, it is possible that its enormity may cause us to neglect the importance of individual acts of aggression, whose consequences in terms of human unhappiness may be much greater.

### Summary

We have seen that many of the difficulties in the study of aggressive behaviour arise from difficulties in definition. Studies of animals permit us to make certain generalizations about factors which increase the probability of aggressive episodes, but to search for generalizations about the causes of aggression is fruitless. However, such studies do indicate that the occurrence of aggression is not so inevitable as "energy models" of motivation suggest. Although aggressive behaviour has been evolved under the influence of natural selection, suggestions that it is a desirable human characteristic rest for the most part on false arguments; and the urgent need is to reduce it. The bases of human aggression resemble in many ways those of aggressive behaviour in animals, though language and the human level of cognitive functioning introduce new dimensions of complexity.

# $\boxed{17}$
# THE DEVELOPMENT OF AGGRESSIVE BEHAVIOUR

In the previous chapter the causation of aggression in adult individuals was considered. Here we shall take up the complementary question—the nature of the developmental factors that determine the tendency of the individual to show aggressive behaviour.

### Genetic factors

As with every other sort of behaviour, genes are amongst the determinants of aggressive behaviour. Genetic studies have shown that different strains of the same species may differ considerably in aggressiveness. Much of the early work was concerned with strains of mice (Ginsburg and Allee, 1942; Scott, 1966), dogs (e.g., Scott and Fuller, 1965), and other domesticated species, but comparable differences in aggressiveness exist between closely related species in nature.

The demonstration that aggressive behaviour is influenced by genes tells us little about how differences in aggressiveness between strains arise. The effects may be indirect—mediated, for instance, by differences in body size, strength, weapons, activity level, sensory capacities, and so on, or by differences in the ease with which aggressive responses are learned, as well as through changes in the immediate central nervous determinants of aggression. Lagerspetz's (1964) selection of mouse strains for aggressiveness seemed to involve an increase in sympathetic tone and arousal, for it was accompanied by changes in motor and exploratory activity, and by changes in metabolism indicated by higher intakes of water and ethanol.

The data of Karczmar and Scudder (1969) show that related rodents differ from one another not only in aggressiveness per se, but in the contexts in which aggression occurs. For example, *Onychomys* mothers are more aggressive than *Mus* in defence of their young and, unlike *Mus*, may be more aggressive than males in a social situation. But *Onychomys* mice, unlike *Mus*, do not fight after isolation.

One important way in which genetic differences affect subsequent aggressiveness has been studied in some detail. It has been known for some years that the nature of the hormones circulating in the young organism before or soon after birth can affect its sexual differentiation and adult sexual behaviour (pages 307–309). Bronson and Desjardins (1968) and Conner and Levine (1969) have shown that similar effects operate in the determination of aggressive behaviour. Neonatally castrated male rats show female-like patterns of shock-induced (see page 260) fighting and, like females but unlike males castrated at weaning, do not show increased fighting in response to injected androgens. Thus the difference between the sexes in both sexual and aggressive behaviour that result ultimately from genetic differences are mediated by differences in hormones circulating around the time of birth. Of course this does not mean that the genetic or hormonal differences determine absolutely the nature of the behaviour shown later—experience can produce marked differences even in the relative extents of male and female behaviour shown (see Chap. 19).

In man, also, some individual differences in aggressiveness may be basically genetic, though precisely how the genetic factors operate is far from understood. There is some evidence that pathological violence may sometimes be due to genetic abnormalities (Brown et al., 1968), but the evidence is controversial (Boelkins and Heiser, 1970). In any case genetic sources of differences in aggressiveness are probably much less important than environmental ones.

## Precursors of aggression

Just because the newborn or newly hatched organism can do fewer things than the adult, we must expect to find the early beginnings of aggressive behaviour to be at first inseparable from, and later closely interwoven with, those of other types of behaviour. Unfortunately there have been very few detailed studies of the ontogeny of aggressive behaviour from its beginnings in young organisms, but one of them makes exactly that point. In his study of the development of behaviour in junglefowl, Kruijt (1964) showed that the precursors of aggressive behaviour occur in the context of locomotion. At about one week the hopping that occurs in the course of general locomotion sometimes results in individuals bumping into one another. A few days later this hopping seems to become oriented toward other individuals, the birds bumping their breasts together. Various stereotyped aggressive patterns—threatening, leaping, aggressive pecking, and kicking—appear between 8 and 21 days after hatching, and during this period the factors controlling fighting seem to be similar to those controlling locomotion. As the pecks become more effective, other chicks come to elicit escape as well as approach responses, and the fights come to involve ambivalence. At about four weeks of age fighting starts to be elicited by the proximity of another individual, and aggressive behaviour comes gradually to be independent of the factors that controlled it in the chick. Although only the outlines of the development of aggressive behaviour in this species are yet available, it is clear that it involves the integration of and interaction between causal factors and movement patterns which were initially independent of each other.

In mammals such evidence as is available indicates that aggressive patterns first appear in play. Play is another category of behaviour with a core about which there is little disagreement, but with extremely shady edges. The aspect important here is that the motor patterns of aggression appear inter-mingled with those of other categories of behaviour and in contexts which suggest considerable independence from the causal factors relevant to them later on. Thus young rhesus monkeys show much "rough-and-tumble" play which includes many aggressive patterns: however, it is not "serious", and is often preceded or accompanied by a special "play-face" (Altmann, 1967b; cf. Fig. 10.6). There is no clear dividing line between "play" aggression and "real" aggression: interactions involving aggressive movement patterns take on more of the character of real aggression as the infant matures (see also Owens, 1973). Once again the development of aggression appears to involve integration of causal factors and movement patterns that were initially independent of each other. To what extent the learning processes involved are constrained by maturational ones is at present an open issue.

Of course, the appearance of aggressive movement patterns in play does not mean that play is a necessary precursor of aggression. As we shall see in a moment, individuals reared in isolation are often exceptionally aggressive.

### Experiential factors

We may now consider some forms of treatment that affect subsequent aggression, proceeding from the crude and gross treatment of rearing in social isolation to those more specifically concerned with aggressive behaviour. As in previous chapters, we shall be forced to draw examples from diverse species, and cross-species generalizations are dangerous: the most that such data can show are the sorts of factors which might operate in any one case.

Rearing in isolation from other members of the species can have profound effects on subsequent aggressive behaviour, but there are no rules about their duration or nature. In some species and circumstances there is a resultant decrease in aggressiveness (e.g., rodents, King and Gurney, 1954; Hutchinson et al., 1965), but more usually there is an increase (e.g., mice, King, 1957; Levine et al., 1965; rats, Seitz, 1954); with some species some workers report a decrease and others an increase (e.g., dogs, Scott and Fuller, 1965; Kuo, 1967); and in some genera the direction of the effect seems to depend on the species (*Peromyscus*, Rosen and Hart, 1963). Rhesus monkeys reared without normal social experience tend to be exceptionally aggressive: in adulthood females brought up under such conditions may attack males who attempt to mate with them and, if they do conceive, behave very aggressively toward their infants (e.g., Harlow and Harlow, 1965; Arling et al., 1969). Monkeys reared in isolation also showed much self-directed aggression. After total social and considerable perceptual isolation for the first 6 months of life, rhesus infants showed intense fear and tried to avoid social contacts, but infants similarly treated only for the second 6 months of life were hyperaggressive (Rowlands cited Boelkins and Heiser, 1970; see also Chap. 16).

The data from experiments involving the rearing of animals in isolation thus show that aggressiveness may be affected by the conditions of rearing, and that the effects are complex, but they provide little further insight. As pointed out in Chap. 15, rearing in total social isolation is an extreme sort of treatment, and it could be expected to affect aggressiveness in a variety of ways. First, in the test a fellow member of the species will initially be strange, and thus likely to evoke fear responses (e.g., King, 1957): fear may augment or inhibit aggression (pages 260–261). Second, social experience normally influences the extent to which aggression is inhibited by fear and by other types of behaviour. Third, the integration between aggressive and fear behaviour which occurs in normally reared animals may be absent in those reared in isolation: Burmese red junglefowl reared in isolation not only show abnormally intense escape and aggressive behaviour, but the change-over from one to the other occurs erratically and is not accompanied by normal ambivalent behaviour (Kruijt, 1964).

Turning to variations in experience somewhat closer to those that might occur normally, the type of maternal care received may influence subsequent aggressiveness. A considerable literature on the effects of mothering on aggressiveness in rodents now exists, and only a few representative studies can be cited. Uyeno (1960) compared the aggressiveness of the offspring of dominant and subordinate rat mothers when the young were reared by mothers of status similar to or different from that of their own. While young with dominant natural mothers proved to be dominant to the offspring of subordinate natural mothers, young reared by subordinate mothers tended to be dominant to those reared by dominant ones: one possibility is that those reared by the more subordinate mothers learnt to be aggressive in interactions with her (Lagerspetz, 1964). Uyeno's results may be compared with those of Southwick (1968), who found that the rearing of mice from a passive strain by foster-mothers of an aggressive one increased the aggressiveness of the pups at maturity.

Another experiment involving cross-fostering between two strains of mice was reported by Lagerspetz (1969). She found a slight tendency for mice reared by mothers of their own strain to be more aggressive than mice reared by mothers of the other strain, though the effect was not large enough to overcome the initial genetic difference in aggressiveness between the strains. Again, mice reared from four days of age by rat mothers fought less than mouse-reared mice (Hudgens et al., 1967). How much this was a consequence or a correlate of the differences observed in weight, activity, and so on has not yet been determined. Nor is it clear whether the difference was due to a difference in the general level of stimulation received by the pups, or to differences in more specifically aggressive episodes.

Though there can be little doubt that the type of mothering received affects subsequent aggressiveness also in primates, there have been few detailed studies. However, the infant rhesus, reared by mothers who had themselves been reared in social isolation and were as a consequence hyperaggressive, were themselves also hyperaggressive in adulthood (Boelkins and Heiser, 1970; see pages 234–237).

Though it is clear that the type of mothering received can affect subsequent aggressiveness, the precise ways in which the effects are produced are certainly diverse. The finding that handling or otherwise disturbing rodent pups for a few minutes each day can have widespread effects on their behaviour in adulthood (pages 230–234) suggests that quite minor changes in maternal care could affect subsequent aggressiveness (Levine, 1967). Indeed, the effect of handling may be mediated by resultant changes in maternal care (e.g., Levine, 1967; Richards, 1967; Thoman and Levine, 1970). The mother may also affect the aggressiveness of her young as a consequence of aggressive interactions with them: this possibility has already been mentioned in connection with Uyeno's experiment. In monkeys a quite different principle seems to operate: the social status of young rhesus monkeys varies with that of their mothers because dominant mothers interfere in disputes on behalf of their young. This may have long-term effects (see Chap. 22).

Experience with social companions other than the mother also may have a profound effect on subsequent aggressiveness. In a study at Wisconsin rhesus infants raised by their own mothers but denied access to peers were hyper-aggressive. The effects were present if access to peers was denied for 4 months, and marked after 8 months (Alexander, cited Harlow and Harlow, 1969): these periods are much what would be expected from the age at which infants begin to spend a considerable proportion of their time in social play. By contrast rhesus infants reared on surrogate mothers or without mothers, but with access to peers, showed near-normal social behaviour (Chamove et al., cited Harlow and Harlow, 1969). The play of many social species contains a high proportion of aggressive play, and is likely to be of considerable importance in influencing not only the level of aggressiveness shown in adulthood, but also the development of the actual techniques of fighting. For example, the scruff-oriented attack in canids depends on social experience (Fox, 1969).

As we have seen, aggressive behaviour may be induced by stimuli previously associated with fighting (Adler and Hogan, 1963; Vernon and Ulrich, 1966; Thompson, 1969). The results of previous fights are also important (Kuo, 1967). Mice subjected to defeats are less likely to be aggressive subsequently, and vice versa. Such effects are perhaps more likely to be long-lasting if they occur early in life than later (Kahn, 1951), but similar ones can certainly be produced in adulthood (e.g., Scott and Fredericson, 1951; McDonald et al., 1968). Lagerspetz (1964) found that defeats decreased the aggressiveness of both aggressive and non-aggressive mice, while victories increased the aggressiveness only of initially aggressive ones: the effects disappeared in the course of a few weeks' isolation. A review of the effects of submissive experience on dominance is given by Thines and Heuts (1968). Experience in fighting can even compensate for the effects of castration: while castration of mice with little fighting experience produces a marked reduction in aggressiveness, the effect is much smaller with experienced fighters (Beeman, 1947).

Where fighting takes place with respect to an object, success in obtaining that object may have a marked effect on subsequent aggressiveness. Fredericson et al. (1955) found that food deprivation and/or food competition in infancy increased the competitive fighting shown by mice over food in adulthood: presumably the animals had learnt to fight in the feeding situation. Kuo (1967) has reported long-term experiments in which dogs were trained as fighters: a large part of the training depended on encounters with weaker individuals at a food bowl. In more controlled situations it has been shown that fighting can be reinforced by both food and water (e.g., Ulrich et al., 1963). If pigeons are reinforced with food for aggressive pecking, there is an increase in the frequency not just of pecking but of the whole complex of aggressive behaviour (Reynolds et al., 1963).

Furthermore, as already mentioned (page 267), each aggressive episode may affect subsequent aggressiveness more or less independently of its consequences, leading to either a decrease or an increase, depending on the time relations and other factors. Animals which have recently been aggressively aroused show more tendency to fight than animals which have not behaved aggressively for some time (e.g., mice, Lagerspetz, 1964; fish, Heiligenberg and Kramer, 1972), but frequent or continuous exposure to a rival may lead to habituation (fish, van den Assem and van den Molen, 1969; Clayton and Hinde, 1968). Isolation may also lead to either an increase or a decrease in aggressiveness (see pages 264–267).

Interactions between positive and negative effects of aggressive encounters have been studied by Noirot and Richards (1966) in the context of the behaviour of adult hamsters to pups. The adults learn to behave aggressively, but at the same time stimuli from the pups prime the adult maternal behaviour. As a result in later tests the adults may attack more readily, but switch over to maternal behaviour earlier in the test.

Finally, the effects of punishment on fighting are complex and not yet fully understood. Pain- or shock-elicited aggression by monkeys may be increased by weak punishment or decreased by strong punishment. Thus the effectiveness of punishment on aggression varies with, among other things, its intensity (Ulrich and Symannek, 1969): of course intense punishment may have other effects in addition to reducing the aggression. Some of the complexities are clearly due to the fact that punishment inevitably has contradictory effects, for it also acts as pain or frustration does in inducing aggression.

It is thus clear that the probability of an animal's behaving aggressively in any particular circumstances may be affected by its experiences in both the immediate and remote past. Most of the experiments cited have involved the manipulation of a particular type of experience and subsequently assessing the consequences on aggression. However, it can be safely assumed that the effect of any one type of experience on subsequent aggression will interact with the effects of other experiences (see pages 230–234).

## Development of aggression in man

It is sometimes suggested that the earliest signs of aggression in man lie in the responses made by young babies when the nose is covered so that the nares are occluded (see page 177). This can happen in the course of breast feeding, or when the baby's face comes into contact with any other part of the mother's body or with some other object. The flailing movements of the infant's arms are functional in that they tend to beat off the obstruction and permit normal respiration (Gunther, 1955). Whether an ontogenetic sequence can be traced from this to adult aggression remains to be seen: a relationship with defensive aggression in the adult seems more plausible than one with unprovoked attack (P. E. Edwards, personal communication). It is also sometimes suggested that infantile tantrums are the primordia of adult aggression: certainly they provide an early means for the infant to control his environment. But, by analogy with lower forms, it seems more likely that aggressive patterns develop out of play behaviour: as in non-human primates, rough-and-tumble play is more common in young males than in young females (Blurton Jones, 1972b).

At older ages, there is little doubt that mechanisms comparable to those demonstrated in animals operate also in man, though their interactions are much more complex. Thus deprivation of maternal care and/or affection can have long-term effects on the aggressiveness of human children (e.g., Ainsworth, 1962; Rutter, 1972). Even amongst children with continuous parental care, the nature of that care affects subsequent aggressiveness. Among the parental characteristics found to be relevant here are parental rejection, family discord, parental inconsistency, punitive discipline, and maternal lack of self-esteem (e.g., Sears et al., 1957; Bandura and Walters, 1959). Similar conclusions were reached from a study of lower-class non-delinquent boys by McCord et al. (1961). In addition these authors found that, compared with non-aggressive children, the aggressive boys were more likely to have been raised by parents who did not impose high demands on them, and were less likely to have been closely supervised by their parents. While non-aggressive boys were raised by mothers who "over-controlled" them, the aggressive ones tended to be raised by mothers who controlled them either more or less than normal. There was also a relationship of parental conformity and inner control with low aggressiveness in the son, though an aggressive parental model seemed to be no more productive of aggression than milder forms of parental deviance, irresponsibility, or escapism.

As McCord et al. (1961) point out, studies based on associations between parental characteristics and filial behaviour are open to a variety of interpretations. The associations could be due to the effects of similar genetic or similar environmental factors on both parents and offspring. Or it could be that aggressive children induce aggressive responses in their parents. Though such explanations can not be entirely ruled out, the weight of evidence is strongly in favour of the view that parental behaviour affects the development of aggressive propensities in the children.

Both inside and outside the family, the degree of frustration experienced by the child, and the consequences of aggressive responses to frustration, are likely to play an important part in subsequent aggressiveness. Of course, insofar as aggressiveness can be traced back to the infant's undirected anger at the frustrations it inevitably encounters, some reinforcement of aggression may be almost inseparable from mothering of any sort. And as the infant's perceptual and motor abilities develop, and the anger response becomes more effectively directed toward the source of frustration, it becomes more likely to be reinforced.

Amongst children aggression may be reinforced by approval from parents, teachers, or peers, but Patterson and Cobb (1971) suggest that a more potent source of reinforcement lies in the behaviour of the victim himself—his crying, giving up an object in dispute, or withdrawing. The reinforcing effectiveness of the perception of pain in others may be secondary, and dependent on its previous association with the removal of frustration (see Feshbach, 1964).

The more successful aggressive behaviour in removing frustrations, the more likely is it to be used subsequently. Patterson and Cobb (1971) suggest that this can lead to an escalation: if one member of a dyad *A* presents to the other *B* a stimulus which *B* perceives to be aversive, *B* may respond by presenting an aversive response to *A*. *A* may respond by increasing his response, to which *B* does likewise. The process may escalate until one member withdraws his aversive stimulus, when the other will do likewise. Thus each presents the other with aversive stimuli from which to escape, and each is reinforced by the withdrawal of the aversive stimuli presented by the other. Patterson and Cobb are concerned primarily with human children, but the parallel with Simpson's description of the duelling of Siamese fighting fish (see pages 87–89) will not have escaped the reader.

In the human case, it must be presumed that children learn which aversive stimuli can be terminated by an aggressive response. Furthermore, stimuli associated with the withdrawal of aversive events could come to serve as positive reinforcers for aggressive or coercive behaviour: thus "little brother's teasing leads to a hit by his older sister; his crying signifies that teasing is terminated . . . crying becomes a conditioned positive reinforcer and the brother a discriminative stimulus setting the occasion for attacks." Thus the stimulus which increases the frequency of the aggressive behaviour could cease to be aversive, and exert positive control on attack. Patterson and Cobb illustrate their hypotheses by a detailed study of family interactions which shows how the behaviour of family members provides stimuli which affect the likelihood that one member of the family will behave aggressively to another.

The role of punishment is far from clear, but it probably results in less aggression toward the punisher but more elsewhere (Bandura and Walters, 1963; Ilfield, 1970), and reward for non-aggressive responses to situations potentially eliciting aggression is probably a more effective procedure. The use of physical punishment by parents is strongly related to the subsequent development of aggressive behaviour (Feshbach, 1970). As childhood and adolescence proceed, the situations which elicit and reinforce aggression, and the nature and intensity of aggressive behaviour, may all be influenced by experience both inside and apart from aggressive situations (see Bender, 1969; Ilfield, 1970).

One effect of experience, whose importance in the aggressive behaviour of animals has not yet been demonstrated, is likely to be of special importance in the human case. This is observational learning. The sight of other people behaving aggressively could predispose the subject toward subsequent aggression. In one experiment nursery school children allowed to witness adults exhibiting verbal and physical aggression toward an inflated plastic doll were subsequently likely to exhibit similar aggression to the doll, whereas children who had seen the adults behaving neutrally toward the doll were not (Bandura and Walters, 1963). It has been argued (Blurton Jones, 1972b) that the children's aggression toward the doll was in fact part of rough-and-tumble play, a category of behaviour motivationally distinct from aggression, so that it is only the acquisition of a *potentially* aggressive movement that has been demonstrated. But even with that limitation, it has great relevance to such debatable subjects as the role of television violence. There are strong reasons for thinking that violence, especially heroic violence and "sanitized" violence, in which the aversive factors associated with fear, agony, and death in real life are removed, may have profound effects on some viewers (see also Siegel, 1970; Feshbach and Singer, 1971).

Another major difference between animal and human aggression, mentioned already in the previous chapter, concerns the development of internalized controls over socially unacceptable behaviour. An important issue here is the process of "identification", revealed in behaviour which involves acting like another person. The extent to which identification with parent or other caretaker occurs is likely to depend on the nature of the relationship. Sears (1951) suggests that imitating parental behaviour or expressing their attitudes is a means for obtaining their attention and approval. Parents who are always warm exact no price for their approval, while cold and rejecting parents do not reinforce the child for identification: on this view, therefore, strong identification is to be expected with moderate parental warmth. That identification with the parent is indeed an important issue in the control of aggression is supported, for example, by a study of Bandura and Walters (1959): aggressive boys showed less identification with their fathers than did a control group.

Further complexity may arise from the fact that, in theory at any rate, the inhibition of aggression may itself serve as a source of frustration. Megargee (1966) has argued that this may be a latent instigation to aggression which, when augmented by additional frustration, leads to paradoxical outbursts of violence in usually quiet and inoffensive individuals.

Thus while the general principles derived from studies of animals can be applied to man, this must be done in a sophisticated manner. To cite some examples,[2] in the human case the manner in which the individual perceives himself is a crucial issue; observational learning is more likely to affect him if it involves an individual he respects; the norms of the groups with which he identifies are likely to have a profound effect on his behaviour; the extent to which he feels himself to be frustrated will be influenced by the extent to which he had acquired self-esteem and security; and the extent to which he avoids violence

---

[2] See also Hartup (1973) and papers in Hartup and de Wit (in press).

will be affected by the guide-lines for behaviour that he has acquired and by his future goals.

## Conclusion

In both animal and man the development of aggressive behaviour depends on a complex interaction between the organism and its environment at each stage in development, with social experience playing a crucial role. Clearly, in the understanding of these social influences lie the best hopes for coming to terms with man's propensities for aggression.

# 18
# SOCIO-SEXUAL
# BEHAVIOUR

## Introduction

In non-human primates many of the activities that appear in a copulatory context, such as presenting, mounting, and male displays (Figs. 18.1 to 18.3), occur also in other social contexts—for instance, in greeting, agonistic, friendly, playful, and mildly alarming situations. Thus sexual behaviour is another category without clear boundaries. In recognition of this fact, the complex of courtship, copulation, and other related activities is often referred to as "socio-sexual" behaviour.[1]

## Breeding seasons

Most primates have an annual birth season, implying that fertile mating is also limited to one time of year (Lancaster and Lee, 1965). The seasonal changes in endocrine condition affect males as well as females (Sade, 1964). As usual there

[1] Recent reviews are given by Rowell (1972c) and Michael et al. (1973).

FIGURE 18.1
*Presenting posture of rhesus female.* (Drawing by
Priscilla Edwards.)

are some exceptions—for instance baboons in South Africa (Hall, 1962) and
Uganda (Rowell, 1966a), and chimpanzees in Tanzania (van Lawick-Goodall,
1968) may give birth at any season. It must be presumed that, as in birds (Lack,
1968), both species differences in the extent to which births are confined to a particular season, and also the limits within any one species, are functionally related
to environmental changes which promote successful reproduction, such as the
availability of food for pregnant females or weanling young.

Human births also show seasonal fluctuations. For instance in England and
Wales, and in Bavaria, the data indicate peaks of conceptions in May/June and,
to a lesser extent, in December. Although this seasonal pattern is reversed in
at least some Southern Hemisphere countries, suggesting a biological explanation, it is also reversed in the United States. From a review of available data on
annual cycles of conception in man, Parkes (1968) came to "the platitudinous
conclusion that conceptions are most frequent when people are most festive and
carefree."

The seasonal changes in non-human primates are presumably triggered by
environmental factors, though these have not been studied in detail in primate
species. In addition the synchronization of breeding between individuals in a
group may be aided by mutual stimulation. For example, rhesus males show
some degree of testicular regression during the off-season (Sade, 1964), but both

FIGURE 18.2

*Rhesus macaque: copulation.* (Drawing by Priscilla Edwards.)

behavioural and testicular activity may be increased by exposure to a hormone-treated or cycling female (Vandenbergh, 1969; Rose et al., 1972; Gordon and Bernstein, 1973). Psychogenic factors augment male hormone production also in man (Anon., 1970), and the menstrual cycles of women living in close proximity in an institution sometimes become synchronized (McClintock, 1971).

The seasonal cycles shown by most non-human primates do not involve merely the occurrence of fertile matings at some times of year and not others. There are also seasonal changes in other activities, such as aggression and play. Furthermore the socio-sexual behaviour itself shows seasonal changes not only in frequency but also in its precise nature, in the sexes and ages of the partners chosen, and in the contexts in which it occurs.

Detailed data on seasonal changes in mounting behaviour have been obtained by Hanby (1972) for the Japanese macaques. The observations were made on a troop living in a large corral in Oregon:

1 Male-female mounting involving adult males was largely limited to the period October–January (Fig. 18.4D). During this period mounts usually

FIGURE 18.3
*Male chimpanzee sexual display and female presentation.* (Drawing by Priscilla Edwards from photograph by D. Bygott.)

occurred in series (see below). With younger males, male-female mountings were more spread out over the year (Fig. 18.4A–C), though series-mounting was again more frequent in October–January.

2 Male-male mounting by adults had a seasonal course opposite to that of male-female mounting: the few male-male mounts that did occur in the October–January period did, however, sometimes involve series of mounts, while those outside this period never did. Seasonal changes were again less conspicuous with younger animals.

3 Female-male and female-female mountings were rarer, so that the data depend on a few idiosyncratic individuals. Nevertheless those mountings that did occur were almost limited to the breeding season.

These data clearly show that though the Japanese macaque shows seasons of fertile mating and of birth, mounting behaviour occurs all the year round. In the breeding season, however, male-female pairings are the rule and mounts

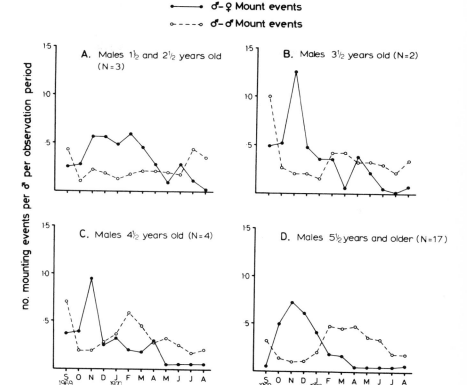

FIGURE 18.4

*Seasonal mounting frequencies in a captive group of Japanese macaques.*
(From Hanby, 1972.)

occur in series which usually lead to ejaculation. Outside the breeding season
mounts are usually single and male-female pairings are relatively rare.

### Monogamy versus polygamy: mate selection

Few primates are monogamous. Among the exceptions are species of Indridae
(Petter, 1965), titi monkeys (Mason, 1968), and gibbons (Carpenter, 1964;
Ellefson, 1968; Chivers, 1972). These species live in family groups in which

there is no clear dominance and in which there are marked social tolerance and continual maintenance of social proximity (Mason, 1968).

Those species that form one-male groups (page 322) could be said to mate polygamously. In multi-male groups mating often appears to be promiscuous: closer study, however, usually shows that this is not the case. Three kinds of constraint are to be found—dominance, and kinship and affiliative relations.

In some species, at least, high-ranking males are more likely to be involved in courtship and copulation than are low-ranking ones (e.g., baboons, DeVore, 1965b). However in most of the species studied the correlation between dominance rank and mounting activity is not absolute: DeVore found that the very highest ranking males were often occupied with controlling the group, and copulated less often than males immediately inferior to them. In another area Saayman (1971) found it was the lowest ranking of three male baboons in a troop which copulated the most. Jay (1965) found an approximate but not a precise correlation between rank and mating activity in langurs, with variation between troops. In free-living rhesus monkeys there seems to be at most a moderate, positive correlation between dominance and mating frequency (Kaufman, 1965; Conaway and Koford, 1965). Loy (1970b, 1971) found no clear correlation at all, for character traits seemed to overshadow effects of age and dominance: however dominant males did tend to mate with older females. The relationship between rank and mating activity varies between troops in vervets (Struhsaker, 1967), and appears to be absent in bonnet macaques (Simonds, 1965). In Japanese macaques the central males do most of the mating, but females sometimes mate with peripheral males (Nishida, 1966). Thus in general there is often some relationship between male dominance and mating in monkeys, but it is often much complicated by other factors. Chimpanzee males sometimes copulate in turn, without reference to rank, though at other times dominant males have precedence (van Lawick-Goodall, 1968; see also page 299 below).

Fewer data are available for females. In the laboratory Goldfoot (1971) found that the dominant of three female pig-tailed macaques in similar endocrine conditions showed the most sexual activity. Whilst in both males and females a relation between dominance and mating could result from natural selection, there appears to be no firm evidence that dominant individuals tend to leave more offspring. The frequency of presenting and mounting vary with dominance also in non-sexual situations (e.g., Japanese macaque, Hanby, 1972).

Turning now to the influence of kinship relations, there is some evidence that incestuous matings occur less often than would be expected by chance. Sade (1968) found this to be the case in free-living rhesus, and Hanby et al. (1971), studying a group of Japanese macaques in a large enclosure, found that sons mounted mothers but did not ejaculate. Loy's (1970b) data showed that interactions between female and adult male rhesus were less correlated with the menstrual cycle if female and male were related than if they were not. Son-mother matings were less common than would be expected by chance, but brother-sister matings were not.

Sade (1972a) has identified three factors which reduce son-mother matings in rhesus. First, many males leave the troop and so are simply not available. Their departure is probably not due to adverse relations with their mothers, since orphans are more likely to leave than sons. Second, within the mother-son relationship female dominance is sufficient to inhibit mating: in the son-mother matings seen the son was dominant to the mother or became so soon afterwards (see also Kortmulder, 1968). Third, son-mother matings are most likely during the last adolescent–early adult stage of the son's life. Sons who had copulated with their mothers in one season were not seen to do so in the next, even though the sons remained dominant.

The third constraint involves the formation of a temporary liaison between a particular male and a particular female: this is usually referred to as "consort behaviour". It usually involves a female, often at the height of behavioural oestrous, associating with a particular male, following and being followed by him, with much mutual grooming and copulation (e.g., rhesus, Bernstein, 1963; Loy, 1970a, b). Even in species where consort relationships are formed, it is by no means the case that all matings are restricted to members of such pairs. Thus oestrous female chimpanzees often travel with a number of males, mating with all of them frequently (van Lawick-Goodall, 1968). However consort pairs are also formed in which the male displays to the female and threatens her if she does not accompany him: such pairs are more common with females whose sexual skin is markedly swollen (see below) than with females at other stages of the cycle (McGinnis, 1973).

In baboons such consort pairs may last for less than a day, or for several days: in rhesus their stability in the wild may be comparable to that in baboons, though pair relationships lasting several years were reported by Kaufmann (1965), and in captivity they may be near-permanent (Reynolds, 1970). The one-male groups of hamadryas baboons (see pages 322–333) involve similar interactions between male and females, but here the male has a permanent liaison with several females.

It must be noted that, apart from the occurrence of copulation, behaviour resembling consort behaviour occurs in many other contexts—for instance,

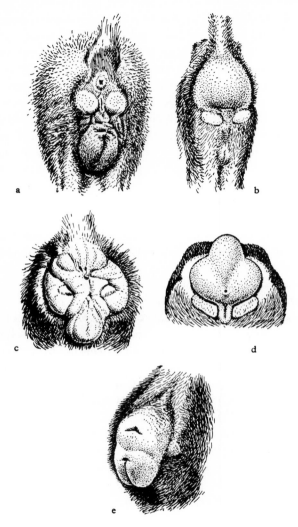

FIGURE 18.5

*Sexual skins of three macaques [(a) rhesus, (b) crab-eating, (d) Celebes]; talapoin monkey (c); and chimpanzee (e). (From Wickler, 1967.)*

between females one of whom has a newborn infant, or between an adult male and a female with a newborn (baboons, Ransom and Ransom, 1971; Rowell, 1972a). In some species affiliative relations between males and young females may influence the formation of later consort pairs. The development of such relations in the hamadryas baboon is described on pages 223–225: Deag (1973) and Ransom and Ransom (1971) have described relationships between males and young females that could affect later choice of consort partners (see page 223).

## The sexual skin, mating, and the menstrual cycle

Some female primates have areas of "sexual skin" which swell and/or change in colour with changes in the reproductive state of the animal (Fig. 18.5). This is particularly conspicuous in baboons, some macaques, and the chimpanzee, but is absent or inconspicuous in most other species. In general the swelling tends to be minimal during menstruation and maximal at ovulation, but there is considerable variation between species (Rowell, 1972a). These changes can be induced by injections of sex hormones (e.g., Saayman, 1972).

Hormone treatment also affects the incidence of female sexual behaviour. In rhesus macaques ovariectomy reduces sexual behaviour, and oestrogen treatment can reinstate it (Michael and Welgella, 1968; see also below).

Such results suggest that mating is under endocrine control, and should therefore be more likely to occur at some stages of the menstrual cycle than at others. This is, however, only partially true. In captivity, copulation occurs throughout the cycle (e.g., rhesus, Rowell, 1963), though there tends to be a peak at the mid-point (rhesus, Michael and Herbert, 1963; Michael, 1968; pig-tailed macaque, Bullock et al., 1972; chimpanzee, Young and Orbison, 1944). This mid-cycle peak, at least under the artificial conditions of tests in which male and female rhesus are paired in a test cage for a limited period, occurs in only some male-female pairs and then not in every cycle (Michael, 1968). The control of female sexual behaviour is evidently more complex than appears at first sight.

One factor here is that hormonal changes in the female influence the occurrence of copulation in two ways, one of which is mediated through the male. Copulation depends on both the attractiveness of the female to the male and on her receptivity: the former is mediated by a vaginal pheromone whose production can be elicited by oestrogen treatment (e.g., Herbert, 1966; Michael and Keverne, 1968), and the latter probably involves adrenal androgens (Everitt and Herbert, 1971; Herbert, 1970). These findings probably have human parallels: it has been suggested that androgens are primarily responsible for sexual motivation in women, oestrogens functioning to promote the lubricant secretions of the vagina (Everitt and Herbert, 1972).

In addition, social preferences complicate the issue. Males show preferences for one female over another (Herbert, 1968), independently of the female's endocrine state. In the pig-tailed macaque the more dominant females tend to copulate more (Goldfoot, 1971).

In the field the relationship between frequency of mating and the menstrual cycle is even less clear. Most and probably all primates show some cyclical variation in the frequency of copulation, but the patterns vary widely. In some species copulation is almost limited to the period of mid-cycle swelling (e.g., anubis baboons, Rowell, 1970; mangabey, Chalmers and Rowell, 1971). In the chacma baboon, the frequency of copulation rises to a mid-cycle peak associated with maximum swelling, and then falls gradually (Saayman, 1970). The mid-cycle peak found in rhesus monkeys tested in small cages (see above) virtually disappears in captive groups (Rowell, 1963). In the field, presenting and copulation tend to be more frequent in mid-cycle, but there is another peak in the latter part of the cycle (Loy, 1970b, 1971). Chimpanzees have an exceptionally well-developed sexual swelling, and copulation is more likely to occur with swollen (mid-cycle) females, but occurs with a reasonable frequency at all stages of the cycle (McGinnis, 1973; Tutin and McGrew, 1973). In man mating occurs fairly evenly through the cycle and even during menstruation, though there are signs of mid-cycle and premenstrual peaks (Udry and Morris, 1968).

Thus considerable variability in the relationship between sexual activity and cyclical hormonal changes in the female occurs amongst primates, and it is difficult to relate the frequency of copulation observed under natural conditions with changes in the controlling hormones as demonstrated in the laboratory. Indeed Loy (1970b) found in rhesus monkeys that copulation was quite frequent during pregnancy. One can only presume, as Rowell (1972a and c) and Goldfoot (1971) suggest, that under natural conditions social factors become more important than hormonal ones—a conclusion which is applicable to our own species.

### Courtship

Copulation is often preceded by a period of "courtship". In some species this may be quite elaborate, with activities such as stalking and parading by the male and even outright attacks on the female (Japanese macaque, Hanby, 1972), or branch-shaking and dashes through the foliage (chimpanzees, Fig. 18.3; van Lawick-Goodall, 1968; McGinnis, 1973). In chimpanzees the male's approach to the female is often accompanied by autonomic behaviour, such as hair-raising, which tends to repel the female. The male is therefore inhibited from approaching the female directly. His courtship behaviour, which includes the erect penis and a variety of gestures, induces the female to cooperate (McGinnis, 1973). Often precopulatory activity involves quiet non-aggressive interactions between male and female. These may be prolonged in baboons, macaques, and chimpanzees, but short or even absent in other species. In howler monkeys courtship is limited to rhythmic tongue movements (Carpenter, 1964), and in Sykes monkeys to an exchange of glances and sometimes mutual nasogenital investigation (Rowell, 1972b). The squirrel monkey, in which the male jumps about from branch to branch near the female with "silent vocalizations" (Baldwin, 1968, 1969, 1971), appears to be intermediate. Since most primates do not form exclusive mating bonds, extensive courtship may not be necessary.

## Copulation

Actual copulation in most primates involves the female's assuming a presentation posture, or at least holding still, while the male mounts from the rear (Fig. 18.2). Intromission, thrusting, and ejaculation can then occur. There are, however, a few exceptions: ventro-ventral mounting has been reported in the siamang (a member of the gibbon group; Koyama, 1971) in the Japanese macaque (Hanby, 1972), and in captive gorillas (Hess, 1973), and is usual in many human cultures. Some monkeys (e.g., Japanese macaque, Fig. 18.6), apes (Zuckerman, 1932; Schaller, 1963; van Lawick-Goodall, 1968), and human beings also use a variety of other postures.

Approaches or mounts do not necessarily end in intromission. A male may merely examine the female's anogenital region, or put a hand on her back, or mount once and then move off.

In some species, such as the rhesus and Japanese macaques and the hamadryas baboon, males usually mount a number of times in series before ejaculation occurs. In most species, however, intromission is achieved on the first or second mount and ejaculation follows a number of thrusts. Even quite closely related species may differ in many aspects of the copulatory sequence (Nadler and Rosenblum, 1973), and species differences appear to be related to anatomical differences in male and female copulatory organs (Kanagawa and Hafez, 1973). In the stump-tailed macaque, in which ejaculation usually occurs

MOUNT POSTURES

**FIGURE 18.6**

*Copulatory positions used by Japanese macaques: (a) double foot-clasp mount; (b) standing mount; (c) bite mount; (d) side mount; (e) and (f) ventro-ventral mounts; (g) and (h) sit-lie on mounts. (From Hanby, 1972.)*

in a single mount, the male sometimes remains tied to the female for a minute or so after ejaculation (Bertrand, 1969), but this is unusual. Whether females of sub-human species achieve orgasm is controversial. A response approximating to physiological orgasm has been induced by experimental manipulation in rhesus females, but the stimulation was excessive (Burton, 1971).

During mounting a couple may be harassed by other members of the troop in various ways. Harassment by adult males has been recorded in rhesus macaques (Altmann, 1962), by juveniles in stump-tailed macaques (Bertrand, 1969), langurs (Jay, 1965), baboons (Rowell, 1967), and chimpanzees (van Lawick-Goodall, 1968), and by adult females in patas monkeys (Hall, 1965). Its significance is obscure.

Copulation itself may be accompanied by certain additional signals in some species. For example in the rhesus monkey the female shows three gestures, the "hand-reach", "head-duck", and "head-bob", which, like the presentation posture, appear to be invitational in nature. They occur most often just before or during mounting and are abolished by ovariectomy (Michael and Zumpe, 1970). These signals do, however, also occur in apparently non-sexual contexts. More detailed observational data are available for other species (e.g., stump-tailed macaque, Bertrand, 1969).

## Mounting and presentation in non-sexual contexts

As noted already, the female's presentation posture, necessary for mounting to be achieved, is also used by many species as a social signal in non-sexual contexts—as a posture of greeting or appeasement, to solicit grooming, and even, in vervets, to assert dominance. Mounting is similarly performed by both sexes and all ages in and out of reproductive condition (Bertrand, 1969; Hanby, 1972). In baboons mounting appears to have different meanings in different contexts. In agonistic situations subordinate males present to dominant ones and may be mounted by them, but in greeting it is often the subordinate male who mounts the dominant one. Subordinates sometimes mount dominants also when they have been engaged in threatening a third, threatening often continuing during the mount (Owens, 1973; macaques, see also Bertrand, 1969; Hanby, 1972).

Both mounting and presenting are clearly functional in the sexual context: presenting displays the genitals, disseminates pheromones, and facilitates intromission; and mounting allows intromission, thrusting, and ejaculation. They are thus usually considered to have been evolved for copulation, other uses being secondary. However, in many species perineal investigation plays an important role in individual recognition, greeting, and so on. It is thus at least possible that the presentation posture has more than one evolutionary origin, the resemblances between sexual and social presenting arising merely from similarity of form (see Bertrand, 1969; Hanby, 1972).

### Conclusion

Two points from these data should perhaps be emphasized. First, sexual behaviour is not a clearly defined category but is closely related to many other aspects of social behaviour. Second, there is great variability between species, and even between the individuals of any one species, in nearly all aspects of sexual behaviour. For both these reasons, generalizations about sexual behaviour demand great caution.

# 19

# THE DEVELOPMENT OF SOCIO-SEXUAL BEHAVIOUR

### Perinatal action of hormones

An increasing volume of evidence demonstrates that the behavioural sex of an animal is in large part determined by the hormonal activity of its own gonads in a fairly brief period before or after birth. Rats are born with a nervous system undifferentiated behaviourally though potentially showing female cyclicity. If it is exposed to testosterone around 4 days after birth, it loses its cyclicity and develops as that of a male. If it is not so exposed, it develops normally as a female. Thus female rats treated with testosterone at four days of age show no oestrous cycles or sexual behaviour in adulthood. Even if ovariectomised and given oestrogen-progesterone therapy they remain sexually unresponsive, but if given testosterone in adulthood they show the complete masculine mating pattern. Treatment of four-day-old males with testosterone has virtually no long-term effect, but neonatally castrated males show ovarian cycles and female sexual behaviour in adulthood if given an ovarian transplant. These perinatal influences of androgenic secretions are not limited to the brain but affect also spinal mechanisms and the external genitalia (Harris and Levine, 1965; Saunders, 1968).[1]

---

[1] In an important review Beach (1971) has stressed the need for conceptual and terminological precision in this area.

In the rat, the brain is most sensitive to sex determination by steroids about 4 days after birth, though the sensitive period probably starts before birth. In the guinea pig, which is born at a more mature stage, the sensitive period is prenatal (Young, 1969). In the monkey, also, the sensitive period is prenatal (Goy, 1968, 1970).

In the rhesus monkey the effects of prenatal androgens on genetic females are not limited to sexual behaviour: they affect also other aspects of behaviour in which the sexes normally differ, including those whose incidence does not depend on the immediate hormone concentration. Thus young male rhesus monkeys show more rough-and-tumble play than do females, and so do females treated prenatally with androgens (Goy, 1970; Goy and Phoenix, 1971). Since the differences depend at least in part on social experience, Goy suggests that the prenatal hormonal influences predispose the individual to acquire the patterns of behaviour characteristic of his sex. For instance they may affect the reinforcing properties of such activities as rough-and-tumble play: the quantitative differences in its incidence between males and females could then be due to a sex difference in the effectiveness of its consequences as a reinforcer.

The finding that sex differences in sub-human forms are determined by hormonal differences early in life does not tell us how far the same is true of man. That there are constitutional sex differences at birth is well established (e.g., Hamburg and Lunde, 1966; Bell et al., 1971), and circumstantial evidence suggests that prenatal hormones may have effects in man similar to those found in other species. For instance Turner's syndrome results in the development of a phenotypic female who, through lack of gonads, fails to show any of the usual changes at puberty. Such individuals will, however, respond to exogenous hormone treatment. Thus in the absence of gonads the nervous system develops as that of a female (review Goy, 1970). However, girls affected by androgens prenatally tend to show tomboyish behaviour (Money and Ehrhardt, 1968).

On the other side the great plasticity of man's behaviour, and the complexity of the cultural factors to which he is exposed, must mean that experiential factors are likely to be more important than in other forms. From their earliest days boys tend to be treated differently from girls. For instance in at least one culture girls are more likely to be breast-fed and are touched more by their mothers (Goldberg and Lewis, 1969). Though prenatal hormones may establish predispositions to acquire the behavioural characteristics of males or females, the type of behaviour which children come to show is due to a complex interaction between genetic factors and experience (Gari and Scheinfeld, 1968; Gray, 1971; Money and Erhardt, 1972). And this interaction is in turn affected by cultural factors: with the increasing emancipation of women and greater equality of the sexes to be found in many societies, many of the social factors promoting behavioural differences between the sexes are diminishing.

### Pubertal and post-pubertal hormones

At puberty there are changes in the production of endogenous gonadal hormones. These may affect behaviour in more than one way. Though the most extensive evidence comes from sub-primate forms, the principles certainly apply also to primates.

1 **Effects on the central nervous system** Perhaps the most important way in which hormones from the gonads affect sexual behaviour is by affecting localized areas of the central nervous system. For example, minute amounts of female sex hormone implanted into the posterior hypothalamus of spayed cats produces full sexual receptiveness (Harris et al., 1958; see also Lisk, 1962). Localized implants of androgens can also induce sex behaviour in male monkeys (Michael, 1971). Such influences of sex hormones on the hypothalamus are probably complex, involving both sensitizing and activating effects (Larsson, 1967; Hutchison, 1969). Sex hormones may also have non-specific effects on the general level of activity in the nervous system, and this may in turn affect sexual behaviour.

2 **Effects on peripheral structures** In some cases hormones affect sexual behaviour by causing changes in a peripheral organ which mediates sensory input to the central nervous system. For instance, ejaculation depends on stimulation received through the penis during intromission. Beach and Levinson (1950) have shown that one way in which male hormone affects the sex behaviour of rats is by increasing the sensitivity of the penis. Male rats given low doses of androgens may copulate but not receive sufficient stimulation from intromission to achieve ejaculation (see also Aronson and Cooper, 1966).

3 **Effects on social signals** Sex hormones may also affect the development of social signals used in mating. As mentioned already (pages 301–302), the attractiveness of the female rhesus monkey to the male is determined in part by a vaginal pheromone, the production of which is under oestrogenic control.

### Experiential factors

As we have seen (pages 301–302), the sexual behaviour of female primates is influenced by hormonal factors but is not solely determined by them. Mating behaviour is not closely tied to the menstrual cycle, suggesting that non-hormonal factors are also important in its control. Similar principles apply to males. Although sexual activity is diminished by gonadectomy, it is not always abolished: it may disappear only slowly in males castrated post-pubertally which have already had mating experience. These facts suggest that social and/or experiential factors play an important part in determining the sexual behaviour an individual shows.

Isolation experiments show that in monkeys and chimpanzees, early social experience is indeed essential for the organization of the components of sexual behaviour into a functional system (e.g., Harlow and Harlow, 1965; Mason, 1965). Such experience may act in a variety of ways. As we have seen (page 284), rhesus monkeys reared in total social isolation show abnormalities in aggressive behaviour and tolerance of physical contact which in themselves make mating impossible. But experience during the performance of elements of the sexual pattern are no doubt also important.

Opportunities for such experience occur from soon after birth. Young male primates show penile erections and pelvic thrusting at an early stage[2] (e.g., rhesus macaques, Harlow and Harlow, 1965; Japanese macaques, Hanby, 1972; chimpanzees, Zuckerman, 1932; man, Freud, 1922): females also show thrusting, but less often (Harlow et al., 1972). Pelvic thrusting is first directed toward the mother's body: in monkeys the movements used in climbing onto the mother's back may approximate to those of mounting. Indeed Hanby (1972) suggests that in the Japanese macaque the pattern of dorsal riding on the mother is a source for the development of both the full copulatory pattern and also the various types of mounting and presenting used in non-sexual contexts. Infants soon

---

[2] Harlow et al. (1972) describe successive oral, anal, and phallic components in the development of the rhesus infant's sexuality; and claim that they are comparable to Freud's postulated stages in human psychosexual development. The oral stage involves non-nutritive sucking. Monkeys raised on surrogate mothers that lactated upon demand showed as much non-nutritional sucking as those raised on surrogate mothers whose nipples were available only on a fixed schedule; and both groups showed more than normally reared monkeys. Harlow et al. therefore conclude that "characteristics of the real maternal breast and/or maternal presence, rather than the feeding schedule, are the primary differentiating variables." The postulation of an anal stage in monkeys is based on the observation that they sometimes manipulate their faeces. However the term "sexual" had wider connotations to Freud than to most contemporary comparative psychologists, and Harlow et al. do not discuss the relations of these oral and anal activities to the development of sexual behaviour in the narrow sense.

start to mount and thrust against each other in the course of play, but at first the mounts are oriented toward the head or side of the partner as often as its rear. In Japanese macaques under a year old most mounts are not accompanied by thrusts, but both sexes will stand still to be mounted (Hanby, 1972). In baboons the full mounting pattern first appears between ten and thirteen months of age (Owens, 1973).

Under natural conditions, mounting and thrusting are seen during interactions with both peers and adult females (e.g., baboons, Anthoney, 1968; Japanese macaques, Hanby, 1972; chimpanzees, van Lawick-Goodall, 1968; McGinnis, 1973; Thorndahl, personal communication). Experimental evidence shows that in the early years, both mother and peers are indeed important in the development of sexual behaviour. The importance of the mother is demonstrated by the finding that rhesus monkeys reared in peer groups have delayed or inadequate copulatory responses compared with monkeys raised in a group with their mothers (Goy and Goldfoot, 1973). The influence of the mother may be exerted in at least two ways: first, components of the sexual pattern occur when the infant is in contact with its mother, and second, she no doubt also provides a secure base (pages 188–189) for interactions with peers. The importance of peers in the development of sexual behaviour is shown by the fact that rhesus infants reared in peer groups without mothers show more normal social and sexual behaviour than those reared in social isolation (pages 234–237).

Thus over the first year or two of life in monkeys, and over a rather longer period in apes, the several components become integrated into the complete copulatory pattern (see also Owens, 1973). In the Japanese macaque, at least, there is also an increasing tendency for males to mount females in the breeding season and males outside it (Fig. 18.4). Although females at this age rarely mount, they will (like males) hold still to be mounted: the full presentation posture develops gradually. During the rest of the juvenile period, mounting becomes more polished, and further changes occur in the selection of the partner and in the extent to which mounting is limited to the breeding season, as described above (Fig. 18.4).

While the copulatory elements of presenting, mounting, thrusting, and intromission are being integrated, presenting and mounting also develop variants that become increasingly common in agonistic and play contexts. These include variations in the postures, in the ages and sexes of the partners, and in the associated gestures (e.g., stump-tailed macaque, Bertrand, 1969; Japanese macaque, Hanby, 1972; chimpanzee, van Lawick-Goodall, 1968). Hanby (1972) therefore emphasizes that the age-changes do not constitute merely the develop-

ment of the complete sexual pattern from an incomplete and often inappro-
priately oriented one, but rather the development and differentiation of two
groups of patterns from one—the complete male-female pattern leading to
ejaculation, and the various other patterns, often occurring outside the breeding
season and involving male-male interactions, which are equally mature but more
social than sexual in nature.

It is clear that a male monkey reaches puberty having already had a great
deal of socio-sexual experience largely independent of immediate hormonal
control. In the male rhesus socio-sexual behaviour in the first year of life is as
frequent in gonadectomised individuals as in intact ones, and thus appears to be
independent of current hormone levels (Joslyn, cited in Goy and Phoenix, 1971).
The Japanese macaque also shows considerable mounting behaviour before the
age at which testosterone levels are believed to increase. And when testosterone
levels do increase, full sexual behaviour does not necessarily appear immediately:
the rhesus male produces spermatozoa and has adult testosterone levels at three
and one-half years of age, but does not show ejaculation until a year or two
later (Hanby, 1972). Thus hormone levels and copulatory behaviour show considerable independence from each other in males. Females, by contrast, show
much less active pre-pubertal sexual behaviour, and a clearer relation between
the onset of regular menstrual cycles and the appearance of full mating behaviour.

Comparative studies indicate that, in both mammals and birds, the role of
experience in mating is greater in males than in females (Beach, 1947). To cite
but one example, experienced male rats prefer the odour of receptive females to
that of non-receptive females, but naive and castrated males do not. By contrast,
the females' preference for the odour of intact males as compared with that of
castrates is determined by hormonal state but not by experience (Carr et al.,
1965). The view that experience plays a greater role in male sexual behaviour
than in female is also in harmony with the finding for rats that cortical ablations
affect the sexual behaviour of males more than that of females (Beach, 1944).
That similar conclusions apply also to primates is suggested by the observation
that the sexual behaviour of males reared in social isolation is much more
disturbed than that of females (Harlow and Harlow, 1969).

Further, it has also been suggested that the role of experience in sexual behaviour is greater in higher than in lower mammals (Beach, 1967). While the conditions of rearing affect subsequent sexual behaviour even in rodents, there is
evidence suggesting that copulatory activity continues in sexually experienced
individuals for longer after castration in the higher mammals (Rosenblatt and

Aronson, 1958). Such a trend would suggest that experience is likely to play an even more vital role in human sexuality. The evidence, though incomplete and confusing, supports this view. Although gonadal hormones are essential for sexual development, a considerable number of post-pubertal castrates retain sexual capacities and responsiveness (e.g., Kinsey et al., 1948; Money, 1961). Furthermore, cultural and other experiential factors have a profound influence on the nature and intensity of the sexual behaviour displayed in adulthood (e.g., Hampson and Hampson, 1961).

## Summary

As with aggressive behaviour, the development of sexual behaviour depends on a complex interaction between organism and environment, with social experience of many sorts playing a crucial role. Hormonal factors are involved both in development and in the expression of sexual behaviour, but in both cases their influence is exerted in interaction with experiential factors. The latter are of course even more important in man.

# SECTION

# F

# GROUP
# STRUCTURE

# 20

# INTRODUCTION
# TO THE PROBLEMS
# OF
# GROUP
# STRUCTURE

### Group structure and individual behaviour

In the preceding chapters we have focussed on the nature of relationships between individuals. Individuals may themselves be members of larger groups, but such groups are not necessarily merely the sum of the individuals composing them. Within each group the relationships between individuals are usually patterned in a characteristic way: the nature, quality and patterning of these relationships is described as the "structure" of the group. It will be noted that this concept of structure involves more than the characteristics of group size and age/sex composition usually considered in this context.

Labels for the relationships between individuals refer to abstractions from their patterns of interactive behaviour and neglect individual characteristics. Thus the parent-child relationship is an abstraction based on the observation of certain types of behaviour involving mutual attachment with loving care by the one and filial responses by the other: the label is independent of the particular individuals involved, of any other relationships that they may have, or of any individually idiosyncratic behaviour that they may show. The structure of a group, i.e., the patterning exhibited by the various types of relationships between the individuals, is also an abstraction (Nadel, 1957). This means that it, too, may be independent of the individuals that compose the group: from moment to moment the members of a monkey troop may change their grooming partners; from day to day the males may change their consorts; from week to week some individuals may leave or join the troop, but its structure endures. Stability of structure exists in spite of, and in fact depends upon, dynamic processes within the group.

As discussed later (pages 327–329), individuals of a social species behave differently when in the society of their fellows from when they are alone, but this must not be taken to indicate that the "structure of the group" necessarily in some way determines their behaviour. To take a simple case, a dozen chicks hatched in an incubator and subsequently reared together in a pen will form a dominance hierarchy—one individual ("alpha") becomes able to supplant and peck all others, a "beta" individual to supplant and peck all except the alpha, and so on down to the omega individual, who does not supplant or peck anyone (see Chap. 22 for further discussion). The social structure arises from the behavioural interactions of the individuals in the flock, and is not an entity which is superimposed on them. Once the dominance structure is there it may be resistant to change, but this is because relationships between individuals are stable, not because the structure has an existence independent of those relationships.

While in this simple case it is clear that the structure of the group is determined by, and in fact *is*, the pattern of relationships between individuals, in more complex groups there may be a sense in which the opposite is the case, the nature of the relationships between individuals being determined by the structure of the group (Durkheim, 1950). In a human society shared beliefs about, for instance, monogamy may determine the patterning of relationships; and an elected parliament, representing the group-as-a-whole, makes laws which govern the behaviour of, and relationships between, the individuals who constitute the society. Of course in these cases the shared beliefs or laws are themselves a product of the individuals in the group: the patterning of relationships may influence beliefs about monogamy. What we have in fact is a system in which the behaviour of individuals generates a superordinated structure, and that structure in turn influences the behaviour of individuals. The structure of any society will be stable so long as it generates behaviour that will re-create the structure: in a changing society individuals develop whose behaviour and relationships generate a new structure.

A parliamentary democracy is clearly a case of immense complexity, involving traditional forms of power and means of choice between candidates to wield that power, the choices being determined by the value systems of the individuals. The juxtaposition of its structure with that of a group of barnyard fowls emphasizes the enormous gulf that separates simple non-human societies from the complex human ones. Clearly, if one is to be discussed in the light of the other, we must tread extremely warily. Yet some attempt in that direction is worthwhile, just because of this difference between them. In the study of human societies, "structure" has been approached from two directions. Some sociologists and anthropologists abstract from the situations that they study enduring relationships, institutions, and organizations, laying stress on the manner in which they constrain the behaviour of individuals. Others, focussing on the individual and the network of relationships in which he participates, examine the manner in which he creates the social world about him (Garbett, 1970). In the latter case, the values and even the institutions characterizing the structure may be seen as emergent from the processes of interaction between individuals (Barth, 1966), though perhaps also with some autonomy. The relationships between these approaches are under debate (Garbett, 1970), and the discussion is of interest just because, in the human case, both have partial validity. Since the differing perspectives lead to different kinds and levels of abstraction, and different types of explanation (e.g., Devons and Gluckman, 1964), the relationships between them are not always easy to perceive. One way out of this difficulty is perhaps to examine social structures where one of these approaches has less validity: it is here that the study of non-human primates may provide a new viewpoint.

Insofar as the institutions and organizations of human society depend upon verbal communication between individuals, comparable organizations must be absent from non-human forms. While the structures of human societies depend on commonly shared beliefs and social norms, that of non-human societies must depend fairly immediately on the behaviour brought forth in individuals by the immediate social situation. Of course this is not to say that social experience plays no part. As we have seen, the temperament of adult monkeys is markedly influenced by the environment in which they grew up (Chap. 15), and this is bound to affect their relationships with one another. Tradition and the cultural transmission of structural forms may also play some role: a rhesus male will have seen older individuals behaving as dominant and as peripheral individuals, and it is an open issue how far he may use them as models. But non-human forms receive no verbal instructions on how to behave, or on the successive positions in the society an individual is likely to occupy: the contributions of culture and tradition to the social structure must be minute, on a quite different scale from those found in human societies.

Of course this does not mean that one can merely subtract the complexity found in non-human social systems from that found in human ones, to leave a remainder which depends on culture and tradition. The structures of human societies are in part determined by, and must be compatible with, the nature of the individuals who comprise them, so that to attempt to separate culturally determined from biologically determined elements of structure is as foolish for societies as it is for individuals or for their behaviour (see Chap. 4). What we can hope for, however, is that the comparative method will provide tools for the teazing out of some of the principles by which structure is determined.

In studying group structure, the first stage must be descriptive: the early stages in both animal sociology and social anthropology must involve description of the structures that occur. But in animal sociology the techniques for description are only just being developed: indeed in this instance it is clear that biologists have much to learn from students of human behaviour. Thus much of this section will be concerned with the techniques that are coming into use and with the preliminary results they are providing.

Descriptions of social structures immediately reveal differences—this monkey troop is composed of adult males each with his own group of females and young, while that has but a single male who is usually to be found on the periphery of the main body. Such differences need to be explained.

From here, two courses are possible. One is to attempt to explain the differences found in relation to the environment in which the group lives, the supposition being that there has been some sort of selection from amongst all possible structures to produce one that maximizes certain desiderata for some or all of the group members. In the case of animal groups the selective agent is usually supposed to be natural selection: with human societies this is somewhat less plausible. To this approach we shall return briefly later (Chap. 26).

The second course is to try to understand the different structures in terms of their causation—that is, in terms of the processes that give rise to them. Those processes are the dynamic inter-relations between the individual group members. To do this we need a conceptual framework with which to describe the various patterns that we see. Various such frameworks have been used: to evaluate them we must first specify the principal dimensions of difference with which we shall be concerned.

## Dimensions of complexity in animal groups

At its simplest and most literal, the structure of a group may involve merely the spatial relations between its members. When a flock of great tits is feeding on the ground in winter, the individuals comprising it hop over the ground a metre or so apart. This "individual distance" (Hediger, 1950) is a consequence of two conflicting behavioural tendencies—to keep fairly near other individuals but to respond negatively (by attack, threat, or avoidance) if another individual approaches too closely (Emlen, 1952; Hinde, 1952). The resultant structure is a loose one, involving merely underdispersion over the range of the flock as a whole (i.e., the individuals are less dispersed, or more clumped, than they would be if randomly distributed over their range), but overdispersion (i.e., less clumping) within the limits of the flock. A somewhat more rigid spatial relationship can be seen in flying swans or egrets: the arrowhead or echelon formations, achieved by each individual positioning itself in a certain position relative to others, is presumably aerodynamically efficient.

As described so far, these two examples are over-simple in at least three ways. First, each group has been described as though it contained individuals of only one type. In practice, of course, this is usually not the case: the great tit flock contains males and females, first- and second-year birds, which, both as classes and as individuals within classes, behave somewhat differently from each other. These differences inevitably complicate the spatial patterning. Second, in both cases only two kinds of social behaviour have so far been mentioned, keeping in company and behaving agonistically. In practice, of course, other types of behaviour also may occur: near the breeding season, for example, sexual behaviour becomes important in the tit flock. Third, each individual may not only show several types of behaviour, but also may direct some types of behaviour more to some classes of individuals than to others: male great tits may be more likely to attack males than females, and more likely to court females than males. Indeed, the members of the group may respond individually to one another, reserving certain categories of behaviour for particular individuals or groups of individuals. For example, flocks of many geese and swans (e.g., Canada goose, Raveling, 1970) consist of family parties. Within each family the members direct certain types of behaviour preferentially amongst themselves, but families, although flocking together, may behave agonistically to one another. Such individual-specific relationships contribute to the structure of the group.

Bird flocks have been mentioned here because in different avian species it is possible to find cases ranging from anonymous flocks, in which individual relationships are unimportant, to societies in which the diversity of relationships between individuals results in a moderately complex social structure. In primates, of course, the complexity is even greater.

In considering the groups of non-human primates, it is essential to remember that their structure and composition vary greatly between species. Only a few non-human primates live in family groups consisting of male and female parents and their sub-adult offspring—for instance the gibbons and siamang, and the marmosets and titi monkeys. In most other species the relationship between male and female is less permanent (pages 297–299).

Some species form troops consisting of a number of females and their young accompanied by one male, the remaining males living solitarily or in bachelor bands. In the patas, some langurs, and forest-living guenons the male is usually to be found on the fringe of the main group of females and young: although he may play an important role in defending the troop, he does not dominate the females. In the hanuman langur the number of males is variable. Under some conditions, when the population density is high, they form one-male groups and bachelor bands. Sometimes a one-male group is invaded by one or more males and a new leader results. But an old male may tolerate his own sons, so that undisturbed groups may come to contain several males (Sugiyama, 1965a, b; Jay, 1965; Yoshiba, 1967; see also Vogel, 1971).

One-male groups also form the basis of the social structure of the hamadryas baboon, but here the total social structure is on three tiers: the troop or herd consists of a number of bands, and each band is composed of smaller one-male groups. The individuals of a herd usually sleep together at night but disperse in these bands to feed during the day time. Although the bands are not apparent as distinct units when the herd is gathered together on the sleeping cliffs, their membership during the day time is constant. Each band consists primarily of a number of one-male units, each of which includes an adult male, a few females with their infants, and sometimes a sub-adult male loosely attached. The band also contains a number of lone adult males. The adult male of each one-male group interacts socially (e.g., in grooming sessions) and sexually primarily with his own females, and they interact socially with one another and with their infants. The infants may form play groups which move freely through the band, but the females interact only briefly with females of other units. The adult males chase and may bite females of their own unit who wander too far away, or who attempt to copulate with one of the sub-adult males (Kummer, 1968). We shall consider these one-male groups later. Kummer's description is of special interest here in that it shows how a quite complex social structure arises in a troop when members of the various age-sex classes behave in different ways to one another, and also individuals behave in special ways to other particular individuals.

In the hamadryas baboon the herds and bands each contain many males only because they contain a number of the one-male groups. In other species several males may be present in the basic social unit. In some of these cases the troop contains several males arranged in a dominance order based on age. Such a situation occurs quite frequently in langurs, and in many other arboreal primates: as we have seen, it may arise from a one-male troop by retention of the offspring. Eisenberg et al. (1972) coined the term "age-graded-male troop" to describe such cases: they differ from one-male troops primarily in that the dominant male is sufficiently tolerant to allow younger males to stay with the troop for some time, but not permanently. The age gradation is thus not continuous.

"Multi-male" troops involve even more inter-male tolerance. These contain an oligarchy of adult males which, though they may form a dominance hierarchy, are roughly equivalent in age and in some circumstances act as a unit (Eisenberg et al., 1972). These central males tolerate a number of younger and sub-dominant males, though the latter are often confined to the periphery of the troop. Such multi-male troops are usual in macaques and baboons: further aspects of the complexity of their structure will be considered later (Chap. 23).

The structure of chimpanzee communities involves a different type of complexity. The size of the groups in which chimpanzees are encountered is extremely variable. Sometimes they travel through the forest and feed alone. Sometimes they are to be found in small groups, consisting perhaps of a mother and her offspring, or a group of males, or a male-female consort pair, but practically any other combination is possible. And sometimes they form larger groups of 20 or 30 or even more individuals, which may have considerable stability. Even if spending most of their time alone or in small groups, the animals meet from time to time in the forest, and their behaviour indicates that all the individuals living in a given area are acquainted with one another and can be regarded as forming a "community" or "unit group". The members of neighbouring communities also know one another, but are less well acquainted and more likely to behave agonistically to each other when they meet. Though the analysis of chimpanzee social relations has not been facilitated by the differences in terminology of those who study them (e.g., van Lawick-Goodall, 1968; Itani and Suzuki, 1967; Suzuki, 1969; Nishida, 1968; Izawa, 1970; Simpson, 1973a) the social structure is clearly both complex and not immediately obvious through the spatial disposition of the members (Sugiyama, 1973). As more species are studied it is becoming apparent that a population structure involving a group divided into sub-groups of varying membership is not limited to chimpanzees: Aldrich-Blake (1970) found that groups of blue monkeys tend to break up into foraging parties of irregular composition, and Klein (1971) noted a similar situation in spider monkeys. Rowell (1973) found that a talapoin troop was habitually divided into subgroups usually differentiated by sex and/or age.

The description of a number of types of troop structure in this way oversimplifies the situation in at least three ways. First, troop structure may be markedly affected by environmental conditions. Baboons, which usually move about in large troops, split up into groups of three to four individuals in the harsh conditions of Ethiopia (Aldrich-Blake et al., 1971): other examples are given later (Chap. 26). Second, structures which appear to differ in kind may in fact differ only in degree: as more species are studied in detail, more intermediate cases are found. Third, the types just described are based on relatively superficial characters. For instance the structures of the one-male units of hamadryas baboon and of patas monkey are quite different: in the hamadryas the male is the focus (page 322), while in the patas he is peripheral.

To emphasize this third point, we may compare the hamadryas baboon also with the fairly closely related gelada baboon. Again, both form one-male units, but these differ in many respects. In the first place, the mechanisms by which the groups are formed differ. In the hamadryas, the male is almost solely responsible for group cohesion, and achieves it by attacking or threatening females who wander off; in the gelada, the senior females also play a part. When males and females were introduced in a captive colony, group formation was initiated by a male and female pairing—the female would present, the male would mount, and the female would then groom him. Subsequent females were accepted only after the first female had gone through a similar pair-forming process, with her in the role of the male. Thus each group consisted of a dominance hierarchy, with the male at the top (Kummer, 1971).

In addition the behaviour of the two species in the field differs greatly. The gelada units wander independently from one another, entering and leaving feeding herds. Within the herds the members of a one-male unit may disperse widely. While the hamadryas male threatens or attacks any of his females that wanders off, the gelada male is more permissive: nevertheless the females all keep watch on him, collect around him from time to time, and move off when he does. When the females are dispersed the male may display and run up to one, who will crouch and then groom him: this apparently serves to reinforce the bonds. While the sub-adult male hamadryas form bonds with infant or juvenile females, this does not happen in the gelada. The young males may either join up with one-male units or form all-male groups. The gelada baboon herds seem not to be structured into bands, as in the hamadryas. Thus although the social structures shown by these closely related species can be described in similar terms, they differ in many important characteristics (Crook, 1970).

For these three reasons schemes for classifying the group structures of non-human primates are of only limited usefulness: more detailed analyses of group structure in terms of interactions between the members are urgently needed.

But the descriptions given will give some impression of the diversity of group structures to be found amongst primate species and even amongst different troops of one species. It will be apparent that they involve far more than conflicting forces of attraction and repulsion between individuals. Apart from size, primate groups may differ in the balance between the social and disruptive forces in their members; the number and relative sizes of categories of individuals showing recognizably distinct types of behaviour; the diversity of types of behaviour which the individuals show to one another; the extent to which behaviour is directed preferentially to specific individuals; and the extent to which this results in the formation of temporary or permanent sub-units.

In human groups, as we have seen, another dimension of complexity enters in that the behaviour of the members may be influenced by rules, conventions, or ideas of what their behaviour or the structure of the group should be. The nature of the interactions between the members of a Western European family, like the nature of interactions in a hamadryas one-male group, is determined in part by their biological properties of maleness and femaleness, adulthood and infancy, as well as by the particular personalities of the individuals involved. But a major difference is that the structure of the human family is also influenced by conventions about how each individual should behave and what families should be like, which are held by one or more of the members. Though it could be argued that both the adult male hamadryas and Victorian parents mould their respective groups according to their own goals, and that in both those goals are constrained by the ecological (economic) factors to which they have been exposed, the overpowering influence of tradition in determining the goals in the human case leads to a difference which is best described as one of kind.

Furthermore, the human family is embedded in a complex society with diverse social institutions. Each of those institutions involves not only traditions and norms, but also special technologies and special roles which affect directly behaviour inside the family. The shift worker or the doctor may be away from home during just those times when family interaction is most intense, and the norms acquired by the child at school affect his behaviour at home. Though the hamadryas one-male group is also embedded within a larger social structure, its influences are both more straightforward and less pervading than those which affect the human family.

In conclusion we see that (1) considerable diversity of structure is to be found amongst non-human primates; (2) their social structure often has considerable complexity; but (3) it nevertheless lacks some of the basic ingredients upon which the richness of human society depends.

### Group density

Individuals of a social species seek the proximity of others—but only up to a point, and not necessarily all the time. Each individual in fact regulates the frequency and duration of his interactions with others, and the intimacy of his relationships with them. As we have seen (page 321), this may result in the maintenance of "individual distance"—the individuals are more spaced out within the limits of the group than they would be if randomly dispersed.

The comparable phenomenon in man is usually referred to as "personal space". Though people like to be with others, they usually also like to keep a certain distance between themselves and others. The extent of this personal space differs considerably between cultures: for instance, Latin Americans on average stand closer together than do United States citizens. It varies also with the nature of the relationship between the individuals concerned, with the type of interaction in which they are involved, and with many other factors (Hall, 1959; Argyle, 1972). These have been studied by both observation (e.g., Hall, 1959) and experiment (e.g., Felipe and Sommer, 1966).

Group-living thus involves almost continuous interactions and mutual adjustment of spatial relations by the individuals within the group: although each may seek the companionship of his fellows, their proximity may involve some degree of stress. "Stress" is another vague term: it is used here as an independent variable linked to changes in the physiological functioning of the individuals concerned. For example, the response of a monkey to stress is mediated in part by the secretion of steroid hormones from the adrenal glands. These in turn are under the control of the pituitary hormone ACTH (adreno-corticotrophic hormone). If an animal is subjected to frequent or prolonged stress, the adrenal glands may enlarge and produce more steroids in response to a given amount of ACTH in the blood reaching them. The responsiveness of the adrenals can be measured by injecting a standard amount of ACTH and measuring the adrenal steroids produced by analysis of the urine. Sassenrath (1970) found that in caged groups of rhesus monkeys the response to ACTH was related to the amount of avoidance behaviour the individuals showed, being lowest in the alpha animals. The responsiveness of the lower animals could be reduced by keeping them in isolation for a while, and that of females fell when they formed a consort relationship with a male (Sassenrath, 1970).

In a natural troop such physiological consequences of interactions with other individuals can usually be kept within limits by behavioural means: an individual who is frequently bullied can retire to the periphery or even leave the troop. But under experimental conditions the effects may become patho-logical. In rodents over-crowding has been found to produce ramifying con-sequences, including adrenal hypertrophy, hypoglycaemia, arteriosclerotic le-sions, and reproductive failure (e.g., Christian and Davis, 1964; Calhoun, 1962; Bruce, 1966; Henry et al., 1967; Chitty, 1967). In tree shrews social stress leads to adrenal hypertrophy and later to death from uraemia due to renal failure (von Holst, 1972). "In man, also, overcrowding can have dramatic consequences, in-cluding an enhanced propensity to aggression" (Hamburg, 1971).

But though too much social stimulation can have pathological effects, social isolation can have equally devastating consequences. These can be seen all too frequently in zoo animals—stereotyped movements, depression, metabolic disturbances, and so on. Under natural conditions the continuous presence of the group companions is normally necessary for most aspects of behaviour.

We have seen how a young primate is enabled to come to terms with novel and potentially frightening situations by the presence of his mother (pages 188–189): group companions play a similar role in adulthood. This was shown in caged groups of rhesus monkeys as follows. The animals were exposed to three mildly disturbing situations—an experimenter of whom they were slightly apprehensive offering them food, staring at them, or making threatening gestures while wear-ing a grotesque mask and a white sheet. The experiments were performed in two conditions—when the animals were in the presence of their group com-

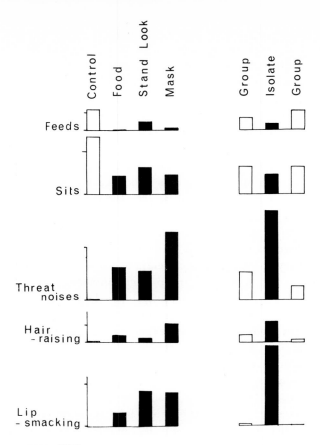

FIGURE 20.1

*Responses of rhesus monkeys to three situations—
an experimenter offering food, an experimenter staring at them, and an experimenter in a mask. Left-
hand column: comparison of the incidence of five
activities in the three experimental situations with
that in a control (undisturbed) period. Right-hand
column: comparison of incidence of the five activities in all three situations when animals were isolated and in a group. (From detailed data in Rowell
and Hinde, 1963.)*

panions, and whilst temporarily isolated from them. As shown in Fig. 20.1, those patterns of behaviour which were decreased by the disturbing stimuli in the group situation were less common when the animals were isolated than when they were in a group, and vice versa. In other words, the presence of the social companions ameliorated the effect of the mildly disturbing situation (Rowell and Hinde, 1963).

Human individuals confined alone often show marked behavioural disturbances and hallucinations (Solomon et al., 1961). While the results of such experiments are often complicated by the fact that the treatment involves general reduction in sensory input as well as social isolation, on a more anecdotal level comparable effects from isolation after shipwreck or other disasters have been recorded (Merrien, 1954; Brownfield, 1964). Situations which involve the crowding of a few individuals in isolation from others, such as the Antarctic explorer's hut or the prisoner-of-war camp, produce other types of breakdown in social behaviour (Gundersen and Nelson, 1963).

These are of course extreme conditions: in normal circumstances individuals are more able to regulate their behaviour to produce a degree of social intercourse congenial to them. While to regard the structure of social relations as the result of such regulations is to neglect its qualitative features, it does call attention to an important point—the possibility and even probability of some degree of stress as individuals attempt to satisfy their several needs within a social group.

## Summary

This chapter has been concerned with three themes. First, the patterning of relationships within a group can be described as the structure of that group. It is possible to regard both the individual relationships as affecting the structure, and the structure as affecting the individual relationships. In man both types of process occur, but in non-human primates the former is much more important than the latter: studies of social structure in non-human primates may thus be of interest just because they reveal the complexity that is possible when the effects of culture and tradition are of minor importance.

Second, the diversity of non-human primate social structures was illustrated; and finally the fact that social life necessarily involves conflict between the desiderata of social contact and some degree of personal space or privacy was emphasized.

# 21
# TROOP COHESION AND FISSION: ALTRUISM

### Cohesion and fission

What is it that keeps a primate group together? As discussed earlier (page 13), some authors have denied the existence of attraction per se, and attempted to account for group cohesiveness in terms of specific activities demanding the presence of other individuals. In one of the earlier studies of primate societies, Zuckerman (1932) suggested that sexual bonding was the main agent that kept individuals together. This was an overstatement. Monkey and ape groups persist through the females' cycles and through non-breeding seasons (Lancaster and Lee, 1965): in any case, mature females are either pregnant or lactating most of the time (Rowell, 1967). Furthermore, hamadryas one-male groups are formed when the females are immature (Kummer, 1967). Though sexual attraction may play some part, its role is small.

Washburn and De Vore (1961) suggested that the attractiveness of infants was an important cohesive force, but this also is an over-simplification. Primate groups can maintain their integrity without infants, and relationships between adults may be entirely independent of their presence.

Yet another mechanism that has been suggested invokes aggression against an outside enemy: individuals may forget their own differences and unite when threatened by an outsider. Kummer (1971) has given a vivid example. Two male gelada baboons, during a pause in a fight, discovered their mirror images in the window of an observation cabin. Both started to threaten the reflections, which of course threatened back. Engaged in the common action against outsiders, the two males gradually shifted closer together and even exchanged friendly lip-smacks. However, while such a mechanism may operate on occasion, it cannot form the basis of all group cohesion.

A more important source of troop integration lies in familial ties. As we shall see (Chap. 23), most of the internal structuring of troops of many species reflects blood relationships, in particular those between mothers and their off-spring. However this again is insufficient to explain the cohesion between family units. It is thus necessary to postulate forces of mutual attraction which may have their ontogenetic origin in intra-familial ties but subsequently extend beyond them.

In most primates positive social attraction is not obviously expressed in overt behaviour other than in the maintenance of proximity. However social grooming occupies much time in many species of non-human primates, and often seems to play a part in cementing social relations (Fig. 21.1). Such a view depends in part on the frequent observation that an individual who has just been attacked will groom his attacker. While it is usually the subordinate individual who carefully approaches the victor and starts to groom him, the victor some-times initiates reconciliation. In the gelada baboon a male who has vanquished another will, when and only when the latter submits, approach him with lip-smacking gestures. After a while the loser may present, the winner mounts, and grooming occurs (Kummer, 1971; see also Goosen, 1973).

When two individuals come together after temporary separation, overt "friendly" displays are especially likely to occur, but their frequency and con-spicuousness differ markedly between species. Both mangabeys and baboons use such gestures frequently, but mangabeys touch only the genital area, baboons anywhere on the body. That mangabeys present their hindquarters only in sexual situations, while baboons do so in a wide variety of social situations, also sug-gests that such gestures are more elaborated in the latter species (Ransom and Rowell, 1973). "Greeting" gestures are most developed in chimpanzees: on meet-ing after a period of separation they may vocalize and greet and embrace each other, using a variety of facial expressions and gestures (Fig. 10.12; van Lawick-Goodall, 1968; Nishida, 1970). The situations in which greetings and conciliatory

FIGURE **21.1**
*Social grooming in macaques.* (Drawing by Priscilla Edwards after Bertrand, 1969.)

gestures are given are usually those of potential aggression. Indeed aggressive displays or threats, as well as greeting gestures, commonly accompany meetings.

A final issue here concerns the positive part sometimes played by dominant individuals in maintaining group cohesion. For instance in macaques adult males may play a large part in breaking up fights between group members: Vandenbergh (1967) reported that groups of rhesus newly imported into Cayo Santiago broke up if one male did not soon become dominant. Again the hamadryas baboon male threatens or attacks females who stray too far from his one-male unit: Kummer has shown experimentally that a male does not attack a female if he has previously seen behaviour indicative of bonding between that female and another male (Kummer, 1968, 1971).

Thus the stability of a primate troop depends on a balance, often a delicate one, between factors making for cohesion and factors promoting disruption. Not surprisingly there are marked differences in stability between species. From Kummer's (1968) account it seems that the constitution of the one-male unit of hamadryas baboons may remain stable for months or years, but in other species organisation is more loose and individuals change troops not infrequently. Rowell (1969), studying Ugandan baboons, found that adult and large juvenile males and adolescent females all sometimes changed troops, while adult females and small juveniles did not. Sade (1972a) gives comparable data for rhesus monkeys: the males are especially likely to leave at the onset of the mating season and in their early reproductive years, suggesting an influence of test-osterone. A long-term study of the stability of rhesus troops has been made by Wilson (1968, cited Crook, 1970).

While the available evidence suggests that the stability of primate groups is due primarily to the females, generalizations must be made with caution: the loosely knit communities or "unit groups" of chimpanzees (see pages 323–324) have a permanent nucleus of males, and it is the females, usually when sexually active, which are most likely to move from one to another (Nishida, 1968; McGinnis, 1973; Bygott, personal communication). In gorilla, also, the females are more likely to change groups than are males, but this seems to be the result of their capture by a dominant silverback (Fossey, personal communication).

How does group fission come about? Eisenberg et al. (1972) believe that most arboreal monkey groups tend to return periodically to a one-male state. As shown in Fig. 21.2, they suggest that the one-male group grows by recruitment to yield a sub-group of juveniles, with the senior males forming another sub-group. As this age-graded male group develops, younger males may form yet another peripheral sub-group of their own, especially if the population density is high. As the troop increases in size, it becomes more unstable, and may split.

Splitting may occur gradually, without fighting between males, by a progressive division into two sub-groups, each under the leadership of a different male. Such sub-groups may at first forage separately for some of the time but continue to sleep together: ultimately, however, they separate completely (e.g., hanuman langur, Muckenhirn, cited in Eisenberg et al., 1972; baboons, Owens, 1973; rhesus, Missakian, 1973).

In other cases, there may be a take-over. The purple-faced leaf monkey tends to live in one-male troops, with peripheral bachelor groups. When the population density is high, the bachelor groups sometimes harass the one-male groups, and this may result in one of the bachelors taking over the females. The new male may kill the young infants in the troop: the females then come into oestrus again (Sugiyama, 1967; see also Sugiyama, 1965b).

In the Japanese macaque individuals may leave the troop in three ways.

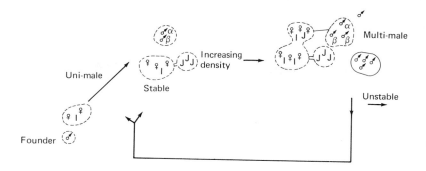

FIGURE 21.2

*Hypothetical diagram of troop growth for arboreal primates. The assumption is that a one-male tendency is the most typical configuration at moderate population densities. Given a founder situation at the left, consider an adult male attached to a cohesive unit of two adult females and their young. The troop grows by recruitment, yielding a sub-group of juveniles and a beta male that is sub-dominant to the alpha male, or father. The two older males form a sub-group in their own right. At greater densities, younger males may form a peripheral sub-group of their own that has no direct contact with the basic sub-group of mothers and their young. The sub-group of adult males may now be augmented slightly to three, with the founding father still dominant. Although the troop now appears to be multi-male, it would be more correct to consider it an age-graded-male group. Splitting of the new unstable troop can lead to the original one-male configuration. (From Eisenberg et al., 1972.)*

Sometimes individual males leave and become solitary. Sometimes several males leave together and form a male group. And sometimes fission occurs, a mixed group of males and females with their offspring forming a branch troop. Fission is especially likely if the troop is large and has a high male-female ratio: usually fission results in the sex ratio of the main troop being restored (Furaya, 1969).

Thus both the forces producing group cohesion and those leading to group fission defy generalization. In attempting to understand cohesion it is necessary, in the absence of other explanations, to postulate forces of mutual attraction between individuals—an explanation with a substantial element of circularity. The mechanisms of group fission clearly differ markedly between species, and even in the same species at different times.

## Altruistic behaviour

In discussing social behaviour, mention must be made of the question of altruism. This has recently been the focus for some discussion, and it will be sufficient here to outline the two main issues. Both of them involve questions of definition.

1  Does altruistic behaviour occur in non-human species? This depends on the precise problems with which one is concerned. If interest centres on the *effects* of one individual's behaviour on others or on group structure, then there are many instances of animals helping others at some cost to themselves. Birds warn others of the approach of predators and may thereby increase the risk to themselves; cetaceans may lift an injured individual to the surface to help it breathe, and chimpanzees may share some of the meat after they have killed a monkey (Teleki, 1973). To cite an example from the laboratory, Masserman et al. (1964) showed that monkeys would consistently refrain from pulling a chain that brought them food if it also gave an electric shock to their cage-mates. Evidently they responded to the signs of distress induced by the shock (cf. pages 100–101). Many anecdotal stories of apparently altruistic behaviour in nature lack adequate support, but some appear to be true. For instance an improbable-sounding story of a hippopotamus rescuing an impala from a crocodile and attempting to nurse it back to health is supported by photographs which appear to be genuine (Reucassel, 1970).

   In all such cases one individual shows behaviour which benefits one or more others at some cost to himself, and on that count the behaviour could be labelled as altruistic. If, however, interest centres on the *motivation* of the behaviour, one may wish to accept the connotations of altruism as applied to man, and limit it to behaviour involving consciously purposeful self-sacrifice for the benefit of others. Many of the cases referred to above could be understood as species-characteristic responses to particular stimulus patterns (e.g., an approaching predator, a drowning member of the school, another individual in pain), and thus would not come within this definition. But in any case conscious purpose is not easy to assess in animals (Krebs, 1970, 1972; see Hebb, 1971, for contrary view).

2 Can altruistic behaviour be produced by natural selection? We take it as a matter of course that one individual may show behaviour which benefits another individual to whom he is closely related, even at some cost to himself. Most parental behaviour, for example, we do not even think of labelling as altruistic. This makes sense from the point of view of natural selection, since the eventual survival of the parents' genes may be better ensured by care of the offspring even though it involves some cost to the parent (see pages 203–205).

Of more interest is behaviour that benefits another individual who is not closely related, while being apparently detrimental to the individual performing the behaviour—benefit and cost once more being defined in terms of inclusive fitness (see page 203). How can one explain, for instance, the behaviour of a man who, at some risk to himself, rescues a drowning child? Why do birds give calls warning others of the approach of danger, when to do so must increase their own vulnerability? To invoke forces of "group selection" (Wynne-Edwards, 1962) is not consistent with our present knowledge of how natural selection works (cf. pages 272–273). One possibility is that such acts are functional when relatives are involved, but sometimes appear in other contexts. This is possible, but one must presume that the cost of occurrences with non-relatives is slight, for otherwise the behaviour would presumably have been eliminated by natural selection. Another possibility is that there is always a reasonable chance that the other individuals are closely related. This could conceivably apply to the case of the birds' warning calls (Maynard Smith, 1965), and even more to primate troops in which many individuals are closely related, but cannot cover cases where genetic relationships are remote. Recently Trivers (1971) has suggested that, in the case of the warning calls, it may be advantageous to the caller to warn others even though they are not related to him. This could happen because a successful predator might

1 be sustained by the meal, or
2 be more likely to search for that prey species in the future, or
3 be more adept at catching that prey species in the future, or
4 be more likely to hunt in the same area in the future, or
5 be more familiar with the area when hunting in the future.

For one or more of these reasons the caller might be more likely to be caught in the future if the predator is successful this time than if he is not. Against this must be weighed the temporary immunity derived from the predator's immediate satisfaction. Similar arguments could be applied to other species.

Evidence for Trivers's suggestions would be hard to obtain, but they provide a plausible hypothesis for many cases of this type that are observed. If he is right, the behaviour is only *apparently* detrimental to the individual concerned, and thus, some would say, not altruistic.

Trivers (1971) has applied comparable principles in discussing the complex selective forces which may have operated in the evolution of human reciprocal altruism.

In summary, the occurrence in animals of behaviour describable as altruistic, with all the human connotations of the term, is at best infrequent. However animals often show behaviour which benefits others at some cost to themselves. The evolution of such behaviour can easily be understood if close relatives are involved, but when relatives are not involved it poses questions which are not yet fully resolved.

# 22

# RANK

### Dominance

Until recently, much biological work on social structure in animals depended on the dominance-subordinance concept. This was largely because of the work of Schjelderup-Ebbe (e.g., 1922) on domestic fowl. If a number of hens are placed together in an enclosure, there is often first a period of agonistic interactions, during which pecking and even actual fighting occur. Gradually, however, overt aggression decreases and relationships between individuals are established such that each accepts a dominant or subordinate position with respect to others. This is then maintained, the subordinates withdrawing or adopting a submissive posture on the approach of a dominant, with only rare attempts at revolt.

Sometimes, as described above, the individuals in the group can be arranged in a straight-line peck order, with the alpha individual dominant to all others, the beta to all except the alpha, and so on down to the omega individual, who is subordinate to all. More often, perhaps, the order is complicated by triangles of the type beta dominant to gamma and gamma to delta, but delta is dominant to beta. The rigidity of the hierarchy also varies. Under some circumstances it may be based on a unidirectional "peck-right" system in which each individual can peck those inferior to it without fear of retaliation, while in other cases relationships are of the peck-dominance type, with pecks going both ways but one individual delivering more pecks than he receives. In the latter case, the relative dominance between two individuals may vary with the location of the encounter, each having absolute peck-right only in one particular area (e.g., Guhl, 1962): the situation then differs only in degree from a territorial one (see page 61). Comparable social relationships have been found in many studies of primates in both the field and the laboratory, and we shall consider several of these shortly.

Now a peck order, derived from observations solely of which individual pecks which, is merely descriptive. In describing social structure in terms of such a peck order, we must beware of circular arguments of the type "A pecks B and so must be higher in the hierarchy. Because A is higher in the hierarchy he can peck B" (cf. Gartlan, 1968). To be useful in an explanatory, as opposed to descriptive, way, the concept of dominance hierarchy must carry the implication that position in the hierarchy depends on relationships between individuals which can be manifest in a variety of types of behaviour. "Dominance" has in fact been measured in many different ways—in terms of some aspect of agonistic behaviour, in terms of priority of access to an incentive such as food or a mate, or in terms of the part played in some other type of interaction such as social grooming. Some of the earlier studies were undertaken in attempts to find a measure that would have a proven generality in different contexts, but insofar as such studies assumed dominance to be an absolute quality they rested on a misapprehension. Dominance has the nature of an intervening variable (see pages 25–28), and is useful in an explanatory way only to the extent that the different ways in which it can be assessed agree with each other. To the extent that they do, dominance can be used to account for a number of aspects of behaviour in an economical way.

We may first consider some studies in which dominance, assessed initially in terms of agonistic interactions, has been found to be related to other types of behaviour. One of the most detailed is Kaufmann's (1967) study of the male rhesus in the free-living troops introduced to Cayo Santiago. The males were organized into a linear dominance hierarchy which included a central hierarchy, a group of four-year-olds in the process of becoming integrated into the central hierarchy, and a group of peripheral males. The dominance order of the males was also related to behaviour in other contexts. For instance, as the mating season approached, dominant males tended to groom proportionately more females, and within the central hierarchy, each male tended to groom females with ranks close to his own. When males groomed males, the groomer tended to be of lower rank than the groomee. Again, males near the top of the order tended to spend less time in trees than peripheral males, and to have more animals sitting near them than animals low in the order (see also Sade, 1967, cited on pages 368–369).

Again, in a baboon troop with a relatively simple social structure and containing only three adult males, one dominated the others in aggressive encounters. He alone mated with females in the fertile phase of their cycles, driving away the others. He tended to be the one who protected the group from outside dangers, and the mothers with newborn infants were supported by him (Hall and DeVore, 1965).

Similarly, Struhsaker (1967) found the dominance concept useful in his study of vervet monkeys. He described a strong tendency toward a linear hierarchy, with only a few triangles and probabilistic relationships. The rank order was similar whether the encounter took place with respect to food, grooming position, or "space". The dominance order was correlated with various other types of behaviour. Thus a particular display, involving pacing with tail aloft and the red perianal region and blue scrotum exposed, was invariably given by dominant to more subordinate males, and seemed to serve to reassert the dominance relations. Copulation was largely limited to the more dominant males.

Yet another example is provided by Simpson's study (1973a) of the relations between free-living male chimpanzees. He found significant correlations between the ranking of males on the basis of the extent to which they supplanted each other, and a number of other measures of rank: the higher the rank as indicated by supplanting, the more often was the male likely to display, the less likely were other males to display in his presence, the more likely were other males to "pant-grunt" to him, and the less likely was he to "pant-grunt" to them. We shall refer later to Simpson's further finding that the rank order as revealed by these measures was also related to the male's grooming behaviour (pages 376–378).

These studies all involved free-living animals in a natural environment. In captivity, hierarchies tend to be even more clearly defined. A study of captive rhesus monkeys by Richards (1972) is of special interest in that 10 different measures were used to assess dominance rankings. Four of these depended on priority of access to incentives, and four on behavioural signs of subordinance in the group: the other two involved the winning of agonistic interactions and the frequency of displays (Fig. 22.1). Although absence of data prevented the use of all measures in all groups, they were in general highly correlated. Of even more interest was the finding that dominance rank in the group was related to certain aspects of the behaviour shown in test situations when the animals were subsequently isolated, such as their latency to respond and persistence in problem situations, and the time spent in manipulative play with the experimental apparatus. This implies the existence of aspects of behaviour relevant both to dominance rank in the group and performance in these tests in social isolation. One possibility is that the common factor was something related to "timidity" or its inverse: in a study of female Japanese macaques, Norikoshi (1971) found that females low in the hierarchy showed stronger fear responses to the observer when offered food than did more dominant animals. This is rendered less probable as an explanation of Richards's results by the absence of a relation between dominance rank in the group and fear of the observer in social isolation. Another possibility is that dominance was related to an individual characteristic of a rather general sort which could be described as "responsiveness" or "persistence". Since the tests in isolation were carried out after the assessment of dominance in the group situation, such a characteristic could be a consequence of the preceding dominance rank or could be causal to both dominance and behaviour in the test situation (see also Angermeier et al., 1968).

In the studies just cited the concept of dominance has been useful both for description and, in that the several measures were correlated, in an explanatory sense. However, the relationship of dominance rank to aggression requires further discussion. When individuals previously unacquainted with each other are first put together, fighting is usually at first frequent, but becomes less so in a day or two (e.g., Bernstein, 1964). The reduction in fighting is accompanied by the emergence of a fairly clear hierarchical structure. In general (and it must be emphasized that many other factors are involved), the characters making for high dominance rank are also those making for success in aggressive episodes— e.g., body size, sex, hormonal status, rearing conditions, and so on (e.g., Bernstein and Mason, 1963a; Tokuda and Jensen, 1969): somewhat surprisingly, the canine teeth appear not to be essential for the attainment or maintenance of high rank in the Japanese macaque, though they may be important in the self-defence of low-ranking males (Alexander and Hughes, 1971).

But although dominance rank depends on aggression or on potential aggressiveness, it is not to be confused with them. The concept of dominance refers to the relationship between individuals, not to the amount of aggressive behaviour that they show. Indeed by a dominance-subordinate relationship, we often mean one in which overt aggression is reduced or absent; and it usually (but not always) happens that the greater the difference in dominance rank between two individuals in a group, the less frequent are agonistic interactions between them (Bernstein, 1970). Indeed the alpha individual may show the least aggression of all. It is as though aggression is shown in relation to the need for asserting rank: in a group of monkeys the alpha male has no need to behave aggressively if his priority is universally accepted, and other individuals show most aggression to those with whom their relationship is least stable (but see Tokuda and Jensen, 1969). In other words, the more uncertain the rank, the greater the need to confirm it. And as in man, confirmation often involves "skewed communication"— that is, over-emphasis of that which confirms the rank and under-emphasis of that which does not (Goffmann, 1959). Perhaps because adequate communication between monkeys probably depends on social experience within a sensitive period (page 235), monkeys reared in individual cages in the laboratory tend not to form stable hierarchies (Mason, 1961b).

But the hierarchy is not maintained solely by the initiative of the top-ranking individuals. Once it is established, self-assertion by the dominants may be less conspicuous than the avoidance of dominants by subordinates. Indeed in a study of captive baboons, Rowell's data (1966b) suggested that "the hierarchy is maintained, or expressed, chiefly by subordinate activities and that it is the lower-ranking animals which do most to perpetuate rank distinctions. . . . It is the subordinate animal which continuously observes and maintains a hierarchy, while a dominant animal could almost be defined as one which does not 'think before it acts' in social situations". Furthermore, Rowell stresses that the hierarchy is potentially always in flux. It is the consequence of learning during every interaction by every individual—learning presumably on the part of both participants and onlookers.

Although the formation of a dominance hierarchy is associated with a reduction in overt aggression, aggression is still potentially present. Any disturbance may precipitate it. Furthermore, aggressive episodes may be infectious: if one individual is attacked or threatened by a superior whom he does not dare attack back, he may re-direct his aggression onto one of his inferiors. Aggressive episodes also become more frequent with crowding (e.g., macaques, Bernstein, 1969): the results of an experiment with captive Japanese macaques by Alexander and Roth (1971) indicated that the effect of crowding on severe aggressive episodes was due primarily to the strange environment in which the animals were confined, while that on mild aggression was due to crowding per se (see also Plotnik et al., 1968).

Though the concept of dominance has proved useful in many studies of primate societies, in others this has been less true. Sometimes it cannot be applied even at the descriptive level. For instance, if agonistic interactions are rare, the existence of a hierarchical organization is difficult to assess. In such cases some authors assume it to be covert, perhaps because dominance relations are so well established that the subordinate individuals have learned not to provoke their superiors. If dominance relations are maintained only by inconspicuous expressive gestures, these might be missed by the field worker. Other observers assume that when agonistic interactions are less conspicuous, dominance relations are less important. For instance on just these grounds it has been suggested that dominance relations are unimportant in arboreal species (DeVore, 1965b; see also Poirier, 1970a), though the data here are of dubious generality. There is of course always the possibility that further observation will reveal a hierarchical structure that was not apparent at first sight. For example, in rhesus monkey troops dominance relations amongst females are less conspicuous than those amongst males, and some observers (e.g. J. H. Kaufmann, 1967) concluded that a hierarchical structure was absent among the females. However, more detailed and longer-term studies indicated not only that female hierarchies were present, but that they were more stable than those of the males (Sade, 1972a). However, in other species dominance interactions do seem to be almost absent—for instance in some lemurs, at any rate during the non-breeding season (Jolly, 1966), in the family groups of titi monkeys (Mason, 1968), amongst the males in some baboon troops (Rowell, 1966a), and in gibbons (see Carpenter, 1964 and Ellefson, 1968).

In addition to such differences in the frequency of dominance interactions between species, there may be marked differences in the nature and extent of the hierarchical structure found in groups of the same species in different situations or at different times. That hierarchical structure is often more conspicuous in caged than in free-living groups of the same species is well established (e.g., patas monkey, Hall et al., 1965; baboon, Rowell, 1966b). Age is also an important variable: Kummer (1957) found that aggressive interactions were good indicators of rank in adult male hamadryas baboons, but not in two-year-olds, and were inappropriate in one-year-olds. Another factor is breeding status: in a troop of semi-free-ranging squirrel monkeys, hierarchies were absent except amongst males during the breeding season (Baldwin, 1971). Thus the dominance concept may be useful for a given species in one context but not in another, and for a given troop at one time but not late.

Situational factors and inter-individual relations also may detract from the value of the dominance hierarchy as a descriptive tool. Alexander and Bowers

FIGURE 22.1

*Displays of high-ranking rhesus male.* (Drawing by Priscilla Edwards.)

(1967, 1969) found that the individuals in a captive troop of Japanese macaques could be divided into classes by age and sex—I, an adult male; II, large males and females; III, adult females that gave birth the previous spring and a few males; IV, infants and juveniles; V and VI, adult males, females without infants, and a few juveniles; VII, a one-year-old orphan. Figure 22.2 shows that the frequency of successful attack decreased with class position. Separate hierarchies existed within each class, forming part of the overall troop hierarchy. It was noticeable that aggression within class II was less than for other classes, probably because all monkeys in that class received protection from the group leader when attacked. But, as shown by the figures to the left of the diagonal in Fig. 22.2, relations within the troop could not be fully described in terms of a linear hierarchy. There were a number of reasons for this. For one thing, dominance was partly situational: a class V or VI male might dominate an infant in an iso-

| | I | II | III | IV | V | VI | VII | TOTAL |
|---|---|---|---|---|---|---|---|---|
| I | | 1.50 | 2.32 | .82 | .93 | .13 | .00 | .124 |
| II | .00 | .20 / .00 | 1.02 | .53 | .64 | .25 | .33 | .63 |
| III | .00 | .00 | .66 / .09 | .32 | .64 | .28 | .26 | .37 |
| IV | .00 | .00 | .01 | .35 / .07 | .15 | .04 | .82 | .11 |
| V | .00 | .00 | .03 | .04 | .29 / .11 | .35 | .27 | .10 |
| VI | .00 | .00 | .02 | .01 | .03 | .43 / .00 | .25 | .04 |
| VII | .00 | .00 | .00 | .00 | .00 | .00 | | .00 |
| TOTAL | .00 | .03 | .24 | .21 | .34 | .22 | .41 | .22 |

FIGURE 22.2

*Density matrix of attacks in a captive group of Japanese macaques. Figures show relative frequency with which animal in class on left attacked animal in class along top.* (From Alexander and Bowers, 1969.)

lated corner, but not when near animals of classes I through III. For another, kinship and affiliative relations much obscured the picture. This question of coalitions is discussed further below.

Such findings indicate that, even as a descriptive concept, dominance/subordinance is not always equally useful in studies of non-human primates. Of greater importance is the extent to which it often falls short as an explanatory concept in that the dependent variables with which it is associated are not adequately correlated with each other. In captive hamadryas baboons, Kummer (1957) found that the rank of males based on success in aggressive encounters was not related to that based on access to oestrous females. Warren and Maroney (1958), in a study of captive monkeys, found that the correlation between priority of access to food and dominance in agonistic encounters was 0.77—a figure which is fairly characteristic and indicates considerable relationship between the two, but certainly not absolute correspondence. This is perhaps not surprising, for in vertebrates of all phyletic levels, access to food depends on subtleties of behaviour, such as opportunism, which cannot be assessed in terms of a unitary intervening variable (e.g., Bernstein, 1969). Similarly in his study of free-living rhesus males, Kaufmann (1967) remarks, "Some monkeys made a good living from bold submissiveness", and Sade (1972a) points out that dominant animals are often distracted by other activities from seizing the food, thereby giving subordinate ones an opportunity to dart in and seize it. Again, Rowell (1966b), in a study of caged baboons, found that even the rankings of individuals in a variety of contexts each involving approach/retreat were not precisely correlated with each other, and these were related hardly at all to the outcomes of non-agonistic interactions.

In perhaps the most detailed study of this type, Bernstein (1970) studied seven captive groups containing six monkey species. In each case he assessed rank orders based on the direction of agonistic encounters, mounting se-quences, and grooming relations. A comparison of these rank orders "failed to reveal a close correlation between any two of the response patterns studied" (see also, for example, Ploog et al., 1963; Conaway and Koford, 1965; Hall and DeVore, 1965; Jolly, 1966; Baldwin, 1968; Loy, 1971; Riopelle et al., 1971).

To the extent that the various dependent variables by which dominance is assessed do not correlate with one another, they cannot be simply related to any basic characteristic of the individual, and the power of the hierarchy to predict outcomes of social interactions is limited. The concept of dominance may thus be deficient both for the description of social structure and for its explanation. Just why it is that dominance proves to be a satisfactory concept in some studies and not in others remains to be determined—presumably through the study of inter-acting variables.

But in any case there is another difficulty in regarding rank based on agonistic encounters as a primary factor determining intra-group relations. The agonistic interactions on which dominance relations are based are basically dis-ruptive of the group and would of themselves lead to a scattering of its members. Indeed in macaque and baboon groups competitive interactions leading to the establishment of a social hierarchy may result in some individuals being forced to the periphery of the troop, or even expelled altogether. In the situations in which dominance has been studied, disruption of the group has not occurred only because either the group was confined, or it was held together by positive social responsiveness between its members. While the establishment of domi-nance relations accepted by the individuals concerned is accompanied by a reduc-tion in intra-group strife and tension, a dominance order cannot in itself be re-sponsible for group cohesiveness. Hierarchical structuring is to be regarded rather as the consequence of the responses of individuals to potentially agonistic situations when withdrawal is rendered impossible either by physical barriers or by other facets of their own behaviour. Agonistic interactions form only one aspect of the inter-relationships between individuals, and a dominance hierarchy is only one aspect of the total pattern of relationships (see also Plutchik, 1964; Gartlan, 1968; Bernstein, 1970).

## Dependent rank and coalitions

One complication in the use of the dominance concept concerns the formation of coalitions. Two animals, acting together, may be able to dominate another which neither could dominate alone; or one animal, normally inferior to another, may be able to dominate it if it can call on the aid of a superior animal. For such reasons Kawai (1958, 1965b), studying Japanese macaques, distinguished between basic rank, which depends on the individual's own prowess, and dependent rank, which depends on association with another individual. When the troop was fed with wheat placed on top of a box, no other individual would approach while the male who was most dominant in agonistic interactions was eating. The second and third males could chase away the most dominant female provided the alpha male was not in the vicinity, but would leave at once if the female's vocalizations brought the alpha male to the spot (see also Altmann, 1962; Imanishi, 1960; Kaufmann, 1965).

Struhsaker's (1967) study of vervet monkeys demonstrates the importance of coalitions in a more natural situation. About 20 percent of all intense intragroup encounters involved more than two individuals, with one soliciting the aid of one or two others against an adversary. At least some of the coalitions occurred more frequently than could be accounted for by chance, and thus indicated individual preferences among the monkeys. Encounters involving such coalitions often had an outcome different from that expected on the basis of the dominance status of the individuals, but only rarely resulted in a permanent change in the dominance order. However where coalitions are more permanent, they may have that effect: Kaufmann (1967) describes how the four-year-old males in a rhesus troop tended to act together as a group and could not be assigned individual ranks (see also Hall and DeVore, 1965).

The relationship most conspicuously giving rise to dependent rank is that between mother and offspring. Observations on a number of species both in captivity (Marsden, 1968) and in the field show that the rank of juveniles is often influenced by that of their mothers, who interfere or are potentially able to interfere in disputes. Thus Kawai (1958) and Kawamura (1958) found that infant Japanese macaques, especially female infants, ranked just below their mothers. Daughters usually ranked in reverse age order, with the youngest over four years of age ranking next to her mother. Sons ranked below daughters but above all members of the next family (Koyama, 1967). Some male offspring of very high-ranking mothers were never forced to the periphery of the troop, as is usually the case during late adolescence, but made a smooth transition from juvenile status to membership of the central male group.

In a study of Japanese macaques in a large corral, Alexander and Bowers (1969) divided the animals into seven classes, as discussed on page 345. There was a strong correlation between the ranks of juveniles is class IV and those of their mothers in classes II and III. However juveniles did not always rank immediately below their mothers, since females in classes II and III did not permit attack by juveniles of higher-ranking mothers.

Sade's long-term studies (1967, 1972a) of rhesus monkeys have confirmed that the dominance relations of the maturing young can be predicted to a greater or lesser extent from those of their mothers (see also Koford, 1963). Juvenile females regularly rose above those females who ranked below their mothers until they occupied a position just below hers. Sade's studies have also shown that, as in the Japanese macaque, younger sisters regularly rise in rank above their older sisters, so that by adulthood sisters rank in inverse order of age. The bases of this appear to be complex, and neither the coalition between mother and youngest daughter nor the physiological events relating to the daughter's first oestrus provide a full explanation. The inverse relationship between age and rank found amongst sisters does not hold amongst brothers, who usually, though not invariably, rank in age order.

The dependent rank resulting from the mother-offspring relationship may thus become basic as the younger animal matures. However not all dependent rank stems immediately from the mother-offspring relationship: other kinship ties, especially that with the mother's sister (Kawai, 1965b), or membership of the same age-sex class, may also be important (Chance, 1954; Hall and DeVore, 1965; Southwick and Siddiqi, 1967). In Japanese macaque consort pairs, the female's rank usually becomes dependent on that of her male (e.g., Kawai, 1965b). Alexander and Bowers (1969) report a case of a male Japanese macaque who formed affiliative relationships with three young monkeys apparently quite unrelated to him. In a captive mixed-species group of bonnet and pig-tail macaques the relative dominance of females depended on whether a male of their species was present (Stynes et al., 1968).

The extent to which such coalitions in primate societies are to be regarded as permanent structures within the society varies with the species and situation in question. The adult males in a rhesus troop form a constant central nucleus, but the situation described by Struhsaker (1967) resembles more "a temporary alliance of distinct parties for a limited purpose"—Boissevain's (1971) definition of a coalition in human societies. Boissevain (1971) has listed seven possible characters of coalitions in human groups:

1  A centrality of focus in the form of a single central ego or leader or clique
2  Presence of clearly defined common goal or
   2a  merely common affection
3  Internal specialization apart from the leader
4  Exclusiveness of membership
5  Shared social relations among members
6  Behavioural norms vis-à-vis other members
7  Presence of rival or competing units

Such a list would seem to provide a substantial basis for assessing the properties of the coalitions to be found within primate groups. For example, the central males of a rhesus group might be found to have (1), (2a), (4), (5), and (6), but coalitions in Struhsaker's vervets perhaps (2), (5), and (7).

### Leadership and control

As we have seen, most primate troops contain an animal who is dominant to all others in agonistic interactions, and it is often that animal who determines what the troop does and the direction it takes in troop movements. The dominant silverback in a gorilla group usually adopts a special stance (Fig. 22.3) before an integrated troop movement, and the other members then follow him (Schaller, 1963; Fossey, personal communication). In many macaques and langurs the dominant male usually moves off first, and the others then follow. In the hamadryas one-male group, the male attacks any female who does not keep near him (Kummer, 1968).

However it cannot always be assumed that the animal which moves first determines the direction of movement. Schaller (1963) describes how the individuals of a gorilla group may move a little way in one direction or another, but not proceed further unless the silverback comes too. In chimpanzees the animal who determines the direction of group movement does not necessarily travel in front. It "may take up a central or rear position while continuing to regulate the movements of the group—if it stops, the others wait; when it moves on, they

FIGURE 22.3

*Stance of silverback gorilla before integrated group movement.* (Drawing by Priscilla Edwards from Schaller, 1963.)

start off again" (van Lawick-Goodall, 1968). The animal who exerts control in this way is often an old male who is not the most dominant member of the group (Bygott, personal communication).

The subtlety of such interactions is seen in Kummer's description of the behaviour of two-male teams in the hamadryas baboon. Each such team consists of an older and a younger male, one or both of which have females accompanying them. Movements are usually initiated by the younger male, who moves off a little way, thereby taking the initiative. Whether he moves further depends on whether or not he is followed by his females, the females of the older male, and the older male himself. Movement by the females is probably controlled also by the older male, since they tend not to move if he remains seated. Only occasionally does the dominant male actually take the lead.

In practice it is often extremely difficult to discover whether any particular individual is responsible for determining the direction in which a troop moves. Individuals may initiate a pseudopodium, now here and now there, the troop following only when one of the control individuals starts to move in a particular direction. Sometimes there seems to be no control animal, the troop following a pseudopodium which contains a substantial minority of the whole. In the slow, drifting movements which troops of monkeys (like bird flocks) often show during feeding, leadership often appears to be absent, though a leader may appear when the troop moves in an integrated fashion from one place to another (Struhsaker, 1967).

It is perhaps especially in arboreal forest monkeys that leadership is least apparent. In squirrel monkeys, Baldwin (1968, 1971) found that there are no troop leaders: troop unity depends on the presence of adult females, not because they enforce order but because other age/sex classes are attracted to them more than vice versa. In howler monkeys leadership may depend on which male first finds a suitable path. Carpenter (1964) describes how, at a choice point in an unfamiliar area, the males explore alternative paths. When one finds a suitable route his vocalizations attract the females and young, and the other males then follow.

Differences in the extent to which leadership occurs can perhaps be understood in functional terms. Where food is evenly dispersed, as in some forest species, it makes less difference which way the troop moves and leadership may therefore be less important. But when food supplies are irregularly available, or when water holes or sleeping cliffs are in short supply, the direction in which the troop moves may be crucial. Even these are not the only issues: for instance, Altmann and Altmann (1970) describe how a baboon troop deserted a sleeping site after predation by a leopard had occurred there.

Such examples indicate that experience may be a more important quality for a leader than physical prowess. As another example, hamadryas baboons may cover 6 or 12 miles in a day, in the course of which they must visit water and finish up at a suitable sleeping cliff: not surprisingly, control depends on the senior males (Kummer, 1971). By contrast, in *anubis* baboons in Uganda it is the senior females who exercise control (Rowell, 1966a); and it is probably more than coincidence that it is these senior females who are the most stable elements in the troop. The silverback mountain gorilla controls his group rather rigidly, even though food is fairly widely dispersed: perhaps in this case the avoidance of enemies places a premium on experienced leadership (Fossey, in press).

Thus it is because the dominant animal is likely to be one of the most experienced in a group, as well as because he is able to impose his will, that dominance and leadership often go together. However they need not, for dominance may respect wisdom when decisions are to be made. Other activities of the senior individuals in a group, such as the disciplinary one of breaking up fights within the group, looking out for enemies, or protecting the group in case of attack, are also often correlated with dominance or leadership, but again they may not be.

## Attention structure

Chance and Jolly (1970) argue that one method for understanding the structure of a social group is to study the direction of attention of the component individuals. For instance, in a group of patas monkeys the single male is usually somewhat detached from the females. The attention of mothers and young is directed toward each other, whereas that of the male is directed outward toward the environment. In a baboon or rhesus group, by contrast, the attention of females is directed primarily toward the adult males. As a descriptive approach, this is unexceptionable.

But Chance and Jolly go further than this. First, they re-define dominance to emphasize its attention-attracting quality rather than the basic aggressiveness, the dominant individual in a group being defined as the one that holds the attention of others. Thus while a straightforward examination of the sequence of events when strangers are placed together indicates that inter-individual agression is replaced by mutual dominance-subordinance relations accompanied by a parallel structuring of the direction of attention of individuals, Chance regards the attention structure as primary (see also Reynolds and Luscombe, 1969). There seems little to be said for this view. True, dominant males in many primate groups (e.g., chimpanzees, van Lawick-Goodall, 1968; Bygott, in preparation; gorilla, Fossey, in preparation; rhesus monkeys, Hinde and Rowell, 1962) do indulge in attention-catching displays, but it can hardly be coincidence that these are all of a type to show off the physical prowess of the displaying individual and to frighten others (Figs. 16.6 and 22.1). When a chimpanzee displays, other animals in the vicinity show signs of fear and avoid the displaying animal. Furthermore, the effectiveness of a display may be enhanced by accompanying loud noises: chimpanzees learn to beat resonating trees or hollow drums, and captive male rhesus learn a variety of techniques for creating a noise with the structures available to them (Fig. 22.1). Thus the displays symbolize potential aggressiveness, and other individuals have ample opportunity to learn their significance.

Second, Chance and Jolly suggest that "attention" has a binding quality.

They write ". . . predominant attention to a single individual can, by acting as a common focus of attention, provide a means whereby a number of individuals cohere". But why should subordinate individuals remain near the dominant animal unless some other factor is involved, except in those cases where his aggressiveness is specifically directed toward punishing them for moving off, as in hamadryas (Kummer, 1968) and consort pairs of chimpanzees (McGinnis, 1973)?

Chance and Jolly do have an answer to this. They refer to Mason's (1965) emphasis (see also Schneirla, 1965) that mildly unfamiliar or threatening objects cause approach, and strongly unfamiliar ones withdrawal. Applying this to primate societies, it is suggested that the females approach the males because the latter give only infrequent threats and only rarely actually attack. But while Mason's line of reasoning could be applicable to very young animals, adult female apes and monkeys are surely too sophisticated consistently to approach a potentially aggressive animal unless attracted in some other way.

Thus while studying the direction of "attention" (a concept which in any case needs precise definition, Terrace, 1966) may provide a useful means of describing group structure, its explanatory power as the crucial factor in determining social relationships is doubtful. The case made by Chance and Jolly for regarding it as primary does not bear examination. These authors may be able to "account for" every kind of social structure by re-describing it in terms of attention structure, but this does not seem a very profound procedure.

### Conclusion

We have seen that the concept of dominance rank is often useful to describe the outcomes of agonistic interactions within primate groups, and that it sometimes has also explanatory value as an intervening variable in relating diverse types of agonistic and non-agonistic encounters. Often, but not always, the dominant animal in a group is also its leader or control animal, and sometimes he performs other functions in the group. The structure of a group as indicated by the direction of attention of its members may result from dominance-subordinance relations, but cannot be regarded as primary.

In any case dominance relations cannot by themselves account for all the subtleties of group structure. To investigate these, better methods for the description of structure are essential. Some of these are discussed in the next chapter.

# 23
# STRUCTURAL COMPLEXITY

### Structure within the troop

The individuals in a primate troop are not dispersed at random (Chance, 1954). In the first place, agonistic interactions promote dispersion and affinities promote cohesion, so that, other things being equal, each pair of animals considered in isolation might remain a preferred distance apart from each other. But each pair of animals cannot be considered in isolation, and it is in principle impossible for preferred spatial equilibria between all members of a troop to be achieved. If A and B sit at their preferred distance apart, C could perhaps find a point which satisfied his preferred distances from each of them, but not one which also satisfied preferred distances from all other neighbours (Kummer, 1971). In any case, proximity to A might affect C's preferred distance from B (page 367). Some degree of social tension seems almost inevitable (cf. pages 326–328). Furthermore special relationships between individuals within or between age-sex classes are associated with clumping in some parts of the troop and increased spacing in others. And non-social factors, such as local food distribution within the troop or the presence of external dangers, may further affect spatial relationships.

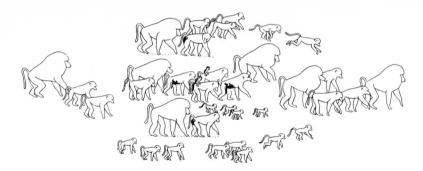

FIGURE 23.1

*Baboon troop, showing characteristic spatial distribution during travel.*
(From Hall and DeVore, 1965.)

Relative spatial position is one outward indicator of the nature of the behavioural relationships between individuals, and is a useful tool for studying the dynamics of group structure. Let us therefore consider some examples of spatial distribution within natural troops. Figure 23.1 shows the description of Hall and DeVore (1965) of a savannah-living baboon troop during movement from one place to another. According to these authors, dominant adult males, females with small infants, and a small group of older infants occupy the centre, with young juveniles on one side and older juveniles on the other. Additional adult males and females precede and follow the centre. In other contexts the groups are arranged differently: for instance, if a young adult male in the front gives an alarm bark, one or more adult males may come up to join him, and if there is a real threat all the central males go to meet it, while the females and young stay behind. Rowell (1966a), studying forest baboons, found less clear signs of organization when the troop was on the move, though there was usually an adult male at front and rear: she also found much less tendency for males to interpose themselves between the troop and potential dangers (see also Rhine and Owens, 1972; Altmann and Altmann, 1970).

Thus although baboons may show a characteristic spatial structure within the troop, its nature varies with the situation. As another example, the females of a hamadryas one-male group typically position themselves between their male and the next one-male group. However if the males start to threaten each other, the females move behind their own males (Kummer, 1968).

Comparable regularities in spatial structure are found also in the Japanese macaque. The adult males, females, and their young are usually in the centre of the troop, the sub-adult males and older juveniles on the periphery (e.g., Sugiyama, 1960). Detailed studies by other workers reveal not only that the structure is actually more complex than this (Imanishi, 1960), but also that it differs between troops (Yamada, 1971). Yamada divided the males into five rough classes—leaders, sub-leaders, ordinary males, semi-solitary males, and young males—according to differences in their social behaviour. The females could similarly be divided into classes. The troops differed markedly both in the proportion of the different classes and in their internal structure: for instance some troops maintained much larger inter-individual distances at the feeding station than did others. They differed also in the extent to which the four-year-old males moved to the periphery of the troop or, having moved, in the extent to which they could re-enter the central area.

The spatial structure of a troop presumably reflects the social relationships among the individuals that compose it: differences in structure pose questions about how the patterns of relationships are determined. As we have seen (pages 17–20), in non-human species a crucial issue is likely to be the temperaments of the component individuals. The question thus arises, can differences in structure be related to differences in the behavioural characteristics of the individuals that compose the group? We may consider two types of study, one concerned with differences within a species, the other with differences between species.

In discussing the differences between the troops of Japanese macaques mentioned above, Yamada (1971) rejected the earlier view that the social structure of a troop depends primarily on the character of the leader, or that it is carried on as a sort of social tradition. Instead he regarded it as a result of dynamic interactions between the individuals present at the time. He emphasized especially attempts by the peripheral males to enter the central area, and the manner in which these are resisted by the animals in the centre. The latter include a few dominant males and a considerably larger number of females: the males are especially likely to attack intruders engaged in agonistic interactions with the females. The nature of the social structure thus depends on the aggressiveness of the high-ranking males and the degree to which the central females reject intrusions from the periphery. If the central males are aggressive and the females rejecting, peripheral males find it hard to enter the centre, and the society is strictly integrated. With an aggressive leader but tolerant females, peripheral males can enter the centre easily provided they keep away from the male, and the society is not integrated. If the leader is mild, intruders are initially superior to the females, who attack them only with support from the leader: the other adult males in the centre avoid getting involved in fights so as not to be attacked by the leader. Thus the character of the leader affects the structure but is by no means the only issue.

Differences in social structure between troops have been reported also in the bonnet macaque. In most troops the young males remain in the troop as they grow to full social and physical activity, and participate actively in social relationships. In some troops, however, there is a network of social relationships which prevents the young males from becoming integrated, and they may become outcasts (Simonds, 1973). Paterson (1973) ascribes the differences he observed between two troops of baboons to a complex interplay between ecological and experiential, including protocultural, factors.

It is also possible to use differences between species to study the relationship between group structure and individual behavioural characteristics. Mason (1973) compared differences in the social structure between two genera of South American monkeys with differences in behaviour shown in encounters between individuals. *Callicebus* species live in small family-like groups consisting of an adult male, adult female, and one or two young and occupying an exclusive territory (page 392). *Saimiri* species (squirrel monkeys) live in groups containing a number of adults of both sexes and their young, occuping an ill-defined home range (page 391). These differences are related to the patterns of affinities and aversions between individuals. *Saimiri* females are strongly attracted to one another, and less strongly to males. The males are moderately attracted to females, and under conditions of prolonged exposure, spend much time with other males. *Callicebus* of both sexes are wary of strangers, but if a male and female live together for a while in isolation from others they form a strong attachment to each other which endures in a group situation.

Another factor affecting the structure of a troop is its absolute size: this may be correlated with the proportions of the various classes of animals, so that individuals in troops of different sizes have different opportunities for interaction. Of course, since troop size is determined in part by the behaviour of the individuals within it (pages 334–335), the influence is reciprocal (page 347). Baldwin and Baldwin (1971), studying squirrel monkeys, emphasize another way in which absolute troop size may affect structure. Citing evidence from the Wisconsin laboratory that rhesus monkeys with extensive experience of playing with peers are more competent in social communication than animals brought up in isolation (e.g., Harlow and Harlow, 1965; Sackett, 1970), they suggest that in a large troop the animals become habituated to more intense and frequent social interaction.

Returning to the Japanese macaque, a major factor determining troop structure is the influence of consanguinity. Blood relations tend to be especially closely associated within the troop, and troop fission may involve a split between consanguineal groups (Koyama, 1970). Matrilines (i.e., mother, daughters, granddaughters) are particularly closely integrated, males being less attached to their relatives. Affiliations based on blood relationships extend to many different activities. Yamada (1963) found that Japanese macaques ate in company with members of their own family more than with members of other families, and this tended to be more clearly the case the more dominant the individual concerned. In rhesus macaques the majority of grooming interactions occurs between members of a family. On Cayo Santiago, Sade (1965) found that 62 percent of grooming during the breeding season, and 64 percent during the non-breeding season, was intra-familial: had grooming occurred at random the figure would have been only 15 percent (see also Koford, 1963; J. H. Kaufmann, 1965; Miller et al., 1973).

The strength of familial ties varies between even closely related species. Rosenblum (1971b) compared a group of pig-tailed macaques with a group of bonnet macaques. Both groups had been in the laboratory for 6 years, and they were of comparable composition, but the pig-tailed macaques interacted much more with family clan members than did bonnets (Fig. 14.1). As mentioned previously, Rosenblum suggests that this difference in familial cohesiveness arises from the fact that pig-tailed macaques establish a more enduring and selective relationship with the mother than do bonnets. It is indeed likely that the mother-offspring relationship forms the basis of most kinship ties, since other relationships, such as those between sibling and sibling or between infant and mother's sister, derive from it (e.g., Yamada, 1963; Koford, 1963; Kaufmann, 1965; Sade, 1968; 1972a). Blood relationships are probably important in determining social structure also in many other primates (e.g., chimpanzees, van Lawick-Goodall, 1968; Thorndahl, personal communication) as well as other species (e.g., African elephant, Douglas-Hamilton, 1972).

The social organization of the Japanese macaque thus depends on positive and negative relationships between members of age-sex classes, and affinities based on blood relationships, with troop differences depending on the temperaments of the component individuals, troop size, and sex ratio. Perhaps Koyama's (1970) remark, "It is not easy to grasp the social organization of the Japanese macaque precisely", is the understatement of the primate literature.

However that is not all, for within any one species, and indeed within one troop, spatial structure may be affected by environmental and seasonal factors.

As we have seen, baboon troops become more closely integrated in situations that involve potential danger or critical "decisions", such as the start of a movement (Altmann and Altmann, 1970). Another important factor is food availability. In some species, at least, aggression decreases if food is scarce (e.g., rhesus, Bernstein, 1969), and this may have profound effects on troop structure. Even the amount of cover during feeding may influence inter-individual interactions (Ripley, 1970). Food availability affects the sizes of chimpanzee groups (Wrangham, in preparation) and of black spider monkey troops (Durham, 1971), as well as the extent to which gelada baboon herds split into one-male groups (Crook, 1966). Anubis baboons also split up into small foraging parties, each of only a few individuals, when food is scarce (Aldrich-Blake et al., 1971). In addition, in areas where food is scarce, baboons need to travel more and have less time for sleep and social interactions. The extent to which baboons sleep in united groups or disperse in smaller parties to sleep varies also with the availability of sleeping sites (Crook and Aldrich-Blake, 1968; Kummer, 1971).[1]

The nature of the environment may affect also the composition of the troop on a longer-term basis. For example juveniles may be more susceptible to disease and predation; and the frequency and success with which females breed, itself affected by environmental factors, will determine the proportion of adults to juveniles in the troop (Rowell, 1972a).

Furthermore most primates have a definite reproductive season (Lancaster and Lee, 1965), and group structure may vary with the reproductive state of its members. Baldwin (1968) found that during the birth season adult male squirrel monkeys were quiet and initiated few interactions: they mostly followed the troop at a distance. But during the mating season they became hyperactive, often approaching females, and became organized in a fiercely contested linear dominance hierarchy. The seasonal differences between the social relations of individuals in the two seasons are shown in Fig. 23.2.

It will be apparent both that regularities in the composition and spatial structure of primate groups can be discerned, and that these characters are markedly influenced by a variety of factors internal and external to the group. Indeed, at the moment field studies are still at a stage where the more that is known about a species, the more complex its social structure appears to be. Students of primate behaviour are still engaged in working out methods for describing social structure: in discussing some of these in the next section, further variations in structure will be mentioned.

[1] See also data on baboons given by Altmann and Altmann, 1970; on langurs by Jay, 1965, Ripley, 1967, and Yoshiba, 1968; and on vervets by Struhsaker, 1967, and by Gartlan and Brain, 1968.

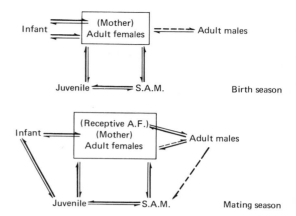

<small>FIGURE</small> 23.2

*The relations between the various age/sex classes of squirrel monkeys. ⟶ indicates the presence and direction of an affinity. — — → indicates the presence and direction of hostility and aggression. Wider arrows indicate stronger relationships. Minor relations (such as infant aggression toward adult males, etc.) are omitted to simplify the diagram. S.A.M. indicates sub-adult males. (From Baldwin, 1968.)*

## Sociograms

We have seen that the structure of a group is the patterning of relationships within that group (page 317). We have seen also that the dominance-subordinance concept is too limited to provide more than a very partial understanding of group structure in primates (page 347). Evidence reviewed in the last section showed that the relationships within a troop may have considerable complexity, and that they may vary not only between species but also between troops of one species and even in the same troop from time to time. Furthermore the spatial relation between two individuals is not necessarily an index of all aspects of their behavioural interactions (e.g. Kummer, 1968). Clearly, therefore, what is needed for the understanding of group structure is a way of mapping the relationships between individuals.

A useful tool here is the "sociogram"—a means of representing pictorially

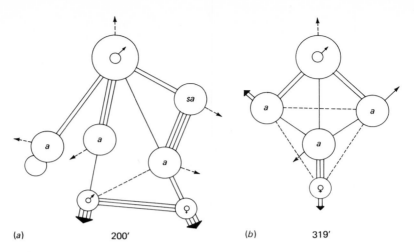

(a)                200'          (b)              319'

**FIGURE 23.3**

*Hamadryas baboon. Sociograms of two one-male units at the peak of their development. (a) Male-female distances were 69, 43, 76, and 50 cm;   (b) male-female distances were 31, 46, and 36 cm. Large circle = adult male; medium circle = female consort; small circle on the radius of a female = her 6- to 18-month-old infant; attached circle = her black infant. a = adult female; sa = sub-adult female; 3 = three-year-old female; 2 = two-year-old female. Connecting lines express the percentage of observation minutes that contained an exchange of the specified gestures. Arrows indicate exchanges with animals outside the unit: – – –, less than 3 percent; ——, 4 to 10 percent; ☰, 11 to 20 percent; ☰, 21 to 30 percent, etc. The graph distance between the leader and each female is proportional to the mean of the recorded distances. The total time of observation is indicated in minutes. (From Kummer, 1968.)*

the frequencies of interactions between individuals in a group. For example, Fig. 23.3 shows the sociograms of two one-male units of the hamadryas baboon (Kummer, 1968). These units contain a male (large circles), several adult or sub-adult females (*a* or *sa* in medium-sized circles), and their young (small circles). The number of lines connecting the circles indicates the proportion of observation minutes in which there was a social interaction between the individuals

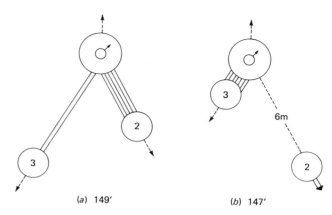

FIGURE 23.4

*Hamadryas baboon. Sociograms of a one-male unit, (a) when the older female was in anoestrus and (b) when she was in oestrus. Male-female distances were 97 and 41 cm in (a) and 9 and 600 cm in (b). See Fig. 23.3 (From Kummer, 1968.)*

concerned. The distance between the circles is related to the mean distance which separated the individuals. It will be apparent that the sociogram provides an immediate picture of the overall relationships between the individuals in the group.

In constructing these sociograms all social interactions in a previously assembled list were included. The great majority of these were positive interactions: even some of the aggressive episodes were considered positive in that they involved attacks by the male on females who wandered away from him. Of course, the precise form of the diagram will depend in part on the method of scoring used: in this case, for example, Kummer scored the initiation of clinging or sucking as one interaction, but not its continuation: had each minute during which the infant continued to suck been scored, the number of lines joining the mothers to their infants would have been much greater.

Sociograms can also be used to portray changes in group structure resulting from changes in the physiological conditions of its members or in the composition of the group. For example, Fig. 23.4 refers to a one-male unit when female 3 was in anoestrus (*a*) and in oestrus (*b*). In the former case, the male watched over both females: he could keep female 3 close to him by threatening

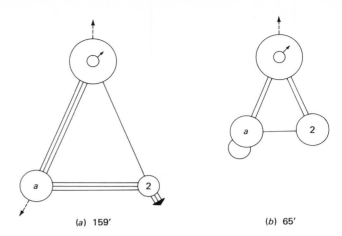

(a) 159'                    (b) 65'

FIGURE 23.5

*Hamadryas baboon. Sociograms of a one-male unit*
*(a) before and (b) after the adult female had given*
*birth. Male-female distances were 93 and 94 cm in*
*(a), 53 and 52 cm in (b). See Fig. 23.3. (From Kummer,*
*1968.)*

her often, but was seldom groomed by her. Female 2 he kept close by occasional glances, and she groomed him often. When female 3 was in oestrus he watched only her, and she often groomed him.

Figure 23.5 refers to another group containing one adult female and her adolescent daughter. After the former gave birth to an infant, and paid less attention to the male, he interacted more with the younger female. By using sociograms in this way to portray changes in social structure, a start can be made on the analysis of process.

Sociograms are one way of reducing the mass of data that it is possible to collect about interactions in a troop, in order to produce a visually comprehensible picture. It is both a virtue and a shortcoming of such a representation that it involves the loss of data. It must also be remembered that, in a group with more than a few individuals, the distances between the symbols cannot be proportional to any measure of their relationships if the diagram is presented in only two dimensions. The overall picture may thus contain an element of subjective assessment by the investigator, even though some of its detailed characteristics, such as the thickness of the lines, are related to hard data.

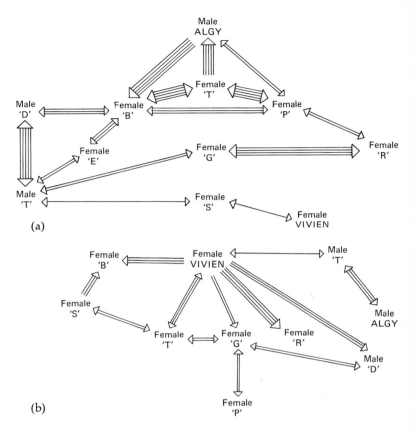

FIGURE 23.6

*Interactions within a captive group of macaques:* (a) *positive relations;* (b) *negative relations.* (From Virgo and Waterhouse, 1969.)

The sociograms discussed so far depict overall affinities between the animals in the group. The distribution of negative interactions amongst individuals is of course not the same as that of the positive ones: furthermore, it is not merely its opposite. One example is provided by Virgo and Waterhouse (1969) from a study of a socially unstable captive colony of macaques. They divided the interactions between individuals of a central group of this colony into positive (promoting association) and negative (avoiding it) and, by a scoring method not explained in their publication, they assessed the strength of positive and negative relations between individuals. Two sociograms were then drawn up (Fig. 23.6a and b): they show that a male, Algy, was the focus for positive inter-actions, and a female, Vivien, provided the centre of negative ones. They comment, "It is apparent that Algy showed some potential for leadership but lacked any aggressive quality, this being found only in Vivien". While the method of scoring adopted here is open to question, it does demonstrate the need for differentiating between qualitatively different kinds of behaviour in constructing sociograms.

Deag's (1974) study of the inter-individual relations within a group of wild Barbary macaques in the non-breeding season is of particular interest not only because it represents one of the most elaborate efforts to portray the relation-ships within a whole troop, but also because he used two independent means for assessing them. In one series of observations he recorded relationships in terms of distances between individuals. He selected subjects in such a manner that each animal was observed on a total of 50 occasions, but with appropriate precautions to ensure independence of the observations on each animal. On each occasion he recorded the three nearest neighbours to the subject selected, an animal qualifying as a neighbour only if it was within 10 m. The data showed that each subject did not associate at random with the various age-sex cate-gories, or with particular individuals within those categories. Deag was thus able to map the web of relationships (as indicated by spatial proximity) within the group using either the data for nearest neighbour or those for all three neigh-bours. The latter are shown in Fig. 23.7. The diagram is drawn so as to minimize the intersections between lines: thus no importance is to be attached to the length of the lines, only to the direction of the arrows. From these data Deag was able to draw a number of conclusions about the relationships between in-dividuals in the troop.

While the individuals of an age-sex class had different associates from each other, the age-sex classes of their associates tended to be similar. For example, each sub-adult female tended to associate with a specific adult female and her unweaned offspring (perhaps a filial tie), while adult males associated with other adult males and adult females.

Some animals tended to occur as neighbours more often than would be expected by chance, others less so: adult and sub-adult males and some females with unweaned offspring tended to be popular, while juveniles, infants, sub-adult females, one female with an unweaned infant, and two with no unweaned offspring were not. The number of neighbours an individual had tended to be related to its dominance status.

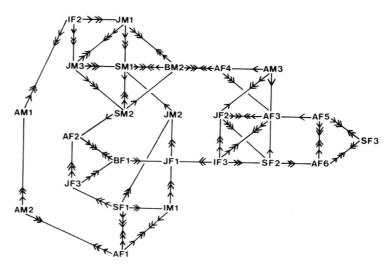

FIGURE 23.7

*The social network in a troop of Barbary macaques. Each symbol refers to an animal, the letters giving its age and sex (A—adult, S—sub-adult, M—male, F—female, etc.) A line joining two animals indicates that they were associates. The single arrow indicates that the animal to whom it points contributes to at least 10 percent of the other's neighbours; the double arrow that the animal from whom it points contributes to at least 10 percent of the other's subjects. Since the network is based on an n × n matrix, two animals can be joined by a line with arrows pointing in both directions. (From Deag, 1974).*

Deag's methods also enabled him to show that some individuals tended to have more neighbours if one other individual was amongst them: thus males tended to have more neighbours if a baby or sub-adult male were present, and females if a baby, infant, or juvenile or adult female were present. These findings are in keeping with Deag's data on the frequency with which males interact with and carry babies in this species (see pages 222–223).

Figure 23.7 is based solely on records of the spatial relations between individuals. However Deag also analysed an independent set of observations of social interactions within the same troop. This gave very similar results to the

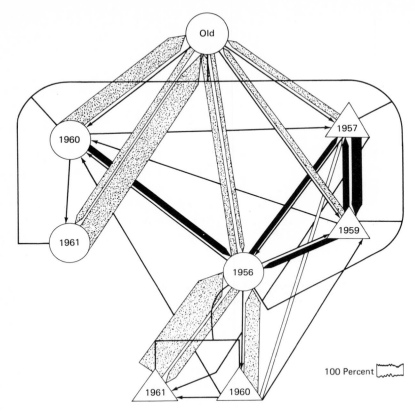

FIGURE 23.8
*Grooming relations in a genealogical group of rhesus monkeys.
See text.* (From Sade, 1965.)

analysis based on distances: animals which were frequently neighbours in the
one set of observations were also found to interact frequently in the other. Thus
spatial relations would seem to be a good guide to social structure.

   In all these studies, the sociograms have been based either on the spatial
relations between individuals, or on a variety of types of behaviour. For a full
understanding of relationships between individuals rather more specific studies
of particular types of activity will be necessary. Sade's (1965) study of grooming
relations within groups of rhesus monkeys is a classic example. Sade showed
that grooming interactions occurred predominantly between related individuals:
in fact with only rare exceptions each monkey did more than half its grooming

with members of its own genealogical group. Figure 23.8 shows the grooming relations within one genealogical group in observations made over 9 months, 1961. The heavy lines represent genealogical relations, the circles females, and the triangles males with their birth years inscribed. The arrows point from groomer to groomee, their width representing the proportion of the groomer's grooming bouts received by the groomee. Arrows represent relationships involving only 1 to 10 percent of the groomer's bouts. Stippled bars connect parent and offspring, shaded bars connect siblings.

Figure 23.8 exemplifies a number of points from Sade's data. For instance, each mother received a larger share of her offsprings' grooming than they did of hers: this is to be expected, since she has a diffuse flock while they focus on her. The grooming relations between parent and subadult or adult daughters (e.g., OLD and 1956 females) are much more reciprocal than those between parent and adult or sub-adult son (e.g., OLD and 1957 male), which tend to be one-sided. It will be apparent that a great deal of information can be contained in sociograms of this type.

By comparing sociograms for successive periods Sade was able to show that the structure of the society, as indicated by the grooming interactions, is constantly changing as individuals alter in status, mature, and join or leave the group.

## The social nexus

Such diagrams can provide a reasonably quantitative picture of the relationships between individuals: they can be made increasingly complex to cope with more precise measurement of behaviour or qualitative distinctions between types of interaction. Furthermore, as Deag has shown, the data on which they are based can reveal how the extent or nature of the interactions between two individuals may be affected by the presence of others.

This last observation bears on a further dimension of complexity: to understand the structure of a group we must understand not only the relationships between individuals, but also how each relationship can affect others. We have already mentioned that a mother can affect the relationship of her offspring with his peers (page 189), that coalitions may affect agonistic relations (pages 348–350), and that the relationship between the leader and the adult females in a troop of Japanese macaques may affect the relations between those females and the sub-adult males (pages 357–358). In this section we shall discuss the complexity that can be generated by such effects of relationships upon relationships even in a small captive group of rhesus monkeys. In such a group the nature of the relationship between a mother and her baby may be influenced by the presence of other adult females or "aunts" (pages 219–221). These aunts may respond to the baby in a number of ways—examining it, grooming it, cuddling it, and so on—but their attentions are on the whole resented by the mother. Thus in mother-infant dyads living in a group, the infants spent less time off their mothers, and went out of arms' reach of their mothers less often, than did infants living alone with their mothers in similar cages (Hinde and Spencer-Booth, 1967b). Since the group-living infants were rejected less often by their mothers when they attempted to obtain the nipple, and played a smaller relative role in staying near her when off her, than did the infants living alone with their mothers, the difference between the two situations must have been due primarily to the mothers (Hinde, 1969b; see Table 13.1, page 200). In brief, the group-living mothers were less permissive of their infants' excursions away from them.

In the group situation, the extent to which a mother permits other females to interact with the infant depends on her relationship with them: she will be more permissive with one of her own grown-up daughters or with a monkey who is one of her own grooming companions. Thus the infant's relationships with individuals other than its mother may be affected by their relationships with her. Since the male often intercedes in disputes, and in doing so is likely to take the side of his own favourite, the extent to which the mother threatens other females away from her infant may be affected by their relationship with the male: thus the male's relationship with a female may affect the mother's relationship with that female, which may affect the female's relationship with the infant, which may affect the mother's relationship with her infant. These and other ways in which relationships may affect relationships are illustrated for a hypothetical group of monkeys in Fig. 23.9. The continuous lines represent the relationships between individuals, their thickness indicating very roughly the amount of interaction in each case. The discontinuous lines show how each interaction may affect other interactions (Hinde, 1972b).

This diagram makes no pretence of being quantitative and, like many sociograms, it implies that qualitatively different interactions between individuals can in some way be summed as indicators of a relationship. But it does go one further than those sociograms in indicating that while group structure depends on the relationships between individuals, it is more than their sum. Each relationship may affect most other relationships, so that each individual lives in a complex social nexus, change in any part of which may have repercussions on all the others. The group involves not merely relationships between individuals, but relationships between relationships.

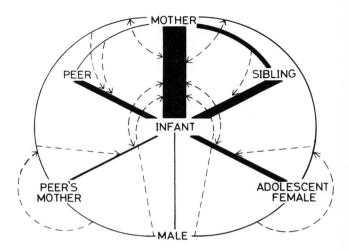

FIGURE 23.9

*Hypothetical diagram of the nexus of relationships between the individuals in a small captive group of rhesus monkeys. The bars indicate relationships between individuals; their thickness is roughly related to their importance. The discontinuous lines show how relationships can affect relationships.*

## Networks

The sociograms used to portray the relationships between individuals of the hamadryas baboon by Kummer can be extended into extensive networks covering a larger group, as shown by Sade's studies of rhesus and Deag's study of the Barbary macaque. The use of networks to portray relationships in non-human primates was preceded by their use in the study of human groups. Some consideration of the latter shows how their more extensive use may provide deeper insight into the structure of the societies of non-human species.

Barnes (1972) traces the use of the network concept back at least to Radcliffe-Brown (1940). Most social scientists, however, have used it as a metaphor in a merely descriptive way: its use as a tool of analysis to distinguish between one network and another, with network parameters being used in the explanation of other social phenomena, is more recent. While the animal work has scarcely passed beyond the metaphor stage, human data are beginning to be adequate for analytical studies. And, as in the animal work, in these studies it is necessary to consider not only the relationships between individuals, but also how relationships affect relationships (e.g., Bott, 1957).

At the simplest level, analysis may start with the selection of an individual and the individuals with whom he is in direct contact. The links he has with them can then be examined. The portion of a network containing an individual and only those others with whom he has direct contact is referred to as his "first-order star". The investigator may search for correlations between the behaviour or beliefs of the individual under scrutiny and the nature of the links he has with others. The process may then be repeated with other individuals.

As a next step, the relationships between the individual's first-order contacts can be examined, or the analysis can be extended to higher-order (i.e., indirect) contacts of the individual first selected. This may lead to a study of paths by which individual A influences another individual Z with whom he never comes into direct contact.

The use of the term "star" implies concern only with links between the individual at the centre and his first- or higher-order contacts. The portion of the network delimiting any set of members and all the relations between them is referred to as a "zone". Thus inclusion of the links between an individual's first-order contacts transforms his first-order star to a first-order zone. The triadic relationships referred to on pages 348–350 would form the simplest type of zone.

The number of possible relationships in a zone increases far more rapidly than the number of units, and the analysis of a network soon becomes a task of great complexity. In practice, it is nearly always necessary to limit the scope of the analysis—for instance, by restricting the number of persons, the situation (e.g., interactions in a factory with neglect of what happens outside), and even the contexts within that situation (e.g., in the workshop but not the canteen).[2] The investigator always has to consider what allowance must be made for links extending beyond his artificially set boundaries.

Within those boundaries, a number of measures may be taken. One concerns the nature of the relationships between individuals—for instance, whether they are single-stranded or multiplex. The former involve only one type of interaction, tend to lack affective involvement, and are usually temporary, while the latter have the opposite characteristics (Parsons, 1951; see pages 16–17). Another type of measure concerns the proportion of possible relationships that do actually occur—the "density" of the network. Yet another is the ratio of the num-

---

[2] Statistical techniques are exemplified by Sade (1972b).

ber of links in an individual's first-order zone to the total number of links in the zone embracing all individuals: this "span" can be regarded as a measure of the individual's influence over the whole group. The network may also be used in studying the use of indirect paths of communication: it is possible to measure both the number of links which must be traversed before one individual can communicate with another, and the number of other individuals which each can reach using up to a given maximum number of links. Where individuals are densely linked (see above) to each other, it may be possible to identify clusters or cliques,[3] and to distinguish the network "effective" for a given individual from the "extended" network of less significance to him. Clearly this distinction is one of degree: boundaries between zones are either artificial, as when the second-order zone of a particular individual is studied, or empirical, in which case their nature is nearly always statistical only.

In what has been said so far the nature of the links between individuals has purposefully been left vague. In animal studies they can be specified only in terms of behavioural interactions between individuals. Barnes (1972) lists three ways in which they can be studied in our own species:

1 **Attitudes** The replies to questions of the type, "Who would you like to work with?" define the attitude of one member of the network to another.

2 **Roles** (see Chap. 24) Individuals in a network may interact in a great variety of ways—friend-friend, parent-child, retailer-customer, and so on. For some purposes (e.g., the spread of epidemic diseases) the nature of the roles may be unimportant, but for others, just as with animals, it may be essential to distinguish them.

3 **Transactional links** These are the links actually called into play in some specific context.

The preceding paragraphs could give at most only a flavour of what has become an important field of inquiry. It is clear that many of the techniques which have been developed in studies of our own species are applicable also to non-human forms. Network analysis would, for instance, be an obvious way of comparing the social organization of different primate species, or of the same

---

[3] The term "set" is sometimes used for the people centering on one individual and classified by him according to particular criteria (e.g., social class): of more interest to students of non-human primates is the term "action set" for those who participate in a particular group of activities centered on one individual: a human example would be the helpers in a political campaign (cf. Mayer, 1966).

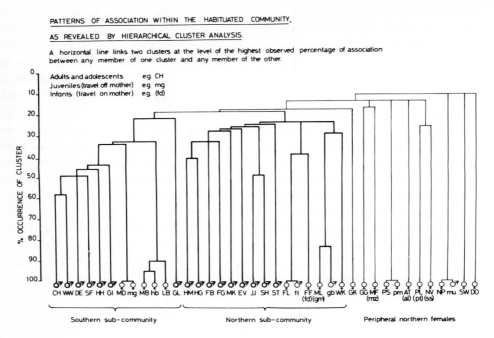

FIGURE 23.10

*Dendrogram showing the relationships between individual chimpanzees in the Gombe Stream National Park. See text.* (From Bygott, personal communication).

species in different areas, if it could be carried to a sufficiently quantitative level: an exploratory study is being made by M. Thorndahl on the chimpanzees of the Gombe Stream Reserve.

### Cluster analysis

Another technique available for understanding the structure of primate groups is cluster analysis. This involves first obtaining an $N \times N$ matrix showing the frequency of social interactions between the $N$ individuals under consideration. This may be based on observations of a particular type of behaviour (e.g., grooming), or of all positive interactions, or of time spent together, according to the problem in hand. For single linkage cluster analysis individuals are withdrawn successively from this matrix as follows. First the pair or pairs of individuals most closely associated are abstracted. Then further individuals closely associated with one member of such pairs, then individuals associated with the clusters thus formed, and so on. In this way a "dendrogram" of the type shown in Fig. 23.10 can be built up to show the individuals connected by a hierarchical scheme based on their closeness of interaction.

Figure 23.10 was based on a measure of the frequency with which chimpanzees were seen in each other's company in the forest of the Gombe Stream National Park, Tanzania. The chimpanzee community there is an open one, with the individuals ranging singly or in small groups over a considerable area, meeting from time to time. The figure shows, for instance, that the adult female *MB* was nearly always observed with her infant *hb*, and both were usually accompanied by the older offspring of *MB*, *LB*. This family group was more closely associated with the individuals to the left on the diagram than with those on the right. The diagram shows that the chimpanzees were divided into two fairly distinct sub-communities, with a number of peripheral females (Bygott, in preparation).

Dendrograms must be interpreted with one reservation. If two clusters are connected at the x percent level, this means only that one individual from one and one from the other are associated at that level, not that all members of both clusters are. However they provide a powerful method for representing relationships within groups. The application of the method to these sorts of data was pioneered by Morgan (1973).

## Rank and transaction

Deag's use of measures of spatial proximity reveals a wealth of information about the structure of the group which is validated by the similar picture provided by study of the positive social interactions themselves (pages 366–367). But the relationship between two individuals is seldom to be assessed along a single dimension. As stressed earlier (pages 16–17), relationships must be characterized in terms of the diversity as well as frequency of the interactions involved. This has been recognized in the study of both human and animal relationships in terms of a polarity between single-stranded and multiplex relationships (pages 379–381).

Now we have seen that in an interaction involving dissimilar but complementary behaviour, such as that between mother and infant rhesus, there may be an imbalance such that one partner would interact in a given way (e.g., cling ventro-ventrally) more than he does if he were given the opportunity to do so (pages 199–203). Similarly, in interactions requiring similar but alternating types of behaviour, such as chasing and being chased, or grooming and being groomed, would either partner take the active role more than he does if he were given the opportunity to do so? Such questions refer to a crucial character of the relationship: to indicate the extreme possibilities, is each partner satisfied with his part, or does one partner merely take from the other, or does one give without gaining (Leach, 1962; Barth, 1966)?

Such questions may be asked not only about particular types of interaction, but also about the whole relationship: an imbalance in one type of interaction may be compensated for or opposed by another facet of the same relationship. We can, in fact, regard the relationship as a transaction, each partner gaining in some respects and giving in others (Barth, 1966). Thus if the mother's tendency to suckle and the infant's to nurse are not quite in balance, one may meet the other's need because of the additional tendency to achieve ventro-ventral contact with the other. Similarly a consort relationship may depend on sexual interactions, grooming interactions, and protective interactions such that the male mounts the female more often than she solicits, the female grooms the male more than vice versa and more than he solicits, and also the male protects the female— each type of interaction contributing to the balance of the overall relationship.

One character of a relationship that affects interactions of many sorts is that of rank. In the human case, the extent to which boss and worker are satisfied by their interchange is determined in part by their relative rank. In non-human primates, as we have already seen, there may be relations between rank and copulatory activity, and two studies have examined the relationship between social grooming and dominance rank in considerable depth. Simpson's (1973a) work was concerned with the relationships between grooming and dominance interactions in free-living male chimpanzees at the Gombe Stream National Park in Tanzania (cf. pages 374–375). We have already referred to his finding that, amongst adult males, rank as indicated by the ability to supplant other males was well correlated with other indications of rank (page 341).

In studying grooming relations between these animals, Simpson used measures of both the frequency and the duration of grooming. There was a slight tendency for males to groom individuals with whom they were more frequently associated on a higher proportion of opportunities, and for longer when they did groom, than individuals with whom they came into contact less. However these correlations were not high, and it was clear that the way in which the males distributed their grooming could not be explained merely in terms of whom they spent their time with.

Tables 23.1 and 23.2 give an idealized representation of the detailed data Simpson obtained on the relationships between dominance rank and the frequency and duration of grooming. The higher-ranking males tended to groom most often, and each male tended to groom high-rank partners more often than low-rank ones. The table also represents the finding that each individual tended to groom each of his several partners about as often as that partner groomed him. Analysis of the starts of grooming sessions indicated that when a very low-rank individual was involved with a high-rank one, it was usually the low-rank one who started the session.

Table 23.2 shows how high-rank individuals tended to groom for shorter sessions than did low-rank ones, and that each individual tended to groom his partners for shorter sessions the lower their rank. It also shows how each male tended to groom a partner of higher rank longer than that partner groomed him. The evidence indicated that this was not a consequence of the partner's behaviour during the grooming session, and it thus seems to represent a more lasting aspect of the relationship.

TABLE 23.1 *Relation between dominance rank and frequency of grooming in chimpanzees*

| Male | Rank | Grooming with partner | Frequency measure of grooming |
|------|------|------------------------|-------------------------------|
| A | 1st | B | ********************* |
|   |     | C | **************** |
|   |     | D | ********** |
| B | 2nd | A | ********************** |
|   |     | C | ************* |
|   |     | D | ********* |
| C | 3rd | A | *************** |
|   |     | B | ************ |
|   |     | D | ******** |
| D | 4th | A | ********** |
|   |     | B | ********* |
|   |     | C | ******** |

SOURCE: From Simpson, 1973.

In this study Simpson concentrated on the higher-ranking males in the community: as we have seen, in chimpanzees it is these who form the stable element (page 334). To include the females in a study of comparable depth would have to be a task of great complexity, but their exclusion does mean that only an isolated part of the social network was studied. Furthermore, it must not be forgotten that other characteristics of the males in addition to grooming may affect grooming interactions: for instance old males who are low-ranking may groom more than high-ranking young ones, suggesting that a maturity factor also is involved (Bygott, personal communication; Simpson, personal communication). The study is however of great interest not only in demonstrating a lack of complete reciprocity in grooming transactions, but also in showing rather precisely the relationship between the departure from reciprocity and rank as assessed by independent criteria.

Sade's (1972b) study was concerned with rhesus monkeys. It was based not on a detailed study of the initiation and duration of grooming episodes, but instead on a measure of "grooming status". This could be assessed in a variety of ways. One simple measure might be the number of individuals by whom each individual was groomed. To eliminate casual grooming, an arbitrary criterion could be used such as the number of individuals who direct more than a certain

TABLE 23.2 *Relation between dominance rank and duration of grooming in chimpanzees*

| Male | Rank | Grooming with partner | Median grooming duration |
|------|------|------------------------|--------------------------|
| A | 1st | B | ****** |
|   |     | C | ***** |
|   |     | D | **** |
| B | 2nd | A | ******** |
|   |     | C | ******* |
|   |     | D | ****** |
| C | 3rd | A | ********** |
|   |     | B | ********* |
|   |     | D | ******** |
| D | 4th | A | *************** |
|   |     | B | ************** |
|   |     | C | ************* |

SOURCE: From Simpson, 1973.

proportion of their grooming bouts to the individual in question. However Sade points out that, by analogy with human groups, a more meaningful measure would be one that took into account not merely the *number* of animals by whom a given individual is groomed, but the statuses of those who groom him. Using the two hypothetical groups shown in Fig. 23.11 he argues that if the number of animals by whom an individual was groomed were the criterion, monkeys *b* and *d* would have similar status. However the monkey who grooms *b* is himself groomed by three monkeys, whereas the monkey who grooms *d* is groomed by only one. Thus *b* is linked to four monkeys by one- and two-step links, but *d* is linked to only two. The same sort of argument can be based on higher-order links, and the procedure can provide a succession of assessments (according to the number of links) of the grooming status of individuals.

Sade used the grooming status of an individual, in terms of the number of one-, two-, and three-step links directed toward him, to assess the relationship between grooming status and dominance (in terms of aggressive and submissive responses) amongst a group of rhesus monkeys. For females the two were clearly correlated: the dominant male had the highest grooming status, but dominance rank and grooming status did not correlate for the males as a whole. Analysis showed that the males were organized in cliques which were not homogeneous in their relations with the group.

Thus Sade's study again shows that dominance status is related to grooming relations within the group, but shows also that, in the case of males, interindividual liaisons may distort the pattern. The methods used by Simpson and by Sade are likely to prove important in teazing apart the complexities of social relationships within groups of primate species.

### Conclusion

At the beginning of this section the structure of a group was referred to as the patterning of relationships within it. In this chapter we have been concerned with the complexity of that patterning within groups of non-human primates. Since the distribution of individuals in space is a consequence of their agonistic and affiliative relationships, the spatial structure of a group can provide insight into the pattern of relationships within it. Characteristic distributions can in fact readily be discerned, but the spatial structure of a group may change with environmental circumstances: changes in the nature of the interactions between

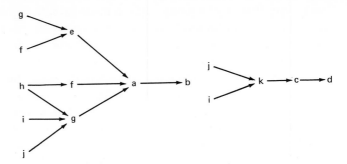

FIGURE 23.11

*Hypothetical grooming relations. The arrows point from groomer to groomee. (After Sade, 1972b.)*

individuals may be both causal to and consequential upon such changes in spatial distribution.

A more direct but more time-consuming method is to study the relationships directly by recording the interactions between individuals. Such a procedure shows that within a group of individuals, the relationship between any two is not merely a product of their individual characteristics: it is affected both by the physical environment and by other individuals. In other words, the structure of the group is not merely the sum of the relationships between individuals, but a consequence of the interactions between relationships.

At the present time the applications of the techniques of network and cluster analysis to the study of groups of non-human primates are opening up exciting possibilities. They should be able to provide not only more precise descriptions of structure, but also understanding of the dynamics of the interacting relationships involved.

As description becomes more precise, the units of description must become finer. We have been using relationship to refer to the pattern of interactions between two individuals, but studies of the interactions between dominance rank and grooming behaviour show that the patterning of one type of interaction (grooming) between two individuals may be affected by that of another (agonistic). Thus within the overall relationship between two individuals, the nature of one type of interaction may affect that of another.

This leads to the view that in order really to understand group structure, it is necessary to analyse at a finer level than that of relationships between individuals. One should first understand the dynamics of each type of interaction between individuals. After that, one should come to terms with the manner in which interaction of one type may affect other types of interaction between the same individuals. Only then could one start to understand the way in which specific interactions between two individuals *A* and *B* are affected by another individual *C*—and only then the manner in which *C*'s interacting with *A* or *B* in specific ways affects *A*'s relationship (i.e., the overall pattern of his interactions) with *B*. Having understood how each relationship affects other relationships, comprehension of the structure of the group should be within our grasp.

Two things must be said about this recipe for understanding group structure. First, nothing in the preceding paragraph should be taken to imply judgments about the relative merits of analysing from group structure to inter-individual interactions on the one hand and of synthesizing from the elements to the whole on the other. Both must proceed hand in hand, and the reductionist fallacy that the whole could be predicted from the parts avoided. Second, the recipe implies an almost hopeless mass of detail: if group structure can be understood only in terms of individual interactions, the task would seem endless. However we are not concerned here with individuals, for structure is independent of individuals: our concern therefore is with characteristic modes of behaviour. For instance structure may be understood in terms of the behaviour of distinguishable age-sex classes. In any case, the problem is one general to all science: the nature of concepts valuable at one level of analysis can be more fully understood by analysis at a finer level, but it remains uneconomical to attempt to comprehend the whole always in terms of interactions between the finest entities into which it can be divided.

A final issue concerns the relationship of the structures of non-human primates to those of primitive human societies. This is a field for almost unlimited speculation, much of it not very profitable. However, certain features commonly found in non-human primates are of interest (e.g., Reynolds, 1968). First, the growing realization of the importance of kinship relationships has not only revealed new dimensions of complexity within primate groups, but provides a close link with man (page 359). Kinship relationships tend to be matrifocal, and in many species (though not chimpanzees) females are the more stable element in the society. Second, there tend to be age/sex groupings—especially play groups of young animals, central hierarchies of adult males, mothers' clubs, and bachelor bands (see also Tiger, 1970, for discussion of human counterparts). Third, mother-son matings are less common than might be expected by chance, and there is a considerable tendency to breed outside the family group. However, it must be remembered that the societies of non-human primates exhibit great diversity between and even within species, so that the drawing of human parallels too easily involves the selection of examples to fit hypotheses.

# 24

# ROLE

A concept recently borrowed by biologists from anthropologists and sociologists is that of "role". In everyday speech we use the term to refer to modes of behaviour which are characteristic of particular relationships in society. Thus a man may have a number of roles—husband, father, doctor, member of the local darts club, and so on. The roles he has may change with age, but each implies interactions with other individuals. In this chapter we will examine the extent to which this concept is likely to be valuable in the study of non-human groups.

Use of the "role" concept in the social sciences involves several strands of emphasis, not necessarily shared by the different disciplines or even by the different contexts in which it is used in any one discipline. In general, it refers to a mode of behaviour that is appropriate to a certain status[1] in the social sys-

[1] It has not so far been necessary to use the term "status" in any technical sense in discussing the structure of non-human primate societies, though it would be quite possible to do so. Amongst sociologists, it refers to a collection of rights and duties which may be ascribed to or achieved by the

tem. It thus implies norms for behaviour in particular situations. The nature of those norms varies with the context. If we are concerned with the behaviour of categories of persons or the holder of an office within a social institution or in the society as a whole, the norms may be specified in terms of the expected consequences of the role behaviour on classes of others. The role of doctors in the health service is to look after the sick: the norms here refer to consequences of their behaviour on their patients. The role of a platoon commander is to interpret orders that he receives from above and to ensure that his men fulfill the intention of those orders: the extent to which he fills his role may be judged by the behaviour of his men. In these cases the "role" concept has reference to the functioning of a social system—the health service or the army. The words "role of" could in fact be replaced by "part played by". But the role concept may tell us little about the determinants of the behaviour of the individual. The doctor may have been motivated by prospects of financial gain, the lieutenant by hopes of promotion or personal glory. And in each case the norm is independent of the identity of the individual: the role is "what the actor does in relation to others seen in the context of its functional significance for the social system" (Parsons, 1951).

But when the concept of role is used primarily with reference to inter-actions between individuals, it usually refers to shared expectations[2] for be-haviour in a particular type of interaction. A man may or may not behave like a "real husband". Here, too, role refers to norms, modes, or idealized goals of behaviour, not to individual idiosyncracies: a role is thus independent of the individual who fills it. And here, too, the norms refer to social consequences for another individual with respect to whom the role is defined. Thus the doctor's roles to patient, nurse, and patient's kin involve shared expectations of the consequences of his behaviour on each of them, but not expectations about the consequences of his behaviour on the golf course. The consequences are not necessarily beneficial to others or to the group: it is not uncommon, for instance, to talk of someone taking an invalid's role. But the focus of interest is always on the expected behaviour of the actor in interaction with others, and thus on the consequences for others: insofar as the actor aims to produce these con-sequences, the role concept *is* relevant to his motivation.

We may now discuss, with considerable reservations, the use to which the term "role" has so far been put in studies of non-human species. In a group of non-human primates, members of the various age-sex classes behave differently.

---

individual: when an individual puts the rights and duties which constitute a status into effect, he is performing a role (Linton, 1936; Nadel, 1957).

[2] The extent to which "expectation" need involve "conscious awareness" is discussed on page 388.

Furthermore, within any one age-sex class some individuals behave differently from others: in a macaque troop, lactating females show some consistent differences in behaviour from oestrous females, and the alpha male behaves differently from other males. The behaviour of individuals is thus to some extent predictable in terms of sex, age, and rank. This has been expressed by saying that the different age-sex categories differ in their "role-patterns" or "role-profiles". For example, in association with his penetrating critique of the dominance concept, Gartlan (1968) used the concept of role in studying the differences in behaviour between age-sex classes of vervet monkeys. He recorded the amount of time members of the various age-sex classes of a troop spent in activities that were of adaptive significance in their habitat. The percentage contributions made by each age-sex class to each activity are shown in Table 24.1. The description of roles in this way resembles the role concept as used by sociologists in two ways. It involves the abstraction of normative aspects of behaviour: individual idiosyncracies are lost insofar as they are submerged in the group averages. And insofar as the types of behaviour are of "adaptive significance", it is the consequences of the behaviour of the various classes for the group that are being examined. But the resemblances relate to the use of role in describing the functioning of a social system, not in understanding the dynamics of behaviour within the group. The norm is merely a group average, and the consequences refer to the well-being of the group, but neither concern "shared expectations" about the behaviour of the incumbents or their immediate motivation.

Used descriptively, Gartlan's procedure is potentially useful in the study of non-human primates in several ways, for example in (1) comparing the ways in

TABLE 24.1 *Percentage contribution of various age-sex classes to certain activities in a troop of* Cercopithecus aethiops

| Activity | Age-sex class | | | | |
| | Adult males | Adult females | Juveniles | Sub-adults | Infants |
|---|---|---|---|---|---|
| Territorial display | 66 | | 33 | | |
| Social vigilance | 35 | 38 | 3 | 12 | 12 |
| Social focus of friendly approaches | 12 | 46 | 4 | 27 | 12 |
| Friendly approach | 3 | 32 | | 47 | 15 |
| Territorial chasing | 66 | | 33 | | |
| Punishing | 100 | | | | |
| Leading | 32 | 49 | | 16 | |

SOURCE: Adapted from Gartlan, 1968.

which the different demographic categories contribute to the dynamics of the behaviour of the group. Thus in one species the adult male may give warning of predators, while in another the subordinate peripheral ones may do so, and in (2) comparing the social structures of different species, or of the same species in different areas.

However one difficulty in this approach, concerning the number of classes of individual to be recognized, must be noted. Gartlan made his initial distinctions in terms of the independent variables of age and sex, and then proceeded to look for differences within each age-sex class on the basis of the data collected. Both of these are entirely proper procedures. Should two age-sex classes give similar data they would be said to have the same role profiles and, for these purposes, could be merged. And within an age-sex class the occurrence of bimodal distributions in the contributions of individuals to the several behaviour categories could be used as a basis for the recognition of new sub-classes with distinct role-profiles. However Gartlan, having described the role-profile of the adult males, went on to do a finer analysis within that age-sex class, comparing the role-profiles of the three individual adult males with one another, and thereby demonstrating that only one of them showed certain types of behaviour. At this point, it must be noted, the normalizing process is necessarily omitted, so that the concept of role loses its reference to a mode or norm of behaviour, and becomes merely behaviour. It is meaningless to talk of the role or role-profile of the dominant male until a number have been studied (contrast Bernstein and Sharpe, 1966).

It must also be noted that Gartlan limited his discussion to aspects of behaviour that he considered to be of "adaptive significance" (although he provided no discussion of the criteria by which this was to be assessed). As we have seen, though the types of consequence implied by "adaptive significance for the group as a whole" provide a useful frame of reference for questions related to the evolution and adaptedness of group structure, or to ecology, they are unlikely to be helpful if intra-group dynamics are the issue.

Other authors have been not wholly consistent in the extent to which the role concept was applied to consequences adaptive for the group. For example Bernstein and Sharpe (1966) describe some of the roles of the dominant male in a group of rhesus monkeys—interfering in aggressive interactions before the dispute becomes disruptive of the group, providing protection against predators, and so on. However, they use "role differentiation" merely to refer to differences between the behaviour of demographic categories: here, as in the case of Gartlan's dominant male, "role" becomes equivalent to behaviour, and merely obfuscates the important issues. Similarly it makes no sense to write of an animal's being in conflict between two roles (Benedict, 1969), when we need only say that two types of behaviour are in conflict. If we are concerned with norms of behaviour that are not related, in the short or long term, to any social consequences, it is preferable not to use the term "role" at all.

Thus while Gartlan's use of "role" is likely to be valuable in comparative studies, it is unlikely to be useful in understanding the dynamics of behaviour within a group. There are thus three issues:

1 To be useful, "role" must refer to norms of behaviour, not to behaviour itself. Used in a merely descriptive sense, "role" becomes synonymous with behaviour and thus redundant.

2 Roles cannot exist *in vacuo*, but only in relation to real or imagined consequences for another individual or for the group. These consequences may be adaptive in a biological sense, or in some cases may be merely facets of the normal behaviour or structure of the group. But roles exist only in a specified social setting, and are related to the complementary roles of others. There can be no leader without a follower, no troop look-out without a troop. Furthermore the specification of roles must depend on the universe being considered: when a male hamadryas baboon walks with his females in a troop he may be leader with respect to the females but follower with respect to other units in the troop.

3 The third issue concerns the "shared expectations" which characterize the concept of role as usually used in understanding inter-individual human relations. Does this imply that conscious awareness is a necessary part of the use of the role concept? If so, one could argue that the term "role" cannot usefully be applied to animals simply because the evidence we can obtain about their conscious intentions is so much less secure than that available in the human case. In man, conscious awareness *may* be paramount: the role may be an idealized pattern of behaviour which the individual strives to achieve, but which may never be realized in "role behaviour" (Newcomb, 1952). In other cases, however, its contribution is more subtle: teenage boys behave differently from teen-age girls in part because they are different and in part because they are expected to behave differently; and those expectations operate to some degree through differences in the opportunities presented to boys and girls, and to some degree through their conscious awareness of what is expected of them. Here the influence of conscious awareness is closely interwoven with other forces moulding the

behaviour. In yet other cases, as we have seen, we use the concept of role with no implication of conscious awareness. The worker may have a role in the plan of the firm, or the soldier in that of the commander, and yet be completely unaware of it. And we may say that a child is taking a maternal role with a younger sibling without implying that she is saying to herself "This is me acting like Mum".

Thus the norms that define role behaviour may be related closely, distantly, or not at all to the factors determining the behaviour of the individuals that fill the role. If the actors are consciously aware of a role which they strive to fulfil, the relationship is a close one, though the behaviour shown (i.e., the mode of all incumbents in the role) may also be affected by other factors, such as social pressures and the limitations of the individuals concerned. At the other extreme, the defining characteristics of the role may be quite unrelated to the causation of the behaviour. For example, the individuals on the periphery of a troop could be good look-outs simply because they are apprehensive individuals: the consequences for the troop are a by-product of behaviour with quite a different causal basis. In such cases, the identification of roles gives us no insight into the factors determining the behaviour of individuals, and is useful only for discussing how the consequences by which the role is defined (in this case, adequate warning of predators) are achieved.

Having raised the question of conscious awareness, we may ask how far it ever enters into the behaviour of non-human species. In many cases there is no need to suppose that it does. Role behaviour can be a result of inherent behaviour tendencies held in check to a greater or lesser extent by social factors. However, lack of evidence does not necessarily mean that conscious awareness of social roles is absent (see page 4), and one occasionally comes across evidence, admittedly observational, suggesting that it is in fact important. For example, the well-integrated groups of the mountain gorilla are usually led by an adult male "silverback"—so called because of the grey hairs which the males develop with age. This dominant silverback normally determines the direction of movements of the group: before moving off he stands stiffly looking in the direction in which he will move (Fig. 22.3). Fossey (personal communication) has described how, when the silverback of one group was temporarily at a distance, his leadership role was taken over by an adult female. In leading the group this female showed behaviour closely similar to that normally shown by the male—behaviour she would very rarely show in his presence. Does this mean that she was always "wanting" to show this behaviour but did not dare? If so the tension was not evident. This is, of course, an isolated observation, but the possibility remains open that, in these sophisticated and intensely social animals, role behaviour may be guided through conscious awareness of the relevant consequences.

In conclusion, if "role" is to be useful in studies of non-human primates it must be reserved for contexts in which we are concerned with (1) norms or modes of behaviour rather than how individuals actually behave, and (2) the consequences of the behaviour on others rather than the particular patterns of behaviour which lead to those consequences. If the roles are defined in terms of consequences adaptive for the group, the concept is likely to be valuable in studies of the evolution and adaptedness of group structure. Where the consequences that define the role are also causal to the role behaviour, perhaps by acting as a conscious or unconscious goal, the role concept helps also in understanding the dynamics of interactions between individuals. But, it must be added, if it leads to too much emphasis on norms, it can distract attention from the individual and from the aspects of personal motivation and idiosyncrasy that determine relationships (Chapple and Arensberg, 1940; Barth, 1966; Goldschmidt, 1972).

If such a concept with so many specifically human connotations is to be applied to non-human forms, the great differences between the two cases must be borne constantly in mind. For example, the limited number of roles (or statuses) that can be distinguished in a monkey group is in sharp contrast to their multiplicity in practically any human society. And insofar as it is useful for pointing to the different types of interaction that one category of animal may have with others, their differentiation lies in their differing emotional orientation rather than in the social rights and duties which determine them (cf. Goodenough's 1967 distinction between personal identity and social identity). Furthermore, roles in non-human societies usually in fact result from natural characteristics—sex, age, parental status—or from competitive interaction. The only evidence that individuals are allocated to or maintained in roles by others refers to the choice of females as consorts by males and to the retention, apparently by popular consent, of leadership roles by aged but weakening individuals (pages 350–352; see Kummer, 1968).

$$\boxed{25}$$

# SPATIAL RELATIONSHIPS BETWEEN GROUPS

In earlier chapters we considered the spatial relationships between the members within primate groups. It is also necessary to consider the spatial relationships between the groups, and of the groups to the habitat.

Probably all primates show some attachment to a localized area. Ring-tailed lemur troops range over an area of around 0.06 sq km (Jolly, 1966); baboons, 4.6 sq km in forest (Rowell, 1966a) and around 25 sq km in savannah (Hall and DeVore, 1965); and chimpanzees, around 35 sq km (van Lawick-Goodall, 1968). The area may or may not be defended from other groups.

Although the inter-group relations of sub-human primates show great diversity, three concepts have been useful in discussing them. These are:

1  **The home range** This is the area over which the group ranges within a given span of time. Since the area used may change with time, it is essential that statements about the home range of a group should be accompanied by information about the time span over which it was assessed

(cf. Burt, 1943; Jewell, 1966). Within any one span of time the different parts of the home range will not be used equally, and careful study is necessary to assess its differential usage (e.g., Mason, 1968; Clutton-Brock, 1972).

2 **The core area** Within the home range there is often one area which the troop visits especially frequently. Often it contains sleeping sites, water, or some other essential. This is termed the "core area" (Kaufmann, 1962; Wilson, 1972).

3 **The territory** The concept of territory, first used extensively in biology in studies of birds (Howard, 1920), has two referents—the restriction of behaviour to a limited area, and defence of the area (Hinde, 1956). The latter is crucial to the distinction from home range. The classic territory is an area whose boundaries are rigidly defended against conspecific individuals, and some primates show territorial behaviour of this sort. The defended area may be restricted to the core area or may encompass the whole home range (Mason, 1968). For example vervet monkeys defend territories with fairly clearly defined boundaries (Struhsaker, 1967). Titi monkeys live in small groups of two to four individuals: when two troops make contact they converge calling, chase, and then mutually withdraw (Mason, 1968). The lutong lives in one-male troops on territories which overlap very narrowly: aggression between males occurs at the boundaries (Bernstein, 1968). The family groups of the white-handed gibbon and siamang occupy territories with clearly defined boundaries (Ellefson, 1968; Chivers, 1972). Klopfer and Jolly (1970) have shown that the boundaries of the territory of a sifaka troop underwent only minor changes over 6 years, but a lemur troop had split into smaller ones with overlapping ranges (Jolly, 1972a).

A great number of variations on this theme are to be found. For instance the Indian langur shows inter-group territoriality in some parts of its range and rank-order relations between troops occupying similar home ranges in others (Sugiyama, 1965a and b; Jay, 1965; Yoshiba, 1967). The difference is primarily one of the extent to which inter-group hostility or avoidance has spatial referents (e.g., Struhsaker, 1967). In some highly territorial species, with relatively stable spatial boundaries, inter-group tolerance may occur especially in particular localities, such as water holes.

In most of the cases so far mentioned, the spacing of groups depends primarily on aggressive interactions. This is not always the case. When several groups inhabit home ranges which overlap more or less extensively, dispersal of groups may be maintained by mutual avoidance. In primates this is often facilitated by the use of loud calls or other auditory signals: these may simply repel other groups, or they may initially attract them, closer proximity being followed by agonistic interactions. The signals may also promote integration of the group: in all cases the function can be described as "locational" (e.g., Struhsaker, 1969; Chivers, 1969; Gautier, 1969; Kawabe, 1970; Fossey, 1972; reviews by Marler, 1968; Bates, 1970). In non-primate species dispersion is often achieved with a minimal amount of aggression by signals in other modalities—for example, visual and auditory signals in birds (Pitelka, 1949), and short-lasting olfactory stimuli in carnivores (Eaton, 1970).

The behaviour of howling monkeys combines several of the characteristics so far mentioned. The home ranges of howling monkey groups do not overlap if assessed over a limited span of time (e.g., 1 month), but do if longer periods are considered. When two groups approach each other, howling increases, and this causes them to change their direction of movement so that the distance between them increases: the howling thus serves to maintain a distance between groups and directs ranging patterns. But within the home range each howling monkey group has temporary exclusive use of a small area, within which other groups are not tolerated (Chivers, 1969).

Territoriality, in the broad sense of exclusive use of a defined area, can thus arise in a number of ways—by the actual defence of an area, including patrolling its boundaries and the active seeking out of intruders (territorial behaviour in a strict sense); by adherence to a home range coupled with aggression toward other groups whenever they happen to be met (i.e., defence of a "mobile territory"); or by adherence to a home range coupled with mutual avoidance between groups. The distinction between the first two, resting on the extent to which intruders are "sought out", is often far from clear; but the evidence required concerns whether a group which becomes aware of another group within the area nearly always moves toward it and attacks it, or whether agonistic interactions occur only if the groups chance to come into close proximity (e.g., rhesus, Vessey, 1968). It seems preferable to accept that territoriality is a concept with different shades of meaning than to expend discussion on precisely what is and is not a territory (see Bates, 1970, for a critical review of the literature on primates; Watson, 1970, for a discussion of aggressive behaviour and population limitation).

Where there is mutual antagonism between groups whose home ranges overlap, the results of the encounters can sometimes be described in terms of a dominance order between troops (e.g., rhesus, Southwick et al., 1965; Altmann, 1962; baboons, Hall and DeVore, 1965); however under both natural conditions and in captivity, the relative dominance of troops may change according to where the encounter takes place (rhesus, Marsden, 1969). In macaques, peripheral males seem to be most often involved in inter-group encounters (rhesus, Vessey, 1968, 1971; Marsden, 1968). Opinion is divided as to the importance of the relative status of the dominant males of each troop in deciding the outcome: Koyama (1970) found that the ranking of two recently separated troops of Japanese macaques reflected the former ranking of the two leaders, but Vessey (1971) found that removal of the alpha male from a rhesus troop did not affect the troop's range or status. Of course, in the former case the status of the adult male could be related to another variable, such as the size of the troop, which was the operative factor.

The most detailed study of inter-group encounters concerns the Barbary macaque (Deag, 1974), and group dominance proved to be much too limited a concept for the diversity of types of encounter seen. The encounters seemed to be well organized, with some males going out to meet and monitor the other troop. The monitoring involved linked movements between the males from one or both troops, and was not always accompanied by agonistic behaviour: Deag suggests that it serves to acquaint the males with the membership of the other group. Each pair of troops tended to have a characteristic type of encounter, probably depending on a variety of factors—the degree of overlap between home ranges, and thus the troops' mutual familiarity; the historical origins of the encounters and their previous history; the kinship relations between the groups; and the individual characters of the males (see also Hausfater, 1972, and Lindburg, 1971, for data on rhesus).

# 26
# ADAPTIVE DIFFERENCES IN GROUP STRUCTURE

As we have seen, primate groups show considerable diversity in structure between species. Within a particular species, however, social structure shows less variability: although the nature of the group may vary with time, place, or conditions, the variations are limited, so that inter-species differences in social organization can be described. That these differences are not wholly imposed by different environments is proved by the fact that species may differ in social structure even though inhabiting the same area, or confined under similar conditions in a zoo. This indicates that differences in group structures may be in part genetically determined. Of course the genetic factors operate through the behaviour of individuals, so that their effect on group structure is quite indirect.

Further evidence for the importance of genetic influences on group structure could come from similarities in group structure between closely related species. Such similarities can sometimes be found—for instance, macaques and baboons tend to form multi-male groups, and *Cercopithecus* monkeys tend to form one-male groups (Struhsaker, 1969)—but there are also many exceptions.

Thus amongst the great apes, orangutans appears to be almost solitary (Rodman, 1973), chimpanzees live in open communities, and gorilla in small groups (page 388). Such cases suggest that social structure is subject fairly immediately to differences produced by natural selection at the species level.

More direct evidence about the role of genetic factors is understandably scarce, but Nadel (1971) has published some important data resulting from a study of a population of hybrids between hamadryas and anubis baboons. The former species lives in one-male groups, the latter in large units each containing many males. The hybrids showed an intermediate type of social organization, with one-male groups that were small and unstable.

Kummer's work (1968, 1971) shows that differences in social structure between these two baboon species may depend on genetically determined differences in only some of the participating individuals. When anubis and hamadryas females were transferred to hamadryas troops, both were herded by the hamadryas males. The anubis females soon learned to follow the one hamadryas male who threatened and attacked them, and not to interact with others. When hamadryas females were transferred to an anubis troop, they readily adapted to life there, ceasing to follow any particular male and grooming one another. Thus the differences between the anubis and hamadryas social structures must depend on differences between the males rather than differences between the females. An adult anubis male who lived in a hamadryas troop for several months did not herd, and as a result obtained no females.

Thus some differences in social structure between species reflect genetic differences between them. Other differences, especially those between different populations of the same species, reflect responses to different environmental conditions (see Jay, 1968): if food becomes scarce or the availability of cover changes, the behaviour of the component individuals and thus the structure of the group may be affected (pages 257, 344, 360). The influence of environmental differences on group structure implies predispositions to respond, for the genetic constitution of every population has been subject to selection for adaptive response by individuals to the environmental conditions they experience. In either case the question arises, how far can the differences in group structure be understood as adaptations to different environments or ways of life? Two issues must be raised.

First, any change in the behaviour of group members will have multiple consequences. The consequences that we identify as a change in group structure may be quite other than the consequence through which natural selection operated to produce the change in behaviour. Thus a change in locomotor activity may affect individual survival through consequences on metabolic balance: it might also produce correlated changes in the spatial structure of the group during progression or in the incidence of grooming behaviour, but these *might* be of quite neutral ecological significance. Differences in characters of group structure, even though based on genetic differences, do not necessarily have functional significance.

And where they do have functional significance, it will be mediated by selective forces acting through changes in success of the individuals in the group. The latter point has been made forcefully by Lack (1968) in considering especially the nature of the dispersion of bird populations. He regards the pattern of dispersion as a consequence of the behaviour of individuals spacing themselves in a manner which maximizes their own reproductive success: selection occurs because there is competition for limited resources, and success is affected by the behaviour which individuals show. This view contrasts with that of Wynne-Edwards (1962), who regards dispersion patterns as produced by group selection to reduce the risk of over-crowding: although Wynne-Edwards supports his view with a mass of descriptive material, there are few well-analysed data to support the importance of group selection as he envisages it, and his views have been much criticized (e.g., Lack, 1966).

The second point is related to the first. The characters of behaviour and structure of the individuals of a species are not independent of each other, but form an adaptive complex such that changes in one may have ramifying consequences through the whole. To take an avian example, those birds that nest in holes tend to lay larger clutches than birds nesting in open sites, and their eggs and young develop more slowly. This is presumably related to the fact that the nest is more protected from predators, so that a more protracted development is possible: this means that the young need less food per day and more young can be reared. With hole-nesting there is also less selection for female crypticity. The marked sexual dimorphism sometimes found in open-nesting species is apparently due to the signal function of conspicuous coloration outweighing the importance of crypticity in males but not in females: in hole-nesting species sexual dimorphism is less common. Thus clutch-size, rapidity of development, nest-site location and sexual dimorphism are linked in such a way that changes in the selection pressure on one would produce also change in that on others— and so on through almost all the characters of the species. Furthermore, selection on each character operates with respect to certain environmental factors, such as the incidence of predation and the presence or absence of other related species with similar coloration.

Similar principles apply to primates. Thus gelada baboons, which feed in open fields, call loudly and bolt for the safety of cliffs when disturbed: being conspicuous on the fields, attempts at concealment would be futile. By contrast, anubis baboons, feeding amongst bushes, slink away silently when disturbed. Thus feeding and escape behaviour are inter-related (Crook and Aldrich-Blake, 1968).

Any one character of group composition or structure may thus be linked adaptively to many others. Consider group size. This may be influenced by the nature of predation pressure, individuals in large groups being more likely to receive warning of the approach of predators and profiting from group action, individuals in small groups being better concealed from them. But this in turn is related to other characters: for instance some species, such as baboons, rely on active defence of the troop by its stronger members, and the effectiveness of this may be related to sex size differences. Sex differences in size may in turn relate to differential use of food resources. In other species, such as the patas monkey and forest guenons (Hall, 1965; Struhsaker, 1967), the males distract predators while the females move off. Group size may also be influenced by food availability and dispersion: living in groups may facilitate the flow of information about food sources, and this may benefit all group members if each food source is not small in comparison with the troop (Kummer, 1971). Group size may also be influenced by the availability of water holes and sleeping sites. In addition to these ecological factors, group size may be affected by the pattern of breeding amongst the males (see below). Any one aspect of social structure is likely to be influenced by multiple selective forces.

The same argument applies to inter-individual behaviour. The different aspects of social behaviour are inter-related: for instance, if selection operates to increase aggressiveness between males, aggression between potential mates may also be augmented (see pages 61–70), with consequent repercussions on the mechanisms of mating (Tinbergen, 1959). Selection must thus operate to fit the social behaviour of individuals to both the physical and the social environment in which they live: the latter includes the social behaviour of their fellows. Where individuals show a number of different patterns of social behaviour, either in succession (infant and adult), or in alternation (consort and maternal), or in accordance with the behaviour of other individuals (dominant and subordinate), the behaviour shown in each case must fit with that of other individuals. Thus natural selection operating on the behaviour of infants will affect also that of mothers, and so on. The fact that all characters of behaviour (social and non-social) and structure form an adaptive complex makes it unlikely that simple correlations between characters of social structure and environmental variables will be found.

With these cautions, it remains the case that group structures differ, and that the differences surely either must themselves be of adaptive significance to the individuals in the groups, or must be related to characters that are. The first step toward their understanding must be a search for correlations between characteristics of group composition and environmental factors—even though simple correlations are unlikely, and the finding of a correlation does not in any case necessarily indicate that characters at the level of group composition are themselves the ones through which natural selection operates.

During the last decade, as data on the social behaviour of more species have become available, students of primates have become increasingly occupied with these questions. Crook's (1970) recent review of the literature shows that present knowledge is adequate to demonstrate that some of the earlier generalizations were premature. For instance it was earlier thought that group sizes were larger in forest species than in savannah ones, but it is now apparent that wide variation in group size exists in both categories, and the validity of the generalization is doubtful (Struhsaker, 1969; Clutton-Brock, 1972). Similarly, it was suggested that one-male groups were an adaptation to savannah with markedly severe seasonal conditions, the supposition being that the exploitation of food by adult males relative to females was reduced to a minimum. But one-male groups are also found in many forest species, where a different mechanism must operate (Crook, 1970).

Such difficulties indicate that attempts to divide primate species according to "levels of adaptation" in different environments (Crook and Gartlan, 1966) are too crude, involving too much heterogeneity within categories to be useful (Struhsaker, 1969; Clutton-Brock, 1972). Both the environmental and the social categories used hitherto have been insufficiently analysed. For instance, while savannah species are primarily terrestrial, forest species may be either terrestrial or arboreal, and the two latter tend to differ in group size (Crook, 1970); and, as we have seen already, superficially similar social structures may turn out to differ very considerably in detail (pages 324–325).

To this must be added the fact that simple correlations between crude characters of group structure and ecology are unlikely to be found just because all the characters of a species are inter-related as an adaptive complex: interactions between characters must be considered, and any one character is likely to be influenced by many ecological factors.

In addition, in a recent paper, Goss-Custard et al. (1972) have pointed out that previous discussions have concentrated on the adaptive significance of social structure for survival, and that its significance for reproductive success is of more fundamental importance. Most female primates are limited to a litter size of one—the operative factor is presumably either food, or the difficulty of carrying more: in species in which more than one are born in a litter, they are kept in a nest. The endurance of the female-offspring bond presumably increases the female's chances of reproductive success (but see pages 203–206). Since the male has been released from feeding the young, he can be responsible for more than one at a time, and can maximize his reproductive success in a number of ways— by dominating other males in the group to ensure his access to the females at the right point in the cycle, as in macaques; or by forming permanent bonds with a small number of females, as in the hamadryas baboon; and in either case by playing a major part in group defence against predators. The one-male troops of patas monkeys and geladas may also be advantageous to the females in that the excess males are not in such immediate competition with them for food (Crook, 1970). If ecological factors favour dispersion in small coherent parties, territorial behaviour by the males of one-male groups may limit access to their females by other males. These and many other interesting suggestions point the way to further study (Crook, in press), but it will be some time before comparisons between species, which invariably differ in a multitude of characters, will lead to more than statements of the type, "The adaptive significance of this difference may possibly be related to that consequence for the reproduction of individuals".

For such reasons it is clear that the search for correlations between group structure and ecological factors requires considerable refinement of the characters so far considered. However the search is clearly worthwhile, for amongst the birds, where the biology of many species is known in detail, attempts to establish generalizations about the relations between social structure and ecology have been revealing (e.g., Crook, 1964; Lack, 1968).

Most hope lies in detailed comparisons between closely related species or between different populations of the same species. For example, red colobus monkeys live in large troops of thirty to eighty individuals in home ranges of about 1 sq km, while black-and-white colobus live in troops of eight to twelve individuals in home ranges about 0.25 sq km. Clutton-Brock (1972) relates this difference to differences in feeding behaviour. While the red colobus feeds on a wide variety of tree species, eating mostly shoots, flowers, and fruit and taking leaves only to a limited extent, the black-and-white colobus specializes on a few tree species, concentrating on the leaves of one of them. Clutton-Brock suggests that the black-and-white colobus must have digestive specializations which permit it to colonize areas where shoots, flowers, and fruit are available for only part of the year. The red colobus may need a large area, and to patrol it regularly, to maintain access to food items seasonally available on different trees in different parts of the range. A large troop presumably represents the most economical way to exploit such an area. The black-and-white colobus, not needing such a large area, may be able to economize on troop movement by living in small troops. Though links in the argument must be speculative, Clutton-Brock's study shows how detailed data are essential if the adaptive significance of differences in social structure are to be understood. Other examples are cited by Crook (1970).

## Summary

The differences in social structure to be found between primate species, and within the same species under different conditions, pose a series of inter-related problems. To what extent are the differences genetically determined, and to what extent environmentally? In either case, are they to be understood as adaptive to local conditions? If they are adaptive, which features of group structure, or rather of the inter-individual relationships that compose that structure, are significant, and which are mere by-products? And in the case of the former, to which environmental features are they relevant? While present knowledge provides some indications of the directions in which answers are to be sought, many more precise data are needed before they are obtained (see, for example, Crook, in press). And the answers may well depend on a deeper understanding of the dynamics of group structure than is at present available for more than a handful of species.

# EPILOGUE

In earlier chapters we have considered the nature of social behaviour, social relationships, and their development. The discussion has been concerned largely with monkeys and apes, and in conclusion it may be as well to emphasize yet again that *of course* studies of non-human species cannot tell us *all* about human social behaviour. But in part because of their similarities to man, and in part because their relative simplicity highlights theoretical and conceptual issues, they can contribute to our understanding of ourselves. We have seen, for instance, how the mother-infant relationship develops from a variety of types of relatively simple interaction between mother and infant: experimental and observational work with non-human forms helps us to understand how each comes to respond to the other as an individual in a continuous but constantly changing dynamic relationship. In normal circumstances this paves the way for interactions with peers, aunts, and other individuals, with some of whom individual relationships may be established.

We have considered also two other types of social interaction—agonistic and sexual behaviour—discussing how the behaviour is moulded during development and how it is controlled in the adult. In each case there have been similarities in principle between the behaviour of non-human primates and that of man. There have also been many differences, arising from the differences in cognitive and intellectual capacities and from the enormous influence of cultural factors in the human case.

The mother-infant relationship, and all subsequent ones, do not exist as independent entities: every relationship is enmeshed in a social nexus, and its nature is affected in some degree (sometimes very little, sometimes profoundly) by every other relationship involving either partner. The last section, concerned primarily with the structure of groups, has focussed entirely on the behaviour of non-human primates. This however does not mean that the material is irrelevant to the human case. The study of the structure of human groups inevitably leads to discussion of how much the structure is determined by, and how much it determines, relationships within the group. In the case of non-human primates the latter is of much less importance than in man. The groups of non-human primates may therefore be of interest not so much because of the ways in which they resemble human groups, nor because they may give hints concerning the social life of protohominids, but precisely because of this difference from human groups. Their structure shows the complexity that can result from the interactions between individuals, with minimal influence of culture or tradition.

# SPECIES MENTIONED IN THE TEXT

### Invertebrata

| | |
|---|---|
| Earthworm | *Lumbricus terrestris* |
| Mosquito | *Aedes* sp. |
| Wasp | Braconidae: various spp. |
| Honey bee | *Apis mellifera* |

### Pisces

| | |
|---|---|
| Three-spined stickleback | *Gasterosteus aculeatus* |
| Siamese fighting fish | *Betta splendens* |
| | *Corynopoma riisei* (Characidae) |
| Damsel fish | *Microspathodon chrysurus* |
| | *Haplochromis burtoni* (Cichlidae) |
| Pike | *Esox lucius* |

### Reptilia

| | |
|---|---|
| Lizard | *Scleropus* spp. |
| Crocodile | *Crocodilus* sp. |

### Aves

| | |
|---|---|
| Great-crested grebe | *Podiceps cristatus* |
| Gannet | *Sula bassana* |

| | |
|---|---|
| Egret | *Egretta garzetta* |
| Whooper swan | *Cygnus cygnus* |
| Canada goose | *Branta canadensis* |
| Greylag goose | *Anser anser* |
| Goldeneye | *Bucephala clangula* |
| Duck (domestic) | *(Anas)* |
| Chicken (domestic) | *(Gallus)* |
| Turkey | *Meleagris* |
| Junglefowl | *Gallus gallus* |
| Moorhen | *Gallinula chloropus* |
| Great skua | *Stercorarius skua* |
| Herring gull | *Larus argentatus* |
| Laughing gull | *Larus atricilla* |
| Black-headed gull | *Larus ridibundus* |
| Kittiwake | *Rissa tridactyla* |
| Ring dove | *Streptopelia risoria* |
| Budgerigar (domestic) | *(Melopsittacus)* |
| Eastern phoebe | *Sayornis phoebe* |
| Swallow | *Hirundo rustica* |
| Dunnock | *Prunella modularis* |
| Robin | *Erithacus rubecula* |
| Flycatcher | *Sayornis phoebe* |
| Great tit | *Parus major* |
| Coal tit | *Parus ater* |
| Blue tit | *Parus caeruleus* |
| Marsh tit | *Parus palustris* |
| Willow tit ⎱<br>Chickadee ⎰ | *Parus atricapillus* ⎱⎰ |
| Towhee | *Pipilio* sp. |
| White-crowned sparrow | *Zonotrichia leucophrys* |
| White-throated sparrow | *Zonotrichia albicollis* |
| Song sparrow | *Melospiza melodia* |
| Canary (domestic) | *(Serinus)* |
| Hawfinch | *Coccothraustes coccothraustes* |
| Bullfinch | *Pyrrhula pyrrhula* |
| Greenfinch | *Chloris chloris* |
| Goldfinch | *Carduelis carduelis* |
| Chaffinch | *Fringilla coelebs* |
| Zebra finch | *Poephila guttata* |
| Quelea | *Quelea quelea* |
| Eastern hill mynah | *Gracula religiosa* |
| Jackdaw | *Corvus monedula* |
| Hooded crow | *Corvus cornix* |

## Mammalia (other than primates)

| | |
|---|---|
| Whales | *(Cetacea)* |
| Hippotamus | *Hippotamus amphibius* |

| African elephant | *Loxodonta africana* |
| Impala | *Aepyceros melampus* |
| Red deer | *Cervus elephas* |
| Rat (laboratory) | *(Rattus)* |
| Mouse (laboratory) | *(Mus)* |
| Mouse | *Onychomys* sp. |
| Deer mouse | *Peromyscus* sp. |
| Hamster | *Mesocricetus auratus* |
| Rabbit (laboratory) | *Oryctolagus* |
| Cat (domestic) | *(Felis)* |
| Dog (domestic) | *[Canis (familiaris)]* |
| Wolf | *Canis lupus* |
| Coyote | *Canis latrans* |
| Red fox | *Vulpes vulpes* |
| Grey fox | *Urocyon cinereoargentatus* |
| Arctic fox | *Alopes lagopus* |

## Primates

| Tree shrew | *(Tupaiidae)* |
| Ring-tailed Lemur | *Lemur catta* |
| Indri | *Indri indri* |
| Sifaka | *Propithecus verreauxi* |
| Galago | *Galago* spp. |
| Goeldi's marmoset | *Callimico goeldii* |
| Marmosets | *Callithrix* spp. |
| Squirrel monkey | *Saimiri sciureus* |
| Titi monkey | *Callicebus moloch* |
| Howler monkey | *Alouetta* sp. |
| Black spider monkey | *Ateles paniscus* |
| Vervet | *Cercopithecus aethiops* |
| Blue monkey } | |
| Sykes monkey } | *Cercopithecus mitis* |
| Lowe's guenon | *Cercopithecus campbelli* |
| Talapoin | *Cerpithecus talapoin* |
| Patas monkey | *Erythrocebus patas* |
| Black mangabey | *Cercocebus aterrimus* |
| Grey-cheeked mangabey | *Cercocebus albigena* |
| Sooty mangabey | *Cercocebus atys* |
| Baboon | *Papio cynocephalus* group |
| Hamadryas baboon | *Papio hamadryas* |
| Gelada baboon | *Theropithecus gelada* |
| Barbary macaque | *Macaca sylvana* |
| Bonnet macaque | *Macaca radiata* |
| Pig-tailed macaque | *Macaca nemestrina* |
| Crab-eating macaque | *Macaca irus* |
| Rhesus macaque | *Macaca mulatta* |
| Stump-tailed macaque | *Macaca speciosa* |

| | |
|---|---|
| Japanese macaque | *Macaca fuscata* |
| Celebes black ape | *Cynopithecus niger* |
| Black-and-white colobus | *Colobus polykomos* |
| Red colobus | *Colobus badius* |
| Douc langur | *Pygathrix nemaeus* |
| Nilgiri langur | *Presbytis johnii* |
| Hanuman langur | *Presbytis entellus* |
| Indian langur | *Presbytis* sp. |
| Purple-faced leaf monkey | *Presbytis senex* |
| Lutong | *Presbytis cristatus* |
| White-handed gibbon | *Hylobates lar* |
| Siamang | *Symphalangus syndactylus* |
| Gorilla | *Gorilla gorilla* |
| Orangutan | *Pongo pygmaeus* |
| Chimpanzee | *Pan troglodytes* |
| Man | *Homo sapiens* |

# BIBLIOGRAPHY

ADLER, N., AND HOGAN, J. N. (1963). Classical conditioning and punishment of an instinctive response in *Betta splendens. Anim. Behav.*, **11**, 351–354.

AHRENS, R. (1954). Beitrage zur Entwicklung des Physiognomie und Mimikerkennes. *Z. Exp. ang. Psychol.*, **2**, 402–454, 599–633.

AINSWORTH, M. D. (1962). The effects of maternal deprivation: a review of findings and controversy in the context of research strategy. In "Deprivation of Maternal Care," World Health Organization, Geneva.

—— (1963). The development of infant-mother interaction among the Ganda. In "Determinants of Infant Behaviour," vol. 2, Ed. B. M. Foss, Methuen, London.

—— (1967). "Infancy in Uganda: Infant Care and the Growth of Attachment." Johns Hopkins, Baltimore.

—— (1969). Object relations, dependency and attachment: a theoretical review of the infant-mother relationship. *Child Devel.*, **40**, 969–1025.

——, AND BELL, S. M. (in press). Mother-infant interaction and the development of competence. In "The Growth of Competence," Eds. K. J. Connolly and J. S. Bruner, Academic, London and New York.

——, BELL, S. M. V., AND STAYTON, D. J. (1971). Individual differences in strange-situation behaviour of one-year olds. In Schaffer (1971a).

——, AND WITTIG, B. A. (1969). Attachment and exploratory behaviour of one-year-olds in a strange situation. In "Determinants of Infant Behaviour," vol. 4, Ed. B. M. Foss, Methuen, London.

ALDRICH-BLAKE, F. P. G. (1970). Problems of social structure in forest monkeys. In "Social Behaviour in Birds and Mammals," Ed. J. H. Crook, Academic, London and New York.

——, DUNN, T. K., DUNBAR, R. I. M., AND HEADLEY, P. M. (1971). Observations on baboons, *Papio anubis*, in an arid region in Ethiopia. *Folia Primatol.*, **15**, 1–35.

ALEXANDER, B. K. (1970). Parental care of adult male Japanese monkeys. *Behaviour*, **36**, 270–285.

——, AND BOWERS, J. M. (1967). The social structure of the Oregon troop of Japanese macaques. *Primates*, **8**, 333–340.

——, AND —— (1969). Social organization of a troop of Japanese monkeys in a two-acre enclosure. *Folia Primatol.*, **10**, 230–242.

——, AND HUGHES, J. (1971). Canine teeth and rank in Japanese monkeys. *Primates*, **12**, 91–93.

————, AND ROTH, E. M. (1971). The effects of acute crowding on aggressive behavior of Japanese monkeys. *Behaviour*, **39**, 73–90.

ALTMANN, S. A. (1962). A field study of the sociobiology of rhesus monkeys, *Macaca mulatta*. *Ann. N.Y. Acad. Sci.*, **102**, 338–435.

———— (1965). Sociobiology of rhesus monkeys. II: Stochastics of social communication. *J. Theor. Biol.*, **8**, 490–522.

———— (Ed.) (1967a). "Social Communication among Primates." The University of Chicago Press, Chicago.

———— (1967b). The structure of primate social communication. In Altmann (1967a).

———— (1968). Sociobiology of rhesus monkeys. III. The basic communication network. *Behaviour*, **32**, 17–32.

————, AND ALTMANN, J. (1970). Baboon ecology. *Bibl. Primatol.*, **12**, 1–220.

AMBROSE, J. A. (1961). The development of the smiling response in early infancy. In "Determinants of Infant Behaviour," vol. 1, Ed. B. M. Foss, Methuen, London.

———— (Ed.) (1969). "Stimulation in Early Infancy." Academic, London and New York.

ANDERSON, J. W. (1972). On the psychological attachment of infants to their mothers. *J. Biosoc. Sci.*, **4**, 197–225.

ANDREW, R. J. (1956). Some remarks on behaviour in conflict situations, with special reference to *Emberiza* spp. *Br. J. Anim. Behav.*, **4**, 41–45.

———— (1957). Influence of hunger on aggressive behavior in certain buntings of the genus *Emberiza*. *Physiol. Zool.*, **30**, 177–185.

———— (1961). The displays given by passerines in courtship and reproductive fighting: a review. *Ibis*, **103a**, 315–348.

———— (1963a). The origin and evolution of the calls and facial expressions of the primates. *Behaviour*, **20**, 1–109.

———— (1963b). Trends apparent in the evolution of vocalization in the Old World monkeys and apes. *Symp. Zool. Soc. Lond.*, **10**, 89–101.

———— (1972). The information potentially available in mammal displays. In Hinde (1972a).

ANGERMEIER, W. F., PHELPS, J. B., REYNOLDS, H. H., AND DAVIS, R. (1968). Dominance in monkeys: effects of social change on performance and biochemistry. *Psychom. Sci.*, **11**, 183–4.

ANON. (1970). Effects of sexual activity on beard growth in man. *Nature*, **226**, 869–870.

ANTHONEY, T. R. (1968). The ontogeny of greeting, grooming and sexual motor patterns in captive baboons. *Behaviour*, **31**, 358–372.

ARDREY, R. (1967). "The Territorial Imperative." Atheneum, New York.

ARGYLE, M. (1969). "Social Interaction." Methuen, London.

———— (1972). Non-verbal communication in human social interaction. In Hinde (1972a).

ARLING, G. L., RUPPENTHAL, G. C., AND MITCHELL, G. D. (1969). Aggressive behaviour of the eight-year-old nulliparous isolate female monkey. *Anim. Behav.*, **17**, 109–113.

ARMSTRONG, J. S., AND SOELBERG, P. (1968). On the interpretation of factor analysis. *Psychol. Bull.*, **70**, 361–364.

ARONSEN, L. R., AND COOPER, M. (1966). The appearance of seasonal cycles in sexual behaviour in domestic male cats following desensitization of the glans penis. *Proc. 18th Int. Cong. Psychol., Moscow*, **1**, 190–197.

ASSEM, J. VAN DEN, AND MOLEN, J. N. VAN DEN (1969). Waning of the aggressive response in the three-spined stickleback upon constant exposure to a conspecific. *Behaviour*, **34**, 286–324.

AUSTIN, J. L. (1962). "How to do Things with Words." Harvard, Cambridge, Mass.

AVERILL, J. R. (1968). Grief: its nature and significance. *Psychol. Bull.*, **70**, 721–748.

AZRIN, N. H., HUTCHINSON, R. R., AND HAKE, D. F. (1966). Extinction-induced aggression. *J. Exp. Anal. Behav.*, **9**, 191–204.

———, HUTCHINSON, R. R., AND McLAUGHLIN, R. (1965). The opportunity for aggression as an operant reinforcer during aversive stimulation. *J. Exp. Anal. Behav.*, **8**, 171–180.

———, ULRICH, R. E., HUTCHINSON, R. R., AND NORMAN, D. G. (1964). Effect of shock duration on shock-induced fighting. *J. Exp. Anal. Behav.*, **7**, 9–11.

BAENNINGER, R. (1970). Visual reinforcement, habituation, and prior social experience of Siamese fighting fish. *J. Comp. Physiol. Psychol.*, **71**, 1–5.

BAERENDS, G. P. (1950). Specializations in organs and movements with a releasing function. *Symp. Soc. Exp. Biol.*, **4**, 337–360.

——— (1973). Contribution to discussion in Hinde and Stevenson-Hinde (1973).

———, AND KRUIJT, J. P. (1973). Stimulus selection. In Hinde and Stevenson-Hinde (1973).

BALDWIN, J. D. (1968). The social behaviour of adult male squirrel monkeys (*Saimiri sciureus*) in a seminatural environment. *Folia Primatol.* **9**, 281–314.

——— (1969). The ontogeny of social behaviour of squirrel monkeys (*Saimiri sciureus*) in a seminatural environment. *Folia Primatol.*, **11**, 35–79.

——— (1971). The social organisation of a semifree-ranging troop of squirrel monkeys (*Saimiri sciureus*). *Folia Primatol.*, **14**, 23–50.

———, AND BALDWIN, J. I. (1971). Squirrel monkeys (*Saimiri*) in natural habitats in Panama, Colombia, Brazil and Peru. *Primates*, **12**, 45–61.

BANDURA, A. (1971). Vicarious and self-reinforcement processes. In "The Nature of Reinforcement," Ed. R. Glaser, Academic, New York and London.

———, AND WALTERS, R. H. (1959). "Adolescent Aggression." Ronald, New York.

———, AND ——— (1963). "The Social Learning of Deviant Behavior." Holt, New York.

BARNES, J. A. (1972). Social networks. *Addison-Wesley Module Anthropol.*, **26**, 1–29.

BARNETT, S. A. (1969). Grouping and dispersive behaviour among wild rats. In Garattini and Sigg (1969).

———, EVANS, C. S., AND STODDART, R. C. (1968). Influence of females on conflict among wild rats. *J. Zool.*, **154**, 391–396.

BARTH, F. (1966). Models of social organization. Roy. Anthropol. Inst. Occasional Paper No. 23, pp. 1–33.

BARTHES, R. (1967). "Systèmes de la mode." Editions du Seuil, Paris.

BATES, B. C. (1970). Territorial behavior in primates: a review of recent field studies. *Primates*, **11**, 271–284.

BATESON, P. P. G. (1964a). Effect of similarity between rearing and testing conditions on chicks' following and avoidance responses. *J. Comp. Physiol. Psychol.*, **57**, 100–103.

——— (1964b). An effect of imprinting on the perceptual development of domestic chicks. *Nature*, **202**, 421–422.

——— (1964c). Changes in the activity of isolated chicks over the first week after hatching. *Anim. Behav.*, **12**, 490–492.

——— (1966). The characteristics and context of imprinting. *Biol. Rev.*, **41**, 177–220.

——— (1971). Imprinting. In "Ontogeny of Vertebrate Behavior," Ed. H. Moltz, Academic, New York and London.

——— (1973). Internal influences on early learning in birds. In Hinde and Stevenson-Hinde (1973).

———, AND CHANTREY, D. F. (1972). Retardation of discrimination learning in monkeys and chicks previously exposed to both stimuli. *Nature,* **237,** 173–174.

————, Horn, G., and Rose, S. P. R. (1972). Effects of early experience on regional incorporation of precursors into RNA and protein in the chick brain. *Brain Res.,* **39,** 449–465.

————, and Reese, E. P. (1969). The reinforcing properties of conspicuous stimuli in the imprinting situation. *Anim. Behav.,* **17,** 692–699.

————, and Wainwright, A. A. P. (1972). The effects of prior exposure to light on the imprinting process in domestic chicks. *Behaviour,* **42,** 279–290.

Beach, F. A. (1944). Relative effects of androgen upon the mating behavior of male rats subjected to forebrain injury or castration. *J. Exp. Zool.,* **97,** 249–295.

———— (1947). A review of physiological and psychological studies of sexual behavior in mammals. *Physiol. Rev.,* **27,** 240–307.

———— (1967). Cerebral and hormonal control of reflexive mechanisms involved in copulatory behavior. *Physiol. Rev.,* **47,** 289–316.

———— (1971). Hormonal factors controlling the differentiation, development and display of copulatory behavior in the ramstergig and related species. In "The Biopsychology of Development," Eds. E. Tobach, L. R. Aronson, and E. Shaw, Academic, New York and London.

————, and Levinson, G. (1950). Effects of androgen on the glans penis and mating behavior of castrated male rats. *J. Exp. Zool.,* **114,** 159–168.

Beeman, E. A. (1947). The effect of male hormone on aggressive behavior in mice. *Physiol. Zool.,* **20,** 373–405.

Beer, C. G. (1970). Individual recognition of voice in the social behavior of birds. *Adv. Study Behav.,* **3,** 27–74.

Bell, R. Q. (1968). A reinterpretation of the direction of effects in studies of socialization. *Psychol. Rev.,* **75,** 81–95.

———— (1971). Stimulus control of parent or caretaker behavior by offspring. *Devel. Psychol.,* **4,** 63–72.

————, Weller, G. M., and Waldrop, M. F. (1971). Newborn and preschooler: organization of behavior and relations between periods. *Monogr. Soc. Res. Child Devel.,* **36,** 1–145.

Bell, S. M., and Ainsworth, M. D. S. (1972). Infant crying and maternal responsiveness. *Child Devel.,* **43,** 1171–1190.

Bender, L. (1969). Hostile aggression in children. In Garattini and Sigg (1969).

Benedict, R. (1969). Role analysis in animals and men. *Man,* **4,** 203–214, 1969.

Bennett, M. A. (1940). Social hierarchy in ring doves. II. The effects of treatment with testosterone propionate. *Ecology,* **21,** 148–165.

Benthall, J. and Polhemus, T. in press. "The Body as a Medium of Expression." Allen Lane and Dutton, London.

Berkowitz, L. (1962). "Aggression." McGraw-Hill, New York.

Bernal, J. D. (1972). Crying during the first ten days of life, and maternal responses. *Devel. Med. Child Neurol.,* **14,** 362–372.

Bernstein, I. S. (1963). Social activities related to rhesus monkey consort behaviour. *Psychol. Rep.,* **13,** 375–379.

———— (1964). The integration of rhesus monkeys introduced to a group. *Folia Primatol.,* **2,** 50–64.

———— (1968). The lutong of Kuala Selongor. *Behaviour,* **32,** 1–15.

———— (1969). Introductory techniques in the formation of pigtail monkey groups. *Folia Primatol.,* **10,** 1–19.

———— (1969). Stability of the status hierarchy in a pigtail monkey group (*Macaca nemestrina*). *Anim. Behav.,* **17,** 452–458.

———— (1970). Primate status hierarchies. In "Primate Behavior," vol. I, Ed. L.

A. Rosenblum, Academic, New York and London.

——, AND MASON, W. A. (1963a). Activity patterns of rhesus monkeys in a social group. *Anim. Behav.*, **11**, 455–460.

——, AND MASON, W. A. (1963b). Group formation by rhesus monkeys. *Anim. Behav.*, **11**, 28–31.

——, AND SHARPE, L. G. (1966). Social roles in a rhesus monkey group. *Behaviour*, **26**, 91–104.

BERTRAM, B. C. R. (1970). The vocal behaviour of the Indian hill mynah, *Gracula religiosa*. *Anim. Behav. Monogr.*, **3**, 2.

BERTRAND, M. (1969). The behavioural repertoire of the stumptail macaque. *Bibl. Primatol.*, **11**, 1–273.

BLEST, D. (1961). The concept of ritualization. In "Current Problems in Animal Behaviour," Eds. W. H. Thorpe and O. L. Zangwill, Cambridge, New York and London.

BLOOM, L. (1970). "Language Development: Form and Function in Emerging Grammars." M.I.T., Cambridge, Mass.

BLURTON JONES, N. G. (1968). Observations and experiments on the causation of threat displays of the great tit *(Parus major)*. *Anim. Behav. Monogr.*, **1**, 2.

—— (Ed.) (1972a). "Ethological Studies of Child Behaviour." Cambridge, New York and London.

—— (1972b). Categories of child–child interaction. In Blurton Jones (1972a).

—— (1972c). Non-verbal communication in children. In Hinde (1972a).

BOELKINS, R. C., AND HEISER, J. F. (1970). Biological bases of aggression. In Daniels et al. (1970).

BOISSEVAIN, J. (1971). Second thoughts on quasi groups, categories and coalitions. *Man*, **6**, 468–472.

BOLLES, R. C. (1967). "Theory of Motivation." Harper & Row, New York.

BOTT, E. (1957). "Family and Social Networks." Tavistock, London.

BOWER, T. G. R. (1966). The visual world of infants. *Sci. Am.*, **215**, 80–97.

—— (1969). Perceptual functioning in early infancy. In "Brain and Early Behaviour," Ed. R. J. Robinson, Academic, New York and London.

—— (1972). Object perception in infants. *Perception*, **1**, 15–30.

BOWLBY, J. (1951). "Maternal Care and Mental Health." World Health Organization, Geneva.

—— (1969). "Attachment and Loss," vol. 1, "Attachment." Hogarth, London.

—— (1973). "Attachment and Loss," vol. 2, "Separation." Hogarth Press, London.

BRACKBILL, Y. (1958). Extinction of the smiling response in infants as a function of reinforcement schedule. *Child Devel.*, **29**, 115–124.

—— (1971). The cumulative effect of continuous stimulation on arousal level in infants. *Child Devel.*, **42**, 17–26.

BRANNIGAN, C. R., AND HUMPHRIES, D. A. (1972). Human non-verbal behaviour, a means of communication. In Blurton Jones (1972a).

BRÉMOND, J-C. (1967). Reconnaissance de schémas réactogènes liés à l'information contenue dans le chant territorial du rouge-gorge. Proc. 14th Int. Ornithol. Congr. (Ed., D. W. Snow), pp. 217–229. Blackwell, Oxford.

BRIDGER, J. H. (1961). Sensory habituation and discrimination in the human neonate. *Am. J. Psychiat.*, **117**, 991–996.

BRINDLEY, C., CLARKE, P., HUTT, C., ROBINSON, I. AND WETHLI, E. (1973). Sex differences in the activities and social interactions of nursery school children. In Michael and Crook (1973).

BRODY, S., AND AXELRAD, S. (1971). Maternal stimulation and social responsiveness of infants. In Schaffer (Ed.) (1971a).

BRONFENBRENNER, U. (1968). Early deprivation in mammals: a cross-species analysis. In "Early Experience and Behavior," Eds. I. Newton, and S. Levine, Charles C Thomas, Springfield, Ill.

BRONSON, F. H., AND DESJARDINS, C. (1968). Aggression in adult mice: modification by neonatal injections of gonadal hormones. *Science*, **161**, 705–706.

BRONSON, G. W. (1971). Fear of the unfamiliar in human infants. In Schaffer (1971a).

BROSSARD, L. M., AND DECARIE, T. G. (1968). Comparative reinforcing effects of eight stimulations on the smiling responses of infants. *J. Child Psychol. Psychiatr.*, **9**, 51–60.

BROWN, J. L. (1969). The control of avian vocalization by the central nervous system. In Hinde (1969a).

BROWN, R. (1970). The first sentences of child and chimpanzee. In "Selected Psycholinguistical Papers." Macmillan, New York.

BROWN, W. L. COURT, JACOBS, R. A., AND PRICE, W. H. (1968). Sex chromosome aneuploidy and criminal behaviour. In Thoday and Parkes (1968).

BROWNFIELD, C. (1964). "Isolation: Clinical and Experimental Approaches." Random House, New York.

BRUCE, H. M. (1966). Smell as an exteroceptive factor. *J. Anim. Sci.*, **25** (suppl.), 83–89.

BRUNER, J. S. (1968). "Processes of Cognitive Growth in Infancy." Clark University Press, Worcester, Mass., 75 pp.

———— (1969a). On voluntary action and its hierarchical structure. In "Beyond Reductionism," Eds. A. Koestler and J. R. Smythies. Hutchinson, London.

———— (1969b). Processes of growth in infancy. In Ambrose (1969).

———— (1970). The growth and structure of skill. In Connolly (1970a).

BULLOCK, D. W., PARIS, C. A., AND GOY, R. W. (1972). Sexual behaviour, swelling of the sex skin and plasma progesterone in the pigtail macaque. *J. Reprod. Fert.*, **31**, 225–236.

BURT, W. H. (1943). Territoriality and home range concepts as applied to mammals. *J. Mammalol.*, **24**, 346–352.

BURTON, F. D. (1971). Sexual climax in female *Macaca mulatta*. Proc. 2d Int. Congr. Primatol. Zurich, 1970, **3**, 180–191.

BUSS, A. H. (1961). "The Psychology of Aggression." Wiley, New York.

BYGOTT, D. (in prep.). Agonistic behaviour in wild male chimpanzees. Ph.D. thesis, Cambridge.

CAIRNS, R. B. (1972a). Attachment and dependency: a psychobiological and social-learning synthesis. In "Attachment and Dependency," Ed. J. L. Gewirtz, Winston, Washington.

———— (1972b). Fighting and punishment from a developmental perspective. *Nebr. Symp. Motiv.*, 59–124.

CALDWELL, B. M. (1964). The effects of infant care. In "Review of Child Development Research," vol. 1, Eds. M. L. Hoffman and L. W. Hoffman, Russell Sage, New York.

CALHOUN, J. B. (1962). Population density and social pathology. *Sci. Am.*, **206**, 139–148.

———— (1963). The ecology and sociology of the Norway rat. Publ. No. 1008, U.S. Dept. of Health, Bethesda.

CAMPBELL, B. A., AND PICKLEMAN, J. R. (1961). The imprinting object as a reinforcing stimulus. *J. Comp. Physiol. Psychol.*, **54**, 592–596.

CAPLAN, N., AND PAIGE, J. M. A. (1968). A study of ghetto rioters. *Sci. Am.*, **219**, 15–21.

CARMICHAEL, L. (1927). A further study of the development of behavior in vertebrates experimentally removed from the influence of external stimulation *Psychol. Rev.*, **34**, 34–47.

CARPENTER, C. R. (1964). "Naturalistic Behaviour of Nonhuman Primates." The Pennsylvania State University Press, University Park.

CARR, W. J., LOEB, L. S., AND WYLIE, N. R. (1965). Responses to feminine odors in normal and castrated male rats. *J. Comp. Physiol. Psychol.*, **62**, 336–338.

CARTHY, J. D., AND EBLING, F. J. (Eds.) (1964). "The Natural History of Aggression." Academic, New York and London.

CARYL, P. G. (1969). Social control of fighting behaviour in the zebra finch, *Taenopygia guttata*. Ph.D. thesis, Cambridge University.

CAUDILL, W., AND WEINSTEIN, H. (1969). Maternal care and infant behavior in Japan and America. *Psychiatry*, **32**, 12–43.

CHALMERS, N. R. (1968). The social behaviour of free living mangabeys in Uganda. *Folia Primatol.*, **8**, 263–281.

————, AND ROWELL, T. E. (1971). Behaviour and female reproductive cycles in a captive group of mangabeys. *Folia Primatol.*, **14**, 1–14.

CHANCE, M. R. A. (1954). Social structure of a colony of *Macaca mulatta*. *Br. J. Anim. Behav.*, **4**, 1–13.

————, AND JOLLY, C. J. (1970). "Social Groups of Monkeys, Apes and Men." Cape, London.

CHANTREY, D. F. (1972). Enhancement and retardation of discrimination learning in chicks after exposure to the discriminanda. *J. Comp. Physiol. Psychol.*, **81**, 256–261.

CHAPPLE, E. D., AND ARENSBERG, C. M. (1940). Measuring human relations. *Genet. Psychol. Monogr.*, **22**.

CHEVALIER-SKOLNIKOFF, S. (1971). The ontogeny of communication in *Macaca speciosa*. Ph.D. thesis, University of California, Berkeley.

CHITTY, D. (1967). The natural selection of self-regulatory behavior in animal populations. *Proc. Ecol. Soc. Aust.*, **2**, 51–78.

CHIVERS, D. J. (1969). On the daily behaviour and spacing of howling monkey groups. *Folia Primatol.*, **10**, 48–102.

———— (1972). The Siamang in Malaya: a field study of a primate in tropical rain forest. Ph.D. thesis, Cambridge University.

CHOMSKY, N. (1959). Review of Skinner, "Verbal Behaviour," *Language*, **35**, 26–58.

———— (1968). "Language and Mind." Harcourt, Brace & World, New York.

CHRISTIAN, J. J., AND DAVIS, D. E. (1964). Endocrines, behavior and population. *Science*, **146**, 1550–1560.

CLANCY, H., AND McBRIDE, G. (1974). The isolation syndrome. *Developmental Medicine and Child Neurology*, **16**, in press.

CLAYTON, F. L., AND HINDE, R. A. (1968). The habituation and recovery of aggressive display in *Betta splendens*. *Behaviour*, **30**, 96–106.

CLEMENTE, C. D., AND LINDSLEY, D. B. (1967). "Aggression and Defense." University of California Press, Los Angeles.

CLUTTON-BROCK, T. H. (1972). Feeding and ranging behaviour of the red colobus monkey. Ph.D. thesis, Cambridge University.

COATES, B., ANDERSON, E. P., AND HARTUP, W. W. (1972a). Interrelations in the attachment behavior of human infants. *Devel. Psychol.*, **6**, 218–230.

————, ————, AND ———— (1972b). The stability of attachment behaviors in the human infant. *Devel. Psychol.*, **6**, 231–237.

COLLIAS, N. E. (1952). The development of social behavior in birds. *Auk*, **69**, 127–159.

COMFORT, A. (1971). Likelihood of human pheromones. *Nature*, **230**, 432–433.

CONAWAY, C. H., AND KOFORD, C. B. (1965). Estrous cycles and mating behavior in a free-ranging band of rhesus monkeys. *J. Mammal.*, **45**, 577–588.

CONNER, R. L., AND LEVINE, S. (1969). Hormonal influences on aggressive behaviour. In Garattini and Sigg (1969).

CONNOLLY, K. V. (Ed.) (1970a). "Mechan-

isms of Motor Skill Development."
Academic, London and New York.

——— (1970b). Skill development: problems and plans. In Connolly (1970a).

——— (1973). Factors influencing the manual skills of young children. In Hinde and Stevenson-Hinde, 1973.

CROOK, J. H. (1964). The evolution of social organization and visual communication in the weaver birds *(Ploceinae). Behavior, suppl.,* **10,** 1–178.

——— (1966). Gelada baboon herd structure and movement. *Symp. Zool. Soc. Lond.,* **18,** 237–258.

——— (1970). The socio-ecology of primates. In "Social Behaviour in Birds and Mammals," Ed. J. H. Crook, Academic, London and New York.

——— (1973). Darwinism and the sexual politics of primates. *Accad. Naz. dei Lincei,* Quad. N. **182,** 199–217.

——— (in press). "Social Systems and Evolutionary Ecology." Macmillan, London and New York.

———, AND ALDRICH-BLAKE, P. (1968). Ecological and behavioural contrasts between sympatric ground-dwelling primates in Ethiopia. *Folia Primatol.,* **8,** 192–227.

———, AND BUTTERFIELD, P. A. (1970). Gender role in the social system of *Quelea.* In "Social Behavior in Birds and Mammals," Ed. J. H. Crook, Academic, London and New York.

———, AND GARTLAN, J. S. (1966). On the evolution of primate societies. *Nature,* **210,** 1200–1203.

CROSS, B. A. (1952). Nursing behaviour and the milk-ejection reflex in rabbits. *J. Endocrinol.,* **8,** xiii.

CULLEN, J. M. (1972). Some principles of animal communication. In Hinde (1972a).

DAANJE, A. (1950). On locomotory movements in birds and the intention movements derived from them. *Behaviour,* **3,** 48–98.

DANIELS, D. N., GILULA, M. F., AND OCHBERG, F. M. (1970). "Violence and

the Struggle for Existence." Little, Brown, Boston.

DARWIN, C. (1872). "The Expression of the Emotions in Man and the Animals." J. Murray, London.

DAVANZO, J. P., (1969). Observations related to drug-induced alterations in aggressive behavior. In Garattini and Sigg (1969).

DAVENPORT, R. K., AND MENZEL, E. W. (1963). Stereotyped behavior of the infant chimpanzee. *Arch. Gen. Psychiatr.,* **8,** 99–104.

DAVIS, D. E. (1940). Social nesting habits of the smooth-billed ani. *Auk,* **57,** 179–217.

DAVIS, J. (1957). Comparative foraging behavior of the spotted and brown towhees. *Auk,* **74,** 129–166.

DAVIS, K. (1947). Final note on a case of extreme isolation. *Am. J. Sociol.,* **52,** 432–437.

DEAG, J. M. (1974). A study of the social behavior and ecology of the wild Barbary macaque, *Macaca sylvanus.* Ph.D. thesis, Bristol University.

———, AND CROOK, J. H. (1971). Social behaviour and "agonistic buffering" in the wild Barbary macaque *Macaca sylvana. Folia Primatol.,* **15,** 183–200.

DEETS, A. C., AND HARLOW, H. F. (1970). Nipple preferences in nursing singleton- and twin-reared rhesus monkey infants. *Devel. Psychol.,* **2,** 159–161.

DELGADO, J. (1969). Offensive-defensive behaviour in free monkeys and chimpanzees induced by radio stimulation of the brain. In Garattini and Sigg (1969).

DENENBERG, V. H. (1970). Experimental programming of life histories and the creation of individual differences. In "Effects of Early Experience," Ed. M. R. Jones, University of Miami Press, Coral Gables, Fla.

———, AND ROSENBERG, K. M. (1967). Nongenetic transmission of information. *Nature,* **216,** 549–550.

DEVONS, E., AND GLUCKMAN, M. (1964). Modes and consequences of limiting a field study. In "Closed Systems and Open Minds," Ed. M. Gluckman, Oliver & Boyd, Edinburgh.

DeVore, I. (1963). Mother-infant relations in free-ranging baboons. In "Maternal Behavior in Mammals," Ed. H. L. Rheingold, Wiley, New York.

—— (Ed.) (1965a). "Primate Behavior." Holt, New York.

—— (1965b). Male dominance and mating behavior in baboons. In "Sex and Behavior," Ed. F. A. Beach, Wiley, New York.

Dollard, J., Doob, L. W., Miller, N. E., Mowrer, O. H., and Sears, R. R. (1939). "Frustration and Aggression." Yale, New Haven, Conn.

Douglas, J. W. B. (in press). Early hospital admission and later disturbances of behaviour and learning.

Douglas-Hamilton, I. (1972). Ecology and behaviour of the African elephant. D.Phil. thesis, Oxford University.

Dunbar, R. I. M., and Nathan, M. F. (1972). Social organization of the Guinea baboon *Papio papio*. *Folia Primatol.,* **17,** 321–334.

Duncan, I. J. H., and Wood-Gush, D. G. M. (1971). Frustration and aggression in the domestic fowl. *Anim. Behav.,* **19,** 500–504.

Duncan, S. (1969). Non-verbal communication. *Psychol. Bull.,* **72,** 118–137.

Durham, N. M. (1969). Sex differences in visual threat displays of West African vervets. *Primates,* **10,** 91–95.

—— (1971). Effects of altitude differences on group organization of wild Black Spider monkeys (*Ateles paniscus*). *Proc. 3d Int. Congr. Primatol., Zurich (1970),* **3,** 32–40.

Durkheim, E. (1938). The rules of sociological method, (8th Ed.). University of Chicago, Chicago.

Eaton, R. L. (1970). Group interactions, spacing and territoriality in cheetahs. *Z. Tierpsychol.,* **27,** 481–491.

Eibl-Eibesfeldt, I. (1971). Zur Ethologie menschlichen Grussverhaltens: II.

Das Grussverhalten und einige andere Muster freundlicher Kontaktaufnahme der Waika. *Z. Tierpsychol.,* **29,** 196–213.

—— (1972). Similarities and differences between cultures in expressive movements. In Hinde (1972a).

Eimas, P. D., Siqueland, E. R., Jusczyk, P., and Vigorito, J. (1971). Speech perception in infants. *Science,* **171,** 303–306.

Eisenberg, J. F., and Dillon, W. S. (Eds.) (1971). "Man and Beast: Comparative Social Behavior." The Smithsonian Institution, Washington.

——, Muckenhirn, N. A., and Rudran, R. (1972). The relation between ecology and social structure in primates. *Science,* **176,** 863–874.

Eisenberg, R. A. (1969). Auditory behaviour in the human neonate: functional properties of sound and their ontogenetic implications. *Int. Audiol.,* **8,** 34–45.

Ekman, P. (1971). Universals and cultural differences in facial expressions of emotion. *Nebr. Symp. Motiv.,* **1970,** 207–284.

—— (1973). Darwin and cross cultural studies of facial expression. In "Darwin and Facial Expression: A Century of Research in Review," Ed. P. Ekman, Academic, New York.

——, and Friesen, W. V. (1969). The repertoire of nonverbal behavior: categories, origins, usage and coding. *Semiotica,* **1,** 49–98.

——, Sorenson, E. R., and Friesen, W. V. (1969). Pan-cultural elements in facial displays of emotion. *Science,* **164,** 86–88.

Ellefson, J. O. (1968). Territorial behavior in the common white-handed gibbon *Hylobates lar.* In Jay (1968).

Emerson, J. (1970). Behavior in private places: sustaining definitions. In Dreitzel, "Recent Sociology," vol. 2, 73–97. Macmillan, New York.

Emlen, J. T. (1952). Flocking behaviour in birds. *Auk,* **69,** 160–170.

EPPLE, G. (1967). Vergleichende Untersuchungen über Sexual- und Sozialverhalten der Krallenaffen (Hapalidae). *Folia Primatol.*, **7**, 37–65.

—— (1968). Comparative studies on vocalization in marmoset monkeys (Hapalidae). *Folia Primatol.*, **8**, 1–40.

ERWIN, J., MOBALDI, J., AND MITCHELL, G. (1971). Separation of rhesus monkey juveniles of the same sex. *J. Abnorm. Psychol.*, **78**, 134–139.

ESCALONA, S. K. (1969). The roots of individuality: normal patterns of development in infancy. Taristock, London.

EVERITT, B. J., AND HERBERT, J. (1971). Sexual receptivity of bilaterally adrenalectomized female rhesus monkeys. *Physiol. Behav.*, **8**, 409–415.

——, AND —— (1972). Hormonal correlates of sexual behaviour in subhuman primates. *Dan. Med. Bull.*, **19**, 246–255.

FADY, J-C. (1969). Les jeux sociaux: le compagnon de jeux chez les jeunes. Observations chez *Macaca irus. Folia Primatol.*, **11**, 134–143.

FALLS, J. B. (1969). Functions of territorial song in the white-throated sparrow. In Hinde (1969a).

FANTZ, R. L. (1965). Visual perception from birth as shown by pattern selectivity. *Ann. N.Y. Acad. Sci.*, **118**, 793–814.

—— (1966). Pattern discrimination and selective attention as determinants of perceptual development from birth. In "Perceptual Development in Children," Eds. A. H. Kidd and J. L. Rivoire. International Universities Press, Inc., New York.

——, AND NEVIS, S. (1967). Pattern preferences and perceptual-cognitive development in early infancy. *Merrill-Palmer Q.*, **13**, 77–108.

FELIPE, N. H., AND SOMMER, R. (1966). Invasions of personal space. *Soc. Prob.*, **14**, 206–214.

FESHBACH, S. (1964). The function of aggression and the regulation of aggressive drive. *Psychol. Rev.*, **71**, 257–272.

—— (1970). Aggression. In "Carmichael's Manual of Child Psychology," vol. 2, Ed. P. H. Mussen, Wiley, New York.

——, AND SINGER, R. D. (1971). "Television and Aggression." Jossey-Bass, San Francisco.

FINDLAY, A. L. R. (1970) Neural and behavioural interactions with lactation. In Proc. Int. Symp. 17th Easter School Agric. Sci., Ed. I. R. Falconer, Butterworth, London.

——, AND ROTH, L. L. (1970). Long-term dissociation of nursing behavior and the condition of the mammary gland in the rabbit. *J. Comp. Physiol. Psychol.*, **72**, 341–344.

——, AND TALLAL, P. A. (1971). Effect of reduced suckling stimulation on the duration of nursing in the rabbit. *J. Comp. Physiol. Psychol.*, **76**, 236–241.

FLANDERS, J. P. (1968). A review of research on imitative behavior. *Psychol. Bull.*, **69**, 316–337.

FLYNN, J. P. (1973). Patterning mechanisms, patterned reflexes, and attack behavior in cats. *Nebr. Symp. Motiv.*, **1972**, 125–153.

FORMBY, D. (1967). Maternal recognition of infant's cry. *Devel. Med. Child Neurol.*, **9**, 293–298.

FOSSEY, D. (1972). Vocalizations of the mountain gorilla (*Gorilla gorilla beringei*). *Anim. Behav.*, **20**, 36–53.

—— (in prep.). Physical and behavioural developments amongst individuals of a troop of mountain gorillas (*Gorilla gorilla beringei*).

FOX, M. W. (1969). The anatomy of aggression and its ritualization in Canidae. *Behaviour*, **35**, 242–258.

—— (1970). A comparative study of the development of facial expressions in canids; wolf, coyote and foxes. *Behaviour*, **36**, 49–73.

FREDERICSON, E., FINK, C. D., AND PARKER, J. R. (1955). Elicitation and inhibition of competitive fighting in food-deprived mice. *J. Genet. Psychol.*, **86**, 131–141.

FREEDMAN, D. G. (1961). The infant's fear of strangers and the flight response. *J. Child Psychol. Psychiatr.*, **2**, 242–248.

FREUD, A. (1949). Certain types and stages of social maladjustment. In "Searchlights on Delinquency," Ed. K. R. Eissler, International Universities Press, Inc., New York.

————— (1949). Aggression in relation to emotional development. *Psychoanal. Study Child.*, **3–4**, 37–41.

FREUD, S. (1922). "Psycho-analysis." Hogarth, London.

VON FRISCH, K. (1954). "The Dancing Bees." Methuen, London.

————— (1968). Do bees really not understand their own language? *Allg. Dtsch. Imkerztg.*, **2**, 35–41.

FURUYA, Y. (1969). On the fission of troops of Japanese monkeys. II. General view of troop fission of Japanese monkeys. *Primates*, **10**, 47–69.

GALLUP, G. (1971). Chimpanzees: self-recognition. *Science*, **167**, 86–87.

GARATTINI, S., AND SIGG, E. B. (Eds.) (1969). "Aggressive Behavior." Excerpta Medica, Amsterdam.

GARBETT, C. K. (1970). The analysis of social situations. *Man*, **5**, 214–227.

GARDNER, B. T., AND GARDNER, R. A. (1971). Two-way communication with an infant chimpanzee. In "Behavior of Nonhuman Primates," vol. 4, Eds. A. Schrier and F. Stollnitz, Academic, New York and London.

————— , AND WALLACH, L. (1965). Shapes of figures identified as a baby's head. *Percept. Motor Skills*, **20**, 135–142.

GARI, J. E., AND SCHEINFELD, A. (1968). Sex differences in mental and behavioral traits. *Gen. Psychol. Monogr.*, **77**, 169–299.

GARTLAN, J. S. (1968). Structure and func-tion in primate society. *Folia Primatol.*, **8**, 89–120.

————— , AND BRAIN, C. K. (1968). Ecology and social variability in *Cercopithecus aethiops* and *C. mitis*. In Jay (1968).

GAUTIER, J-P. (1969). Emissions sonores d'espacement et de ralliement par deux *Cercopithèques arboricolles*. *Rev. Biol. Gabonica*, **2**, 117–145.

GAUTIER-HION, A. (1973). Social and ecological features of talapoin monkey—comparisons with sympatric cercopithecines. In Michael and Crook (1973).

GEWIRTZ, J. L. (1961). A learning analysis of the effects of normal stimulation, privation and deprivation on the acquisition of social motivation and attachment. In "Determinants of Infant Behaviour, vol. 1, Ed. B. M. Foss, Methuen, London.

————— (1965). The course of infant smiling in four child-rearing environments in Israel. In "Determinants of Infant Behaviour," vol. 3, Methuen, London.

————— (1971). Conditional responding as a paradigm for observational, imitative learning and vicarious reinforcement. *Adv. Child Devel. Behav.*, **6**, 273–304.

GIBSON, E. J., AND WALK, R. D. (1956). The effect of prolonged exposure to visually presented patterns on learning to discriminate them. *J. Comp. Physiol. Psychol.*, **49**, 239–242.

————— , —————, AND TIGHE, T. J. (1959). Enhancement and deprivation of visual stimulation during rearing as factors in visual discrimination learning. *J. Comp. Physiol. Psychol.*, **52**, 74–81.

GINSBURG, B., AND ALLEE, W. C. (1942). Some effects of conditioning on social dominance and subordination in inbred strains of mice. *Physiol. Zool.*, **15**, 485–506.

GINSBURG, N. (1960). Conditioned vocalization in the budgerigar. *J. Comp. Physiol. Psychol.*, **53**, 183–186.

GLEASON, K. K., AND REYNIERSE, J. H. (1969). The behavioral significance of pheromones in vertebrates. *Psychol. Bull.*, **71**, 58–73.

GOFFMANN, E. (1959). "The Presentation of Self in Everyday Life." Doubleday, Garden City, N.Y.

GOLDBERG, S., AND LEWIS, M. (1969). Play behaviour in the one year old infant: early sex differences. *Child Devel.*, **40**, 21–31.

GOLDFOOT, D. A. (1971). Hormonal and social determinants of sexual behavior in the pigtail monkey (*Macaca nemestrina*). In "Normal and Abnormal Development of Brain and Behavior," Eds. G. B. A. Stoelinger and J. J. van der Werff ten Bosch, University of Leiden Press.

GOLDSCHMIDT, W. (1972). An ethnography of encounters: a methodology for the enquiry into the relation between the individual and Society. *Curr. Anthropol.*, **13**, 59–71.

GOMBRICH, E. H. (1972). Action and expression in western art. In Hinde (1972a).

GOODENOUGH, W. H. (1967). Rethinking "status" and "role." The relevance of models for social anthropology. *Assoc. Soc. Anthropol.*, **1**, 1–24.

GOODY, E. (1972). "Greeting," "begging," and the presentation of respect. In "The Interpretation of Ritual," Ed. J. S. La Fontaine, Tavistock, London.

GOOSEN, C. (1973). Experimental analysis of causal relationships between grooming behaviour and inter-individual proximity in the stump-tailed macaque. *Am. J. Physiol. Anthropol.*, **38**, 531–536.

GORDON, T. P., AND BERNSTEIN, I. S. (1973). Seasonal variation in sexual behavior in all-male rhesus troops. *Am. J. Physiol. Anthropol.*, **38**, 221–226.

GOSS-CUSTARD, J. D., DUNBAR, R. I. M., AND ALDRICH-BLAKE, F. P. G. (1972). Survival, mating and rearing strategies in the evolution of primate social structure. *Folia Primatol.*, **17**, 1–19.

GOTTLIEB, G. (1971). "Development of Species Identification in Birds." The University of Chicago Press, Chicago.

GOULD, J. E., HENEREY, M., AND MacLEOD, M. C. (1970). Communication of direction by the honey bee. *Science*, **169**, 544–554.

GOY, R. W. (1968). Organizing effects of androgen on the behaviour of rhesus monkeys. In "Endocrinology and Human Behaviour," Ed. R. P. Michael, Oxford, London.

——— (1970). Experimental control of psychosexuality. *Philos. Trans. Roy. Soc. Lond. B*, **259**, 149–162.

———, AND GOLDFOOT, D. A. (1973). Experiential and hormonal factors influencing development of sexual behaviour in the male rhesus monkey. In "The Neurosciences, Third Study, Program," M. I. T. Press, Cambridge, Mass.

———, AND PHOENIX, C. H. (1971). The effects of testosterone propionate administered before birth on the development of behavior in genetic female rhesus monkeys. In "Steroid Hormones and Brain Function," Eds. C. H. Sawyer and R. A. Gaski, University of California Press.

GRANT, E. C. (1969). Human facial expression. *Man* (N. S.), **4**, 525–536.

GRAY, J. A. (1971). Sex differences in emotional and cognitive behaviour in mammals including man: adaptive and neural bases. *Acta Psychol.*, **35**, 89–111.

GREEN, S. (in press). Variation of vocal pattern with social situation in the Japanese monkey (*Macaca fuscata*). In "Primate Behavior," vol. 4, Ed. L.

Rosenblum, Academic, New York and London.

GRIFFIN, G. A. (1966). The effects of multiple mothering on the infant-mother and infant-infant affectional systems. Ph.D. thesis, University of Wisconsin, Madison.

GUHL, A. M. (1962). The behaviour of chickens. In "The Behaviour of Domestic Animals," Ed. E. S. E. Hafez, Baillière, London.

GUITON, P. (1961). The influence of imprinting on the agonistic and courtship responses of the brown leghorn cock. *Anim. Behav.*, **9**, 167–177.

GUNDERSEN, E. K. E., AND NELSON, P. (1963). Adaptations of small groups to extreme environments. *Aerosp. Med.*, **34**, 1111–1115.

GUNTHER, M. (1955). Instinct and the nursing couple. *Lancet*, 1955, 575–578.

HAILMAN, J. P. (1967). The ontogeny of an instinct. *Behaviour*, suppl., **15**.

HALL, E. T. (1959). "The Silent Language." Doubleday, New York.

HALL, K. R. L. (1962). The sexual, agonistic and derived social behaviour patterns of the wild chacma baboon *Papio ursinus*. *Proc. Zool. Soc. Lond.*, **139**, 283–327.

——— (1965). Behaviour and ecology of the wild patas monkey, *Erythrocebus patas*, in Uganda. *J. Zool.*, **148**, 15–87.

———, BOELKINS, R. C., AND GOSWELL, M. J. (1965). Behaviour of patas monkeys, *Erythrocebus patas*, in captivity, with notes on the natural habitat. *Folia Primatol.*, **3**, 22–49.

———, AND DEVORE, I. (1965). Baboon social behavior. In DeVore (1965a).

HALL-CRAGGS, J. (1969). The aesthetic content of bird song. In Hinde (1969a).

HAMBURG, D. A. (1971). Crowding, stranger contact and aggressive behaviour. In "Society, Stress and Disease," Ed. L. Levi, vol. 1, pp. 209–218. Oxford University Press.

———, AND LUNDE, D. T. (1966). Sex hormones in the development of sex differences in human behavior. In "The Development of Sex Differences," Ed. E. E. Maccoby, Stanford, Stanford, Calif.

HAMILTON, W. D. (1964). The genetical evolution of social behaviour. *J. Theoret. Biol.*, **7**, 1–52.

HAMPSON, J. L., AND HAMPSON, J. G. (1961). The ontogenesis of sexual behavior in man. In Young (1961).

HAMPTON, J. K., HAMPTON, S. H., AND LANDWEHR, B. T. (1966). Observations on a successful breeding colony of the marmoset *Oedipomidas oedipus*. *Folia Primatol.*, **4**, 265–287.

HANBY, J. P. (1972). The sociosexual nature of mounting and related behaviors in a confined troop of Japanese macaques *(Macaca fuscata)*. Ph.D. thesis, University of Oregon.

———, ROBERTSON, L. T., AND PHOENIX, C. H. (1971). The sexual behaviour of a confined troop of Japanese macaques. *Folia Primatol.*, **16**, 123–143.

HANSEN, E. W. (1966). The development of maternal and infant behavior in the rhesus monkey. *Behaviour*, **27**, 107–149.

———, AND MASON, W. A. (1962). Socially mediated changes in lever-responding of rhesus monkeys. *Psychol. Rep.*, **11**, 647–654.

HARLOW, H. F. (1969). Age-mate or peer affectional system. *Adv. Study Behav.*, **2**, 333–383.

———, AND HARLOW, M. K. (1965). The affectional systems. In "Behavior of Nonhuman Primates," vol. 2, Eds. A. M. Schrier, H. F. Harlow, and F. Stollnitz, Academic, New York and London.

———, AND ——— (1969). Effects of various mother-infant relationships on rhesus monkey behaviors. In "Determinants of Infant Behaviour," vol. 4, Ed. B. M. Foss, Methuen, London.

——, ——, HANSEN, E. W., AND SUOMI, S. J. (1972). Infantile sexuality in monkeys. *Arch. Sex. Behav.*, **2**, 1–7.

——, AND SUOMI, S. J. (1970). Nature of love—simplified. *Am. Psychol.*, **25**, 161–168.

——, AND SUOMI, S. J. (1971a). From thought to therapy: lessons from a primate laboratory. *Am. Sci.*, **59**, 538–549.

——, AND —— (1971b). Social recovery by isolation-reared monkeys. *Proc. Natl. Acad. Sci.*, **68**, 1534–1538.

——, AND ZIMMERMANN, R. R. (1959). Affectional responses in the infant monkey. *Science*, **130**, 421–432.

HARPER, L. V. (1970). Ontogenetic and phylogenetic functions of the parent-offspring relationship in mammals. *Adv. Study Behav.*, **3**, 75–119.

HARRIS, G. W., AND LEVINE, S. (1965). Sexual differentiation of the brain and its experimental control. *J. Physiol.*, **181**, 379–400.

——, MICHAEL, R. P., AND SCOTT, P. P. (1958). Neurological site of action of stilboestrol in eliciting sexual behaviour. In Ciba Foundation Symposium, "Neurological Basis of Behaviour." Churchill, London.

HARTUP, W. W. (1973). Violence in development: the functions of aggression in childhood. In *Address to Amer. Psychol. Ass.*, Montreal.

——, AND DE WIT, J. (Eds.) (in press). "Aggression: origins and determinants." Mouton, The Hague.

HATCH, A., BALAZS, T., WIBERG, G. S., AND GRICE, H. C. (1963). Long-term isolation stress in rats. *Science*, **142**, 507.

HAUGAN, G. M., AND McINTIRE, R. W. (1972). Comparisons of vocal imitation, tactile stimulation and food as reinforcers for infant vocalizations. *Devel. Psychol.*, **6**, 201–209.

HAUSFATER, G. (1972). Intergroup behavior of free-ranging rhesus monkeys (*Macaca mulatta*). *Folia Primatol.*, **18**, 78–107.

HAYES, K. J., AND HAYES, C. (1952). Imitation in a home-raised chimpanzee. *J. Comp. Physiol. Psychol.*, **45**, 450–459.

HAYNES, H., WHITE, B. L., AND HELD, R. (1965). Visual accommodation in human infants. *Science*, **148**, 528–530.

HEBB, D. O. (1949). "The Organization of Behavior." Wiley, New York.

—— (1971). Comment on altruism. *Psychol. Bull.*, **76**, 409–410.

——, LAMBERT, W. E., AND TUCKER, G. R. (1971). Language, thought and experience. *Mod. Lang. J.*, **55**, 212–222.

HEDIGER, H. (1950). "Wild Animals in Captivity." Butterworth, London.

HEILIGENBERG, W. (1973). Personal communication.

——, AND KRAMER, U. (1972). Aggressiveness as a function of external stimulation. *J. Comp. Physiol.*, **77**, 332–340.

HELD, R., AND BAUER, J. (1967). Visually guided reaching in infant monkeys after restricted rearing. *Science*, **155**, 718–720.

HELTNE, P. G., TURNER, D. C., AND WOLHANDLER, J. (1973). Maternal and paternal periods in the development of infant *Collimico goeldii*. *Am. J. Physiol. Anthropol.*, **38**, 555–560.

VAN HEMEL, P. E., AND MYER, J. S. (1970). Satiation of mouse killing by rats in an operant situation. *Psychonom. Sci,.* **21**, 129–130.

HENRY, J. P., MEEHAN, J. P., AND STEPHENS, P. M. (1967). The use of psychosocial stimuli to induce prolonged systolic hypertension in mice. *Psychosom. Med.*, **29**, 408–433.

HERBERT, J. (1968). Sexual preference in the rhesus monkey (*Macaca mulatta*) in the laboratory. *Anim. Behav.*, **16**, 120–128.

——. (1966). The effect of oestrogen applied directly to the genitalia upon the sexual attractiveness of the female rhesus monkey. *Excerpta. Med. Int. Congr.*, **111**, 212.

———— (1970). Hormones and reproductive behaviour in rhesus and talapoin monkeys. *J. Reprod. Fertil.*, suppl., **11**, 119–140.

————, AND TRIMBLE, M. R. (1967). Effect of oestradiol and testosterone on the sexual receptivity and attractiveness of the female rhesus monkey. *Nature*, **216**, 165–166.

HERRNSTEIN, R. J. (1966). Superstition: a corollary of the principles of operant conditioning. In "Operant Behavior," Ed. W. K. Honig, Appleton-Century-Crofts, New York.

HESS, E. H. (1959). Imprinting. *Science*, **130**, 133–141.

HESS, J. P. (1973). Some observations on the sexual behaviour of captive low-land gorillas. In Michael and Crook (1973).

HILL, C. A. (1972). Infant sharing in the family Colobidae emphasizing *Pygathrix*. *Primates 13*.

HINDE, R. A. (1952). The behaviour of the great tit *(Parus major)* and some other related species. *Behaviour*, suppl., **2**.

———— (1953). The conflict between drives in the courtship and copulation of the chaffinch. *Behaviour*, **5**, 1–31.

———— (1956). The biological significance of the territories of birds. *Ibis*, **98**, 340–369.

———— (1959). Behaviour and speciation in birds and lower vertebrates. *Biol. Rev.*, **34**, 85–128.

———— (1960). Energy models of motivation. *Symp. Soc. Exp. Biol.*, **14**, 199–213.

———— (1961) The establishment of the parent-offspring relation in birds, with some mammalian analogies. In "Current Problems in Animal Behaviour," Eds. W. H. Thorpe and O. L. Zangwill, Cambridge, New York and London.

———— (1962). Some aspects of the im-printing problem. *Symp. Zool. Soc. Lond.*, **8**, 129–138.

———— (1965). Interaction of internal and external factors in the integration of canary reproduction. In "Sex and Behavior," Ed. F. A. Beach, Wiley, New York.

———— (1968). Dichotomies in the study of development. In Thoday and Parkes (1968).

———— (Ed.) (1969a). "Bird Vocalizations." Cambridge, New York and London.

———— (1969b). Analysing the roles of the partners in a behavioural interaction — mother-infant relations in rhesus macaques. *Ann. N.Y. Acad. Sci.*, **159**, 651–667.

———— (1970). "Animal Behaviour: A Synthesis of Ethology and Comparative Psychology," 2d ed. McGraw-Hill, New York.

———— (Ed.) (1972a). "Non-verbal Communication." Cambridge, New York and London.

———— (1972b). Social behavior and its development in subhuman primates. Condon Lectures. Oregon State System Higher Education. Eugene, Ore.

———— (in prep.) The concept of function.

————, AND ATKINSON, S. (1970). Assessing the roles of social partners in maintaining mutual proximity, as exemplified by mother/infant relations in monkeys. *Anim. Behav.*, **18**, 169–176.

————, AND DAVIES, L. (1972a). Removing infant rhesus from mother for 13 days compared with removing mother from infant. *J. Child Psychol. Psychiatr.*, **13**, 227–237.

————, AND ———— (1972b). Changes in mother-infant relationship after separation in rhesus monkeys. *Nature*, **239**, 41–42.

————, AND FISHER, J. (1951). Further observations on the opening of milk bottles by birds. *Br. Birds*, **44**, 393–396.

————, AND ROWELL, T. E. (1962). Communication by postures and facial expressions in the rhesus monkey

(*Macaca mulatta*). *Proc. Zool. Soc. Lond.*, **138**, 1–21.

———, ROWELL, T. E., AND SPENCER-BOOTH, Y. (1964). Behaviour of socially living rhesus monkeys in their first six months. *Proc. Zool. Soc. Lond.*, **143**, 609–649.

———, AND SPENCER-BOOTH, Y. (1967a). The behaviour of socially living rhesus monkeys in their first two and a half years. *Anim. Behav.*, **15**, 169–196.

———, AND ——— (1967b). The effect of social companions on mother-infant relations in rhesus monkeys. In "Primate Ethology," Ed. D. Morris, Weidenfeld and Nicolson, London.

———, AND ——— (1970). Individual differences in the responses of rhesus monkeys to a period of separation from their mothers. *J. Child Psychol. Psychiatr.*, **11**, 159–176.

———, AND ——— (1971a). Effects of brief separation from mother on rhesus monkeys. *Science*, **173**, 111–118.

———, AND ——— (1971b). Towards understanding individual differences in rhesus mother-infant interaction. *Anim. Behav.*, **19**, 165–173.

———, AND STEVENSON, J. G. (1969). Goals and response control. In "Development and Evolution of Behavior," vol. 1, Eds. L. R. Aronson, E. Tobach, J. S. Rosenblatt, and D. S. Lehrman, Freeman, San Francisco.

———, AND STEVENSON-HINDE, J. (Eds.) (1973). "Constraints on Learning: Limitations and Predispositions." Academic, London and New York.

———, THORPE, W. H., AND VINCE, M. A. (1956). The following response of young coots and moorhens. *Behaviour*, **9**, 214–242.

———, AND WHITE, L. (1974). The dynamics of a relationship—rhesus monkey ventro-ventral contact. *J. Comp. Physiol. Psychol.*; in proof.

HOCKETT, C. F. (1960). Logical considerations in the study of animal communication. In "Animal Sounds and Communication," Ed. T. A. Sebeok, Indiana University Press, Bloomington.

———, AND ALTMANN, S. A. (1968). A note on design features. In "Animal Communication," Ed. T. A. Sebeok, Indiana University Press, Bloomington, Indiana.

HOFFMAN, H. S., AND KOZMA, F. (1967). Behavioral control by an imprinted stimulus: long-term effects. *J. Exp. Anal. Behav.*, **10**, 495–501.

———, SEARLE, J. L., TOFFEY, S., AND KOZMA, F. (1966). Behavioral control by an imprinted stimulus. *J. Exp. Anal. Behav.*, **9**, 177–189.

HOFFMEISTER, F., AND WUTTKE, W. (1969). On the actions of psychotropic drugs on the attack- and aggressive-defensive behaviour of mice and cats. In Garattini and Sigg (1969).

HOGAN, J. A. (1967). Fighting and reinforcement in the Siamese fighting fish (*Betta splendens*). *J. Comp. Physiol. Psychol.*, **64**, 356–359.

HOKANSON, J. E. (1970). Psychophysiological evaluation of the catharsis hypothesis. In "The Dynamics of Aggression," Eds. E. I. Megargee and J. E. Hokanson. Harper & Row, New York.

HOLST, D. VON (1972). Renal failure as the cause of death in *Tupaiabelangeri* exposed to persistent social stress. *J. Comp. Physiol.*, **78**, 236–273.

HOLST, E. VON, AND SAINT PAUL, U. VON (1963). On the functional organization of drives. *Anim. Behav.*, **11**, 1–20.

HOOFF, J. A. R. A. M. VAN (1962). Facial expressions in higher primates. *Symp. Zool. Soc. Lond.*, **8**, 97–125.

——— (1972). A comparative approach to the phylogeny of laughter and smiling. In Hinde (1972a).

HORN, G., AND HINDE, R. A. (1970). "Short-term Changes in Neural Activity and Behaviour." Cambridge, New York and London.

HOVLAND, C. I., AND SEARS, R. R. (1940). Minor studies in aggression. VI. Correlation of lynchings with economic indices. *J. Pers.,* **9,** 301–310.

HOWARD, H. E. (1920). "Territory in Bird Life." J. Murray, London.

HOWELLS, J. G. (1970). Fallacies in child care. 1. That "separation" is synonymous with "deprivation." *Acta Paedopsychiatr.,* **37,** 3–14.

HRDY, S. B. (in press). The care and exploitation of non-human primate infants by conspecifics other than the mother. *Adv. Study Behav.*

HUBEL, D. H. (1963). The visual cortex of the brain. *Sci. Am.,* November 1963.

———, AND WIESEL, A. N. (1968). Receptive fields and functional architecture of monkey striate cortex. *J. Physiol.,* **195,** 215–243.

HUDGENS, G. A., DENENBERG, V. H., AND ZARROW, M. X. (1967). Mice reared with rats: relations between mothers' activity level and offspring's behavior. *J. Comp. Physiol. Psychol.,* **63,** 304–308.

HUNKELER, C. BOURLIÉRE, F., AND BERTRAND, M. (1972). Le comportement social de la Mone de Lowe (*Cercopithecus campbelli lowei*). *Folia Primatol.,* **17,** 218–236.

HUNSAKER, D. (1962). Ethological isolating mechanisms in the *Scleropus torquatus* group of lizards. *Evolution,* **16,** 62–74.

HUNT, J. McV. (1964). The psychological basis for using pre-school enrichment as an antidote for cultural deprivation. *Merrill-Palmer Q.,* **10,** 209–248.

——— (1967). How children develop intellectually. In "Readings in Human Development," Eds. H. W. Bernard and W. C. Huckins, Allyn & Bacon, Boston. (not consulted).

HUTCHINSON, R. R., AND RENFREW, J. W. (1966). Stalking attack and eating behaviors elicited from the same sites in the hypothalamus. *J. Comp. Physiol. Psychol.,* **61,** 360–367.

———, ULRICH, R. E., AND AZRIN, N. H. (1965). Effects of age and related factors on the pain-aggression reaction.

*J. Comp. Physiol. Psychol.,* **59,** 365–369.

HUTCHISON, J. B. (1969). Changes in hypothalamic responsiveness to testosterone in male Barbary doves (*Streptopelia risoria*). *Nature,* **222,** 176.

HUTT, C. (1970). Specific and diversive exploration. *Adv. Child Devel. Behav.,* **5,** 119–180.

HUTT, S. J., HUTT, C., LENARD, H. G., BERNUTH, H. VON, AND MUNTJEWERFF, W. J. (1968). Auditory responsivity in the human neonate. *Nature,* **218,** 888–890.

ILFIELD, F. W. (1970). Environmental theories of violence. In Daniels et al. (1970).

IMANISHI, K. (1960). Social organization of subhuman primates in their natural habitat. *Curr. Anthropol.,* **1,** 393.

——— (1965). The origin of the human family: A primatological approach. In "Japanese monkeys," Ed. Altmann, S. A., Pub. Altmann, S. A., Alberta, Canada.

IMMELMANN, K. (1969). Song development in the zebra finch and other Estrildid finches. In Hinde (1969a).

ITANI, J. (1958). On the acquisition and propagation of a new food habit in the troop of Japanese monkeys at Takasakiyama. Eng. translation in "Japanese Monkeys, a Collection of Translations," 1965, Ed. S. A. Altmann, Yerkes Regional Primate Center, Atlanta.

——— (1963). Paternal care in the wild Japanese monkey. In "Primate Social Behavior," Ed. C. H. Southwick, Van Nostrand, Princeton, N.J.

———, AND SUZUKI, A. (1967). The social unit of chimpanzees. *Primates,* **8,** 355–381.

IZAWA, K. (1970). Unit groups of chimpanzees and their nomadism in the savannah woodland. *Primates,* **11,** 1–46.

JAMES, W. (1892). "Textbook of Psychology." Macmillan, London.

JAMES, W. T., AND GILBERT, T. F. (1956). The effect of social facilitation on food intake of puppies fed separately and together for the first ninety days of life. *Br. J. Anim. Behav.*, **3**, 131–133.

JAY, P. (1965). The common langur in Northern India. In DeVore (1965).

———— (Ed.) (1968). "Primates." Holt, New York.

JENSEN, G. D. (1965). Mother-infant relationship in the monkey *Macaca nemestrina*: development of specificity of maternal response to own infant. *J. Comp. Physiol. Psychol.*, **59**, 305–308.

————, BOBBITT, R. A., AND GORDON, B. N. (1968). Effects of environment on the relationship between mother and infant pigtailed monkeys (*Macaca nemestrina*). *J. Comp. Physiol. Psychol.*, **66**, 259–263.

————, AND TOLMAN, C. W. (1962). Mother-infant relationship in the monkey *Macaca nemestrina*: the effect of brief separation and mother-infant specificity. *J. Comp. Physiol. Psychol.*, **55**, 131–136.

JEWELL, P. A. (1966). The concept of home range in mammals. *Symp. Zool. Soc. Lond.*, **18**, 85–110.

JOHNSON, D. L. (1967). Honey bees: do they use the direction information contained in their dance maneuver? *Science*, **155**, 844–847.

JOHNSON, R. N. (1972). "Aggression in Man and Animals." Saunders, Philadelphia.

JOLLY, A. (1966). "Lemur Behavior." The University of Chicago Press, Chicago.

———— (1972a). Troop continuity and troop spacing in *Propithecus verreauxi* and *Lemur catta* at Berenty (Madagascar). *Folia Primatol.*, **17**, 335–362.

———— (1972b). "The Evolution of Primate Behavior." Macmillan, New York.

JOSLIN, J., FLETCHER, H., AND EMLEN, J. (1964). A comparison of the responses to snakes of lab- and wild-reared rhesus macaques. *Anim. Behav.*, **12**, 348–352.

KAGAN, J., AND LEWIS, M. (1965). Studies of attention in the human infant. *Merrill-Palmer Q.*, **11**, 95–122.

————, (1970). Attention and psychological change in the child. *Science*, **170**, 826–832.

————, HENKER, B. A., HEN-TOV, A., LEVINE, J., AND LEWIS, M. (1966). Infants' differential reactions to familiar and distorted faces. *Child Devel.*, **37**, 519–532.

————, AND TULKIN, S. R. (1971). Social class differences in child rearing during the first year. In Schaffer (1971a).

KAHN, M. W. (1951). The effect of severe defeat at various age levels on the aggressive behavior of mice. *J. Genet. Psychol.*, **79**, 117–130.

KANAGAWA, H., AND HAFEZ, E. S. E. (1973). Copulatory behavior in relation to anatomical characteristics of three macaques. *Am. J. Physiol. Anthropol.*, **38**, 233–240.

KAPLAN, J. (1970). The effects of separation and reunion on the behavior of mother and infant squirrel monkeys. *Devel. Psychobiol.*, **3**, 43–52.

KARCZMAR, A. G., AND SCUDDER, C. L. (1969). Aggression and neurochemical changes in different strains and genera of mice. In Garattini and Sigg (1969).

KAUFMAN, I. C., AND HINDE, R. A. (1961). Factors influencing distress calling in chicks, with special reference to temperature changes and social isolation. *Anim. Behav.*, **9**, 197–204.

————, AND ROSENBLUM, L. A. (1969a). Effects of separation from mother on the emotional behavior of infant monkeys. *Ann. N.Y. Acad. Sci.*, **159**, 681–695.

————, AND ———— (1969b). The waning of the mother-infant bond in two species of macaque. In "Determinants of Infant Behaviour," vol. 4, Ed. B. M. Foss, Methuen, London.

KAUFMANN, J. H. (1962). Ecology and social behavior of the Coati, *Nasua narica* on Barro Colorado Island, Panama. *Univ. Calif. Publ. Zool.,* **60,** 95–222.

———— (1965). A 3-year study of mating behavior in a free ranging band of rhesus monkeys. *Ecology,* **46,** 500–512.

———— (1967). Social relations of adult males in a free-ranging band of rhesus monkeys. In Altmann (1967a).

KAWABE, M. (1970). A preliminary study of the wild Siamang gibbon *(Hylobates syndactylus)* at Fraser's Hill, Malaysia. *Primates,* **11,** 285–291.

KAWAI, M. (1958). On the system of social ranks in a natural group of Japanese monkeys. *Primates,* **1,** 111–148.

———— (1963). On the newly acquired behaviors of the natural troop of Japanese monkeys on Koshima Island. *Primates,* **4,** 113–115.

———— (1965a). Newly acquired pre-cultural behavior of the natural troop of Japanese monkeys on Koshima island. *Primates,* **6,** 1–30.

———— (1965b). On the system of social ranks in a natural troop of Japanese monkeys, 1. Basic rank and dependent rank. In "Japanese Monkeys: a Collection of Translations," Eds. K. Imanishi and S. A. Altmann, Yerkes Regional Primate Center, Atlanta, Ga.

KAWAMURA, S. (1958). Matriarchal social ranks in the Minoo-B troop: a study of the rank system of Japanese monkeys. *Primates,* **2,** 181–252.

———— (1963). The process of sub-culture propagation among Japanese macaques. In "Primate Social Behaviour," Ed. E. Southwick, Van Nostrand, Princeton, N. J.

KEAR, J. (1962). Food selection in finches with special reference to interspecific differences. *Proc. Zool. Soc. Lond.,* **138,** 163–204.

KELLOGG, W. N., AND KELLOGG, L. (1933). "The Ape and the Child: a study of Environmental Influence upon Early Behavior." McGraw-Hill, New York.

KENDON, A. (1973). A description of some human greetings. In Michael and Crook (1973).

KESSEN, W., AND MANDLER, G. (1961). Anxiety, pain and the inhibition of distress. *Psychol. Rev.,* **68,** 396–404.

KING, J. A. (1956). Sexual behaviour of C$_{57}$BL/10 mice and its relation to early social experience. *J. Genet. Psychol.,* **88,** 223–229.

———— (1957). Relation between early social experience and adult aggressive behaviour in inbred mice. *J. Genet. Psychol.,* **90,** 151–166.

————, AND GURNEY, N. L. (1954). Effect of early social experience on adult aggressive behavior in C$_{57}$BL/10 mice. *J. Comp. Physiol. Psychol.,* **47,** 326–330.

KINSEY, A. C., POMEROY, W. B., AND MARTIN, C. E. (1948). "Sexual Behavior in the Human Male." Saunders, Philadelphia.

KISLACK, J. W., AND BEACH, F. A. (1955). Inhibition of aggressiveness by ovarian hormones. *Endocrinology,* **56,** 684–692.

KLAUS, M. H., AND KENNELL, J. H. (1970). Mothers separated from their newborn infants. *Pediatr. Clin. N. Am.,* **17,** 1015–1037.

KLEIN, L. (1971). Observations on copulation and seasonal reproduction in two species of spider monkeys, *Ateles belzebuth* and *A. geoffroyi. Folia Primatol.,* **15,** 233–248.

KLEIN, M. (1948). "Contributions to Psycho-analysis, 1921–1945." Hogarth, London.

KLOPFER, P. H. (1959). Social interactions in discrimination learning with special reference to feeding behavior in birds. *Behaviour,* **14,** 282–299.

——— (1970). Discrimination of young in galagos. *Folia Primatol.*, **13**, 137–143.

———, AND JOLLY, A. (1970). The stability of territorial boundaries in a lemur troop. *Folia Primatol.*, **12**, 199–208.

KNIGHT, W. R., HOLTZ, J. R., AND SPROGIS, G. R. (1963). Acetophenazine and fighting behavior in mice. *Science*, **141**, 830.

KOFORD, C. B. (1963). Rank of mothers and sons in bands of rhesus monkeys. *Science*, **141**, 356–357.

KOHLBERG, L. (1969). Stage and sequence: the cognitive-developmental approach to socialization. In "Handbook of Socialization Theory and Research," Ed. D. A. Goslin, Rand McNally, Chicago.

KÖHLER, O. (1952). "Wolfskinder", Affen im Haus und vergleichende Verhaltensforschung. *Folia Phoniatr.*, **4**, 29–53.

——— (1955). "Zahlende" Voegel und vergleichende Verhaltensforschung. Acta XI Congr. Ornithol., **1954**, 588–598.

KONISHI, M. (1963). The role of auditory feedback in the vocal behavior of the domestic fowl. *Z. Tierpsychol.*, **20**, 349–367.

———, AND NOTTEBOHM, F. (1969). Experimental studies in the ontogeny of avian vocalizations. In Hinde (1969a).

KORNER, A. F., AND THOMAN, E. B. (1970). Visual alertness in neonates as evoked by maternal care. *J. Exp. Child Psychol.*, **10**, 67–78.

KORTMULDER, K. (1968). An ethological theory of the incest taboo and exogamy. *Curr. Anthropol.*, **9**, 437–449.

KOVACK, J. K. (1964). Effects of autonomic drugs on imprinting. *J. Comp. Physiol. Psychol.*, **57**, 183–187.

KOYAMA, N. (1967). On dominance rank and kinship of a wild Japanese monkey troop in Arashiyama. *Primates*, **8**, 189–216.

——— (1970). Changes in dominance rank and division of a wild Japanese mon-key troop in Arashiyama. *Primates*, **11**, 335–390.

——— (1971). Observations on mating behavior of wild Siamang gibbons at Fraser's Hill, Malaysia. *Primates*, **12**, 183–190.

KREBS, D. L. (1970). Altruism—an examination of the concept and a review of the literature. *Psychol. Bull.*, **73**, 258–302.

——— (1972). Intrahuman altruism. *Psychol. Bull.*, **76**, 411–414.

KRON, R. E., STEIN, M., AND GODDARD, K. E. (1963). A method of measuring sucking behavior of newborn infants. *Psychosomat. Med.*, **25**, 181–191.

KRŠIAK, M., AND JANKU, I. (1969). The development of aggressive behaviour by mice in isolation. In Garattini and Sigg, 1969.

———, AND STEINBERG, H. (1969). Psychopharmacological aspects of aggression. *J. Psychosomat. Res.*, **13**, 243–252.

KRUIJT, J. P. (1964). Ontogeny of social behaviour in Burmese red junglefowl. *Behaviour*, suppl. 12.

KULKA, A. M. (1968). Observations and data on mother-infant interaction. *Israel Ann. Psychiatr. & Allied Disciplines*, **1**, 70–83.

KUMMER, H. (1957). Soziales Verhalten einer Mantelpavian-Gruppe. *Beih. Schweiz. Z. Psychol. ihre Anwend.*, **33**, 1–91.

——— (1967). Tripartite relations in hamadryas baboons. In Altmann (1967a).

——— (1968). "Social Organization of Hamadryas Baboons." The University of Chicago Press, Chicago.

——— (1971). "Primate Societies: Group Techniques of Ecological Adaptation." Aldine-Atherton, Inc., Chicago.

———, AND KURT, F. (1963). Social units of a free-living population of Hamadryas baboons. *Folia Primat.*, **1**, 4–19.

KUO, Z. Y. (1967). "The Dynamics of

Behavior Development." Random House, New York.

LA BARRE, W. (1947). The cultural basis of emotions and gestures. *J. Pers.*, **16**.

—— (1964). Paralinguistics, kinesics and cultural anthropology. In "Approaches to Semiotics," Eds. T. A. Sebeok, A. S. Hayes, and M. C. Bateson, Mouton, The Hague.

LACK, D. (1939). The behaviour of the robin: I and II. *Proc. Zool. Soc. Lond., A*, **109**, 169–178.

—— (1966). "Population Studies of Birds." Oxford, New York and London.

—— (1968). "Ecological Adaptations for Breeding in Birds." Methuen, London.

—— (1969). Of birds and men. *New Sci.*, 16 Jan. 1969, 121–122.

LADE, B. I., AND THORPE, W. H. (1964). Dove songs as innately coded patterns of specific behaviour. *Nature*, **202**, 366–368.

LAGERSPETZ, K. (1964). Studies on the aggressive behaviour of mice. *Suom. Tiedeakat. Toim. Ann. Acad. Sci. Fenn., B*, **131**, 1–131.

—— (1969). Aggression and aggresiveness in laboratory mice. In Garattini and Sigg (1969).

LANCASTER, J. B. (1971). Play mothering: the relations between juvenile females and young infants among free-ranging vervet monkeys (*Cercopithecus aethiops*). *Folia Primat.* **15**, 161–182.

——, AND LEE, R. (1965). The annual reproductive cycle in monkeys and apes. In DeVore (1965).

LARSSON, K. (1967). Testicular hormone and developmental changes in mating behaviour of the male rat. *J. Comp. Physiol. Psychol.*, **63**, 223–230.

LÁT, J., WIDDOWSON, E. M., AND McCANCE, R. A. (1960). Some effects of accelerating growth. III. Behaviour and ner-

vous activity. *Proc. Roy. Soc. B.*, **153**, 347–356.

LAWICK-GOODALL, J. VAN (1968). Behaviour of free-living chimpanzees of the Gombe Stream area. *Anim. Behav. Monogr.*, **3**.

—— (1971a). "In the Shadow of Man." Houghton Mifflin, Boston.

—— (1971b). Some aspects of mother-infant relationships in a group of wild chimpanzees. In Schaffer (1971a).

LEACH, E. R. (1962). On certain unconsidered aspects of double descent systems. *Man*, **62**, 130–134.

—— (1972). The influence of cultural context on non-verbal communication in man. In Hinde (1972a).

LEHRMAN, D. S. (1965). Interaction between internal and external environments in the regulation of the reproductive cycle of the ring dove. In "Sex and Behavior," Ed. F. A. Beach, Wiley, New York.

—— (1970). Semantic and conceptual issues in the nature-nurture problem. In "Development and Evolution of Behavior," Eds. L. R. Aronson, E. Tobach, D. S. Lehrman, and J. S. Rosenblatt, Freeman, San Francisco.

LEMMON, W. B. (1971). Deprivation and enrichment in the development of primates. *Proc. 3d Int. Congr. Primatol., Zurich, 1970*, **3**, 108–115.

LENNEBERG, E. H. (1967). "Biological Foundations of Languages." Wiley, New York.

LESKES, A., AND ACHESON, N. H. (1971). Social organisation of a free-ranging troop of Black and White Colobus monkeys (*Colobus abyssinicus*). *Proc. 3d Int. Congr. Primatol., Zurich, 1970*, **3**, 22–31.

LEVINE, L., BARSEL, G. E., AND DRAKOW, C. A. (1965). Interaction of aggressive and sexual behavior in male mice. *Behaviour*, **25**, 272–280.

LEVINE, S. (1967). Maternal and environmental influences on the adrenocortical response to stress in weanling rats. *Science*, **156**, 258–260.

—— (1969). An endocrine theory of infantile stimulation. In Ambrose (1969).

Lévi-Strauss, C. (1966). The culinary triangle. *New Soc.*, 22 Dec., 937–940.

Lieberson, S., and Silverman, A. R. (1965). The precipitants and underlying conditions of race riots. *Am. Sociol. Rev.*, **30**, 887–898.

Lincoln, G. A., Youngson, R. W., and Short, R. V. (1970). The social and sexual behaviour of the red deer stag. *J. Reprod. Fertil.*, suppl., **11**, 71–103.

Lindburg, D. G. (1971). The rhesus monkey in North India: an ecological and behavioral study. In "Primate Behavior," vol. 2, Ed. L. A. Rosenblum, Academic, New York and London.

Linton, R. (1936). "The Study of Man: an Introduction." Appleton-Century-Crofts, New York.

Lipsitt, L. P. (1966). Learning processes of human newborns. *Merrill-Palmer Q.*, **12**, 45–71.

Lisk, R. D. (1962). Testosterone sensitive centers in the hypothalamus of the rat. *Acta Endocrinol.*, **41**, 195–204.

Littenberg, R., Tulkin, S. R., and Kagan, J. (1971). Cognitive components of separation anxiety. *Devel. Psychol.*, **4**, 387–388.

Lorenz, K. (1931). Beiträge zur Ethologie sozialer Corviden. *J. Ornithol.*, **79**, translated in "Studies in Animal and Human Behaviour," vol. I, Ed. R. B. Martin, Harvard, Cambridge, Mass.

—— (1935). Der Kumpan in der Umwelt des Vogels. *J. Ornithol.*, **83**, 137–213, 289–413, translated in "Studies in Animal and Human Behaviour," vol. I, Ed. R. B. Martin, Harvard, Cambridge, Mass.

—— (1943). Die angeborenen Formen möglicher Erfahrung. *Z. Tierpsychol.*, **5**, 235–409.

—— (1950). The comparative method in studying innate behaviour patterns. *Symp. Soc. Exp. Biol.*, **4**, 221–268.

—— (1965). "Evolution and Modification of Behaviour." The University of Chicago Press, Chicago.

—— (1966). "On Aggression." Methuen, London.

Loy, J. (1970a). Behavioral responses of free-ranging rhesus monkeys to food shortage. *Am. J. Phys. Anthropol.*, **33**, 263–271.

—— (1970b). Perimenstrual sexual behavior among rhesus monkeys. *Folia Primatol.*, **13**, 286–297.

—— (1971). Estrous behavior of free-ranging rhesus monkeys. *Primates*, **12**, 1–31.

Lyons, J. (1972). "Human Language." In Hinde (1972a).

McCall, G. J., and Simmons, J. L. (1966). "Identities and Interactions." Collier-Macmillan, New York. Excerpts in "Sociological Perspectives," 1971, Eds. K. Thompson and J. Tunstall, Penguin, Harmonsworth.

McCall, R. B., and Kagan, J. (1969). Individual differences in the infant's distribution of attention to stimulus discrepancy. *Devel. Psychol.*, **2**, 90–98.

——, and Melson, W. H. (1969). Attention in infants as a function of magnitude of discrepancy and habituation rate. *Psychonom. Sci.*, **17**, 317–319.

McClintock, M. K. (1971). Menstrual synchrony and suppression. *Nature*, **229**, 244–245.

McCord, W., McCord, J., and Howard, A. (1961). Familial correlates of aggression in nondelinquent male children. *J. Abnorm. Soc. Psychol.*, **63**, 493–503.

McDonald, A. L., Heimstra, N. W., and Damkot, D. K. (1968). Social modification of agonistic behavior in fish. *Anim. Behav.*, **16**, 437–441.

MacDonnell, M. F., and Flynn, J. P. (1966). Sensory control of hypothalamic attack. *Anim. Behav.*, **14**, 399–405.

McDougall, W. (1923). "An Outline of Psychology." Methuen, London.

McGinnis, L. (in prep.). Analysis of factors involved in mother-infant separation in rhesus monkeys. Ph.D. thesis, Cambridge University.

McGinnis, P. (1973). Sexual behaviour of chimpanzees. Ph.D. thesis, Cambridge University.

McGrew, W. C. (1972). "An Ethological study of children's behaviour." Academic, New York and London.

——— (1972). Aspects of social development in nursery school children, with emphasis on introduction to the group. In Blurton Jones (1972a).

MacKay, D. M. (1972). Formal analysis of communicative processes. In Hinde (1972a).

McKinney, W. T., Suomi, S. J., and Harlow, H. F. (1971). Depression in primates. *Am. J. Psychiatr.*, **127**, 1313–1320.

Marler, P. (1956a). Behaviour of the chaffinch *(Fringilla coelebs). Behaviour,* suppl. **5**, 1–184.

——— (1956b). Studies of fighting in chaffinches. 3. Proximity as a cause of aggression. *Br. J. Anim. Behav.*, **4**, 23–30.

——— (1959). Developments in the study of animal communication. In "Darwin's Biological Work," Ed. P. R. Bell, Cambridge, New York and London.

——— (1960). Bird songs and mate selection. In "Animal Sounds and Communication." American Institute of Biological Sciences, vol. 7, pp. 348–367.

——— (1965). Communication in monkeys and apes. In DeVore 1965a).

——— (1968). Aggregation and dispersal: two functions in primate communication. In Jay (1968).

——— (1970). A comparative approach to vocal learning: song development in white-crowned sparrows. *J. Comp.*

*Physiol. Psychol.*, **71**, Monogr., 1–25.

———, and Hamilton, W. J. (1966). "Mechanisms of Animal Behavior." Wiley, New York.

Marsden, H. M. (1968). Agonistic behaviour of young rhesus monkeys after changes induced in social rank of their mothers. *Anim. Behav.*, **16**, 38–44.

——— (1969). Dominance order reversal of two groups of rhesus monkeys in tunnel-connected enclosures. *Proc. 2d Int. Congr. Primatol.*, **1**, 52–58.

Mason, W. A. (1960). The effects of social restriction on the behavior of rhesus monkeys. 1. Free social behaviour. *J. Comp. Physiol. Psychol.*, **53**, 582–589.

——— (1961a). The effects of social restriction on the behavior of rhesus monkeys. 2. Tests of gregariousness. *J. Comp. Physiol. Psychol.*, **54**, 287–290.

——— (1961b). The effects of social restriction on the behavior of rhesus monkeys. 3. Dominance tests. *J. Comp. Physiol. Psychol.*, **54**, 694–699.

——— (1962). The effects of social restriction on the behavior of rhesus monkeys. 4. Responses to a novel environment and to an alien species. *J. Comp. Physiol. Psychol.*, **55**, 363–368.

——— (1965). The social behavior of monkeys and apes. In DeVore (1965a).

——— (1967). Motivational aspects of social responsiveness in young chimpanzees. In "Early Behavior," Ed. M. W. Stevenson, Wiley, New York.

——— (1968). Use of space by *Callicebus* groups. In Jay (1968).

——— (1973). Field and laboratory studies of social organization in *Saimiri* and *Callicebus*. In "Primate Behavior," vol. 2, Ed. L. A. Rosenblum, Academic, New York and London.

———, and Berkson, G. (1962). Conditions affecting vocal responsiveness of infant chimpanzees. *Science,* **137,** 127–128.

———, AND HARLOW, H. F. (1958). Learned approach by infant rhesus monkeys to the sucking situation. *Psychol. Rep.,* **4,** 79–82.

———, AND ——— (1959). Initial responses of infant rhesus monkeys to solid foods. *Psychol. Rep.,* **5,** 193–199.

———, ———, AND RUEPING, R. R. (1959). The development of manipulatory responsiveness in the infant rhesus monkey. *J. Comp. Physiol. Psychol.,* **52,** 555–558.

———, HILL, S. D., AND THOMSEN, C. E. (1971). Perceptual factors in the development of filial attachment. *Proc. 3d Int. Congr. Primatol., Zurich, 1970,* **3,** 125–133.

———, AND HOLLIS, J. H. (1962). Communication between young rhesus monkeys. *Anim. Behav.,* **10,** 211–221.

MASSERMAN, J. H., WECHKIN, S., AND TERRIS, W. (1964). "Altruistic" behavior in rhesus monkeys. *Am. J. Psychiatr.,* **121,** 584–585.

MATTINGLY, I. G. (1972). Speech cues and sign stimuli. *Am. Sci.,* **60,** 327–337.

MAYER, A. C. (1966). The significance of quasi-groups in the study of complex societies. *Assoc. Soc. Anthropol.,* **4,** 97–122.

MAYNARD SMITH, J. (1965). The evolution of alarm calls. *Am. Nat.,* **99,** 59–63.

MAXIM, P. E., AND BUETTNER-JANISCH, J. (1963). A field study of the Kenya baboon. *Am. J. Phys. Anthropol.,* **21,** 165–180.

MEGARGEE, E. I. (1966). Undercontrolled and overcontrolled personality types in extreme antisocial aggression. *Psychol. Monogr.,* **80,** no. 611.

———, AND HOKANSON, J. E. (1970). "The Dynamics of Aggression." Harper & Row, New York.

MEHRABIAN, A. (1969). Significance of posture and position in the communication of attitude and status re-

lationships. *Psychol. Bull.,* **71,** 359–372.

MENZEL, E. W. (1964). Responsiveness to object-movement in young chimpanzees. *Behaviour,* **24,** 147–160.

——— (1966). Responsiveness to objects in free-ranging Japanese monkeys. *Behaviour,* **26,** 130–150.

——— (1971). Communication about the environment in a group of young chimpanzees. *Folia Primatol.,* **15,** 220–232.

——— (1972). Spontaneous invention of ladders in a group of young chimpanzees. *Folia Primatol.,* **17,** 87–106.

——— (in press). A group of young chimpanzees. In "Behavior of Nonhuman Primates," vol. 5, Eds. A. Schrier and F. Stollnitz.

———, DAVENPORT, R. K., AND ROGERS, C. M. (1970). The development of tool using in wild-born and restriction-reared chimpanzees. *Folia Primatol.,* **12,** 273–283.

———, ———, AND ——— (1972). Protocultural aspects of chimpanzees' responsiveness to novel objects. *Folia Primatol.,* **17,** 161–170.

MERRIEN, J. (1954). "Lonely Voyagers." Putnam, London.

MICHAEL, R. P. (1968). Gonadal hormones and the control of primate behaviour. In "Endocrinology and Human Behaviour," Ed. R. P. Michael, Oxford, New York and London.

——— (1971). Neuroendocrine factors regulating primate behaviour. In "Frontiers in Neuroendocrinology," Eds. L. Martini and W. F. Genong, Oxford, New York and London.

———, AND CROOK, J. H. (Eds.) (1973). "Comparative Ecology and Behaviour of Primates." Academic Press, London.

———, AND HERBERT, J. (1963). Menstrual cycle influences grooming behaviour and sexual activity in the rhesus monkey. *Science,* **140,** 500–501.

———, AND KEVERNE, E. B. (1968). Pheromones in the communication of sexual status in primates. *Nature*, **218**, 746–749.

———, AND WELEGALLA, J. (1968). Ovarian hormones and the sexual behaviour of the female rhesus monkey (*Macaca mulatta*) under laboratory conditions. *J. Endocr.* **41**, 407–420.

———, WILSON, M., AND PLANT, T. M. (1973). Sexual behaviour of male primates and the rôle of testosterone. In Michael and Crook (1973).

———, AND ZUMPE, D. (1970). Sexual initiating behaviour by female rhesus monkeys (*Macaca mulatta*) under laboratory conditions. *Behaviour*, **36**, 168–186.

MICHENER, C. D. (1969). Comparative social behavior of bees. *Ann. Rev. Entomol.*, **14**, 299–342.

MILLER, M. H., KLING, A., AND DICKS, D. (1973). Familial interactions of male rhesus monkeys in a semi-free-ranging troop. *Am. J. Physiol. Anthropol.*, **38**, 605–612.

MILLER, N. E. (1959). Liberalization of basic S-R concepts. In "Psychology, a Study of a Science," Study 1, vol. 2, Ed. S. Koch, McGraw-Hill, New York.

MILLER, R. E., CAUL, W. F., AND MIRSKY, I. F. (1967). Communication of affect between feral and socially isolated monkeys. *J. Pers. Soc. Psychol.*, **7**, 231–239.

MISSAKIAN, E. A. (1969). Reproductive behavior of socially deprived rhesus monkeys. *J. Comp. Physiol. Psychol.*, **69**, 403–407.

——— (1973). The timing of fission among free-ranging rhesus monkeys. *Am. J. Physiol. Anthropol.*, **38**, 621–624.

MITCHELL, G. D. (1968). Persistent behavior pathology in rhesus monkeys following early social isolation. *Folia Primatol.*, **8**, 132–147.

——— (1969). Paternalistic behaviour in primates. *Psychol. Bull.*, **71**, 399–417.

———, AND BRANDT, E. M. (1972). Paternal behavior in primates. In "Primate Socialization," Ed. F. Poirier, New York, Random House.

———, AND STEVENS, C. W. (1969). Primiparous and multiparous monkey mothers in a mildly stressful social situation: first 3 months. *Devel. Psychobiol.*, **1**, 280–286.

MØLLER, G. W., HARLOW, H. F., AND MITCHELL, G. D. (1968). Factors affecting agonistic communication in rhesus monkeys (*Macaca mulatta*). *Behaviour*, **31**, 339–357.

MOLTZ, H., AND STETTNER, L. J. (1961). The influence of patterned-light deprivation on the critical period for imprinting. *J. Comp. Physiol. Psychol.*, **54**, 279–283.

MONEY, J. W. (1961). Sex hormones and human eroticism. In Young (1961).

———, AND EHRHARDT, A. A. (1968). Prenatal hormonal exposure: possible effects on behaviour in man. In "Endocrinology and Human Behaviour," Ed. R. P. Michael, Oxford, New York and London.

———, ———, (1972). "Man and Woman, Boy and Girl." Johns Hopkins University Press, Baltimore and London.

MOORE, C. R. (1942). The physiology of the testis and the application of male sex hormone. *J. Urol.*, **47**, 31–44.

MORGAN, B. J. T. (1973). Cluster analyses of two acoustic confusion matrices. *Percept. Psychophys.*, **13**, 13–24.

MOSS, H. A., ROBSON, K. S., AND PEDERSEN, F. (1969). Determinants of maternal stimulation of infants and consequences of treatment for later reactions to strangers. *Devel. Psychol.*, **1**, 239–246.

MOYER, K. E. (1968). Kinds of aggression and their physiological basis. *Commun. Behav. Biol.*, **2**, 65–87.

MOYNIHAN, M. (1955). Some aspects of reproductive behavior in the black-headed gull (*Larus ridibundus* L.) and related species. *Behaviour*, suppl. **4**, 1–201.

——— (1970). Control, suppression, decay, disappearance and replacement of displays. *J. Theor. Biol.*, **29**, 85–112.

MUGFORD, R. A., AND NOWELL, N. W. (1971). Endocrine control over production and activity of the anti-aggression pheromone from female mice. *J. Endocrinol.*, **49**, 225–232.

MULLIGAN, J. A. (1966). Singing behavior and its development in the song sparrow *(Melospiza melodia)*. *Univ. Calif. Publ. Zool.*, **81**, 1–76.

NADEL, S. F. (1957). "The Theory of Social Structure." Free Press, New York.

NADLER, R. D., AND ROSENBLUM, L. E. (1973). Sexual behavior during successive ejaculations in bonnet and pigtail macaques. *Am. J. Phys. Anthropol.*, **38**, 217–220.

NAGEL, U. (1971). Social organization in a baboon hybrid zone. *Proc. 2d Int. Congr. Primatol., Zurich, 1970,* **3**, 48–57.

NELSON, J. B. (1964). Factors influencing clutch-size and chick growth in the North Atlantic gannet, *Sula bassana. Ibis,* **106**, 63–77.

NELSON, K. (1964). The temporal patterning of courtship behaviour in the glandulocaudine fishes (Ostariophysi, Characidae). *Behaviour,* **24**, 90–146.

NEWCOMB, T. M. (1952). "Social Psychology." Tavistock, London.

NEWSON, J., AND NEWSON, E. (1963). Four years old in an urban community. Allen and Unwin, London.

NEWTON, I. (1967). The adaptive radiation and feeding ecology of some British finches. *Ibis,* **109**, 33–98.

NICOLAI, J. (1964). Der Brutparasitismus der Viduinae als ethologisches Problem. *Z. Tierpsychol.,* **21**, 129–204.

NISHIDA, T. (1966). A sociological study of solitary male monkeys. *Primates,* **7**, 141–204.

—— (1968). The social group of wild chimpanzees in the Mahali mountains. *Primates,* **9**, 167–227.

—— (1970). Social behaviour and relationship among wild chimpanzees of the Mahali mountains. *Primates,* **11**, 47–87.

NOIROT, E. (1972). The onset of maternal behavior in rats, hamsters, and mice: a selective review. *Adv. Study Behav.,* **4**, 107–146.

——, AND RICHARDS, M. P. M. (1966). Maternal behaviour in virgin female golden hamsters. Changes consequent upon initial contact with pups. *Anim. Behav.,* **14**, 7–10.

NORIKOSHI, K. (1971). Tests to determine the responsiveness of free-ranging Japanese monkeys in food-getting situations. *Primates,* **12**, 113–124.

NOTTEBOHM, F. (1970). Ontogeny of bird song. *Science,* **167**, 950–956.

—— (1972a). Neural lateralization of vocal control in a passerine bird. II. Subsong, calls, and a theory of vocal learning. *J. Exp. Zool.,* **179**, 35–49.

—— (1972b). The origins of vocal learning. *Am. Nat.,* **106**, 116–140.

——, AND NOTTEBOHM, M. (1971). Vocalizations and breeding behaviour of surgically deafened ring doves, *Streptopelia risoria. Anim. Behav.,* **19**, 313–328.

OVERALL, J. E. (1964). Note on the scientific status of factors. *Psychol. Bull.,* **61**, 270–276.

OWENS, N. W. (1973). The development of behaviour in free-living baboons. Ph.D. thesis, Cambridge University.

PAPOUSEK, H. (1966). Conditioning during early postnatal development. In "Behavior in Infancy and Early Childhood," Eds. Y. Brackbill and G. G. Thompson, Free Press, New York.

PARKES, A. S. (1968). Seasonal variation in human sexual activity. In Thoday and Parkes (1968).

PARSONS, T. (1951). "The Social System." Free Press, Glencoe, Ill.

PATERSON, J. D. (1973). Ecologically differentiated patterns of aggressive and sexual behavior in two troops of Ugandan baboons, *Papio anubis. Am. J. Phys. Anthropol.*, **38**, 641–648.

PATTERSON, G. R., AND COBB, J. A. (1971). A dyadic analysis of "aggressive" behaviors. In *Minn. Symp. Child Psychol., Ed. J. P. Hill*, **5**, 72–129

PAYNE, A. P., AND SWANSON, H. H. (1971). Hormonal control of aggressive dominance in the female hamster. *Physiol. Behav.*, **6**, 355–357.

PELKWIJK, J. J. TER, AND TINBERGEN, N. (1937). Eine reizbiologische Analyse einiger Verhaltensweisen von *Gasterosteus aculeatus* L. *Z. Tierpsychol.*, **1**, 193–200.

PETTER, J. (1965). The lemurs of Madagascar. In DeVore (1965a).

PHOENIX, C. H. (1973). The role of testosterone in the sexual behavior of laboratory male rhesus. *Proc. IVth Int. Cong. Primatol.*, Oregon.

PIAGET, J., AND INHELDER, B. (1948; Eng. trans., 1956). "The Child's Conception of Space." Routledge, London.

—— (1953). "The Origins of Intelligence in the Child." Routledge and Kegan Paul, London.

PITELKA, F. A. (1949). Numbers, breeding schedule, and territoriality in pectoral sandpipers in Northern Alaska. *Condor*, **61**, 233–264.

PLOOG, D. W., BLITZ, J., AND PLOOG, F. (1963). Studies on social and sexual behaviour of the squirrel monkey *(Siamiri sciureus). Folia Primatol.*, **1**, 29–66.

PLOTNIK, R., KING, F. A., AND ROBERTS, L. (1968). Effect of competition on the aggressive behavior of squirrel and cebus monkeys. *Behaviour*, **32**, 315–332.

PLUTCHIK, R. (1964). The study of social behavior in primates. *Folia Primatol.*, **2**, 67–92.

POIRIER, F. E. (1968). The Nilgor langur *(Presbytis johnii)* mother-infant dyad. *Primates*, **9**, 45–68.

—— (1970a). Dominance structure of the Nilgiri langur *(Presbytis johnii)* of South India. *Folia Primatol.*, **12**, 161–186.

—— (1970b). The communication matrix of the Nilgiri langur *(Presbytis johnii)* of South India. *Folia Primatol.*, **13**, 92–136.

PRECHTL, H. F. R. (1958). The directed head turning response and allied movements of the human baby. *Behaviour*, **13**, 212–242.

—— (1965). Problems of behavioural studies in the newborn infant. *Adv. Study Behav.*, **1**, 75–99.

—— AND LENARD, H. G. (1967). A study of eye movements in sleeping newborn infants. *Brain Res.*, **5**, 477–493.

PREMACK, D. (1965). Reinforcement theory. In "Nebraska Symposium on Motivation," Ed. D. Levine, University of Nebraska Press, Lincoln.

—— (1971). The assessment of language competence in the chimpanzee. In "Behavior of Nonhuman Primates," vol. 4, Eds. A. Schrier and F. Stollnitz, Academic, New York.

PRESTON, D. G., BAKER, R. P., AND LEAY, B. (1970). Mother-infant separation in the patas monkey. *Devel. Psychobiol.*, **3**, 298–306.

RADCLIFFE-BROWN, A. R. (1940). On social structure. *J. Roy. Anthropol. Inst.*, **70**, 1–12

RANDOLPH, M. C., AND BROOKS, B. A. (1967). Conditioning of a vocal response in a chimpanzee through social reinforcement. *Folia Primatol.*, **5**, 70–79.

——, AND MASON, W. A. (1969). Effects of rearing conditions on distress vocalizations in chimpanzees. *Folia Primatol.*, **10**, 103–112.

RANSFORD, H. E. (1968). Isolation, powerlessness, and violence: a study of attitudes and participation in the Watts riots. *Am. J. Sociol.*, **73**, 581–591.

RANSOM, T. W., AND RANSOM, B. S. (1971). Adult male-infant relations among baboons (*Papio anubis*). *Folia Primatol.*, **16**, 179–195.

——, AND ROWELL, T. E. (1973). Early social development of feral baboons. In "Primate Socialization," Ed. F. Poirier, Random House, New York.

RASA, O. A. E. (1971). Appetence for aggression in juvenile damsel fish. *Z. Tierpsychol.*, Beiheft **7**, 1–70.

RAVELING, D. G. (1970). Dominance relationships and agonistic behavior of Canada geese in winter. *Behaviour*, **37**, 291–319.

REDICAN, W. K., AND MITCHELL, G. (1973). The social behavior of adult male-infant pairs of rhesus macaques in a laboratory environment. *Am. J. Phys. Anthropol.*, **38**, 523–526.

REESE, E. P., SCHOTTÉ, C. S., BECHTOLD, R. E., AND COWLEY, V. L. (1972). Initial preference of chicks from five rearing conditions for a hen or a rotating light. *J. Comp. Physiol. Psychol.*, **81**, 76–83.

RESSLER, R. H. (1963). Genotype-correlated parental influences in two strains of mice. *J. Comp. Physiol. Psychol.*, **56**, 882–886.

—— (1966). Inherited environmental influences on the operant behavior of mice. *J. Comp. Physiol. Psychol.*, **61**, 264–267.

REUCASSEL, D. (1970). A fight for life is won and lost. *Scope*, Dec. 25, 1970.

REYNOLDS, G. S., CATANIA, A. C., AND SKINNER, B. F. (1963). Conditioned and unconditioned aggression in pigeons. *J. Exp. Anal. Behav.*, **1**, 73–75.

REYNOLDS, V. (1968). Kinship and the family in monkeys, apes and man. *Man*, **3**, 209–223.

—— (1970). Roles and role change in monkey society: the consort relationship of rhesus monkeys. *Man*, **5** (NS), 449–465.

——, AND LUSCOMBE, G. (1969). "Chimpanzee Rank Order and the Function of Displays," 2d Conf. Int. Primatol., Soc., vol. 1. Karger, Basel.

RHEINGOLD, H. (Ed.) (1963). "Maternal Behavior in Mammals." Wiley, New York.

—— (1968). The social and socializing infant. In "Handbook of Socialization Theory and Research," Ed. D. A. Goslin. Rand McNally, Chicago.

——, AND ECKERMAN, C. O. (1971). Departures from the mother. In Schaffer (1971a).

——, GEWIRTZ, J. L., AND ROSS, H. W. (1959). Social conditioning of vocalizations in the infant. *J. Comp. Physiol. Psychol.*, **52**, 68–73.

RHINE, R. J., AND OWENS, N. W. (1972). The order of movement of adult male and black infant baboons (*Papio anubis*) entering and leaving a potentially dangerous clearing. *Folia Primatol.*, **18**, 276–283.

RICHARDS, M. P. M. (1967). Maternal behaviour in rodents and lagomorphs. *Adv. Reprod. Physiol.*, **2**, 53–110.

—— (1971). A comment on the social context of mother-infant interaction. In Schaffer (1971a).

RICHARDS, S. (1972). Tests for behavioural characteristics in rhesus monkeys. Ph.D. thesis, Cambridge University.

RIOPELLE, A. J., NOS, R., AND JONCH, A. (1971). Situational determinants of dominance in captive young gorillas. *Proc. 3d Int. Congr. Primatol. Zurich, 1970*, **3**, 86–91.

RIPLEY, S. (1967). Intertroop encounters among Ceylon gray langurs *Presbytis entellus*. In Altmann (1967a).

—— (1970). Leaves and leaf-monkeys: the social organization of foraging in grey langurs (*Presbytis entellus thersites*). In "Old World Monkeys," Eds. J. and P. Napier, Academic, New York.

ROBSON, K. S., PEDERSEN, F. A., AND MOSS, H. A. (1969). Developmental observations of diadic gazing in relation to the fear of strangers and social approach behavior. *Child Devel.*, **40**, 619–627.

RODMAN, P. S. (1973). Population composition and adaptive organisation among orang-utans of the Kutai Reserve. In Michael and Crook (1973).

ROPARTZ, PH. (1968). Olfaction et comportement social chez les rongeurs. *Mammalia*, **32**, 550–569.

———— (1968). The relation between olfactory stimulation and aggressive behaviour in mice. *Anim. Behav.*, **16**, 97–100.

ROSE, R. M., GORDON, T. P., AND BERNSTEIN, I. S. (1972). Plasma testosterone levels in the male rhesus: influences of sexual and social stimuli. *Science*, **178**, 643–645.

ROSEN, J., AND HART, F. M. (1963). Effects of early social isolation upon adult timidity and dominance in *Peromyscus. Psychol. Rep.*, **13**, 47–50.

ROSENBLATT, J. S. (1965). The basis of synchrony in the behavioural interaction between the mother and her offspring in the laboratory rat. In "Determinants of Infant Behaviour," vol. 3, Ed. B. M. Foss, Methuen, London.

———— (1967). Nonhormonal basis of maternal behavior in the rat. *Science*, **156**, 1512–1514.

———— (1970). Views on the onset and maintenance of maternal behavior in the rat. In "Development and Evolution of Behavior," Ed. L. R. Aronson et al, Freeman, San Francisco.

———— (1972). Learning in newborn kittens. *Sci. Am.*, **227**, 18–25.

————, AND ARONSON, L. R. (1958). The decline of sexual behavior in male rats after castration with special reference to the role of prior sexual experience. *Behaviour*, **12**, 285–338.

————, AND LEHRMAN, D. S. (1963). Maternal behavior of the laboratory rat. In Rheingold (1963).

ROSENBLUM, L. A. (1971a). Kinship interaction patterns in pigtail and bonnet macaques. *Proc. 3d Int. Congr. Primatol., Zurich, 1971*, **3**, 79–84.

———— (1971b). Infant attachment in monkeys. In Schaffer (1971a).

ROTH, L. L., AND ROSENBLATT, J. S. (1967). Changes in self-licking during pregnancy in the rat. *J. Comp. Physiol. Psychol.*, **63**, 397–400.

ROWELL, T. E. (1962). Agonistic noises of the rhesus monkey (*Macaca mulatta*). *Symp. Zool. Soc. Lond.*, **8**, 91–96.

———— (1963). Behaviour and reproductive cycles of rhesus macaques. *J. Reprod. Fertil.*, **6**, 193–203.

———— (1965). Some observations on a hand-reared baboon. In "Determinants of Infant Behaviour," vol. 3, Ed. B. M. Foss, Methuen, London.

———— (1966a). Forest living baboons in Uganda. *J. Zool.*, **147**, 344–364.

———— (1966b). Hierarchy in the organization of a captive baboon group. *Anim. Behav.*, **14**, 430–433.

———— (1967). A quantitative comparison of the behaviour of a wild and a caged baboon troop. *Anim. Behav.*, **15**, 499–509.

———— (1970). Baboon menstrual cycles affected by social environment. *J. Reprod. Fertil.*, **21**, 133–141.

———— (1972a). "Social Behaviour of Monkeys." Penguin, Harmondsworth.

———— (1972b). Organization of caged groups of *Cercopithecus* monkeys. *Anim. Behav.*, **19**, 625–645.

———— (1972c). Female reproduction cycles and social behavior in primates. *Adv. Study Behav.*, **4**, 69–105.

———— (1973b). Toward a natural history of the talapoin monkey in Cameroon. *Ann. de la Fac. des Sci. du Cameroun*, **10**, 121–131.

———— (1973a). Social organization of wild talapoin monkeys. *Am. J. Phys. Anthropol.*, **38**, 593–598.

————, AND HINDE, R. A. (1962). Vocal communication by the rhesus monkey *(Macaca mulatta). Proc. Zool. Soc. Lond.*, **138**, 279–294.

————, AND ———— (1963). Responses of rhesus monkeys to mildly stressful situations. *Anim. Behav.*, **11**, 235–243.

ROZENZWEIG, S. (1944). An outline of frustration theory. In "Personality and the Behavior Disorders," Ed. J. McV. Hunt. Ronald, New York.

RUTTER, M. (1972). "Maternal Deprivation." Penguin, Harmondsworth.

RYAN, J. (1973). Interpretation and imitation in early language development. In Hinde and Stevenson-Hinde (1973).

SAAYMAN, G. S. (1970). The menstrual cycle and sexual behaviour in a troop of free-living chacma baboons, *Papio ursinus. Folia Primatol.*, **12**, 81–110.

———— (1971). Behaviour of the adult males in a troop of free-ranging chacma baboons. *Folia Primat.*, **15**, 36–57.

———— (1972). Effects of ovarian hormones upon the sexual skin and mounting behaviour in the free-ranging chacma baboon. *Folia Primatol.*, **17**, 297–303.

SACKETT, G. P. (1963). A neural mechanism underlying unlearned, critical period and developmental aspects of visually controlled behaviour. *Psychol. Rec.*, **70**, 40–50.

———— (1966). Monkeys reared in visual isolation with pictures as visual input: evidence for an innate releasing mechanism. *Science*, **154**, 1468–1472.

———— (1968). The persistence of abnormal behaviour in monkeys following isolation rearing. In "The Role of Learning in Psychotherapy," Ed. R. Porter, Churchill, London.

———— (1970). Unlearned responses, differential recurring experiences and the development of social attachments by rhesus monkeys. In "Pri-mate Behavior," vol. I, L. A. Rosenblum, Academic, New York and London.

————, AND RUPPENTHAL, G. C. (1973). Development of monkeys after varied experiences during infancy. In "Ethology and Development," Ed. S. A. Barnett, Heinemann, London.

SADE, D. S. (1964). Seasonal cycle in size of testes of free-ranging *Macaca mulatta. Folia Primatol.*, **2**, 171–180.

———— (1965). Some aspects of parent-offspring and sibling relations in a group of rhesus monkeys, with a discussion of grooming. *Am. J. Phys. Anthropol.*, **23**, 1–18.

———— (1967). Determinants of dominance in a group of free ranging rhesus monkeys. In Altmann (1967a).

———— (1968). Inhibition of son-mother mating among free-ranging rhesus monkeys. *Sci. Psychoanal.*, **12**, 18–38.

———— (1972a). A longitudinal study of social behavior of rhesus monkeys. In "The Functional and Evolutionary Biology of Primates," Aldine Atherton, Chicago.

———— (1972b). Sociometrics of *Macaca mulatta*. I. Linkages and cliques in grooming matrices. *Folia Primatol.*, **18**, 196–223.

SALK, L. (1973). The role of the heart beat in the relations between mother and infant. *Sci. Am.*, **228**, 24–29.

SALZEN, E. A. (1967). Imprinting in birds and primates. *Behaviour*, **28**, 232–254.

SANDER, L. W. (1969). Regulation and organization in the early infant-caretaker system. In "Brain and Early Behaviour," Ed. R. J. Robinson, Academic, London and New York.

———— (1970). *J. Am. Acad. Child Psychiatr.*, **9**, 103.

SASSENRATH, E. N. (1970). Increased adrenal responsiveness related to social stress in rhesus monkeys. *Horm. Behav.*, **1**, 283–298.

SAUNDERS, F. J. (1968). Effects of sex steroids and related compounds on pregnancy and on development of the young. *Physiol. Rev.*, **48**, 601–643.

SCHAFFER, H. R. (1966). The onset of fear of strangers and the incongruity hypothesis. *J. Child Psychol. Psychiatr.*, **7**, 95–106.

―――― (Ed.) (1971a). "The Origins of Human Social Relations." Academic, London and New York.

―――― (1971b). "The Growth of Sociability." Penguin, Harmondsworth.

―――― (1973). The multivariate approach to early learning. In Hinde and Stevenson-Hinde (1973).

――――, AND EMERSON, P. E. (1964). The development of social attachments in infancy. *Monogr. Soc. Res. Child Devel.*, **29**, 3.

――――, GREENWOOD, A., AND PARRY, M. H. (1972). The onset of wariness. *Child Devel.*, **43**, 165–175.

SCHALLER, G. B. (1963). "The Mountain Gorilla: Ecology and Behavior." The University of Chicago Press, Chicago.

SCHJELDERUP-EBBE, T. (1922). Beiträge zur Sozialpsychologie des Haushühns. *Z. Psychol.*, **88**, 225–252.

SCHNEIRLA, T. C. (1949). Levels in the psychological capacities of animals. In "Philosophy for the Future," Ed. R. W. Sellars et al., Macmillan, New York.

―――― (1965). Aspects of stimulation and organisation in approach/withdrawal processes underlying vertebrate behavioral development. *Adv. Study Behav.*, **1**, 1–74.

――――, ROSENBLATT, J. S., AND TOBACH, E. (1963). Maternal behavior in the cat. In "Maternal Behavior in Mammals," Ed. H. Rheingold, Wiley, New York.

SCOTT, J. P. (1958). "Aggression." The University of Chicago Press, Chicago.

―――― (1962). Hostility and aggression in animals. In "Roots of Behavior," Ed.

E. L. Bliss, Harper & Row, New York.

―――― (1966). Agonistic behavior in mice and rats: a review. *Am. Zool.*, **6**, 683–701.

―――― (1971). Attachment and separation in dog and man: theoretical propositions. In Schaffer (1971a).

――――, AND FREDERICSON, E. (1951). The causes of fighting in mice and rats. *Physiol. Zool.*, **24**, 273–309.

――――, AND FULLER, J. L. (1965). "Genetics and the Social Behavior of the Dog." The University of Chicago Press, Chicago.

SEARS, R. (1951). Doll play aggression in normal young children: influence of sex, age, sibling status, and father's absence. *Psychol. Monogr.*, **65**, 1–42.

―――― (1957). Identification as a form of behavioral development. In "The Concept of Development," Ed. D. B. Harris, University of Minnesota Press, Minneapolis.

――――, MACCOBY, E. E., AND LEVIN, H. (1957). "Patterns of Child-rearing." Row Peterson, Evanston, Ill.

SEAY, B., HANSEN, E. W., AND HARLOW, H. F. (1962). Mother-infant separation in monkeys. *J. Child Psychol. Psychiatr.*, **3**, 123–132.

――――, AND HARLOW, H. F. (1965). Maternal separation in the rhesus monkey. *J. Nerv. Ment. Dis.*, **140**, 434–441.

SEBEOK, T. A. (1968) "Animal Communication." Indiana University Press, Bloomington.

SEITZ, P. E. D. (1954). The effects of infantile experiences upon adult behavior in animal subjects. I. Effects of litter size during infancy upon adult behavior in the rat. *Am. J. Psychiatr.*, **110**, 916–927.

SEVENSTER, P. (1961). A causal analysis of a displacement activity: fanning in *Gasterosteus aculeatus*. *Behaviour*, suppl., **9**, 1–170.

―――― (1973). Incompatibility of response

and reward. In Hinde and Stevenson-Hinde (1973).

SEVENSTER-BOL, A. C. A. (1962). On the causation of drive reduction after a consummatory act. *Arch. Néerl. Zool.,* **15,** 175–236.

SHERIF, M., AND SHERIF, C. W. (1953). "Groups in Harmony and Tension." Harper & Row, New York.

SIEGEL, A. E. (1970). Violence in the mass media. In Daniels et al. (1970).

SIGG, E. B. (1969) Relationship of aggressive behaviour to adrenal and gonadal function in male mice. In Garattini and Sigg (1969).

SIMONDS, P. E. (1965). The bonnet macaque in south India. In DeVore (1965a).

——— (1973). Outcast males and social structure among bonnet macaques. *Am. J. Phys. Anthropol.,* **38,** 599–604.

SIMPSON, M. J. A. (1968). The display of the Siamese fighting fish, *Betta splendens. Anim. Behav. Monogr.,* **1,** 1.

——— (1973a). The social grooming of male chimpanzees. In "The Comparative Ecology and Behaviour of Primates," Eds. J. H. Crook and R. P. Michael, Academic, London and New York.

——— (1973b). Social displays and the recognition of individuals.

SINCLAIR, H. (1973). Some remarks on the Genevan point of view on learning with special reference to language learning. In Hinde and Stevenson-Hinde (1973).

SKINNER, B. F. (1948). "Superstition" in the pigeon. *J. Exp. Psychol.,* **38,** 168–172.

SLUCKIN, W. (1962). Perceptual and associative learning. *Symp. Zool. Soc. Lond.,* **8,** 193–198.

———, AND SALZEN, E. A. (1961). Imprinting and perceptual learning. *Q. J. Exp. Psychol.,* **13,** 65–77.

SMITH, P. K., AND CONNOLLY, K. (1972). Patterns of play and social interaction in pre-school children. In Blurton Jones (1972a).

SMITH, W. J. (1965). Message, meaning and context in ethology. *Am. Nat.,* **99,** 405–409.

——— (1969a). Displays of *Sayornis phoebe* (Aves, Tyrannidae). *Behaviour,* **33,** 283–322.

——— (1969b). Messages of vertebrate communication. *Science,* **165,** 145–150.

SOLOMON, G. F. (1970). Psychodynamic aspects of aggression, hostility, and violence. In Daniels et al. (1970).

SOLOMON, P. et al. (1961). "Sensory Deprivation." Harvard, Cambridge, Mass.

SOUTHWICK, C. H. (1968). Effect of maternal environment on aggressive behavior of inbred mice. *Commun. Behav. Biol., A.,* **1,** 129–132.

——— (1969). Aggressive behaviour of rhesus monkeys in natural and captive groups. In Garattini and Sigg (1969).

———, BEG, M. A., AND SIDDIQI, M. R. (1965). Rhesus monkeys in north India. In DeVore (1965a).

———, AND SIDDIQI, M. R. (1967). The role of social tradition in the maintenance of dominance in a wild rhesus group. *Primates,* **8,** 341–353.

SPENCER-BOOTH, Y. (1968a). The behaviour of twin rhesus monkeys and comparisons with the behaviour of single infants. *Primates,* **9,** 75–84.

——— (1968b). The behaviour of group companions towards rhesus monkey infants. *Anim. Behav.,* **16,** 541–557.

——— (1969). The effects of rearing rhesus monkey infants in isolation with their mothers on their subsequent behaviour in a group situation. *Mammalia,* **33,** 80–86.

——— (1970). The relationships between mammalian young and conspecifics other than mothers and peers: a review. *Adv. Study Behav.,* **3,** 120–194.

———, AND HINDE, R. A. (1971a). Effects of 6 days separation from mother on

18- to 32-week old rhesus monkeys. *Anim. Behav.*, **19**, 174–191.

———, AND ——— (1971b). Effects of brief separations from mothers during infancy on behaviour of rhesus monkeys 6-24 months later. *J. Child Psychol. Psychiatr.*, **12**, 157–172.

SPITZ, R. A. (1946). Anaclitic depression. *Psychoanal. Study Child*, **2**, 313–342.

——— (1950). Anxiety in infancy: a study of its manifestations in the first year of life. *Int. J. Psychonanal.*, **31**, 138–143.

——— (1965). "The First Year of Life." International Universities Press, Inc., New York.

STAYTON, D. J., HOGAN, R., AND AINSWORTH, M. D. S. (1971). Infant obedience and maternal behavior: the origins of socialization reconsidered. *Child Devel.*, **42**, 1057–1069.

STEPHENSON, G. R. (1967). Cultural acquisition of a specific learned response among rhesus monkeys. In "Progress in Primatology," Eds. D. Starck, R. Schneider, and H-J. Kuhn, Fischer, Stuttgart.

STEVENS, A. G. (1971). Attachment behaviour, separation anxiety, and stranger anxiety of polymatrically reared infants. In Schaffer (Ed.) (1971a).

STEVENSON, J. G. (1969). Song as a reinforcer. In Hinde (1969a).

———, HUTCHISON, R. E., HUTCHISON, J., BERTRAM, B. C. R., AND THORPE, W. H. (1970). Individual recognition by auditory cries in the common tern (*Sterna hirundo*). *Nature*, **226**, 562–563.

STEVENSON-HINDE, J. (1972). Effects of early experience and testosterone on song as a reinforcer. *Anim. Behav.*, **20**, 430–435.

STOKES, A. W. (1962). Agonistic behaviour among blue tits at a winter feeding station. *Behaviour*, **19**, 118–138.

———, AND COX, L. M. (1969). Aggressive man and aggressive beast. *Bioscience*, **20**, 1092–1093.

STORR, A. (1968). "Human Aggression." Penguin Press, Allen Lane, London.

STRUHSAKER, T. T. (1967). Social structure among Vervet monkeys (*Cercopithecus aethiops*). *Behaviour*, **29**, 83–121.

——— (1969). Correlates of ecology and social organization among African cercopithecines. *Folia Primatol.*, **11**, 80–118.

STYNES, A. J., ROSENBLUM, L. A., AND KAUFMAN, I. C. (1968). The dominant male and behavior within heterospecific monkey groups. *Folia Primatol.*, **9**, 123–134.

SUGIYAMA, Y. (1960). On the division of a natural troop of Japanese monkeys at Tagasakiyama. *Primates*, **2**, 109–148.

——— (1965a). Behavioral development and social structure in two troops of hanuman langurs (*Presbytis entellus*). *Primates*, **6**, 213–247.

——— (1965b). On the social change of hanuman langurs (*Presbytis entellus*) in their natural condition. *Primates*, **6**, 381–418.

——— (1966). An artificial change in a hanuman langur troop *Presbytis entellus*. *Primates*, **7**, 41–73.

——— (1967). Social organization of hanuman langurs. In Altmann (1967a).

——— (1973). The social structure of wild chimpanzees: a review of field studies. In Michael and Crook (1973).

SUOMI, S. J., HARLOW, H. F., AND DOMEK, C. J. (1970). Effect of repetitive infant-infant separation of young monkeys. *J. Abnorm. Psychol.*, **76**, 161–172.

SUZUKI, A. (1969). An ecological study of chimpanzees in a savannah woodland. *Primates*, **10**, 103–148.

TELEKI, G. (1973). The omnivorous chimpanzee. *Sci. Am.*, **228**(1), 33–42.

TERKEL, J., AND ROSENBLATT, J. S. (1968). Maternal behaviour induced by maternal blood plasma injected into virgin rats. *J. Comp. Physiol. Psychol.*, **65**, 479–482.

TERRACE, H. S. (1966). Stimulus control. In "Operant Behavior," Ed. W. K. Honig, Appleton - Century - Crofts, New York.

THINES, G., AND HEUTS, B. (1968). The effect of submissive experience on dominance and aggressive behaviour of *Xiphophorus*. *Z. Tierpsychol.*, **25**, 139–154.

THODAY, J. M., AND PARKES, A. S. (Eds.) (1968). "Genetic and Environmental Influences on Behaviour." Oliver & Boyd, Edinburgh.

THOMAN, E. B., CONNER, R. L., AND LEVINE, S. (1970). Lactation suppresses adrenal corticosteroid activity and aggressiveness in rats. *J. Comp. Physiol. Psychol.*, **70**, 364–369.

———, LEIDERMAN, P. N., AND OLSON, J. P. (1972). Neonate-mother interaction during breast-feeding. *Devel. Psychol.*, **6**, 110–118.

———, AND LEVINE, S. (1970). Hormonal and behavioral changes in the rat mother as a function of early experience treatments of the offspring. *Physiol. Behav.*, **5**, 1417–1421.

THOMPSON, N. S. (1967). Some variables affecting the behaviour of Irus macaques in dyadic encounters. *Anim. Behav.*, **15**, 307–311.

——— (1969). The motivations underlying the social structure of *Macaca irus*. *Anim. Behav.*, **17**, 459–467.

THOMPSON, T. I. (1963). Visual reinforcement in Siamese fighting fish. *Science*, **141**, 55–57.

——— (1969). Aggressive behavior of Siamese fighting fish: analysis and synthesis of conditioned and unconditioned components. In Garattini and Sigg (1969).

THORPE, W. H. (1961). "Bird-song." Cambridge, New York and London.

——— (1972). Duetting and antiphonal song in birds. *Behaviour*, suppl., **18**, 1–197.

———, AND ZANGWILL, O. L. (Eds.) (1961). "Current Problems in Animal Behaviour." Cambridge, New York and London.

TIGER, L. (1969). "Men in Groups." Nelson, London.

———, AND FOX, R. W. (1972). "The Imperial Animal." Secker and Warburg, London.

TINBERGEN, E. A., AND TINBERGEN, N. (1972). Early childhood autism—an ethological approach. *Z. Tierpsychol.*, Beiheft **10**, 1–53.

TINBERGEN, N. (1951). "The Study of Instinct." Oxford, New York and London.

——— (1952). Derived activities: their causation, biological significance, origin and emancipation during evolution. *Q. Rev. Biol.*, **27**, 1–32.

——— (1953). "The Herring Gull's World." Collins, London.

——— (1956). On the functions of territory in gulls. *Ibis*, **98**, 401–411.

——— (1959). Comparative studies of the behaviour of gulls (Laridae): a progress report. *Behaviour*, **15**, 1–70.

——— (1968). On war and peace in animals and man. *Science*, **160**, 1411–1418.

———, AND PERDECK, A. C. (1950). On the stimulus situation releasing the begging response in the newly hatched herring gull chick (*Larus argentatus argentatus* Pont.). *Behaviour*, **3**, 1–39.

TIZARD, J., AND TIZARD, B. (1971). The social development of two-year-old children in residential nurseries. In Schaffer (1971a).

TOKUDA, A., AND JENSEN, G. D. (1969). Determinants of dominance hierarchy in a captive group of pigtailed monkeys (*Macaca nemestrina*). *Primates*, **10**, 227–236.

TOLMAN, C. W. (1968). The varieties of social stimulation in the feeding behaviour of domestic chicks. *Behaviour*, **30**, 275–286.

TOMKINS, S. S., AND McCARTER, R. (1964). What and where are the primary affects? Some evidence for a theory. *Percept. Motor Skills*, **18**, 119–158.

TRIVERS, R. L. (1971). The evolution of reciprocal altruism. *Q. Rev. Biol.*, **46**, 35–57.

———— (in press) Parent-offspring conflict. *Am. Zool.*

TSUMORI, A. (1966). Delayed response of wild Japanese monkeys by the sand-digging method. II. Cases of the Tokasakiyama troops and the Chirayama troop. *Primates*, **7**, 363–380.

———— (1967). Newly acquired behavior and social interactions of Japanese monkeys. In Altmann (1967a).

TURNER, E. R. A. (1965). Social feeding in birds. *Behaviour*, **24**, 1–46.

TUTIN, C. E. G. AND McGREW, W. C. (1973). Sexual behaviour of group-living adolescent chimpanzees. *Am. J. Phys. Anthropol.*, **38**, 195–200.

TWITCHELL, T. E. (1970). Reflex mechanisms and the development of prehension. In "Mechanisms of Motor Skill Development," Ed. K. J. Connolly, Academic, London and New York.

UDRY, J. R., AND MORRIS, N. M. (1968). Distribution of coitus in the menstrual cycle. *Nature*, **220**, 593–596.

UEXKÜLL, J. VON (1934). "Streifzuge durch die Umwelten von Tieren und Menschen." Springer, Berlin. Translated in "Instinctive Behaviour" (1957), Ed. C. H. Schiller, Methuen, London.

ULRICH, R. E. (1966). Pain as a cause of aggression. *Am. Zool.*, **6**, 643–662.

————, JOHNSTON, M., RICHARDSON, J., AND WOLFF, P. C. (1963). The operant conditioning of fighting behavior in rats. *Psychol. Rec.*, **13**, 465–470.

————, AND SYMANNEK, B. (1969). Pain as a stimulus for aggression. In Garattini and Sigg (1969).

UYENO, E. T. (1960). Hereditary and environmental aspects of dominant behavior in the albino rat. *J. Comp. Physiol.*, **53**, 138–141.

VALZELLI, L. (1969). Aggressive behaviour induced by isolation. In Garattini and Sigg (1969).

VANDENBERGH, J. G. (1967). The development of social structure in free-ranging rhesus monkeys. *Behaviour*, **29**, 179–194.

———— (1969). Endocrine coordination in monkeys: male sexual responses to females. *Physiol. Behav.*, **4**, 261–264.

VERNON, W., AND ULRICH, R. (1966). Classical conditioning of pain-elicited aggression. *Science*, **152**, 668.

VESSEY, S. H. (1968). Interactions between free-ranging groups of rhesus monkeys. *Folia Primatol.*, **8**, 228–239.

———— (1971). Free-ranging rhesus monkeys: behavioural effects of removal, separation and reintroduction of group members. *Behaviour*, **40**, 216–227.

VINCE, M. A. (1964). Use of the feet in feeding by the great tit *Parus major*. *Ibis*, **106**, 508–529.

VIRGO, H. B., AND WATERHOUSE, M. J. (1969). The emergence of attention structure amongst rhesus macaques. *Man (N.S.)*, **4**, 85–93.

VOGEL, C. (1971). Behavioral differences of *Presbytis entellus* in two different habitats. *Proc. 3d Int. Congr. Primatol., Zurich, 1970*, **3**, 41–47.

VOWLES, D. (1970). "The Psychobiology of Aggression." Edinburgh University Press, Edinburgh.

————, AND HARWOOD, D. (1966). The effect of exogenous hormones on aggressive and defensive behaviour in the ring dove (*Streptopelia risoria*). *J. Endocrinol.*, **36**, 35–51.

WARREN, J. M., AND MARONEY, R. J. (1958). Competitive social interaction between monkeys. *J. Soc. Psychol.*, **48**, 223–233.

WASHBURN, S. L., AND DeVORE, I. (1961). The social life of baboons. *Sci. Am.*, **204**, 62–71.

———, AND HAMBURG, D. A. (1968). Aggressive behavior in Old World monkeys and apes. In Jay (1968).

WATSON, A. (1970). Dominance, spacing behaviour and aggression in relation to population limitation in vertebrates. In "Animal Populations in Relation to their Food Resources," Blackwell, Oxford.

WEBER, I. (1973). Tactile communication among free-ranging langurs. *Am. J. Phys. Anthropol.*, **38**, 481–486.

WEILAND, I. H., AND SPERBER, Z. (1970). Patterns of mother-infant contact: the significance of lateral preference. *J. Genet. Psychol.*, **117**, 157–165.

WEISKRANTZ, L., AND COWEY, A. (1960). The aetiology of food reward in monkeys. *Anim. Behav.*, **11**, 225–234.

WEIZMAN, F., COHEN, L. B., AND PRATT, R. J. (1971). Novelty, familiarity and the development of infant attention. *Devel. Psychol.*, **4**, 149–154.

WELCH, B. L. AND WELCH, A. S. (1969). Aggression and the biogenic amine neuro-humors. In Garattini and Sigg (1969).

WENNER, A. M. (1967). Honey bees: do they use the distance information contained in their dance maneuver? *Science*, **155**, 847–849.

WHEELER, L., AND CAGGIULA, A. R. (1966). The contagion of aggression. *J. Exp. Soc. Psychol.*, **2**, 1–10.

WHITE, B. L. (1970). Experience and the development of motor mechanisms in infancy. In Connolly (1970a).

WICKLER, W. (1967). Socio-sexual signals and their intra-specific imitation among primates. In "Primate Ethology," Ed. D. Morris, Weidenfeld & Nicolson, London.

——— (1968). "Mimicry." Weidenfeld & Nicolson, London.

WIEPKEMA, P. R. (1961). An ethological analysis of the reproductive behaviour of the bitterling. *Arch. Néerl. Zool.*, **14**, 103–199.

WIESNER, B. P., AND SHEARD, N. M. (1933). "Maternal Behaviour in the Rat." Oliver & Boyd, Edinburgh.

WILDER, J. (1947). Sugar metabolism in its relation to criminology. In "Handbook of Correctional Psychology," Eds. Lindner and Seliger, Philosophical Library, New York.

WILSON, A. P., AND VESSEY, S. H. (1968). Behavior of free-ranging castrated rhesus monkeys. *Folia Primatol.*, **9**, 1–14.

WILSON, C. C. (1972). Spatial factors and the behavior of nonhuman primates. *Folia Primatol.*, **18**, 256–275.

WILSON, E. O. (1971). Competitive and aggressive behavior. In Eisenberg and Dillon (1971).

WILZ, K. J. (1972). Causal relationships between aggression and the sexual and nest behaviours in the three-spined stickleback (*Gasterosteus aculeatus*). *Anim. Behav.*, **20**, 335–340.

WOLFF, P. H. (1963). Observations on the early development of smiling. In "Determinants of Infant Behaviour," vol. 2, Ed. B. M. Foss, Methuen, London.

——— (1968). The serial organization of sucking in the young infant. *Pediatrics*, **42**, 943–956.

——— (1969). The natural history of crying and other vocalizations in early infancy. In "Determinants of Infant Behaviour," vol. 4, Ed. B. M. Foss, Methuen, London.

WORCHEL, P. (1957). Catharsis and the relief of hostility. *J. Abnorm. Soc. Psychol.*, **55**, 238–243.

WRANGHAM, R. (in prep. a). Feeding ecology and behaviour of chimpanzees. Ph.D. thesis, Cambridge University.

——— (in prep. b). Some effects of supplying bananas to wild ·chimpanzees and baboons.

WÜNSCHMANN, A. (1963). Quantitative Untersuchungen zur Neugierverhalten von Wirbeltieren. *Z. Tierpsychol.,* **20,** 80–109.

WYNNE-EDWARDS, V. C. (1962). "Animal Dispersion in Relation to Social Behaviour." Oliver & Boyd, Edinburgh.

—— (1972). Ecology and the evolution of social ethics. In "Biology and the Human Sciences," Ed. J. W. S. Pringle, Oxford, New York and London.

YAMADA, M. (1963). A study of blood-relationship in the natural society of the Japanese macaque. *Primates,* **4,** 43–65.

—— (1971). Five natural troops of Japanese monkeys on Stodoshima Island. II. A comparison of social structure. *Primates,* **12,** 125–150.

YARROW, L. J. (1964). Separation from parents during early childhood. *Rev. Child Devel. Res.,* vol. 1, Eds. M. L. Hoffman and L. W. Hoffman, Russell Sage, New York

—— (1967). The development of focused relationships during infancy. In *"Exceptional Infant,"* vol. 1, Ed. J. Hollmuth, Special Child Publications.

——, RUBENSTEIN, J. L., PEDERSEN, F. A., AND JANKOWSKI, J. J. (1972). Dimensions of early stimulation and their differential effects on infant development. *Merrill-Palmer Q.,* **18,** 205–218.

YOSHIBA, K. (1967). An ecological study of hanuman langurs, *Presbytis entellus. Primates,* **8,** 127–154.

—— (1968). Local and intertroop variability in ecology and social behavior of common Indian langurs. In Jay (1968).

YOUNG, W. C. (Ed.) (1961). "Sex and Internal Secretions." Williams & Wilkins, Baltimore.

—— (1969). Psychobiology of sexual behavior in the guinea pig. *Adv. Study Behav.,* **2,** 1–111.

——, AND ORBISON, W. D. (1944). Changes in selected features of behavior in pairs of oppositely sexed chimpanzees during the sexual cycle and after ovariectomy. *J. Comp. Psychol.,* **37,** 107–143.

ZARROW, M. X., DENENBERG, V. H., AND ANDERSON, C. O. (1965). Rabbit: frequency of suckling in the pup. *Science,* **150,** 1835–1836.

ZUCKERMAN, S. (1932). "The Social Life of Monkeys and Apes." Routledge, London.

# NAME INDEX

# SUBJECT INDEX